CHOOSING A LOVE THAT WILL LAST by Glory Chapman
Copyright © 1987 by Glory Chapman, United States Copyright Office. All rights reserved. No part of this publication may be reproduced, stored in a retrieval system, or transmitted in any form or by any means—electronic, mechanical, photocopy, recording, or any other—except for brief quotations in printed reviews, without the prior permission of the publisher.

All Scripture references are from *The Living Bible* unless otherwise indicated. Copyright 1971 owned by assignment by Illinois Regional Bank N.A. (as trustee). Used by permission of Tyndale House Publishers, Inc., Wheaton, Illinois 60189. All rights reserved.

Some of the names in this book have been changed.

Library of Congress Catalog Card Number: 96-67598
Chapman, Glory.
Choosing A Love That Will Last by Glory Chapman.

ISBN 0-9651143-0-9

1. Choosing A Love That Will Last- Non-Fiction- Love and Marriage.

Printed in the United States of America

CHOOSING

A LOVE

THAT WILL LAST

FOR MARRIAGE AND REMARRIAGE

GLORY CHAPMAN

SP

SOUTHWICK PUBLISHING
Houston

ACKNOWLEDGMENTS

To Bob Slosser, author of twelve books, including *Miracle in Darien and Child of Satan, Child of God,* who critiqued the first five chapters and wrote: "Dear Glory: This looks quite good to me. You write well: lucidly and with feeling. I urge you to press on and constantly make it clear in the manuscript what the book is all about. Drop little reminders in, so the reader won't drift off. Keep reminding him why he is reading this book. Blessings. Bob Slosser."

To Nancy Horner of Waco, Texas, for her constant enthusiasm in cheering me on when the going was tough, making me believe it was not only good, but it also helped her.

To Chappy, my husband, who lovingly bore with me patiently through the many months (even years) spent writing this book. For his ability to convey to me his faith that I could transfer my thoughts onto paper.

To all nine of my beloved children.

To my editor, Brenda Ritter, who worked tirelessly while giving me her love and encouragement.

There were others who contributed greatly in the birth of this manuscript through positive remarks. My thanks to them!

Uppermost and singlemost is my desire that this book be of value to those experiencing deep traumas, tragedies and hurts, pointing them to the One who in the ultimate has *all* the answers to life's baffling happenings. Please read this book twice or very slowly.

GLORY CHAPMAN

TABLE OF CONTENTS

CHAPTER

1. HUMPTY-DUMPTY FELL OFF THE WALL
2. CRY BABY CRY!
3. INLOVENESS
4. APPEAL YOUR CASE
5. SHOULDER TO KNEE
6. GOODBYE MISS GOODY TWO SHOES
7. THE WAITING GAME
8. ANGEL UNAWARE
9. SILENCE OF GOD
10. OKLAHOMA SNIPE HUNTING AND WILD INDIANS
11. BELOVED JUNIOR, PRECIOUS JUNIOR
12. CHILDREN ARE A BLESSING FROM GOD?
13. SCHOOL DAYS! SCHOOL DAYS! DEAR OLD GOLDEN RULE DAYS!
14. RELATIONSHIPS
15. PORT MANSFIELD, TEXAS
16. RUN BABY RUN!
17. TURN IN THE ROAD
18. BAD THINGS DON'T HAPPEN TO GOOD PEOPLE
19. MY TRACK RECORD ON GOD
20. PARTING
21. HIS NEEDS HER NEEDS
22. ME A PHARISEE?
23. THE GREAT DEBATE

CHOOSING A LOVE THAT WILL LAST

CHAPTER

24 A KNIGHT
25 OUR LAST SUPPER
26 A REAL ANGEL
27 SPECIAL GIFTS
28 MAMA'S WEDDING GOWN
29 CONFRONTATIONS
30 A TRIBUTE TO GEORGIA MARIE
31 LIVING AGAIN AFTER DIVORCE
32 NORMY, ABBY NORM AND SUBY NORM
33 WHEN DOES A MOTHER RETIRE?
34 ISLE OF VIEW
35 YOURS, MINE PLUS THREE MAKES TWELVE

GLORY CHAPMAN

CHAPTER 1

HUMPTY-DUMPTY FELL OFF THE WALL

The stormy turbulent sky that hung over McAllen, Texas was as gloomy and impetuous as my spirit. Nothing was right with my world it seemed. I had had it with life! I had had it with religion! I had had it with marriage! Was there any area in my life which was meaningful?

I was even contemplating whether there was a God. Only my dad's experience, which happened many years before, convinced me there must be a *living* God. But where was He now that I needed Him? In much frustration it was more than difficult to hear that still small voice above the roar of the storm and the waves that dashed against my very soul. It was as if I was being pushed beyond the limits of my endurance--that breaking point some say everyone has. Pain, as C. S. Lewis said, is God's megaphone, "He whispers to us in our joys, speaks to us in our conscience, and shouts to us in our pain."

Mr. Troubles came to visit and overstayed his welcome. Much confusion about marriage and life had been brewing inside me for sometime. Without warning all hell broke loose with my forebodings, tearing down the dam of security and everything I held dear. My life hadn't gone the way I had planned it at all. My cup ran dry! I had no more to give. Had I not tried very hard to live by the principles and rules given me by my parents and by the church? Where had it gotten me all these years later? They were middle-age years by now. The wrong time in life for divorce, especially with six young children who were being torpedoed out of their faith and security.

What I could never reconcile with myself was the fact I had envisioned my life as always being right, but certainly not by

CHOOSING A LOVE THAT WILL LAST

accident. I had worked untiringly in obeying and caring, placing God first and teaching our children to do the same by example and doctrine. I honored my father and mother and was faithful to my husband in marriage. On and on paraded my self-righteous deeds. Too bad God didn't ask me for my resume'. He would have been impressed. However, I was to learn; my perception of myself and God's differed somewhat.

To me, divorce is worse than death; it is worse than anything I can think of. Not ever entertaining such a possibility, I was thrown into an insolvable situation with no happy ending. Nowadays, it seems divorce is not considered such a tragedy, but it still remains an incalculable hurt to the ones involved.

I've found in any impossible situation, it's wise to analyze any and all alternatives. It seemed that I had two choices--divorce or death. Quite frankly, death seemed a great deal more preferable than divorce, though both seemed unthinkable to me. It was like being asked on a personality test, "Would you rather watch the hogs eat your brother or would you prefer to see your mother slowly die of some horrible disease?" You are supposed to give an answer. You can't leave it blank, and there is no way you can answer *neither*. You must choose between those two repugnant options.

During the worst time in our marriage, there seemed a simple enough solution. Let me die, or better still, let my husband die. It really didn't matter which one. Escaping would be convenient. What a coward! No matter, that was my secret wish, even my prayer.

One afternoon, with but one thing on my mind, I walked down the hallway into my daughter Shari's bedroom, placed myself on her bed and prayed clearly, earnestly and distinctly, "Please God let me just stop breathing. You could have life--I would take death by choice."

Even in my despair, there was the haunting thought of who would take care of the precious children God had given us. They were all planned and wanted desperately. To me, each one was exceptional, and each birthing sent me into an euphoric state that made the trees look greener, the flowers more afire and brilliant. The children are and have been the one bright spot in my life. Certainly I was responsible for bringing all six of them into this world. How could I abandon them now or ever? Their age spread now was from six years old to twenty.

A brief plan that was certainly spoken to no one began to take shape in the private chambers of my mind. There was a way to spare my children anymore pain. For the first time I understood and could identify with the desperate frame of mind of a parent who kills all her children, then herself. The children would go straight to heaven. I would be the only one lost. Well, were not all eight of us going to be lost if we stayed in this impossible situation? Fortunately, this kind of insanity didn't last long. It has been said that given just the right set of circumstances with the appropriately timed strikes, we could all commit murder. No doubt there are many in prison today who saw no other alternative at the moment of crisis. There is no way to fully describe this kind of trauma. No way!

After much soul searching, I decided there was no choice but to file for divorce due to truly irreconcilable differences. Need I say more? Though they aren't aware of this, many days my children were singularly responsible for keeping me together. They are the love of my life. Although we were unusually quiet around the house, there were hugs, pats and expressions of love between the children and me. They were very perceptive and sensitive, giving me little cause for concern though their sad and downcast faces broke my heart. Perhaps this was one of the few times I was unable to fix things for them. It was as if I was drowning and somehow couldn't get to shore to help them. I see now things that I could have said and done, but given the circumstances then, I fought with all my might with what was left in me. Emotionally, I was far too traumatized over my disappointment in marriage.

It was good, I see now, that life didn't slow down. There was the regular hustle-bustle of cooking, shopping, cleaning, disciplining, repairing and homework, all of which gave life some semblance of stability and normality.

Also, there were finances to be considered. Should I return to my old job with the Shary-Shivers Organization, or try for something new? Eventually four job openings were available, mostly from former business associates, but it had been 11 years since I had worked. When I worked for former Governor Allan Shivers; his mother-in-law, Mrs. John H. Shary; and Blaine Holcomb, their Chief Executive Officer; it was on a half-day basis. Most of what I know I learned from them, having started to work with them in my teens. They are very beloved to me, especially Bee Bud (Allan Shivers, Jr.). Their driver, Oliver Garza, would bring Bee Bud into the office every morning and he would make a beeline for my office, jump up on my lap and try and pry into everything in and on my desk. He was five at the time.

Just the fact I was offered these jobs greatly encouraged me. However, I remember telling one of the prospective employers that I had to be home by 3:30 every afternoon when the children were out of school. "That would certainly not be fair to the other employees," he countered, and to which I sighed, "Yes, but the children are all I have."

So I finally decided not to go back to work yet, but go to school and take some classes at Pan American University. The property settlement provided us with enough income if we were frugal, but there were heavy debt payments which had to be paid. It was nip and tuck. I remember some months we had little left after paying debts and charges. Later it improved some. In all my struggles neither family offered or asked if we needed help, which surprised me. So I borrowed money from the bank. However, my mother was an angel and did babysit the children when I needed her. Everyone presumed we were doing fine. To others, we looked brave and strong as we put on fairly happy faces for their benefit.

At this time, Herby and Shari were in college; Tari, eighth grade; Tami, sixth; Tom, second; Lori, first grade. Not having an abundance certainly taught me how to manage. The good news was I gained a graduate degree in money management. The bad news was, it was constant.

While the children were in school, I had more time to try to figure out what went wrong in my life. I had been taught that God loved all His creation, but I longed that He love me individually and unconditionally here and now. I wanted Him to know me personally and I to know Him; for God to know where I was and to help me when I called. I believed that bad things didn't happen to good people. It was a very confusing time for me to sort out. Do bad things happen to Christians? More about this dilemma later.

Having been in the church all of my life, the Scriptures weren't foreign to me. Yes, I knew Jesus said, "I will never leave you nor forsake you." Knowing that word is much like knowing about President Bush. Yet it is quite another thing to know God or President Bush to the extent they will respond to me. At this point, my own insignificance swallowed up what little faith I had. Just think how many millions of people are in the world and have been from the beginning of time. Sure, I know He created the universe and all that's in it, but it's beyond my grasp to know how He keeps up with all of it. Guess if I did; I would be God, but I seemed to be lost in all the vastness. The Bible says no detail escapes God's knowing and seeing. Even the tiny unwanted sparrow is noticed when he drops. God knows the number of hairs on my head. That is what I would call pretty constant attention, considering the daily fallout rate.

Also, I had been taught God is love. That means He isn't sometimes loving, but His whole person is all love through and through--the very epitome of love. Sometimes love has to be tough love, but it is still love. In other words, LOVE IS A PERSON. This is incomprehensible to me. Who can fully understand that kind of love?

To put it more to the point, I wanted to know if God really involved Himself in my everyday happenings? Really? Although

CHOOSING A LOVE THAT WILL LAST

I had heard it mouthed all my life, I wanted to know if God would answer my questions with real answers? I didn't want a feeling, an impression, but wanted a definite response, especially to the big decisions of life?

Perhaps I tried too hard to find the solutions to life. Tried too hard to be super righteous! To be a super person! To be a super mom!

In reading *My Utmost For His Highest*, a devotional by Oswald Chambers, there was a small paragraph that caught my attention.

"Cast that 'He hath given thee' upon the Lord. We ought never to bear the burden of sin or of doubt, but there are burdens placed on us by God which He does not intend to lift off. He wants us to roll them back on Him. If we roll back on God that which He has put upon us, He takes away the sense of responsibility of bringing in the 'realization of Himself.' Commit to God 'that He hath given thee;' not fling it off, but put it over onto Him and yourself with it, and the burden is lightened by the 'sense of companionship'."[1]

There would be many miles to go before I would learn how to apply this truth. Strange how much knowledge I can acquire, even memorize, and yet fail to know how to activate those principles in my particular situation. Certainly I can know the Ten Commandments backwards and forwards without being able to keep them. What is needed is application. Application is putting into practice what I already know.

There was a running dialogue I had with myself that went something like this. "Glory, just take one day at a time. Can you make it until 5 p.m. today? Of course. Then do the same thing tomorrow and the next." There was no fear for that *one* day. Someone has said *fear* is the knowledge of our own inadequacies. I felt totally inadequate for what lay ahead of me. What I was not so peaceful about were possibly the hundreds of days, perhaps even 40 to 50 years ahead. All those long, endless, unknown years in the future. If only I was 70, there wouldn't be so many years left. As my good friend Jeannette Clift George says, "Life is so daily."

Why had this happened to me? Had I not prayed about whom I was to marry? Yes, many times. I see now I didn't wait for an answer. I did the choosing and asked God to bless my choice. It should have been the other way round, ASKING FOR GOD'S CHOICE AND HIS BLESSINGS WOULD FOLLOW.

From hearing different speakers, I knew self-pity was to be avoided because no sin is worse than the sin of self-pity because it obliterates God and puts self-interest upon the throne.

God's response to my self-pity probably would be: "Would you like some cheese with your whine?"

Oswald Chambers says, "Where I will not trust where I cannot see, that is where infidelity begins. I must abandon myself to God." Chambers also says that worry is to be bypassed because it is not only wrong to worry, it too is infidelity since worrying means that I do not think that God can look after the everyday details of my life.

When the chips were down, I quickly discovered all my best efforts and work were not enough. It would certainly take more than all the king's horses and all the king's men to put this Humpty-Dumpty back together again--along with her six little egglets.

MUCH HEART SEARCHING MUST BEGIN!

CHOOSING A LOVE THAT WILL LAST

CHAPTER 2

CRY BABY CRY!

Deeply embedded within me was the conviction that my children were entitled to a happy childhood just as I had had--at all costs. Since I was given total custody of the children, the responsibility was all mine. There could be no big misjudgments on my part now. Since their father lived a distance away, there would be few visitations.

To get some direction, many afternoons I would walk across the street from our home on North Tenth Street to St. John's Episcopal Church. I found the sanctuary particularly beautiful with its blood-red carpeting and huge stained-glass window behind the altar depicting Christ holding a lamb in His arms. When I entered the silent chapel, I would go to the second row from the front on the right-hand side and kneel on the prie-dieu. Each time, I would promise myself not to cry and would take no Kleenex with me, believing I couldn't possibly sob again today. It was disastrous because I would inevitably end up wiping my tears and runny nose on either my skirt or sleeve. Yuck!

I'd spend the time before God in deep contemplation and meditation, and pray for guidance about what to do next and how to handle the children. The Bible says that we are to seek first the Kingdom of God and his righteousness and all these things shall be added unto us. Matt. 6:33.

As I looked at the stained-glass Jesus, much comfort was given to me in that little church. Often the time would get away and I wouldn't realize I had been there so long. One time the secretary of the church stepped in to ask me if I was all right. Of course I wasn't all right, but there was no one who could help me except God. And I felt I was in the right place.

From talking over every detail of my life with God, I drew tremendous strength. There were no secrets. There was nothing I couldn't share with Him. He would never betray me.

Occasionally, I would leave that small sanctuary feeling peaceful, other times numb. Mostly, it was a conscious effort to put one foot in front of the other to get back home.

At that time, Barbara Johnson, a friend whom I will write about later, was teaching me how to be open and honest with God and express just how I felt. In other words, no pious or formal prayers. One time she was telling me what she had told God that morning, and I gasped, "You told God what?"

She said, "Of course, He knows that is the real way I feel deep inside. I just told Him that life wasn't fair and that I deserved better."

This openness was all very strange to me because my dad had taught me to be very careful with whom I shared my secrets, because those secrets might come back to me for years to come but not as I told them. Also, my dad cautioned me not to let my friends confide in me too much either. He said that if your friends feel you know too much about them, they will avoid you, and very likely you will end up odd man out with the black eye. The same advice was given for staying out of other people's affairs.

Maybe I should insert something a little off the subject, but it was a surprise to me to find that the motto on the first coin ever issued in the United States (the 1787 penny) was, "Mind Your Own Business."

THE PACT

As I grew more comfortable baring my soul to God, I eventually made a pact with Him. It was something like this, "I don't trust my judgment. I want You to take care of my life and the lives of my children. You choose for me the big decisions even if I cry, scream and resist. No matter how much it hurts me, You decide what is best for all seven of us. If marriage should be in my future, then You choose a love that will last. I need a clear answer; some way I will know for sure it is from You. I want Your FIRST choice, not second or third, but first. I hereby give

CHOOSING A LOVE THAT WILL LAST

You my permission."

I had some hesitations about not putting some restrictions on this pact.

For example, I didn't want to be sent to India or be asked to do some kind of religious work. Strange how I wanted God's best and yet I wanted to have some say in it too, which certainly showed my lack of faith in God's wisdom. As to religious work, it seemed to me there was a lack of joy in those who were doing such work.

This story explains my feelings at that time. For many years, the Northups were missionaries to Pueblo, Mexico. Every six months they'd return to the United States to have their passports renewed. On one particular crossing into the U. S., an American immigration official asked them what they had been doing all this time in Mexico. Mrs. Northup smiling sweetly replied, "We are missionaries."

The agent quickly replied, "Oh, no, you can't be." Whereupon she stated very emphatically that they really were missionaries. He unflinchingly repeated that they couldn't possibly be and informed her, "I can tell the ones who are missionaries."

"How?" she pleaded.

"You're too happy. I know the faces of missionaries, and they're not happy," he announced.

Back to my quest, something spurred me on, something certainly beyond myself. It was adventure of the highest sort since I knew of no one who approached God like this. I was careful not to share this with anyone except Barbara.

With my pact made, all I had to do was to wait and see what pathway God would lead me down. I had asked the question and made the petition, but the real miracle would be in the answer, HIS ANSWER. Many times I wondered just how I would receive or know the answer. Many ways crossed my mind, but I was open to any avenue or method by which He might choose to bring it. How it came or by whom He used was of no consequence to me. What I was after was God's direction and plan for my life. It seems to me, we have a problem in life when we don't have any orders, no commitments and no plan for our lives. We are defensive because we haven't heard from God, or because we are unsure and have no place of our own with God.

I wanted to know if faith really worked when you lose your most precious thing? Would faith be viable for the 70's and 80's? This quest was of great importance to me.

And too, it is always assumed if you ask a question of someone that an answer will be forthcoming, right? Perhaps this is the most profound sentence in this book. The sum total of this book is about, "WAITING FOR AN ANSWER." I had asked the question or request of God, now I had to wait for His response. This really hit me when I shared with a friend that I was waiting for advice from God, and gave her no other details. Her quizzical look told me volumes, like, "Isn't that why God gave us brains?"

Sure, we all pray I dare say, but there are many ways to interpret an answer. True, but to pray and expect no answer translates into no answer is expected. In other words, we are making one-sided conversation. Why? Let's be sane about this. If we are talking to someone and pose a question, then we must wait for a reply.

It is my contention that almost everyone in the world prays at one time or another. Sometimes they are *help me* or *crisis* prayers to a God who is for the most part a stranger to us, because we've spent so little time with Him. We run in with our emergency, without even saying *hello* first. Since God isn't visible we feel we can get away with that kind of behavior. We should ask ourselves, "Do I pray only in the disturbances of my life, or only when things go wrong? What am I offering back to God on a daily basis?" There is a right way and a wrong way to approach God in prayer. David says our posture first of all should be that of worship with a joyful heart, then thanksgiving and praise. Psalms 100:1,4. I am learning that my thanks should exceed my requests.

A close high school friend of mine, Jody Hudson, told me one

CHOOSING A LOVE THAT WILL LAST

day she was praying for a husband and a man knocked on the door. She interpreted it to mean he was the one. Later she was confused as to whether he was the right one. Telling God, "If you don't stop me, I think you mean for me to go ahead." That is certainly very presumptuous and dangerous. For instance, if no one knocks on the door within ten minutes, then I am going ahead and sin. God will not play our games.

I know some who take stories from the Bible and fit them into their own particular situation. If I were impressed or given a Scripture by the Holy Spirit to look up, then that would be different. But to go and open the Bible on my own and say, *"I will take whatever passage my finger lands on as my answer"* is deluding myself. I tried this only once because my finger landed on, "Today thou shalt be with me in paradise." That cured me as that proved not to be true guidance.

Frequently, we go by feelings. In other words, if we feel good after we have prayed, we interpret that as a *yes* and if fearful or uneasy a *no*. I definitely needed much more specific and clear direction than that. I wanted God to deliver the message to my spirit in such a way that it would be unmistakable--more than guesswork or feelings.

God is spirit and He has placed His Holy Spirit within us. It is in the blending of these two spirits, who have a language all their own, that gives us the inner knowledge beyond a shadow of a doubt. WAIT FOR THE INNER KNOWING OF YOUR SPIRIT WITHIN. It will be strong and become stronger with time, and there will be no mistaking His answer.

But usually there is a waiting period. Is there any work in life so hard as waiting? All motion is easier than calm waiting. However, it takes time, sometimes longer than we think or want, but it is wise not to take a shortcut or put a time limit on God. We must hang tough until we receive a distinguishable answer from God. Otherwise we will have to support our own decision. Surely we all have had quite enough of supporting our own wrong decisions.

When I was wanting a certain thing from God, it was more than easy to try to twist or read into the situation what I wanted the answer to be. For instance when I was wanting a certain person to be chosen as God's choice as a husband. However, I never acted on that because I knew deep within I didn't really have a distinct answer, or any answer for that matter.

If indeed God is not dumb so that He cannot speak, nor blind that He cannot see, is there any reason why God would want me to muddle around second-guessing His will? This God who has no limits in the entire universe can make abundantly transparent His exact plan for my life, or there is no God--not for me--at least not the one I had been taught about.

God says in several places in the Bible, "Is there anything too hard for Me?" Gen. 18:14, Jer. 32:17-27. Anything? WOW! He invites us to prove Him to see if He will not do as He says and promises. We are somewhat hesitant to try to prove God for some reason. Perhaps we have learned more reverence and piety than we have in developing a close relationship with Him.

Scripture says we are to fear God and we do to the extent we fear to draw near to Him--for many reasons. We are truly afraid, I believe, to get familiar with such a high God. God invites us to draw close to Him and He will draw close to us. James 4:8. The checks of the Spirit come in the most gentle ways. If we aren't sensitive enough to detect His voice, we will not hear it. Or could it be possible that we aren't in close enough proximity to Him to hear anything? There must be the *listening* ear, as well as the still small voice.

It is in the getting to know and drawing close to one another that enables the deep longings of the heart to merge and blend together. I always imagine it this way. Any kind of affection and touch between lovers is in close proximity. Can you visualize lovers yelling sweet nothings back and forth from the car to the front porch? The most rewarding and comforting times are those spent in close embrace or when communication is either whispered or spoken very quietly and tenderly to each other. A

CHOOSING A LOVE THAT WILL LAST

step beyond that is perhaps when two hearts are intertwined to the degree there is no need for verbalization. That is how close God wants us to be to Him.

> "Love's in the merest look, the lightest touch,
> The thought almost too subtle to recall;
> When love is deepest, words may be too much.
> True lovers do not need a sign at all;
> They have, and do not even have to reach.
> When love says most, it has least need of speech."
> James Dillet Freeman [1]

"The apprehension of the divine voice depends upon man's capacity for hearing," as Elisabeth Elliot quotes in *A Chance to Die*. It is doubtful God will yell His instructions to us. It takes two persons to form a love relationship. One can love with all her heart, soul and body, but only when it is reciprocated by the loved one is it truly a relationship. To form a complete love bond, it takes two. I can envision God standing with His arms outstretched with a heart full of love for each of His children. He is waiting and longing for each child to come up very close and let there flow between them trust and love. There is no disappointment or betrayal in God's kind of love. It is everlasting, unconditional and trustworthy.

There is a Scripture that lists all the ways that cannot separate us from the love of God: tribulation, distress, persecution, famine, nakedness, peril or sword. Romans 8:35 KJV. However, we can make the decision to walk away from His love ourselves. We have that prerogative since we have been given free wills to do as we choose. The prodigal was loved by the father, but the son chose to leave. He was still his son and still loved, but he was a lost son inasmuch as the father's love was not reciprocated, and he would receive no inheritance until he returned. C. S. Lewis in *Mere Christianity* says,

"If a thing is free to be good, it is also free to be bad. And free will is what has made evil possible. Why, then, did God give them free will? Because free will, though it makes evil possible, is also the only thing that makes possible any love or goodness or joy worth having. The happiness which God designs for his higher creatures is the happiness of being freely, voluntarily united to him and to each other in an ecstasy of love and delight compared with which the most rapturous love between a man and a woman on this earth is mere milk and water. And for that they must be free. Why did God make a creature of such rotten stuff that it went wrong? The better stuff a creature is made of--the cleverer and stronger and freer it is--then the better it will be if it goes right, but also the worse it will be if it goes wrong."[2]

I heard Billy Graham say in a crusade, "Man is infinitely lonely until he comes into communion with his maker." We were made by God for God--for His pleasure and fellowship. That's why man gets so depraved when he gets away from the purpose for which he was created.

In *Angelwalk* Roger Elwood, says, "It is free will only, not an enslavement but a dedication, not an obsession but a devotion."[3]

Try this sometime. For a period of say 30 days give your husband or wife the same amount of time, attention and love you give to God. At the end of the 30 days, see if the relationship is progressing as you want it. God is all love, but that love is not activated until our love is released back towards the object of our love. The two loves intermix and meld. That's what makes two spirits one.

Perhaps it is not too difficult to observe a person and ascertain what that person loves most in life. Who or what would come out in first place? Spouse, golf, God, business or self?

God says, "If you will begin to search again for God, you shall find him when you search for him with ALL your hearts and souls." Deut. 4:29.

Why does it seem that most worthwhile things in life are not instant, but take either time, pain, effort or learning? For instance an education, courtship, marriage, profession, baby, voyage, language, maturity and wisdom, to name a few.

Somewhere there was borne in me this determination to hasten towards this source of all love, and I was not to be disappointed.

Having turned my entire case over to God, I knew it would be ludicrous to consult with man, any man. Many of my friends earlier had advised me to seek counsel with some minister. No way! It was too late and besides they could only offer their sympathy. I needed someone with the ability to change things. However, I did confide with my friend Barbara. My desperate need was to find the One who made me, who caused me to come into being, that One who loved me unconditionally. The Psalmist put it so succinctly.

"You made all the delicate, inner parts of my body, and knit them together in my mother's womb. Thank you for making me so wonderfully complex! It is amazing to think about. Your workmanship is marvelous--and how well I know it. You were there while I was being formed in utter seclusion. You saw me before I was born and SCHEDULED EACH DAY OF MY LIFE BEFORE I BEGAN TO BREATHE. Every day was recorded in your Book. How precious it is, Lord, to realize you are thinking about me constantly! I can't even count how many times a day your thoughts turn towards me. And when I waken in the morning, you are still thinking about me." Psalms 139:13,18.

How close or how far I have veered from His schedule for my life gives me much food for thought.

Also, sounds as if our names are all written down in the Book of Life before we are born, but apparently after the age of accountability our names can be blotted out of that book by God if we refuse to accept his Son. I John 2:23, Rev. 3:5, Deut. 29:20, Psa. 69:28, Exodus 32:32.

In the meantime, I must pick up the pieces of my life and carry on until more direction is received.

MORE INTENSE SEARCHING WITH MY WHOLE HEART IS NEEDED IF I AM TO FIND GOD'S BEST FOR MY LIFE!

CHOOSING A LOVE THAT WILL LAST

CHAPTER 3

INLOVENESS

Of all wishes of the human heart, no doubt finding a love that will last tops them all, but isn't it sad that we have received so little training to prepare us for such a love and marriage? Twelve to twenty years goes into a profession while almost zero years are spent in learning about marriage and the person to whom we will pledge to live with for the balance of our lives. Our professional lives outlive our vows many times.

If only at sixteen I had had the book *Finding The Love Of Your Life* by Dr. Neil Clark Warren, it would have helped me immeasurably. He outlines the ten principles for choosing the right marriage partner:

1. Eliminate the seven primary causes of faulty mate selection.
2 Find a person to love who is a lot like you.
3. Get yourself emotionally healthy before you get yourself married.
4. Develop a clear mental image of your "perfect person."
5. Find love that you can feel in your bones, and express it with great wisdom.
6. Let passionate love mature before you decide.
7. Master the art of intimacy.
8. Learn how to resolve differences before you get married.
9. Refuse to proceed until you can genuinely pledge your life-long commitment.
10. Celebrate your marriage with the full support of your family and friends.

Under principle #1 Dr. Warren lists the seven faulty decisions.

"1. The decision to get married is made too quickly.
2. The decision is made at too young an age.
3. One or both persons are too eager to be married.
4. One or both may be choosing a mate to please someone else.
5. The experience base is too narrow.
6. The couple has unrealistic expectations.
7. One or both may have unaddressed significant personality or behavior problems." [1]

It would appear our whole lives are pivotal around our professions while in fact it is our marriages or relationships that can indeed make or break a person. It might appear otherwise, but insurance companies take off anywhere from four to five years of a person's life expectancy for a divorce. The trauma cannot be underestimated. It not only affects the divorced themselves, but their children and their children's children. Its ravages are far reaching and the trauma is immeasurable. I know.

Hence, the necessity to better prepare for such commitment. In an area where we are for the most part untrained, unskilled and yes, even ignorant, there is a need to learn much and be guided on more than infatuation, physical attraction, in-loveness and feelings. Some suggest that most of our decision should be based on being in-love. Many can attest to the fact that we can fall *out* of love as easily as we fall *in* if the relationship is not properly nourished.

The divorce statistics clearly indicate we are failing in the area of interpersonal relationships. Some marriages bumble along until they are at a point of no return when the analyzation process begins to learn just what a marriage should be. Should it not be the other way round? Lawyers and doctors practice and are tested in the classroom and hospital over a period of years before they are permitted a license. Not so with the practice of marriage. Three days' waiting is all that is required in Texas. Why not put our relationship to the test before marriage--we will be forced to

CHOOSING A LOVE THAT WILL LAST

afterwards. All cards should be put on the table, being open and honest with no hint of changing the other person after marriage. This does not include living together before marriage. It seems to me much more time should be spent in evaluating what we expect and need in marriage--after sex! Life has many facets besides sex. As George Burns says, "It's not what you do in bed that makes a marriage." Yet many a marriage is unknowingly based on hormones—one set of glands chasing another set of glands.

I found the book, *A Severe Mercy* by Sheldon Vanauken very interesting. "The smile of inloveness seemed to promise forever, but friends who had been in love last year were parting this year. The divorce rate was in the news. It must be that, whatever its promises, love does not by itself endure. But why? What was the failure behind the failure of love?

Mr. Vanauken goes on to say, "The killer of love is creeping separateness. Inloveness is a gift, but then it is up to the lovers to cherish or to ruin. This is done by taking love for granted, especially after marriage; ceasing to do things together; finding separate interests; we turning into I; self; self-regard: what I want to do. Actual selfishness is only a hop away."[2]

In this same book. Sheldon and Davy had what they called 'The Shining Barrier'--the shield of their love--to guard their love. They would be us centered, not self-centered. What will be best for our love? Total sharing, they felt, was the ultimate secret of a love that would last forever.

James D. Bryden puts forth, "Love does not die easily. It is a living thing. It thrives in the face of all life's hazards, save one-- neglect."

In the book, *The Laws of Lasting Love,* by Dr. Paul Pearsall gives these laws:

1. Put time where love is. If we hope to find love, we must first find time for loving. To make a lasting marriage we have to overcome self-centeredness.

2. In crisis, become as one, especially in illness, loss of children or other tragedies.

3. Take a loving look. How we see our partners often depends more on how *we* are than how *they* are. Look for love instead of flaws. It's a way of seeing.

4. Try another perspective. People in lasting-love marriages begin with the premise that there are many realities. They learn to accept different points of view.

5. Look out for No. 2. There is a powerful healing energy that emanates from loving. Bad energy springs from conflicts that arise when two egos collide.

6. Grow up, stop fighting, and start loving. It is better to learn how to love than how to fight. Don't try to win *in* your marriage, win *for* your marriage.

7. Marriage is designed primarily for giving rather than taking. It is meant to be a permanent union of two unselfish people.

8. If you fight for yourself, only you can win. When you fight for your marriage, you both win.[7]

It is my opinion that selfishness and divorce are synonymous. If there was some way to annihilate selfishness, divorce could be eradicated.

According to the *1989 Marital Status of Population*, U. S. Department of Commerce, Bureau of Census, in 1987 there were 13.6 million divorced persons between the ages of 18 and older in the United States.

These 13.6 million divorced people need ministering to. There is forgiveness available. The Father stands with outstretched arms welcoming all who will come to Him and He will freely pardon, and remake their lives. Sometimes I wonder if the church is fearful of addressing the problem of divorce, sensing it may increase the divorce rate among its parishioners, as well as its clergy. It seems the church would rather address suicide than divorce. Death is simpler and more final!

It was reported on television that by the Year 2000 there will be more divorced families in America than first families. What a

CHOOSING A LOVE THAT WILL LAST

shocking statistic!

I want to emphasize that divorce is not the unforgivable sin, regardless of whatever else it is. There is plenteous forgiveness available to these millions. Full pardon--else Jesus died in vain. Make no mistake about it, Jesus died for all sins and all people. Do not permit anyone to tell you that Christ will turn you away for any reason except one--the sin against the Holy Spirit, because Jesus said, "...and him that cometh to Me I will in no wise cast out." John 6:38 KJV. For *man*, this is the beauty of redemption.

Can you imagine being forgiven for murder if we truly repent and ask for Christ's forgiveness-- having our slate wiped clean just as if we had never done it? That is mercy and unmerited love beyond my comprehension. Stop and think about this for a moment. No other religion offers such hope, forgiveness and rehabilitation. Sometimes Christians don't offer their forgiveness but Christ does.

God said in Isaiah 1:18, "Come, let's talk this over! No matter how deep the stain of your sins, I can take it out and make you as clean as freshly fallen snow. Even if you are stained as red as crimson, I can make you white as wool."

Satan would love for these millions of divorced (as well as others) to believe they can't be forgiven. It increases his kingdom. If Christians don't forgive divorce or other sins, neither will their sins be forgiven them, according to Mark 11:26 KJV. In fact, we don't have to commit the cardinal sins to be lost. If we don't love others, that is sin. Therefore, the majority of the world ends up on the devil's team through just such a fluke. How disheartening because Jesus repeated over and over that He came to the evil and sick--not to the good and well. Don't permit God's worst enemy to dupe us. Repentance plus believing that Jesus Christ took that sin for us when He died on the cross is all that is required.

King David didn't divorce--he murdered and committed adultery. However, David was a man after God's own heart, not because of his deeds but because of his repentant heart. David never turned against God, nor turned to God's worst enemy for advice. David took responsibility for his sin--something Adam and Eve didn't do. David didn't blame others. Incidentally, that is why I think the father so totally forgave the prodigal. His son took full responsibility for running away. He returned and repented. What parent would not love and forgive such a son? No doubt the father wouldn't have suggested giving him a ring, a robe and a feast if the prodigal had come back demanding more of his inheritance to waste. The way I see the prodigal son and the eldest brother is--the prodigal committed sins of the body while his brother committed sins of the disposition. Adam was thrown out of his Garden of Eden home because of disobeying God's command not to eat from a certain tree. Adam blamed Eve, and Eve blamed the serpent. I notice that didn't save their explusion from the Garden. The prodigal regained his home through taking full responsibility for his own wayward behavior.

God let David keep Bathsheba and she was even included in the bloodline of Jesus Christ, along with the harlot, Rahab, who lied to those who were against God. So there is certainly hope for the divorced and remarried. Jesus was never pious. I love that about Him. He is also sovereign. "God does whatever pleases Him throughout all of heaven and earth and in the deepest seas." Psalms 135:6.

Of course, there are consequences to divorce as there are to all sins. If we get drunk and are involved in an accident, resulting in our leg being cut off, chances are our limb won't grow back, but God takes what remains and makes the best with what's left, if given to Him.

Marriage or a family unit can be likened to a wheel with a hub and many spokes. Life presents various happenings to a family throughout a lifetime, indeed some very sad things. These events can be compared to knocking out one or several of the spokes. Whereas, divorce is catastrophic, striking and crushing the hub or center of the wheel, rending the entire wheel inoperative. The damage of divorce is incalculable when the long term effects are considered in the lives of each individual in that family. Broken relationships of any kind are always devastating. "We all long for stability and that secure sense of knowing things are right in the center--even when it's all wrong on the edges," states Alice Byram in *Healing In Broken Places*.[3]

This is what the J. B. Phillips text says, "It has been well said by several modern psychologists that it is not the outward storms and stresses of life that defeat and disrupt personality, but its inner conflicts and miseries. If a man is happy and stable at heart, he can normally cope, even with zest, with difficulties that lie outside his personality. For example, a man who is happily married and can return daily to a happy home is not likely to be defeated by outward trials and strains. But the same man could quite easily go to pieces and find life altogether too much for him if his marriage, for instance, were to collapse--if in fact the center of his operations were destroyed."[4]

This is why, first of all, we must have a secure center of operations within, which faith in God provides.

This is not to say we cannot be healed and be made even stronger after each problem. At no occurrence in our lives are we to give up and throw in the towel regardless of what horrendous things happen to us. To me, divorce is the worst possible thing that can happen in life, but even so, it can be overcome with God's participation of inner and outer healing. Your *worst thing* may be something else. There is nothing too hard for God if given to Him.

Earlier, this is what I prayed, "God, there will be no divorce, even when happenings were out of my control. Anything else, but definitely no divorce. It is against your Word. Certainly You were the one who started the whole institution of the family in the first place. It was all Your plan and idea."

Indirectly, I guess I tried to make God responsible in some way for the divorce. I quoted some other Scriptures to Him, indicating He didn't know what He wrote. Never entered my mind how insulting it was to remind God of His own plan for mankind. It would soon be evident that I must face up to the responsibility of my own choices and decisions.

In life, each of us is presented with many choices. It's in the choosing that determines our destiny in life and after life. At each fork of the road there are decisions we must make. Yet it is unfathomable what consequences are produced by one single choice--whether good or bad.

Prior to this time, divorce was not in my vocabulary. It was never an option I would consider. Even pagans didn't divorce, I reasoned. God said He hates divorce. Mal. 2:16. He didn't say He hated divorced people. I felt I detested it more since it was happening to me. No, not till death do us part, I reaffirmed. Well, death almost parted us, but not the kind of death that is acceptable to God.

Before I actually filed for divorce, there was a turmoil and a thrashing about for the right decision. In the end I knew I had to file. It was a definite inner knowing that was unmistakable. *Perhaps if I weren't so resistant and immovable to divorce, God would restore my marriage,* I thought.

About this time the verse in Psalms kept coming to me, "Oh Lord My God, in thee do I put my trust." I clung to the hope that God, whom I had loved since childhood, would intervene in the madness of my life. Total and complete trust requires few questions.

In my mind, I kept seeing a scene of a cemetery with seven caskets lined up. The cemetery grounds were all burned and blackened as by fire. It was the most desolate place imaginable. I was so bereft as I beheld it all I could hardly get my breath. Then suddenly I sensed I was not alone. A presence was with me, and it was bearable only so long as He stayed with me. The shock of it all did not seem to reach the hurting part of me. I was shielded by this comforting presence.

Through it all, I sensed God was there, though I didn't see or hear Him. It was more like a distant vague knowing, but at times too far away somehow to reach. Realizing that if I was to triumph over the worst tragedy that can happen to a human being, I would have to stake my whole life in getting a response from God--this God who is there.

Death at this point would have been like singing in the rain compared to divorce. Even the word *divorce* is detestable to me.

I fully realize that other types of tragedies would be considered by many to be worse than divorce--losing children, having a dreaded disease, being disgraced, or someone you love spending life in prison.

I was given an opportunity to prove if I meant death would be preferable to divorce. It was while my son, Tommy, who was seven at the time, and I were flying back from Fort Collins, Colorado. We had gone to see Dr. N. C. Kephart, concerning Tommy's hearing loss problem. We were approaching Oklahoma City when the pilot advised that we would have to fly around for about 20 minutes to burn up most of the fuel before making an emergency landing because either one or two tires blew out on take-off. Since it was a very cold January evening with snow on the ground, I woke Tommy up and put his heavy coat and cap on him, and bundled up myself.

After confessing all my sins, I had a little time left (very little) to think. There were many signs of the Cross being made in the cabin as the pilot kept us informed as to what to expect next. The strangest thought consumed me totally. To myself, I mused, *This is perfect. Really perfect that Tommy and I should go together because I felt there would be no one else who would help Tommy with the hours of tutoring he needed to catch up.*

As we eventually came down for the landing, I was totally happy and relieved that it would all soon be over. Also, I remember wishing there was some way I could let my family know that it was the best answer, and to please not grieve for us.

In a few seconds the plane came in for a smooth landing with all the fire trucks and ambulances standing by. Only one tire had blown out. The other tire carried the plane so the wing tips were kept level. Was I ever disappointed! Given 20 minutes, that is how I felt at the moment of truth.

There are many ways to cope with problems, and if tears could have mended our lives, then we wouldn't have needed anything else. There were many more tears than words. We were all crushed and unhappy. That is the way we handled it. I like where it says in Scripture that our tears are bottled up in heaven, and He records each one in His book. Psalms 56:8. The children and I have a mega-supply stored there. Mother mentioned to me several times, "Glory, please don't cry anymore. You will get old looking." But dear old Tear River kept right on flowing and overflowing many times. Mostly when no one else was around.

The children seldom saw me looking depressed. In fact, Shari told me later the thing she resented the most was making her think life was a bowl of cherries when it wasn't. It was my belief that burdening their happy childhoods would have been both cruel and unnecessary, especially when they could do nothing to change things. From my observation, friends of mine who had similar problems with fewer children did go into deeper problems, and some are still in unfulfilled lives many years later.

"DEAR GOD, HELP ME! OH, LORD GOD OF HEAVEN AND EARTH, DON'T LET MY HURTS BE INSIGNIFICANT TO YOU," I cried.

In the worst episode of my life, it seemed I was in a tiny little sturdy bubble boat, far out at sea with no land in sight. The little capsule tossed furiously to and fro, flipping from side to side. No matter how much the winds and waves beat upon that little bubble boat, I was snug, dry and safe inside. Nothing disturbed me. I was witnessing all the havoc about me, but somehow it was not reaching my consciousness. My little bubble was just bouncing and rolling with the storm. It was incredible. Let the ocean and all the world roar, I was safe inside. I was not the captain of this boat!

At other times and in other crises, I found I did not function nearly as bravely as I showed outwardly. When my mother and father heard of the divorce, they couldn't believe it. "Impossible," they exclaimed in great dismay. "How could we not have known what was going on when we were so close to them? Glory should be awarded an Academy Award."

All the while my mind, body and spirit was searching, reaching, grasping for the way out of this nightmare of a family shipwrecked.

What with the church's view on divorce, my own undying view of marriage, my family being very verbal with many crossviews on what happened or what should have happened, I was caught in an insurmountable position. It was a no-win situation.

In an article in the Wall Street Journal, Faye Crosby, a Smith College psychologist, says that divorce interferes with work more than any other trauma in a person's life. During the first three months after a spouse walks out, the other spouse usually is incapable of focusing on work. But the shattered spouse gets back on track once it's accepted that the divorce is a reality. Statistics also show that 90% of couples who lose a child end up in divorce within five years.

First it was a glimmer, then more and more came the realization I had to arrange an audience with God, much like people do with the Pope in Rome, to get a ruling on my case before going any farther. I was certainly incapable of handling life alone with six children. I seemed lost to myself. I needed my husband to shoulder some of the responsibility.

God was my court of last resort. All other sources and resources had been exhausted. Does not the Bible teach that we have an advocate with the Father, Jesus Christ, the righteous? I John 2:1,2. IF GOD COULD NOT HELP ME, THEN I WAS SUNK!

For Christmas, the children gave me the new Living Version of the Bible now called *The Book*. It is written in contemporary American English--not the King's English--hence much more rapid comprehension. The wording and phrasing is so easily understood. I attempted to clear my mind of any and all doctrine I had learned per se, and began reading only from the viewpoint of discovering what God was like.

I ran across James 1:5,8. It was thrilling! Really thrilling to me! Many times I was hesitant to bother God with such small things, only I didn't consider them small to me. To my happy relief, I found God does not mind us asking. It goes like this.

"If you want to know what God wants you to do, ask Him, and He will gladly tell you, for He is always ready to give a bountiful supply of wisdom to all who ask Him; HE WILL NOT RESENT IT. But when you ask Him, be sure that you really expect Him to tell you, for a doubtful mind will be as unsettled as a wave of the sea that is driven and tossed by the wind; and every decision you then make will be uncertain, as you turn first this way, and then that. If you don't ask with faith, don't expect the Lord to give you any solid answer."

Somewhere in the back of my mind, I felt God helped those who helped themselves. Now, I felt no guilt in asking God what He wanted me to do with the rest of my life, and I knew He would not *resent* telling me. I loved that verse and read and reread it many times.

"The power of faith is in its object, not in faith itself, much less in our imagination. Our positive attitude should come from Christ-confidence instead of a humanly produced self-confidence."[5]

With my mind and heart in agreement, I decided I would approach God the Father through His son, Jesus. Why not test and see if God was who I had been taught to believe He was? At least give Him a chance. What did I have to lose? Either He was very much alive with no limitations as the Bible presents, or the whole story was fabricated and was one of the greatest farces ever perpetrated upon mankind. If this God who made ears and eyes is now deaf and blind, (Psalms 94:9) why keep up all the prayers and rituals? I thought prayer meant conversation. Does it not take two to converse? I wanted God to talk to me, and to give me solid answers. In Malachi 3:10, God said, "...Try me! Let me prove it to you!...." referring in this instance to tithes and

CHOOSING A LOVE THAT WILL LAST

offerings. Then I ran across this verse in Isaiah 48:8.

"And don't forget the many times I clearly told you what was going to happen in the future. For I am God--I only--and there is no other like me who can tell you what is going to happen in the future. All I say will come to pass, for I do whatever I wish."

Now armed with more information, I dared to ask God to prove Himself to me. In reading a number of books, I noted this was what some of the authors had also done.

These books whetted my appetite and I started reading marathons; all kind of books, attempting to discern what other people did in times of crises. So many lives have been changed by reading books; perhaps more than by sermons. A book requires our participation and takes several days to read while only about 10 percent of any sermon is retained. According to Guy P. Leavitt in *Teach With Success*, there are five ways we learn.

> Seeing   75 percent
> Hearing 13 percent
> Touching 6 percent
> Tasting 3 percent
> Smelling 3 percent

If these percentages can be believed, television has the greater ministries, with perhaps Christian bookstores a close second.

Most of these authors touched me deeply, much to my surprise. The books that changed my life were authored by C. S. Lewis, Bruce Olsson, Charles L. Allen, Pat Robertson, Harald Bredesen, Charles Colson, Robert Schuller, Betty Malz, Lydia Prince, Corrie ten Boom, Catherine Marshall, Agnes Sanford, Frances Hunter, Dale Evans, Pat Boone, Watchman Nee and Francis Schaeffer, to name a few.

It is my personal belief that there are some writers today who are inspired (not inerrant) by the Holy Spirit just as authors of the Bible were. Why not? The Holy Spirit is God--the third person of the Trinity--alive and well, still helping, still teaching, still running alongside us, and still leading us into all truth.

The one book that actually convinced me to wait for an answer from God was potent. It was *Bruchko* by Bruce Olsson. That story proved to be the pivotal point in my life. Bruce was a 19-year old boy from Minneapolis, Minnesota, with only a year of college, little money and not knowing one word of the Motilone language. Yet God directed Bruce to minister to some Indians in Colombia. He won the entire village to Christ in about seven years. *Bruchko* is a classic on God's guidance--sovereign divine guidance. I read that book over and over.

There was also one LP record that ministered to me in a profound way. Late at night, I would close my bedroom door, place a pillow over my head, so the children wouldn't hear me crying, and play the record, *Joe Mulford Sings*. My favorite songs were, *He Looked Beyond My Faults and Saw My Need*, *Sheltered In the Arms of God*, *My Savior Cares* and *In the Beginning*.

It has been 15 years now since I played that record. In getting it out and listening to it recently, it was but a distant melancholy from this point in time. Back then, I hung onto the words of those songs like a drowning man clings to a rope. Some say it is weak to hang onto a crutch. Whee, I clung and clung tight. Man, it seems, has not invented any better device for a broken limb than a crutch. I say if you are broken, grab a couple of good strong crutches and hold on for dear life until you are well again.

God is certainly more than a crutch: He is the whole pillar upon which to lean. He invites us to become weak so He can become strong on our behalf. The weaker we are the more He can show us His strength. Could we ever forget the man who threw us a rope when we were drowning? He will even pick us up and carry us in His arms if need be. The poem *Footprints* is relevant to a needy person. *Well* people do not need a physician or a hospital.

CHOOSING A LOVE THAT WILL LAST

FOOTPRINTS

"One night a man had a dream. He dreamed he was walking along the beach with the Lord. Across the sky flashed scenes from his life. For each scene, he noticed two sets of footprints in the sand; one belonged to him, and the other to the Lord.

When the last scene of his life flashed before him, he looked back at the footprints in the sand. He noticed that many times along the path of his life there was only one set of footprints. He also noticed that it happened at the very lowest and saddest times in his life.

This really bothered him and he questioned the Lord about it. "Lord, you said that once I decided to follow you, you'd walk with me all the way. But I have noticed that during the most troublesome times in my life, there is only one set of footprints. I don't understand why, when I needed you most, you would leave me."

The Lord replied, "My precious, precious child, I love you and I would never leave you. During your times of trial and suffering, when you see only one set of footprints, it was then that I carried you." [6]

Looking back on all this, it is very grievous to me that I didn't do certain things at the time of the divorce. At that particular time, I couldn't face taking each of my six children aside or together and explain what was happening. They knew something was wrong. Herby and Shari knew more than I knew they knew. We never discussed openly about what would happen to us. We just hung in there together, mostly silent. Sometimes quiet determination and standing still is enough glue for the moment. However, in retrospect, I would recommend sharing with them, but perhaps without all the details. There are some things a mother cannot share with her children. However, if you don't share with them, others will. One relative even went so far as to divide the children's loyalties. Knowing the children were in no way responsible for the divorce was my reason, I told myself, for not making accusations to them against their dad. Dads are very important people to their children. As I have confessed before, I am not a confronter, but I am learning.

Someone at school told Tami, 12, and she was heartbroken and cried secretly for days. Only then did she tell me. Tari Alice, 14, was unusually quiet, withdrawn and downcast. While driving the kids to school, Tommy, 7, out of the clear blue said, "Daddy must have done something really bad." I didn't answer. Little Lori who was 5 sensed something was wrong. She was an angel and demanded little attention.

Looking back, it seems I could have set them all down and had a long talk, but I just couldn't do it. There was no way I could bear to see them in any more pain. And too, a part of me said it would be an unfair advantage over the other parent.

There had to be a solution somewhere. But where?

Sensing and searching more and more where to turn for help, I discovered it's not in man's ability to correct some things. They may want to help but they are severely limited. Man can do natural things, but it takes God to do the supernatural. For big problems you need big help; for little problems you need little help.

A very startling realization hit me full force as I was awakening early one morning. Nothing unusual happened to cause it, but there was this overwhelming sense that there was no one in all the world who could help me--not my father, mother, in-laws, sisters or brother. No one! I was all alone. It was chilling. NO ONE! Turning with more earnestness than ever to the only source I knew who could rescue the seven of us, I began a journey I had not anticipated.

Either God was who He said He was or He was not. I would ask, seek and knock, like it says, and wait.

Life was not very normal during those days. It seemed there were many unexpected calls. Unusual how sorrow comes in

CHOOSING A LOVE THAT WILL LAST

multiples.

"When sorrows come, they come not single spies,
 But in battalions!" Shakepeare, Hamlet IV.

About two miles from home, Herby then 19, totalled his new car (new to him) and walked away unscratched.

A few weeks later, I got a call that Lori, 6, was hit by a car. The teenager was driving too fast on newly graveled Main Street at Westway, tossing Lori from her bicycle into the air, where she landed in some carrisa thorn bushes. The car narrowly missed running over her. After carefully twizzing the thorns out of her back and legs and soaking her in a tub of boric acid, she recovered fast but was very sore.

Next came the call from the women in our Dinner Club informing me I was no longer a member. We had formed this club some 11 years before. It was a close-knit group of friends made up of seven couples. Some of our happiest times were shared with these friends. I didn't know whether to laugh or cry after hearing their reason. They were afraid of my singleness.

What happened to the world I knew? It seemed as if I was on another planet. Nothing was familiar anymore. At this time, I wanted to leave McAllen more than anything else. Escape--just run away--anywhere. After several attempts that didn't work out, we decided to stay. But earlier, Hawaii seemed to be the answer. A doctor and his family wanted to rent our home in McAllen, and they would rent us their home in Hawaii. Next I went to Austin, Texas to try to rent an apartment, but the fire code forbade anyone with so many children renting the size apartment I could afford.

MY SEARCH WAS ON BIG TIME!

CHAPTER 4

APPEAL YOUR CASE

Some years ago, the author, Horatio G. Spafford received the news that his four daughters had all gone down at sea on the S. S. Ville de Havre on its way to Europe. Only his wife survived. Spafford could not rest until he hired a ship and had the captain point out the place where the tragedy occurred. Then Spafford went to his cabin and wrote the stanzas of the song, *It Is Well With My Soul.*

> When peace like a river attendeth my way;
> When sorrows like sea billows roll;
> Whatever my lot, thou hast taught me to say,
> It is well, it is well with my soul.

I didn't have trouble singing that song until I heard the story behind it. But although I feel compassion for Spafford, I can't feel his deepest pain and anguish because it didn't happen to *me*.

Let me interject here a little bit about things not discomfitting us until they happen to us. Divorce is not as painful to those who haven't been through it. Someone else's daughter being pregnant out of wedlock isn't as painful unless it happens to your daughter. Leukemia holds no personal terror until it has your 10-year old's name on it. We certainly can feel compassion and sorrow for others, but the tragedy would not wrench our hearts in the same way.

It took me more than eight years to use the word *divorce* without consciously flinching inwardly. I hate divorce and all the consequential happenings connected with it. It gives me no comfort to know that God hates divorce. Incidentally, there are other things God hates, such as lying, murdering, haughtiness,

CHOOSING A LOVE THAT WILL LAST

plotting evil, eagerness to do wrong, a false witness and sowing discord among brothers. Prov. 6:17. My comfort comes from knowing God said He would forgive these.

God knew there would be divorcees, murderers, liars and troublemakers. Of course God hates these things, knowing how much they are going to hurt us. That is why forgiveness is so necessary in order to rid us of guilt. That's why God's forgiveness was so important to me. The Bible says every person has need to be forgiven. That leaves no one out. We all have sinned. The great price God paid for this absolution was His only Son being given as a once and for all sacrifice in order to bring countless millions back into a right relationship with Himself. How truly marvelous for mankind! It was so important for me to cling to that truth.

I found that God knows all the circumstances and facts of our lives and will rule in total justice for all parties involved. However, I pray that He use more mercy than justice. But if God is to make a ruling, the case first must be handed over for His sole examination. Remember God doesn't intrude into our personal affairs unless invited to do so.

I didn't feel forgiveness until I realized how much He had forgiven me. If it is true God will not forgive my sins if I don't forgive others, then it is significant to me.

So I appealed my case to the righteous judge and ruler of all mankind and waited to be governed accordingly. I found He can be trusted with the right verdict, and I'm convinced He knows some things I don't! He is the only one who keeps books. I hereby rest my case and let my eternal destiny rest in the highest court of the universe. But coming to these conclusions wasn't easy as you shall see.

LORD, MAKE ME MORE LIKE YOURSELF, LESS LIKE MYSELF.

GLORY CHAPMAN

CHAPTER 5

SHOULDER TO KNEE

Sensing that getting an eight to five job right now was not to be, I enrolled at Pan American University located in Edinburg, Texas, a town nine miles from home. One of the graduate courses I audited was "Creative Writing." It was both stimulating and exciting to discern what I could learn from hearing the students' work critiqued in class.

Dr. Clyde Miller showed us how easy it was for a reader to detect the credibility of a writer right away, and that we were to write from a retrospective viewpoint only.

Some of my feelings at that time were expressed in this villanelle which I wrote.

LIFE OR DEATH

To live or to die
What should it be?
It could mean goodbye!

Forever is nigh
Old man, don't you see?
To live or to die.

With a heavy sigh
Down on bended knee
It could mean goodbye!

Life could be like pie
Left to you and me
To live or to die.

CHOOSING A LOVE THAT WILL LAST

Happiness cannot lie
It goes like one, two, three
It could mean goodbye!

Birth and death race to tie
In the conflict you see
To live or to die
Could mean goodbye!

This villanelle certainly exposed my feelings. It was a low time in my life. However, I wasn't the only one. I will never forget the morning the class was critiquing a short story written by Wilma, a young student who had taught school for one year. After hearing her story read aloud, Jack, another young student, turned to Wilma and blurted out accusingly, "Why don't you like kids?"

She flinched as if hit, and with wide round black eyes finally responded, "What do you mean?"

Jack explained that she had written about every aspect of her work with children, except the children themselves. He went on further to point out she had mentioned the other teachers, the principal, the room and the reams of paperwork, but not one single sentence about the children. Then he looked pleadingly into her eyes, "Did you not have just one close contact or special feeling for any child during the entire year you taught them?" Wilma was silent and dejected as if someone had stripped off her real self for all to see.

But Wilma wasn't the only student stripping off her real self. Here is another poem I wrote and turned in.

RESURRECTION

In happier days I often thought
Life does not seem such a trial
Peace, love and contentment sought

Were apparent with many a smile.

Now thru dark deep valleys I wander
In search of a place where I belong
Long, long days and nights to ponder
To fight, to conquer and to long.

Sorrow! Sorrow! Sorrow!
I wish I knew another word
Seems forever till tomorrow
Keep me from falling on my sword.

To be released from grief so deep
There are no words with which to tell
If happiness were mine to keep
Resurrection! Ring that bell.

A few days later, Dr. Miller asked me to stay after class. "If I interpret you correctly, you couldn't have written that poem," he explained. "It is something out of a 16th century melodrama," insinuating I had copied it. Rather than disclose to him my deep feelings, I turned and walked out the classroom door. I did return to the class the next week, but this poem was never mentioned again.

Here is the first story I wrote and turned in to the class for its critiquing.

SHOULDER TO KNEE

It was predawn when I awakened on this September morn of what promised to be a beautiful Indian summer day, but it came much too soon. More importantly, this day was the day of my *first* book review. I had chosen the book, *Forty Odd* by Mary Bard. I liked funny entertaining books. Unfortunately, as a novice, I was unaware this was a bad choice.

CHOOSING A LOVE THAT WILL LAST

Mentally, I was toying with an idea that I couldn't shake. However embarrassing and contrary to my former self, I just would not show up. When they called to check on me, temporary amnesia would be my plea. Or would it be accepted more readily if I hinted that it was just more than I could physically handle. There was a third alternative I had seen used before, but it was not popularly accepted by the group; in fact, not acceptable at all. I shuddered when I thought of it--resignation at the last minute.

NO! NO! I could not and would not allow myself to become so intimidated. Who was I afraid of? Perhaps if I could analyze the root problem I could coax the symptoms into going away.

Public speaking is listed as number one among fears, and I became a firm believer of that fact that day.

It all started out well over a year ago when I received a letter of invitation to join the McAllen Reviewers' Guild. Though it was a feeling of elation and anticipation at the time, the only lingering sensation of that day is but a distant memory in this present-day nightmare of uncertainty and increasing queasiness.

President Margaret Baltis and Secretary Peggy Nix had both assured me there was nothing much to joining this club; mostly pleasure, a lot of social contact, and hopefully some literary growth and development. What I liked was the intimate size of the club--15 but no more than 20 members--which met fortnightly in the different homes on a rotating basis. The clincher for me was that a new member had a one year's sabbatical in which to observe, learn and prepare for her first review.

My letter of acceptance was written with an eager, happy and carefree spirit, which is extinct today. Then I had reasoned that the timing had been so right. The last of my six precious children--little petite blonde Lori--would be in the first grade. That first year did prove to be an interesting and fascinating honeymoon into the literary world limited. This afforded me enough time to form many impressions from each book review and reviewer.

The books chosen were a stimulating mixture of fiction, drama, poetry and nonfiction. *Black Like Me* was reviewed by Martha Dizdar, *The Pearl* was chosen by Barbara Northcutt, and *The Life of Thomas Jefferson* was reviewed by the only redhead in the club, Joan Tavarez.

Then a bag of tricks was presented by Barbara Gower on the *Joys of Chocolate,* who tempted all her subjects by pulling every kind of chocolate imaginable out of a big brown paper bag. Jackie Hanshaw especially enjoyed each temptation, knowing her own lean body would not inflate one inch. I took special notice when Nora Kelly reviewed. She was infectious with her choice of *Dressing for Success* and brought a whole wardrobe of men's clothes from Jones & Jones to show what the well-dressed male should wear.

One of the first clear observations I made was that each reviewer was immaculately dressed, with unusually attractive hair. What did they do to their make-up to give their faces that transparent glow and young suppleness of tone? Why didn't they look like that at every meeting?

Also, there were quite a few no-no's I picked up. I was concerned that I was learning more from negative mannerisms than positive ones. Making a mental note to do some more probing on that angle of learning, I was becoming more stern with myself now. Today is not the day for analytical or critical judgments. Today is the day for my first book review. Someone has said, "Today is the first day of the rest of your life." At this pace? My mental computer is jamming all its circuits.

Deadlines seem to trigger the desire in me to do too many things at once. There were many leisure days I could have looked up the meaning of the words *fear* and *stage fright,* but, no, I didn't. Today I can think of nothing else. No matter, I can do that after cooking breakfast.

It is now 7:20 a.m. and I roll out of my king-sized bed with a bounce. Double checking our chiming Seth Thomas, it is exactly five hours, ten minutes and 40 seconds until 1:30 p.m. Real-life consciousness is breaking in upon me now, bringing with it a ball

CHOOSING A LOVE THAT WILL LAST

in the pit of my stomach. It is becoming restless and is doing the only thing a ball can do. This has to be fear more than stage fright I thought. Stage fright would indicate a stage. Private, cozy, nice homes didn't suggest stage to me.

Earlier, while lying in bed, I had planned to prepare a wonderfully delicious and nutritious breakfast for our whole household (eight counting our housekeeper, Maria, from Tampico, Mexico, who sulks if I send my little *chula ninos* to school without a good breakfast).

By the time I reach the kitchen, I notice it is 7:45 and things are closing in on me. Surely orange juice and apple danish rolls will get the *little ninos* through this day to the *rest of their life* part. At rapid two-minute intervals each ate, grabbed and ran, and as if by magic the house was still as a mouse by 7:56.

Taking my orange juice and roll into the library, I grab *Webster's New World Dictionary*. It says *fear* is: sudden attack, ambush, snare, akin to OHG, danger, peril, a feeling of anxiety, timidity, dread, terror, fright, concern, doubtful. Webster sure is right because I have all those symptoms--except one. I don't know what OHG is. If I don't know what that is, then the power of suggestion can't go to work on me.

Only recently I learned about the power of suggestion first-hand when on a 10-country tour with Mother and my double cousin, Happy Gettings from Yukon, Oklahoma. (borrowing the money from the bank for the trip). It was on a big 747 jet. Seated next to me was a tall, distinguished and intelligent looking couple in their mid 50's.

The plane seemed to be late in leaving London's Lyton Airport for Madrid, Spain. After a few minutes, the stewardess advised that they were giving oxygen to a woman on the front seat because she was having difficulty breathing in such close quarters. The three of us had been chatting away about where we were from, how many children and hobbies, when the husband started waving his hands and pressing the stewardess button frantically. I asked, "What is the matter?" Before he could answer, I noticed his wife was colorless and her forehead beaded with perspiration. The stewardess arrived shortly with an oxygen mask and quickly fastened it onto the woman's face. In a few minutes the woman opened her eyes and the color returned to her cheeks. After she had settled back and we were airborne, I expressed my concern for her health to her husband. Whispering very low, he murmured, "It's the power of suggestion, you know." No, I didn't know, but now I do.

Picking the dictionary up again, I found the word *stage fright*, hoping it wouldn't be as foreboding and terrifying as the word *fear*. My eyes fell down two words too many and in my haste I read, 'having an intense desire to become an actor or actress." I almost closed the book when I discovered that meaning belonged to the word *stage struck*. Laughing at how ridiculous that was, I carefully placed my ragged nail-bitten finger on the word *stage fright* and read, "nervousness felt when appearing before an audience, as by an inexperienced performer." That's all it said. What an understatement! How could I be experienced and not nervous if I was inexperienced and very nervous?

It is becoming obvious to me now that it is time for what Mother calls my drastic therapy, so I begin repeating over and over, "It's better than terminal cancer. IT'S MUCH BETTER THAN TERMINAL CANCER."

Skipping two steps at a time with increased adrenalin pumping power, I shower, dry off and dress in a two-piece carnation-red ensemble with a very wide belt squeezing my middle more than is comfortable. To me, red is a cheerful and strong color, projecting vitality and life. Oh yes, I am wearing high-heeled black patent shoes to match the color of my hair and eyes, but more importantly they make me look taller than five feet three and a half inches and thinner than 122 libros or is it libras? Maria says one means pounds and the other books.

Thank goodness I can wear my own hair, even if it is sort of a tamed Phyllis Diller style. It is cooler and more secure than the popularly worn wigs. All in all my physical appearance is more secure than my emotional whole. I say whole because my emotions at this moment seem to be the whole of me, spelled two ways: *hold and whole.* No one in the entire club is aware that I have never stood, sat or knelt before a real live audience and said or read a word in the whole of my 29 years, plus 60 months. It's of high priority that they don't find out how nervous I really am.

Gathering up my prized typed manuscript, I go cautiously out the back door to my car. I do want to improve and overcome! Ignorance is bliss at this point because what I don't know is that I have chosen a very satirical book which can be disastrous for first time reviewers.

Earlier, Millie Robicheaux called to ask if she could pick me up, to which I told her, "Thanks, Millie, for thinking of me, but I think I will need my car later--*for a fast getaway.*" Though I didn't say the last words audibly until I hung up the phone.

It was only a short drive of four blocks to Reba Showers' home on Highland Drive, but it was time enough to think of sad and funny things, and I was beginning to feel giddy. Something I hadn't thought of for a long time came unbidden to me as I approached Reba's lush green carpeted lawn and parked my car. It was about the story of a young nervous minister who stood up to speak for the very first time to his new congregation. His mouth worked perfectly well in every way, except no sound came out. He kept mouthing the words when a little old lady stood up in the back and said, "Pardon me, sir, but would you pray for me? I think I just lost my hearing."

Sitting in the car for a minute, I repeat slowly several times. "It's better than terminal cancer." Like lightning I wondered where in the garden of my mind did I dig up all these insecurities. I am acutely aware that I like individual people--it's public people that terrify me. Perhaps this is a lack of ego. Wouldn't a person have to possess a big ego to speak in public and enjoy it? Taking up the listeners precious time to simply listen to what they have to say. How I wish I had done more research during my sabbatical, and it wouldn't all be crowding in on me today. I am suddenly curious about my lack of self-confidence.

Slowly walking up to the double front doors, I wonder if my dread came from being in a large close-knit family. We were seven children who all wanted to talk at once. Being number five, I wasn't asked much to be answered. Before I could attempt to reply, the others had gone on to someone who didn't hesitate and roll big blank soulful eyes around. They suggested my eyes stated all that needed to be said. That used to worry me, and I would squint in school thinking that the eyes were the windows through which you saw the soul.

WHERE AND WHAT was the soul? Never mind.

No one day in my entire life has forced so much thought and reflection. Could that be why people choose public speaking?

One thought triggers another, and I can't handle it in bunches like this with no pencil. However, I told myself, don't forget to call the school superintendent to request that public speaking be made mandatory, instead of an elective, from kindergarten all the way through grade twelve.

Hostess Reba greets me with, "Hi there, are we ever glad to see you." Together we enter her formal living room done in soft muted tones of biege and blue, complimenting her antique furniture. Everyone is happily talking at once. I feel at home.

However, I'm not talking much and take no strawberry shortcake or coffee as I am busy glancing about the room to decide where I will stand to feel just right giving my maiden review.

I'm not only glancing about, but I'm doing some first-time perspiring. This greatly surprises me as I NEVER perspire. I've made quite a point of this fact. Now it is soon going to be obvious I am a liar, as well as a very nervous wet one. Why don't I temper my statements with seldom?

Vice-President Peggy Yancy rises to introduce me. Peggy is the club's own published author of poetry titled, *Then Let It Spill*. Peggy used her own poem to announce me.

CHOOSING A LOVE THAT WILL LAST

GLORY

For this week's meeting
We will have a story
By last year's new member
Our girl named Glory.

She has many talents
Such as decorating her home
And keeping it all clean
Even when she's alone.

We have found out her secret
To raise children galore
Just tell your husband
'Open another food store'

Forty Odd by Mary Bard
Is the book she will do
So Glory we're waiting
To hear your review.

    Vaguely I hear the words of that poem as from afar. Right now I must breathe in deeply three times, as someone suggested, and dry my palms against my pleated skirt so my manila folder won't slip around. Peggy says, "Now h-e-r-e's Glory," imitating the voice inflection like they do on the *Johnny Carson Show*.
    Slowly I get up and stand beside a big solid wing chair, wrap and brace one leg to the other and open my condensed 40-minute story and begin.
    "*Forty Odd* by Mary Bard." My mouth opens. I know because I can feel a draft on my teeth, but what I hear is no voice I have ever heard before. It is high-pitched with a quivering trilling sound. That scares me! I stop briefly to clear my throat to

camouflage my audio difficulties. My upper lip seems to be stuck on something and won't come down, although I make every effort to do so. Taking my right hand from my limp folder, I slip it up to assist my stubborn lip. When I pull it down hard, there is no saliva. None! I quickly suppose it has gone into my armpits as it is very wet there now.

New Secretary Lois Kelly grasps the situation, and thoughtfully hands me a glass of water from the silver tray on the marble-topped table near her. I take one big gulp. Seems to be a day for gulping! I'm not seemingly aware that Betty Faust is seated close to my right hand, nor that she is so very pregnant until I keep seeing a right foot drawn taut with toes pointing straight up--less than three feet from me. That distracts me greatly as I'm not sure if she is in pain for herself or for me! No matter, I must continue, however bad.

All 17 girls are waiting for no one but me. I take one anxious look about the room, and I am struck by 17 pair of motionless expectant eyes glued to only *my* face--much like expressions people wear to bad accidents.

No matter, I plunge in again very soberly and determinedly, and after a very long hard five minutes, my voice becomes more like my own musical normal one. I am tuning out my former friends and making real headway with Mary Bard. The plot is revealing when Mary awakens on her 40th birthday and feels like Marie Antionette must have felt when she awoke and knew that this was the day she was to be guillotined. Her motive in relating how ghastly she feels upon reaching 40 is still a mystery. However, it is becoming clearer and clearer as she unfolds blow-by-blow how each part of the body just goes to pot: organs, pipes and all. Mary Bard is amusing and humorous. I'm amazingly controlled and calm, and my audience is in deep personal thought. Without looking, I unlock my legs and now each leg is on its own with very little trembling visible.

Still reading but thinking to myself, "shaky voice, dry mouth, trembly legs, sweaty armpits, shortness of breath, clammy hands,

CHOOSING A LOVE THAT WILL LAST

tennis-match stomach." What else could there possibly be? There was plenty more though I didn't suspect it. How innocently we walk along the pathway to our destiny.

The review cruised along on course until I read these words, "It wasn't encouraging. How would he like to have hair which had once been red but was now the color and texture of hemp? Today's fashions for women were obviously designed so that middle-aged woman had her choice of girdling herself from shoulder to knee and looking like a shootin' cracker as Granny used to say, or pretending she didn't need a girdle and looking like a lurchin' feed sack."

Just as I reached the words, *shoulder to knee* I went into premature hysterics and couldn't stop. I attempted to keep on reading between uncontrolled spasms of laughter and managed with jerky squeaky starts to finish the paragraph. Realizing I couldn't regain my composure--all the while desperately trying by any and all means to get myself back on track--I burst out crying, and tears made dark rivulets down both my cheeks. My lashes were limp from all the moisture. I was now laughing and crying. I couldn't tell which, or for what, nor why!

Carolyn Cathey, full by this time with much empathy, makes a loving gesture with her eyes to mine. Greatly strengthened by this show of concern, I try once more. About the time it seemed I could regain some composure again, I would start this uncontrollable laughing and make low gurgling hubble-bubble sounds.

Co-hostess Nita Calvert, slips out of the room quietly and quickly. I stare in disbelief when she returns with a super-sized box of yellow Kleenex in her hand. That upsets me. She offers me the first one. I pull out two and use both of them, thinking I need a Scot towel instead. Turning around, she places the cardboard box in the lap of Nancy Brimberry with instructions to pass it along. The next sounds that reach me are in this order: muffled popping of paper moving, a snort or two; shuffling of the big yellow box until all 17 had blown their noses and wiped their eyes. Our guests, Peggy Reidland and Ruth Jung participated like members, though with some puzzlement.

This spontaneous interruption touches me where I have not previously been touched. How could they identify so completely and compassionately with my inability, misery and to my predicament? Curiously, it made me feel warm, loved and accepted in my inexperience.

Everyone is now refreshed and willing to try again. I read for almost another 18 minutes covering many clever and downright funny incidents, but after that last bad scene, this audience is in complete charge. They are helping poor Glory get through it--as if to say, she can't so we must.

Close to the end of my review I read, "Evelyn said Jean tried that, Mary, but after she had hysterics at Penney's White Sale she was more than willing to cough up her symptoms. Dr. Hank is a darling, and I wouldn't think of letting anybody else monkey with my kidneys, but just because he can't see it with a cystoscope, Hank thinks change of life doesn't exist. Edith had advised that I start on the afternoon of my 40th birthday making lists of everything--you have no idea how muddleheaded you can get. Start now. By the time you develop severe symptoms you won't be able to remember your own name. Don't get discouraged if everything you do seems futile. That hopeless feeling is the first sign of C of L, but it does go away."

During the entire remaining part of the review, there was no response. Catatonic expressions! In fact, they were all now very relaxed. All pointed toes were down. That made me feel better. As I glanced to my left, Liz Compere had quiet tears in her eyes.

On this note I conclude my review. But before I make a hurried departure, I turn and look deep into each woman's face, and am convinced that suffering is not individual. Would you believe that I'm of the same opinion still--IT'S SO MUCH BETTER THAN TERMINAL CANCER?

Apparently, Dr. Miller liked this story better than my poems

CHOOSING A LOVE THAT WILL LAST

because he gave me an A-.

If I thought creative writing was difficult, it was nothing compared to what was ahead.

GLORY CHAPMAN

CHAPTER 6

GOODBYE MISS GOODY-TWO-SHOES

Divorce is such an enigma. At the time of my divorce, the picture I kept seeing in my mind was that of being hung high in city square for all to see and deride, "Ha! Ha! Miss Goody-Two-Shoes. See what happened to her. Where is her wonderful God *now*?" No need to tell you, my self-righteousness had a very prolonged and painful funeral. She didn't want to be buried. I've found self-righteousness is sort of like humility, "Them that has it don't know it."

"A noble heart, like the sun, showeth its greatest countenance in its lowest estate." Sir P. Sidney. [1]

It is never wise to bottle up more feeling than a heart can contain. Many times my emotions gushed out of control, sometimes so unexpectedly it was impossible to hold in check. At a book review meeting something set me off, and I was awash before I reached my car. However, most of the time I could make it to the car or home first.

For months, I was much like a storm victim picking through the rubble of her home after a tornado, stumbling around in shock trying to realize it really did happen. Any major crisis takes a bit of readjusting time to get back to normal actions and reactions.

To me, divorce is like a funeral, only much, much worse. With divorce there is no ceremony, no cards, no flowers, no food and measured love. There can't be--not for failure. You are cut in half with no anesthesia. You are bleeding to death, but no one seems to be alarmed since you seem to be handling it outwardly fairly well.

Besides what can you say to someone in divorce? Taking sides is not wise. Usually there isn't enough information to know what to say. So everyone stumbles around and muddles through the

CHOOSING A LOVE THAT WILL LAST

most tragic happening in the lives of their loved ones.

At this time, Susan Delaney called me to come over to her home. She cautioned me repeatedly about men and the propositions I might receive now that I was single. Though I assured her I didn't think that would be a problem, we made a bet of $100.00. She was trying to be kind and helpful, I am sure. Incidentally, I need to collect the $100.00 from her. She insisted that I listen to the warning. It didn't set too well with me because the visual picture I had at that time was: here I am bleeding to death and she says, "Anyone for sex?" Men and their advances were very remote to me at that particular time.

However, it wasn't long before I had to deal with them. One man upon learning that I was divorced, blurted out without thinking, "Oh, we will have to get together. My wife has cancer." Another time a man knocked on my door pretending to be there on business. I thought it best to keep standing on the front porch after he said that what his wife didn't know couldn't hurt her.

Late one night some male voice on the telephone said very distinctly, "I love you," and hung up. I didn't know who it was.

Another person dropped a note in my mailbox without ringing the doorbell. It said, "I love you." That made me cry but it was a good kind of release. Some men wanted someone else to introduce me to them, instead of calling me direct. Another man told me he was getting a divorce and wanted to start dating around, starting with me. No way! There were many intriguing encounters. In spite of the many interesting calls and situations during those years, I would have to say that I definitely found men in general more decent than they are given credit.

In a lengthy test given by an insurance company, it says that a divorce will take off five years of your life. The toll is incalculable. At least in death there is a finality to be accepted along with the many expressions of love, sympathies, thoughtfulnesses and condolences. YOU EVEN MAKE A SCRAPBOOK TO REMEMBER.

Early one morning Ruth Schweer came by the house. She is

GLORY CHAPMAN

considered perhaps a *live* saint. Everyone calls her *sweet Ruthie*. She was so dear and said, "The most important thing at this time, Glory, is not to lose your faith."

"Oh, Ruthie, I've already determined this is the worst time of all to lose my faith in God since that is all I am hanging onto," was my reply. I thought about my poster which says, "Faith isn't faith until it's all you're holding onto."

As Oswald Chambers says, "The basis of things is tragic." Sometimes it can be and when Herby was 20 and Lori 6, I was fully awake to the enormity of the responsibility of rearing six children alone.

MY JOURNEY INTO MY SEARCH MUST CONTINUE.

CHOOSING A LOVE THAT WILL LAST

CHAPTER 7

THE WAITING GAME

I have often thought of Rose Kennedy. There is no one lady in all the world that I know of who has experienced life to the fullest, both in the good things and the bad. Of course, I don't know her personally, but from reading about her, I've learned she has experienced having nine children, having a mentally retarded child, being the wife of an ambassador to England, having a strong husband and father, being the wife of an affluent husband, betrayal, caring for an invalid husband for nine years, and being a widow for many, many years.

Although her children seem to be her source of joy and strength, they often were the source of her pain. Her daughter, Kathleen, was killed in an airplane crash. Her son, Joe, Jr., was killed in World War II. Ted, the youngest son was in an airplane crash and brought her humiliation with the Chappaquiddick incident. She experienced more than any mother should endure when her sons, Jack, President of the United States, and Robert, the U. S. Attorney General, were assassinated. These things were so devastating to her that the other family tragedies seemed trivial, such as Ted's and Pat's divorces, her grandson dying from drugs, another grandson losing a leg to cancer while grandson, Willie Smith, was on trial for rape. But through it all, the public sees a smiling Rose whose radiant face hides the pain.

Perhaps I, too, project a different exterior than what is being experienced within. My dear friend, Peggy Yancy, wrote this poem for me.

GLORY CHAPMAN

GLORY

Glory is a robot...
I'm positive she is!
Only one mechanical
Could be such a whiz.

Always gracious...
Always nice...
Always gorgeous...
Not a vice...
Always pleasant...
And serene...
Effervescent...
Even lean...
Always healthy...
Never hurried...
Somehow wealthy...
And not worried...
Calculating and alert...
Managerial and pert...
Always clever...
Always bright...
Each endeavor
Seeming right...
And around her such a calm...
Holy even as a psalm...

Glory is a robot!
I'm absolutely sure.
To think of her as human
My ego can't endure!

    There are days when I am bone tired and have gone nonstop for many hours, and someone will say, "You don't even look tired,"

CHOOSING A LOVE THAT WILL LAST

or "You must be Samson."

The good news is that makes me feel good because it doesn't show, but on the other hand the bad news is, I might drop dead and no one will know why.

Feeling insecure, it is of special importance to portray confidence. Since I was a little kid and cried so much, I have prayed that I wouldn't show so much emotion in front of people. My prayers have been answered in that I'm not embarrassed nearly as often in public anymore. However, the squeaky wheel and the beaten look do get the oil, make no mistake about it. I sometimes wish I wasn't so good at hiding my pain. But, thanks to God, He knows what I need and provides for me without squeaking. His system of reward and provision is based on His resources and love for me, and in turn upon my trust and love for Him.

In the Bible it says, "No matter what happens, *always* be thankful, for this is God's will for you who belong to Christ Jesus." I Thes. 5:18. I can read those words without any pain at all, and I can even say those words easily. But to believe and act on those words beyond my understanding is tougher than tough when the worst happens. It takes super help to believe against lost hope. And without hope the spirit shrivels to inertness rapidly.

For example, do you know that 30 diseases are caused by animals being kept in the house, and that toxoplasmosis is caused by cat feces and is very dangerous to pregnant women and causes damage to children? If you keep the animals in the house after reading this, then you apparently don't believe it is dangerous or true, or you are willing to take the risk. However, knowledge has to precede action. The proof of learning and assimilating knowledge comes only in experiencing what has been taught. Giving assent to the gospel is saying you know what it says, but taking action is the evidence of that knowledge. So even if you know what causes toxoplasmosis, until you put the animals out of the house, there is no evidence of that knowledge.

GLORY CHAPMAN

> To 'look' is one thing.
> To 'see' what you look at is another.
> To 'understand' what you see is a third.
> To 'learn' from what you understand is
>   still something else.
> But to 'act' on what you learn is all
>   that really matters, isn't it?
> Harvard Business Review [1]

A young girl in-love may *believe* in her mind that the young man may marry her since he has stated he loves her. But until he *acts* to have the marriage ceremony performed, there is no wedding. Talk is cheap--actions more costly.

Now it was time to stop reciting over and over what I had learned and to make the leap of faith. I felt like the man who had a wheelbarrow and was going to cross Niagara Falls on a tight wire in it. He asked the onlookers if they believed he could do it. Their decision was unanimous. "Okay," he summoned, "Come on over and get in the wheelbarrow with me."

When Herby was 5 and Shari 3, they took swimming lessons from a super teacher, Ada Toland. Herby watched and listened while one by one each new swimmer jumped into the water from the edge of the pool, later all jumped off the diving board. The brave little scout thought it was wonderful and insisted he knew how just from watching. He thought it was especially fine that Shari jumped in. Herby was content to say he had been to swimming classes--never mind the jumping off part. Finally Ada had to throw him in. His knowledge didn't push him to action. He had to have help. Sometimes a crisis pushes us to action. It is very difficult to crucify one's self. Given a choice, we will climb down every time.

Another thing that kept me from acting on my faith were the thoughts, *Why do you think God will come to you? Why are you so special? You know of other people in the same situation or worse and nothing changed or happened for them.* Those thoughts played over more than once and became a spiritual obstacle course.

However, I kept on knocking, asking and seeking. There was this inner assurance that I had a lot to gain and nothing to lose--if I could *believe*. There must be a way I could find my secret hiding place with God. That was the main reason I didn't talk about my problems. The Lord was my confidante.

"Lord, how you have helped me before! You took me safely from my mother's womb and brought me through the years of infancy. I have depended upon you since birth; you have always been my God. Don't leave me now, for trouble is near and no one else can possibly help." Psalms 22:9-11.

Placing all my confidence and trust in Him, I knew I could trust Him totally. He would not betray me. When in trouble head towards someone who has the resources and the capability to help. Much the same thought as Abraham Lincoln disclosed, "Never make the mistake of arguing with anyone whose opinion you do not value." Otherwise, you are wasting your time. The quicker you reach this decision the sooner His strength and love will flow towards you to begin the process of inner and outer healing.

When we are desperately ill, we don't go to a nurse's aide. She can only keep us comfortable and refer us to a medical doctor. The nurse's aide might be sympathetic and gentle, but what we need is for someone to properly diagnose our pain--someone qualified to proceed with the treatment--internal medicine or possibly major surgery. Many people turn to the pastor, who in turn must refer them to his superior--God.

As much as I was capable of, I consciously and deliberately deposited all the faith I possessed into the person of Jesus Christ of Nazareth. Scripture tells me nothing in the spirit world works without faith. Nothing! Without faith it is impossible to please God. Heb. 11:6. Anyone who wants to come to God must believe that there is a God and that He rewards those who sincerely look for Him. <u>Faith is the fuel of the spirit world</u>. Faith is believing I will receive whatever I ask for before I actually receive it. Matt. 21:21. It is imperative that I believe what God says if I am to receive. There is no other alternative available. Sounds simple, doesn't it? We either believe or we don't believe. Only God knows when we really are serious and mean it. Talk is so easy, believing is a different animal.

"What is faith? It is the confident assurance that something we want is going to happen. It is the certainty that what we hope for is waiting for us, even though we cannot see it up ahead." Heb. 11:1.

Where do I get this faith to believe? "Faith comes by hearing and hearing by the Word of God." Rom. 10:17 KJV. "The message didn't do them any good because they didn't believe it. They didn't mix it with faith." Heb. 4:2. Each one of us has been given a deposit of faith at birth. Rom. 12:3 KJV. God placed it there, but guess who has to exercise it? We do. Physically, we are born with little arms and legs to begin life, but if they are not exercised they shrivel and lose their muscle tone.

There is no one formula or set of rules on faith because it is a relationship between each man and his God. Each friendship is different. "Friendship with God is reserved for those who reverence Him. With them alone He shares the secrets of His promises." Psa. 25:14. Friendship of any sort requires time and attention. We can't run in once a year or when in trouble and think any awards will be handed out. Deep and lasting relationships are cultivated and watered day by day with thoughtfulness, kindness, trust, care and attention.

C. S. Lewis wrote in *Mere Christianity*, "Your natural life is derived from your parents; that does not mean it will stay there if you do nothing about it. You can lose it by neglect, or you can drive it away by committing suicide. You have to feed it and look after it: but always remember you are not making it, you are only keeping up a life you got from someone else. In the same way a Christian can lose the Christ-life which has been put into him, and he has to make efforts to keep it. But even the best Christian that ever lived is not acting on his own steam--he is only nourishing or protecting a life he could never have acquired by his own efforts. A live body is not one that never gets hurt, but one that can to some extent repair itself. In the same way a Christian is not a man who never goes wrong, but a man who is enabled to repent and pick himself up and begin over again after each stumble--because the Christ-life is inside him, repairing him all the time. There is no good trying to be more spiritual than God. God never meant man to be a purely spiritual creature. That is why he uses material things like bread and wine to put the new life in us. God invented eating."[2]

And, too, waiting is almost always involved and is not easy in our fast paced life. If we can't touch-tone it, then we won't dial it. Possibly, there is no work in life so hard as waiting. Certainly, waiting can eat away at our faith, little by little. But remember, delay is not necessarily denial. Take a look at the following persons who had long waiting periods before their answers and provisions came.

Joseph had several prophetic dreams, (promise) as well as a special coat of many colors, which made his ten half brothers envious. At the first opportunity his brothers sold 17-year old Joseph to some foreigners from Egypt. He didn't even know their language. Later he was accused of seducing his boss' wife and spent time in prison for a crime he didn't commit (problem). Joseph was required to interpret four dreams for other people before his own long-ago dream came true. It must have given him pause many times in trying to figure out why all of this was happening to him. Sometimes we are required to plant in other people's lives and help them with their dreams before ours are fulfilled. And, too, all great leaders must be painstakingly trained and disciplined.

In the end, the 13-year plan was made perfect when through Joseph (by way of exile, imprisonment and trial) his whole family was saved from starvation (provision). I notice where it says

Joseph prospered in prison. Incidentally, prison is not where most of us want to prosper, right? Later, it was worth it all when he was made second in command of all Egypt under Pharaoh. Joseph declared to his brothers, "You thought evil against me; but God meant it for good--to save the lives of *many* people." Gen. 50:20 KJV. God will do the best for us where the most people are involved. Sometimes it takes bad circumstances to bring God's best plan into being. However, that is not how most of us interpret the 13 years of bad things that happen to us. Joseph was used to save his whole family and nation from starvation. It was pain, alienation and imprisonment, but God did the best for Joseph considering the greater number of people God wanted to save.

David was minding his own business as a young lad taking care of his dad's sheep when the prophet Samuel came looking for him to anoint him to be the next King over Israel (promise). For the next 13 years he was on the run for his life trying to escape from the then present King Saul, who was jealous of him and wanted to kill him (problem). The wait and fight paid off when he was finally crowned King, which came along on God's timetable, though not without a lot of testing and severe training first (provision). Just a side note, I notice God didn't dethrone David even though he committed adultery and murder. David wasn't even put on probation because he was truly sorry and repented. But there were other consequences for his sin that passed on down to his children.

Moses was 80 when he was finally given the go-ahead to deliver the three plus million Jews out of Egyptian slavery back to their land of Canaan (promise). Moses blew it earlier when he killed an Egyptian boy and hid his body. Would you want a murderer for a leader? Moses had to be ground to powder so he could be blown by the wind of the spirit to fulfill that mighty feat of delivering such a crowd (problem). God's daily miracles weren't enough to keep those millions from murmuring and complaining. Poor old stuttering Moses was tried to the utmost.

CHOOSING A LOVE THAT WILL LAST

Their grumbling about God's provision is at the least attributing more power to circumstances and to evil than to God. In the end, Moses got to see the provision but he couldn't enter into Canaan. The Jews tried him sorely to the point of losing his temper. Those 40 years of training in the wilderness weren't enough! I do observe that God didn't replace Moses as his chosen leader even after Moses committed murder.

Consider Abraham's waiting. God told him he would have a son by Sarah 20 years before he received the son (promise). Later, God repeated the promise closer to the time. Why did God tell him so far in advance? That way his faith was severely stretched. Time can disintegrate my faith. Waiting puts my faith on trial. Abraham realized both he and Sarah were getting older every year--hope was fading along with the body. So Abraham put an alternate plan into effect by having an heir, Ishmael, by Sarah's maid. That was a big misjudgment because the sons of Isaac, the promised son, and the sons of Ishmael are still at war these some 4,000 years later.

Finally, at the age of 90 Sarah becomes pregnant. She has never had a baby. God's timing is not our timing. "For my thoughts are not your thoughts, neither are your ways my ways, saith the Lord." Isa. 55:8 KJV. Then to cap it all off, when Isaac was 12 years old, guess what God asked Abraham to do with Isaac? Make a burnt offering of him! How could He? Why didn't God ask him to sacrifice Ishmael? After all, he wasn't supposed to be born anyway. No, God asked Abraham to sacrifice the one he loved most.

Also, Abraham could have answered by saying, "No, God. This is the miraculous baby you gave Sarah and me. I cannot sacrifice him." We don't read where Abraham so much as discussed with Sarah what he was going to do to Isaac. He immediately obeyed and began walking the three days journey to reach Mount Moriah, where God told him to offer Isaac. Abraham got so far as to raise the knife to kill Isaac when the angel of God SHOUTED to him from heaven, "Abraham, don't hurt the boy, for I know that God is first in your life--you have not withheld even your beloved son from me." Gen. 22:11,12.

In chapter 22:1 of Genesis, it says that God tested Abraham's faith. In Isaiah 41:8, God says that Abraham was his friend. And, too, I notice that God didn't take back his covenant or contract with Abraham, even though Abraham lied earlier, saying Sarah was his sister. Neither does the Bible reveal if he repented of this lie. All happenings are not recorded in Scripture. In fact, it states in John 21:25, "And there are also many other things Jesus did, which if they were written in detail, I suppose that the world itself would not contain the books which were written."

After reading these stories, I wondered how my faith would be rated in such a test. Would my family, the law, my church allow me to obey such an order from God?

Then there was Noah who went about the new business of building a boat in anticipation of a great flood. It had never rained up to that time. They didn't even know what rain was. Nonetheless dear old faithful Noah proceeded to do exactly what God asked him to do, even if it was ridiculous to those who laughed and chided him. Apparently these great men knew who was speaking to them. Seems nowadays we wonder whether it is God or the devil talking to us. Certainly, it paid off for Noah when 120 years later, he and his sons and their wives were the only ones saved in the ark from the great flood, along with every kind of fowl and animal, but no fish since Noah had an outdoor aquarium. Notice Noah had the *promise*, then came the *problem* and lastly the *provision*. In that order! Having confidence that God knows what He is doing is imperative on my part.

Even the disciples, along with Mary, the mother of Jesus, and others had to go to the Upper Room and *wait* for the Day of Pentecost. Why all the waiting? God seldom gives us the reason why. That's where our trust in Him begins. Possibly, there was being produced in them obedience, faith, as well as unity, during the wait.

Here is a thought. Ask yourself, how obedient will I be if it

CHOOSING A LOVE THAT WILL LAST

makes me look bad? However, take a look at one of my favorite persons in the Bible, Mary, the mother of Jesus. Here is another example of God doing the best for Mary given the number of people who would eventually benefit. Her suffering, ridicule and exile were tough, but it was necessary because God was going to bring manifold blessings out of this obedience for *millions* of people. Unfortunately, the angel, Gabriel, didn't announce in a loud voice over the entire little town of Nazareth the message that Mary was chosen to bear the Son of God. If he did, everyone in town would have known it was truly from God and not from her fiance´, Joseph.

Gabriel told only little teenaged Mary in private (promise). Mary believed what was told her. She knew within herself and that was enough for her to bear the Messiah, whatever the consequences. Making matters worse, she left town to visit her Aunt Elizabeth and returned three to four months later obviously pregnant (problem).

Remember Joseph did not go with her. She was made to look very immoral when in fact she was most virtuous and innocent. She was chosen to carry the Savior of all mankind. Mary had no doubt read that a Messiah would be born to a Jewish maiden someday, but it's quite another matter when you are *the one* chosen. With this blessing and promise came the cloud of suspicion and shame. What defense did she have? I can just hear Mary explaining to her girlfriends that she was pregnant by the Holy Spirit coming upon her. "Sure, Mary, sure!"

In *Two From Galilee*, Marjorie Holmes has Mary's own mother saying to Mary after she arrived back home, "Oh, Mary, how could you?"[3]

I imagine Joseph was having a hard time until he had an angel visitation himself. I notice throughout Scripture that whenever an angel of God appeared or came to a person, the angel's word always proved true and men were punished for disobeying them. Heb. 2:2.

Zacharias said to Gabriel upon delivering news that his wife

Elizabeth would have a baby (John the Baptist) in her old age, "But this is impossible." He was stricken silent, unable to speak until the child was born.

Mary could have protested to the angel, arguing about becoming pregnant before marriage. "Please tell my mother, father and sisters so they will understand. It will appear I am sinful." She was doing the highest good when she appeared to have done the greatest wrong. A wrong punishable in those days by being stoned to death. Our love and faith in what God is telling us must exceed the consequences or what others think. This special road can sometimes be lonely.

How many people in Mary's town of Nazareth do you suppose believed Mary was pregnant by the Holy Spirit coming upon her? No doubt she was suspect while in the center of God's perfect will. THE EVIL IN US MAKES US SUSPICIOUS OF THE GOOD IN OTHERS. Apparently God is little concerned with what man thinks as to how He chooses to do things. GOD IS GOD! Who can change that? Let's permit God to have His mysteries! "For all God's words are right and everything He does is worthy of our trust." Psa. 33:4.

God plainly tells us over and over, we are not to be judges. He is. If we insist on passing judgments along with sentences, we can fill that position. Only one problem, He declares that with what judgment (and gossip?) we mete out will be returned to us in the exact same measure. Matt. 7:1,2 KJV. Isn't it magnanimous of Jesus to be our judge--not our prosecuting attorney?

Surely Mary would at least have the best suite in the hospital with angels in attendance for the delivery. Certainly there should be no hardships if God asks me to do it. Where do I keep getting the idea if God asks me to do something, there will be no problems? Where? All progress and growth includes problems and pain. No, Mary couldn't even find a decent home, much less a hospital, and the Savior of the world was born in a smelly cave with animals. No matter! No germs could touch this divine

CHOOSING A LOVE THAT WILL LAST

baby!

All during Jesus' lifetime He was made to look illegitimate. Mary was forced to watch the discrimination and ridicule of her precious son, finally leading up to His being arrested, given the death sentence and crucified publicly between two common criminals, when she knew the truth of this son of hers. Mary believed the angel despite a lifetime of unbelievable problems. Those religious priests and church leaders seemed to be right until the earth quaked when Jesus died on the cross, and again when Jesus was resurrected. Can you imagine their expressions when all those people who were resurrected, along with Jesus, walked around Jerusalem? Matt. 27:52. How did they explain that? Even then, were they convinced that Jesus was the true Messiah? Some people are never convinced, no matter what.

Mary was vindicated (provision) for all time and eternity, but it was much later. EXTREME BLESSINGS SEEM TO INSURE EXTREME TESTINGS. The greater the leadership-- the more severe the training. Every great work must have this great test-time.

In *Daily Blessings*, Roberta Roberts Potts states, "How quickly do things change? We wonder at times whether circumstances will ever change for the better. The Scripture evidences that even though things may seem to take a long time to build up, the actual change often happens in *one* day.

"One night the children of Israel went to bed in Egypt as slaves, and the next morning they awoke free. Enoch walked with the Lord and in *one* day the Bible says, 'He was not.'

"Haman had built gallows for Mordecai, but in *one* day things changed. Haman himself hung on those gallows and the children of Israel were saved from certain death.

"In *one* day, Joseph went from a prison to the palace. In *one* day, his chains were removed and he was next in line to the Pharaoh of Egypt.

"Remember change can come sooner than we think. It can happen in *one* day." [4]

Who is created to question the creator? God's ways are past finding out. Romans 11:33 KJV. None of us would choose to be tested if left up to us. We resist pain and change at all costs. We would use rubber nails every time. Testing brings out what is inside. Before gold is pure, it has to go through a purification process. This evaluation is painful when we can't hide anything from God. He knows our every thought, plan and action before we do. Remember though, we only stay in the crucible until the impurities are gone, thereby creating greater value and are in greater demand. Has it ever crossed my mind that if God didn't keep books on me, there would be no records kept? The children sort of smart when I say I'm not keeping books on them, "Don't clear it with me, clear it with the bookkeeper!"

Can it be true there is no gain without pain?

Time and again in Scripture I notice where it says God was testing them--not tempting them. Heb. 3:8 and Job 23:10 KJV. The more I search and study the more convinced I am that God can and does whatever He pleases. No one can stop Him or challenge Him. Daniel 4. However, the very fact that He is so powerful gives me faith to believe He is capable of doing anything He pleases to help me. Really good news for man. Another verse that gives me hope that I didn't know before was Psalms 75:6,7. "For promotion and power come from nowhere on earth, but only from God. He promotes one and deposes another," referring to individuals, kings, presidents and governments.

Just trying to comprehend such sovereignty gives me fresh hope and anticipation.

Whenever I have the slightest doubt about the Bible's authenticity, there are several facts that convince me of the infallibility of the Holy Scriptures. One is the fulfillment of the prophecies about the State and people of Israel. Many, perhaps countless, events were foretold about them as a people and nation, and to watch during my lifetime alone the accurate unfolding of these ancient prophesies by different men is proof enough for me. Remember these events were foretold some 1,500 years or more ago. This has to be supernatural--to prohesy about them, and for them to come to pass in such a distant future and so precisely.

The other fact is the resurrection of Jesus Christ. A fact proven by many witnesses and historians, as well as documented in the Bible. No other leader of any religion has accomplished this feat. Moreover, there were numerous prophecies over a period of 1500 years concerning his birth, life, death and resurrection; all of which came to pass accurately and as predicted. The details were so explicit, they could not have happened by accident.

Old Testament Prediction	**Nature of Prophecy**	**New Testament Fulfillment**
Isa. 7:14	Born of a virgin	Matt. 1:22,23
2 Sam. 7:11,12; Psa. 132:11; Isa. 9:6; 16:5; Jer. 23:5	Given throne of David	Luke 1:31,32
Dan. 2:44; 7:14,27; Mic. 4:7	Throne to be eternal	Luke 1:33
Isa. 7:14	Called Emmanuel	Matt. 1:23
Isa. 40:3-5; Mal. 3:1	Have a forerunner	Luke 1:76-78; 3:3-6; Matt. 3:1-3
Mic. 5:2	Be born in Bethlehem	Matt. 2:5,6
Ps. 72:10; Isa. 60:3,6,9	Be worshipped by wise men & presented gifts	Matt. 2:11

GLORY CHAPMAN

Num. 24:8; Hos. 11:1	Be in Egypt a season	Matt. 2:15
Jer. 31:15	Birthplace to suffer a massacre of infants	Matt. 2:17,18
Isa. 11:1	Be called a Nazarene	Matt. 2:23
Ps.69:9; 119;139	Be zealous for the Father	John 2:16,17
Isa. 11:2; 61:1,2; Ps. 45:7	Be filled with God's Spirit	Luke 4:18,19
Isa. 53:4	To heal many	Matt. 8:16,17
Isa. 9:1,2; 42:1-3	To deal gently with the Gentiles	Matt. 12:17-21; 4:13-16
Isa. 6:9,10	To speak in parables	Matt. 13:10-15
Isa. 53:3; Ps. 69:8	Be rejected by his own	John 1:11; 7:5
Zech. 9:9	Make triumphal entry into Jerusalem	Matt. 21:4,5
Ps. 8:2	Be praised by children	Matt. 21:16
Ps. 118:22,23	Be rejected cornerstone	Matt. 21:42
Isa. 53:1	His miracles would not be believed	John 12:37,38
Ps. 41:9; 55:12-14	Be betrayed by his friend for 30 pieces of silver	Matt. 26:14-16, 21-25
Isa. 53:3	To be a man of sorrows	Matt. 26:37,38
Zech. 13:7	Be forsaken by his disciples	Matt. 26:31,56
Isa. 50:6	Be scourged & spat upon	Matt. 26:67;27-36
Zech. 11:12,13; Jer. 18:1-4; 19:1-4	His price money to be used to buy potter's field	Matt, 27:9,10
Isa. 53:12	To be crucified middle 2 thieves	Matt. 27:38
Ps. 69:21	Be given vinegar to drink	Matt. 27:34,48 John 19:28-30

CHOOSING A LOVE THAT WILL LAST

Ps. 22:16 Zech. 12:10	Suffer the piercing of hands and feet	Mark 15:25 John 19:34,37 20:25-27
Ps. 22:18	His garments to be parted & gambled for	Luke 23:34; John 19:23,24
Ps. 22:7,8	Be surrounded & ridi- culed by his enemies	Matt. 27:39-44; Mark 15:29-32
Ps. 22:15	That He would thirst	John 19:28
Ps. 31:5	To commend His spirit to the Father	Luke 23:46
Ps. 34:20; Ex. 12:46; Num. 9:12	No bones broken	John 19:33-36
Zech. 12:10	To be stared at in death	John 19:37; Matt. 27:36
Isa. 53:9	To be buried with the rich	Matt. 27:57-60
Ps. 16:10	TO BE RAISED FROM THE DEAD	Matt. 28:2-8
Ps. 24:7-10; Isa. 52:13	TO ASCEND	Mark 16:19; Luke 24:51

Harold Willmington

GLORY CHAPMAN

Who in all of human history stepped forward and offered man a way out of his sins (volunteering to die in our place)? Jesus Christ brought man back to God, thereby assuring us that we will *live happily ever after* for all eternity. That is an offer we can't refuse!

Unique among the books of the world is the Bible. The perennial best seller, the Bible is to the believer the Word of God (God-breathed). Sir Walter Scott wrote this poem about the Bible.

Within that awful volume lies
The mystery of mysteries!
Happiest they of the human race
To whom their God has granted grace
To read, to fear, to hope, to pray,
To lift the latch, and force the way;
And better had they ne'er been born
Who read to doubt, or read to scorn.

The literary style of the Bible portrays a sublimity and unity that is startling. Men such as H. G. Wells have tried to duplicate it but have given up the attempts in hopeless frustration. This is remarkable since the Bible was produced over a period of some fifteen centuries by a variety of authors.

The person of the Holy Spirit was the real author of the Bible. Such an authorship is responsible for this unique literary style and the inability of any human author to duplicate it because of its supernatural authority, inspiration and inerrancy.

The three funamental questions that face every man are answered profoundly by the Bible: From whence did I come? Who am I? What is my destiny?

CHOOSING A LOVE THAT WILL LAST

Someone has said, "Never make the mistake of having your god precede you in death." OUR GOD IS ALIVE AND WELL!

The fact that boggles my mind is that God chose to indwell each believer with *His presence* via the person of the Holy Spirit. This is unmatched in all other religions known to man. Each individual believer has *His presence* within them, so we are never alone and have constant accessibility.

It might appear I have strayed from my text on finding a love that will last, but unless we are totally convinced that God's Word is true, we render God unable to answer and help us. Faith in God and His Son is absolutely essential if we are to receive.

I was gaining all this knowledge and exercising my faith muscles but it seemed difficult for me to act on it.

"O Lord, I know it is not within the power of man to map his life and plan his course—so you correct me, Lord; but please be gentle." Jer. 10:23,24.

THIS SEARCHING JOURNEY IS TAKING A LOT OF TIME1

CHAPTER 8

ANGEL UNAWARE

It is a marvel to me now that I didn't recognize God's intervention from the very first day of my deepest distress. It's a little like the old man who was very sick in the hospital and prayed time and again for the Lord to please send an angel to him. The Lord told him, "I did send an angel," to which he replied, "I never saw any angel." God informed him that the little old lady who came to visit and read him some Scripture was the angel He sent. She had delivered the word he needed. Too bad because he had never thought much of her and was looking for someone more to his own liking.

I found my angel standing on my front porch on the October afternoon I filed for divorce. That day I was unaware of the significant role Barbara Johnson would play in my life as teacher and friend.

Barbara attended the same church I did, but I knew her only by name and face and that she was married to Harry Johnson, a builder. We had spoken very briefly with each other. Little did I suspect that this was my angel unaware and that she would be the catalyst for my big leap of faith.

Let me back up just a bit. On one prior occasion to her ringing my doorbell in late October, she had casually invited me to stop by her home if I was ever in the neighborhood. Some weeks later I found myself driving West of McAllen on the expressway all alone. I was very upset. When my cup spilled over, I would drive and drive, sometimes to nowhere in particular, at other times I drove a well worn circuit. Not much praying, mostly tears as I drove with only a few words, "I TRUST YOU. I TRUST YOU. I TRUST YOU. OH LORD, MY GOD, IN YOU DO I PUT MY TRUST."

CHOOSING A LOVE THAT WILL LAST

As I approached Bentsen Road, I looked over and realized it was the area where Barbara said she lived. Turning on impulse, I turned into her driveway, went up to the door and rang. She greeted me warmly and invited me in.

For the next couple of hours we shared a lot of girl talk--mostly about antiques, pets, decorating, children, etc. Out of the blue, Barbara began telling me the story of her life. Towards the end, she moved back slowly and thoughtfully in the large wing chair and mentioned to me that it was strange because she didn't often share her life with anyone.

What she ended up saying last is still very vivid in my memory. In fact, that last sentence upset me so much I excused myself and hurriedly rushed to my car before I burst into sobbing. I recall saying out loud to myself, *I certainly didn't go out there to hear that.* What she had talked about was how she stayed up all night with some friends. They cried and prayed that Barbara's husband would not go through with a divorce--that God would stop him. She finished by saying, "I was to learn that God does not always put some marriages back together." Wow! I thought He did. Firmly so! All the way home I wept uncontrollably.

This might shock some people as it did me. What I later discovered was that God gave each of us a will to do as we choose. We have total control over our own will, but not the other person's will. It takes two to stay married. God doesn't force His will on us--not ever or under any circumstance. However, He may keep presenting us with problems to try to get our attention.

Again, love not freely given is not love at all. Force will not produce love. God is very patient and long-suffering and woos us, but the ultimate choice is ours. We have sole authority over our own will, either to love God and obey what He asks of us, or to ignore Him altogether. God gave us that free choice. One spouse can choose another path. Perhaps it would have been better for man if God had made us robots since man has proved to be so rebellious. "God is so sovereign. He gave us free wills,"

GLORY CHAPMAN

Francis Schaeffer said.

Back to Barbara! During the afternoon spent in her home, I never once said a word about having any problems in my marriage. For all she knew, I had a wonderful husband and life. With that visit, my life was to change, though I was unaware of it at the time. It dawned on me gradually over the next few years how much.

Several weeks passed between the time of my visit to Barbara's house and the afternoon she rang my doorbell. Barbara and I talked about many things that humid fall afternoon. Again, there was no revealing on my part about any of my own problems. Of course, she suspected nothing. All looked good to her.

It was about time for her to leave, and I was being inwardly prodded by the fact I knew the divorce proceedings would be published in our local newspaper sometime that week. I thought, *She will read it in the paper and say, 'No, that couldn't be,' having spent several hours with me today.* Churning inside and being compelled to be honest, I mumbled haltingly that I felt I needed to tell her something. She fastened her Irish face on mine, waiting expectantly for more information. I could tell she was caught off-guard by my somber expression. "I filed for divorce today," I eked out slowly.

Her reaction was worse than I had anticipated. She turned pale and with frightened blue eyes quickly cried out, "We have to pray." I knew the word *divorce* to her was the worst possible word in the English language. The afternoon I spent with her revealed what utter devastation and agony she suffered during and after her divorce.

Seeing her so undone and surprised, I sat down on the chaise lounge nearby because to deliver bad news is very distasteful to me. Unknown to me at the time was Barbara's ability to pray. I don't mean a pious formal prayer. I mean a prayer from the heart. Whereupon, I discovered she was using several gifts of the Holy Spirit; namely, the gift of prophesy, the gift of the word of wisdom and the gift of the word of knowledge. These gifts are spoken of in the Bible in I Cor. 12 and 14 in detail. Throughout my life I had known or heard of people having certain gifts like these, but didn't realize they could minister so personally and specifically to an individual. These are the words Barbara spoke as she placed her hands on my head:

"My daughter, I have had compassion on you. I know your trust, and I AM WORTHY OF *YOUR* TRUST. Have I ever failed you? I will be with you when you walk through the valley. Your path is not a dead end, but there is an opening at the end. There is light and I will cause your feet to walk in broad places. I will lead you in green pastures and beside the still waters, and you shall have joy and peace. I AM WORTHY OF *YOUR* TRUST. I am in control."

All I could seem to remember at the moment were the words, "I am worthy of *your* trust."

These words were puzzling to me. I asked Barbara, "What did you say? Did I hear you correctly?"

She repeated, "The Lord says that I am worthy of *your* trust--*your* trust."

It took a few seconds for that to sink in. I was filled with awe at God's thoughtfulness in using the word *trust*.

In the weeks to follow, those words would return again and again to bathe my spirit when I was distressed or perplexed. I wanted God to give me some very specific directions on what to do next. However, Barbara's words got me through to the next stage of growth. There is no way to express how calming and quieting those few words were as they nourished my inner self day after day. They were more effective than Valium. It was like being wrapped in a fuzzy soft warm blanket when you are shivering from the cold. As I said, what I wanted most was some advice on how to proceed with my life. That request was to be answered in unexpected and mysterious ways over the next four years and not at all like I would have ever guessed.

Upon receiving these first words from the Lord, I hungrily anticipated the next words; like a lover who anxiously awaits the next sign of affection, a look or a touch. I couldn't wait to see what was next! My Father was in charge now and I knew He did *impossible* things.

GOD CAN DO NOTHING FOR ME UNTIL I GET TO THE LIMIT OF THE POSSIBLE.

Because God had spoken to me through Barbara about my trusting Him, I was convinced deep within that God was aware of who and where I was. He was alive! Alive to me! He knew me! Remembering that God wanted me to draw close to Him spurred me on. God would not mind if I kept talking to Him, even praying without ceasing.

The answer to my deepest longings would prove to be fulfilled little by little as I followed his leading. I felt I must be in close proximity for Him to speak to me.

A computer may contain all the right kind of knowledge, but if the right motions are not made in pushing certain keys, the end result is the same as if there were no knowledge stored within, or worse. God has all knowledge. However, to transfer that knowledge to me, I must use the manual correctly if the benefits are to be forthcoming.

The Bible says, "In everything you do, acknowledge God first, and He will direct you and crown your efforts with success." Proverbs 3:6.

Early one morning while reading the devotional book, *God Calling*, these words helped me understand losses and suffering.

> "There does come a joy known to those who suffer with Me. But that is not the result of the suffering, but the result of the close intimacy with Me, to which SUFFERING DROVE YOU." [1]

"Yes, Lord, let your constant love surround me, for my hope is in you alone." Psalms 33:22.

I TRUST YOU IN MY SEARCH!

CHAPTER 9

SILENCE OF GOD

Perhaps I was like the little seed which was planted beneath the earth where it was all dark and no one would ever see it again, at least not in seed form. At one point in my life, it felt as if I had bled to death and even my blood had sunk into the dry cracked earth, never to be seen again. Worse still, no one knew where I had poured into the ground. There was no trace left of me. My life had all been for nothing. What a waste!

That little seed had not only to be planted but also had to die. If there is no dying there can be no fruit produced. And a tiny handful of seeds can produce bushels of either weeds or flowers. Only in the dying to myself and my desires is real life possible. That seems to be a paradox, but it is the principle of the law of sowing and reaping. Maybe it's a little like chasing wildly after the butterfly of happiness, and only when I stop driving so hard, does it come and settle on my shoulder.

Seeds are hard to digest and you can't drink grapes. It's only in the breaking and squeezing that the fullness of flavor is brought out. We can only reproduce ourselves after death to self. Then we are poured as wine to enrich others.

Jesus speaks of his own life as a seed, "I must fall and die like a kernel of wheat that falls into the furrows of the earth. Unless I die I will be alone--a single seed. But my death will produce many new wheat kernels--a plentiful harvest of new lives. If you love your life down here--you will lose it. If you despise your life down here--you will exchange it for eternal glory." John 12:24,25.

One ingredient is required between planting, dying and harvesting and that is TIME. I was between seasons!

Time, no doubt, produces more than we are fully aware of in our lives. Many battles have to be waged before the victory celebration can begin. The greater the battle the greater the celebration. Graduation from kindergarten calls for small refreshments and treats, high school greater reward, ending perhaps with a doctorate deserving much applause, reward and celebration.

Actually I see now that I was on a quest to know God all through my life. As I was learning more about Him, the greater my search intensified. In my silent contemplative moments, I wondered, *Is He really there for me?* I had no trouble believing He did marvelous miracles for His own people long ago, but would He be here for me individually in McAllen, Texas? There was no doubt I felt His presence when I was converted at the age of nine, experiencing the sensation of walking a foot off the ground, which happened about an hour after returning home from church. It was something I never forgot and which has kept me from ever doubting that I belonged to God. In my early teens, I rededicated my life and was filled with the Holy Spirit. His presence enveloped me. He and I were closer than friends. But why couldn't I feel His presence like that everyday now, especially now?

If in my deep desperation I could not reach the God who is there, then I would quit the whole futile search. You can only search so long. The ritual and ceremony of church attendance and religion was monotonous to me now. Without finding some present meaning in it all, I felt I could not play charades forever. If God is not there, it is totally meaningless and boring to pretend He is. There must be a way my Creator and I can communicate in a significant and consequential way.

Again the book, *God Calling* helped me.

> "Sometimes weariness and exhaustion
> are not signs of lack of spirit but
> of the guiding of the Spirit."[1]

It seems there is no big struggle with our faith until we run up against unbelievable odds. Then definite and specific answers are needed. This is not babyhood or adulthood--this is womanhood spiritually. It's the point where my faith hits the fire--the fires of life.

I AM CONVINCED I COULD GRADUATE SUMMA CUM LAUDE--IF THEY WOULDN'T MAKE ME TAKE THE TESTS!

Barbara's words gave me renewed stamina and hope. So many evidences of God--my own limited experience, in nature, testimonies of others, and of course the Word of God. I had loved God from early childhood, but why was He so silent? Why couldn't I hear His voice when I was so distressed?"

Under May 1 of *God Calling* it says:

> "Delay is not denial--not even withholding. It is the opportunity for God to work out our problems and accomplish your desires in the most wonderful way possible for you." [1]

I MISTOOK SILENCE FOR ABSENCE!

Could it be likened to a glorious honeymoon, only to return to everyday life to very little closeness and deep communing? After while you are emotionally famished. Love is constantly needed for daily nourishment to keep the emotions sensitive and healthy--just like the body. My desire was to find this God who was love personified, all knowing, all powerful, present everywhere--the God with no limits in any way. If I couldn't get this God to respond to me, then why would I want anymore to do with an impotent religion and church? Why? Someone has said that when Christianity gets off track, it becomes religion. Religion is what the Pharisees and Sadducees had. They had the Book--not the Author; the Law--not the Life; the Letter--not the relationship.

CHOOSING A LOVE THAT WILL LAST

Catherine Marshall is the first author I recall reading about who thought it should be perfectly normal for the creator to talk to His creation, just as He did with Adam and Eve, the prophets, kings, His disciples and many others all down through the ages. We are to pray or talk to Him without ceasing and that His eyes are constantly searching throughout the whole earth for those who love Him. I Thes. 5:17 KJV.

Before Jesus ascended to heaven the last time, He even told those standing there to go and wait for the Holy Spirit, providing them with a person to walk alongside--even to be *in* them to communicate more perfectly. We are praying to someone who is listening, and we want a response from the listener. I wanted God in some manner to converse with me.

Lois Kelly, a member of Reviewers' Guild, reviewed the book, *Four Women In A Violent Time* by Deborah Crawford. Apparently the Puritans in Massachusetts at that time held to the rule that if anyone claimed that God spoke to them, it was considered heresy, punishable by hanging. I am no history buff, but this bit of information certainly startled me. Evidently, there wasn't religious freedom in America until the Constitution was signed in 1787.

In 1660 Mary Dyer, a Quaker, along with two men, were to be hanged in Boston Commons. The execution was carried out on the two men first. Then they bound Mary's arms behind her, tied her skirt around her ankles, covered her face and lifted her to the ladder. At the top of the ladder she felt the noose tighten against her throat. At the drum roll, the ladder was not pulled out from under her as with the two men. She was advised it was intended to give her a severe scare. She was then to leave the Massachusetts Bay Colony and not to ever return. One of Mary's crimes was attending meetings at her friend's house. Anne Hutchinson's is where Anne claimed the Holy Spirit was *within* every believer and that the Holy Spirit spoke with her direct. The Puritans claimed that only through the Bible could God's Word be heard and only through interpretation of ordained ministers could ordinary folk understand its meaning.

Upon hearing of all the reports of continued floggings, mutilations, cutting off ears and tattooing 'S.L.' (seditions libeler) on their cheeks, Mary Dyer did return a few months later with a roll of clean linen under her arm. She told her executioners it was for the wrapping of her body. So Mary was condemned to be hanged at nine the next morning. Her body dropped hard into the noose when the ladder was pulled away at the drum roll.

King Charles II stopped the Puritan intolerance with stern edicts in both England and New England. Today across from Boston Commons are two statues of the martyrs: Mary Dyer and Anne Hutchinson.

Incidentally, a heretic believes too much while an apostate believes too little.

What reason and how much truth would there be in teaching that God is Almighty and speaks to His children if, in fact, He does not? Or He used to, but quit? When? Why did He quit?

This search would lead me into paths I had not planned on exploring. Now I realize why God cannot reveal too much too soon to us. We would ruin it every time. Perhaps if I had known where God was indeed directing my steps and had known where they were heading, I wouldn't have had the good judgment to follow. However, the fact of having made so many unwise choices certainly made me pay closer attention now.

The next four years were crammed with much new learning and unlearning. Sometimes I felt the pace too slow and at other times the pace much too swift. I was often jerked from my cliches' and narrow views about God. Cliches' are big faith eaters I discovered.

I prayed, "Lord, give me enough courage to *will* to give the reins of my life over to You and stick with it." I continually told God that I would let Him make my big decisions, fully realizing that with that would come the necessity of some changes. Change is painful.

Dr. Ed Young says in *Against All Odds*, "Our response to the challenge of change is critical. We can view change as a threat and put up resistance, resign, or remove ourselves, or we can rescript the negative implications of change and see it as an opportunity for growth. The choice is ours."

I wonder if there is anything more frightening in human experience than change and the unknown? Some psychologists have suggested there can be no change without pain. It is indeed painful to grow out of longtime habit patterns and attitudes. In fact, I believe it requires anywhere from 21 to 30 days to break or change a habit. Truly no one but God would have the patience to keep putting us back on His potter's wheel again and again. We lose hope in ourselves long before He does. God never ceases to keep trying to make of us what we claim we want to be. It is impossible to crucify ourselves. Usually when the pain begins, we wiggle off the wheel. Thank God that He never despairs of us so long as we *will* to stay on His molding wheel. What love!

I didn't know what lengths God would take me through to see if I really meant He could control my life. At least anticipating and looking forward to a change with someone so powerful and capable was certainly far better than the despair I was feeling. What did I have to lose by trading my despair for hope?

"Hope deferred makes the heart sick; but when dreams come true at last, there is life and joy." Proverbs 13:12.

"Hope is the thing with feathers/ that perches in the soul/ that sings the tune without the words/ and never stops at all," so aptly put by poet Emily Dickinson.

It has been said that man can live about 40 days without food, about six days without water and about five minutes without oxygen--but ONLY ONE SECOND WITHOUT HOPE.

After many years, I discovered that as long as we don't lose the dearest person or thing in our lives, we don't despair. When we find that certain special relationship that makes us feel esteemed and worthwhile, it enables us to withstand much adversity and pressure. It is when we feel all is lost that we succumb to despondency.

So long as we have and hold the most precious thing which we treasure above all else, there is always hope. If our relationship is personal and meaningful with God, and we love Him above all else in this life, and He is our highest joy, then we can lose all and not be destroyed because we still have and hold the thing we value most. On the other hand, if the most precious thing happens to be a child, a mate, money, position or reputation, and they are stripped away, then we can be distressed to the point of being pauperized--destitute of any meaning to life.

Perhaps that is why Job survived his ordeal. He never lost his faith in the relationship he prized above all else in life. It is when we lose the most idealized thing that we are bereft and distraught to the point of despair and suicide. Hope and anticipation are always present when we are holding the most cherished thing close to our hearts. I am struggling to say that a person cannot lose everything meaningful to him and remain untouched or unmoved.

Hopelessness rapidly overtakes us when there is nothing in view and all seems lost--pushed or backed into a corner with no way out. Damned if you do and damned if you don't! No-win situations can have devastating results.

It was a startling revelation to realize that my family did indeed hold a place of greater importance and security than did my relationship with God. My family seemed most precious and God somehow more distant--there, but somehow far away too. No doubt, that is why I was almost blown away when tragedy struck. My priorities needed to be overhauled and realigned!

Now, my most precious One is holding my hand. I am safe, secure, protected and know all will be well, even in trouble, because I am not alone. My treasure will always be there to help and assist no matter what. There is no limit to His wondrous power. Years later I experienced this safe protection when a terrible storm hit Houston and I was alone. I fixed a bed with pillows under the stairway and went to sleep!

When someone asked Ann Landers her favorite quotation or

maxim about life, she shared this, "My single most useful bit of advice to humanity is this: Expect trouble as an inevitable part of your life, and when it comes, hold your head high, look it squarely in the eye and say, 'I will be bigger than you. You cannot defeat me.' Then repeat to yourself the most comforting of all words, 'This too shall pass.'"[2]

"There is no medicine like hope, no incentive so great, and no tonic so powerful as expectation of something better tomorrow,"[3] writes Orison Marden. Most of all, there must be meaning, purpose, and direction in our lives.

God would turn on my light. "This God who with a breath can scatter the plans of *all* the nations." Psalms 33:10.

SEARCHING CERTAINLY TAKES TIME AND PAYING ATTENTION!

GLORY CHAPMAN

CHAPTER 10

OKLAHOMA SNIPE HUNTING & WILD INDIANS

Let me break away here, and go back to my childhood and the many happenings which helped to shape my life.

My first memories are filled with carefree happy days shared with two brothers and lots of sisters on an Oklahoma wheat and cotton farm on the east side of Yukon. The population was about 1200 then. Yukon is now a suburb of Oklahoma City.

Being the fifth child of eight born to Thomas Powell and Alice Lucy James Taylor, I certainly never experienced being lonely. It was the reverse, always trying to find some quiet corner to be alone to read or think. If that was to be any indication of what my life would be, I am still trying to find some quiet space. Even while I am trying to write this book, it is perhaps the busiest time of my life. Strange how I always thought when my six *small* children got to be six *big* children, I would have lots of leisure time. At every juncture in life I keep thinking the next phase will be more quiet and less busy.

Back to the farm--there was always something happening, what with horses to ride, especially Prince our gentle paint horse, and with Buster, our mongrel dog, jumping and bouncing alongside.

My brothers were second and fourth in birth order sandwiched between six sisters. It was a tight, close-knit group experience.

When we weren't playing jacks, walking on stilts, hopscotching, jumping rope, sliding down the roof, swinging from trees or riding bikes, we were down in the silo or climbing up into the hayloft or wheat bin, burying ourselves. Also, not to be forgotten were the hundreds of mud pies we made, as well as throwing them at each other! Riding curled up inside an old tire was a thrill too.

My mother tells me, there were plenty of chores, but we four younger girls were too little to be of much help. Mainly we just played and swam in the horse tank connected to the back of our garage.

However, one of the favorite things my brother Norlyne enjoyed was taking his little sisters and cousins (and any friends who fell for the ploy) snipe hunting about dusk way out in the east pasture near the little creek. We especially loved to play this trick on our city cousins who turned absolutely into the wildest of wild Indians from the time their feet touched our driveway until the time they were pulled away. No let up! If we kids whooped and hollered like that when they weren't there, we got slowed down. There were seven or eight of us kids and cousins running up the stairs, heading for the bedroom windows, whipping off the screens, climbing out onto the sloping shingled roof to go sailing off to the ground below, only to repeat without stopping. This was such an exhilarated feeling of freedom as to almost feel like flying.

The Jameses; Earl, Jr., Franky and little Mary, our city cousins, were gung-ho for snipe hunting, and it lasted several hours into the night or when we finally went back for them. They would be asleep, still holding tight to keep the gunnysack open so the snipes could fly in, according to specific instructions given them. What fun we all had when they caught on and chased us to get even!

Franky spotted the small pond across the street on the south forty, and insisted on taking a swim. Before my brother Norlyne could say *Jack Robinson*, he went down a clean white cousin and came up a soggy reddish one. It was an Oklahoma mud hole!

There was another even steeper roof over the cellar at the back of our two-story white frame farmhouse, which was off-limits to us kids. However, when Mother pulled out of the driveway and headed towards town, we ran for our stashed away flat cardboards, dashed for the ancient maple tree overhanging the steep roof, shinnied up the big old trunk, leapt out onto the highest pitch of the roof, adjusted our cardboards to our anatomies, and sailed off faster than wind, only to land on our buns full force.

The miracle of it all is that none of us ever got so much as a sprained ankle or arm from this kind of whoopee. The only restraining note we felt was the lookout one of us had to keep for our Mama's approaching car. When the signal was given, we and our cardboards vanished quicker than a magician's rabbit.

Another exciting exercise was climbing to the top of the windmill and waving to Mother from the high platform some 50 feet above. Of course, there was one catch. While we had no trouble scaling up, we couldn't seem to get back down by ourselves. One day Mother looked and looked for me, but couldn't find me anywhere. Eventually I was compelled to call for Mother from high on my little perch atop the old turning windmill. Mother cast her eyes heavenward to see a child of three or four waving, silhouetted against the blue sky. Waving and crying, I might add. Looking downward had quickly drained all my spunkiness away. It was Daddy who finally rescued me.

My sister Alice and I often begged and begged to go to work with daddy or wherever he was going. After patiently explaining to us he would be gone too long, we would sneak down into the back seat of his car and cover ourselves up. Several hours later, the farmer that Daddy had gone to see would say, "Tom, have the girls go on inside."

Daddy quipped, "I don't have any girls with me."

Whereupon his friend would point towards the car, "Who is that in your car?"

Much to Dad's chagrin he had to take us miles back home. I don't remember him ever spanking us though. Probably that is why we did it so often!

With eight children, all approximately 18 months apart in age, you can imagine the many escapades. Fortunately we never seemed to get injured or were ill very often, except for Junior. All of us were slight in build when young, but for some reason I was more frail looking than the others. In fact, I was downright skinny with blonde curls and huge brown eyes. My brother Norlyne would sometimes call me *Slats* which I disliked a lot.

Also, I remember the fun time we all had in our front room hospital! All seven of us came down with the measles at the same time, so our beds were all brought downstairs where Mother could play and work at being nurse. All the beds were lined up side by side like in a hospital ward. We four younger children were not very sick like the three older ones--Monita, Lahoma and Norlyne. They kept pleading with Mother to keep us from jumping on all the beds, chasing each other, laughing and making noise. It was so much fun to be out of school and to have this excitable and captive audience. Remember, we had no television. We wished we could always have our beds close like this.

Going into the milk barn in the evenings proved a real challenge, mostly for Norlyne, whose job was milking the cows. He would squirt milk direct from the cow's udder fingers at us if we so much as put our heads around the doorway to the barn. Norlyne was about ten at the time. We four little girls were driving him nuts, so at the least provocation, he would do us one-upmanship. He was quick and many times when we didn't think he could see us sneaking up behind him, he would turn and take aim with the cow's teat, delivering yucky warm milk into our open squealing mouths. We would run like scalded dogs to tell Mother and Daddy what a hideous person Norlyne was. Of course, we didn't reveal what we had done. When quizzed a bit about it, we would usually mumble something about just standing there minding our own business when he just shot us with Betsy's bag of milk.

Junior had died several years earlier, and on more than one occasion, Norlyne thought it was disastrous being the only boy in the middle of six girls. Norlyne was always in motion, doing something either mischievous or fiddling with some mechanical tool. Missing from the house at night, my parents would often find him most any place asleep--one time over the milk house in the loft, another time asleep in the manure spreader out in the corral, in the haystack, or down in the ground silo. He wasn't afraid of anything, literally, though he was only about five-feet tall, probably weighing no more than 60 pounds at ten years of age.

Later, while in the Marines, having enlisted at the age of 17, Norlyne was itching to get to the real battlefront after boot camp at Camp Pendleton in San Diego. His wish was answered as he fought in several beachheads: Saipan, Tinian and Okinawa. At Saipan he was shot in his left arm. On Okinawa he landed in a machine-gun nest and was shot more seriously in his right arm. That took the fight out of him. There was only one man from the 8th Marine Regiment that was not wounded. About half of them came home. Returning to the United States looked pretty good to Norlyne. He left home with straight dark brown hair and returned with wavy curly hair. Interesting as to what made it curl!

In our family, it was sort of like the big kids and the four little kids. I had an interesting vantage point--up three and down three. There were five years between the four little kids from top to bottom.

There is no memory of helping around the house, barn, milk house, garden, animals, etc. before the age of 10 or 12, but life was hard for my parents with long hours--up before daybreak and to bed late into the night after finishing all the farm chores. In the winter it was worse, of course. We younger kids were left to run free within the confines of the home place. Other than occasional guests, usually on Sundays, we were in our own little world of fun and games to run barefoot over hill and dale.

On many hot, still, summer evenings, we kids would drag our mattresses and springs out the upstairs windows, slide them down the sloping roof to sleep out on the front lawn.

The dark heavens were so vast accenting the brightness of the millions of stars by contrast. We fell asleep trying to locate the Little and Big Dippers, and counting the shooting stars. I still get an ethereal feeling when I think of how we used to look up into the gigantic galaxies. Other times, from our front bedroom windows we had contests to see who could come up with the most cars going east or west on Highway 66. We would often be carried off by the sandman still mumbling.

My grandparents, T.Jack and Lola Taylor, lived a quarter of a mile towards town on another farm, whereas, my mother's parents, Lewis and Belle James, lived in Oklahoma City and visited only on some weekends. However, they did live in a small house on our farm during one period of time. So, of course, we knew Grandpa and Grandma Taylor better.

The Oklahoma hills were mostly gentle rolling ones, and what sheer delight to look forward to spring so we could go wiggle our toes in the freshly turned soil with little wheat shoots peaking their heads above the winter's hibernation.

Summer was by far our favorite season with swimming, walking on tall stilts, having our city and country cousins visit, and lots of homemade ice cream being cranked by hand out in the west yard. We little kids had to take turns sitting on the gunnysack to keep the freezer from moving around while the big kids groaned and cranked away. There was always lots of delicious fried chicken and big juicy messy watermelons too.

For my parents, summer meant harvest time with thrashers, combiners and harvesters to be fed. Never shall I forget when several truckloads of black people pulled up in our driveway to pick our cotton. We were told not to get out of the hurricane fenced yard, so we little kids just sort of fastened our bodies into the steel fence, peering with wide curious eyes, at those coffee-colored people. I learned later the reason they were trucked in was because Yukon had a city ordinance that prohibited blacks from spending the night. They had to be out of town by sundown. So, of course, our city and schools had no black people, and only one Mexican-American family. Yukon was mostly a mixture of English, Irish, German and Czech, often only a generation or two removed from their mother country.

Mother tells me our family was semi-religious protestant. I say semi because church was something they did for an hour or so on

Sunday mornings, having done their duty and paid their respects to God for the week. My parents were good moral people, hard-working and benevolent, teaching us kids to observe man's as well as God's laws.

However, something happened in our little town of about 1200 people that was to impact my family's faith. It was not gradual with a slight change, but fast with a big transition in our family life after this.

Two evangelists came to our town and set up a big tent on the north side of Yukon: a Brother Enos and a Brother Solon Welch. Grandpa and Grandma Taylor attended one night before any of the other family did just to see what it was all about. On the third night my Grandma Lola went forward to accept Jesus Christ as her Lord and was filled with the Holy Spirit. She had thought herself a Christian until she attended the meetings. After hearing the evangelist, she knew she was not. After this happened, some talk in town was she was so good she didn't need to be saved. Everyone loved my dear sweet wonderful, almost perfect, Grandma. Grandpa Jack was something else. He mostly observed!

Upon hearing what happened to Grandma, my parents went to see her for themselves. They were perplexed and surprised to see her so expressive. They marveled at the exuberance in her personality and countenance. She was bubbling over with joy and love, which continued.

After seeing Grandma, both my parents decided to attend. Mother said that she wasn't particularly interested in the meeting at first, but when Bro. Welch gave a call to come forward, she found herself responding almost without realizing she was moving forward. Something propelled her to the front. She knelt down at the makeshift wooden altar in the sawdust. After rededicating her life to Jesus Christ (she had accepted Christ as a child) there came this overwhelming and unmistakable sense that she was being asked to promise to have as many children as God wanted her to have.

CHOOSING A LOVE THAT WILL LAST

She already had three children; ages one, three and five. My parents had not planned nor wanted a large family. Three was just right. Mother had never been taught whether it was right or wrong to use contraceptives. In fact, she had just ordered some device from her doctor. Mother related that the request was unmistakable. She would have to make a decision. "You cannot *think* a spiritual matter clear, you have to *obey* it clear. In intellectual matters you can think things out, but in spiritual matters you will think yourself into cotton wool. If there is something upon which God puts his pressure, obey in that matter, and everything will become as clear as daylight." Oswald Chambers.

When Mother made the commitment, she too was filled with the Holy Spirit. She has told all of us many times how she was flooded with so much joy and love. She loved the whole world! It was almost more than she could contain. After this, Mother said that the Bible was so easy to understand; whereas before she just couldn't comprehend what it was all about. She could also find scriptures easily, actually without really knowing where certain passages were found. Mother was always very shy, but now she was much more forward and bold in speaking about what had happened to her.

Meanwhile, my daddy watched from the rear of the tent, and frankly didn't know what to make of any of this, not to mention he was very busy taking care of three small children during the services. He didn't know what had happened to his mother, and now his little pristine wife. He said little on the way home as the horses' hooves clapped along the dusty country road, pulling the buggy carrying all five of them.

However, as time went by, the church expostulated more and more rules of conduct of do's and don'ts. It was pointed out that if a man couldn't govern his own house well, meaning his wife and children, then how could he govern the house of God. Strange how small things can create such differences, but it seems the pastor thought all the girls should wear long stockings instead of anklets. Well, that idea did not appeal nor was bought by my sister, Monita, since all the other girls at school wore short socks.

It didn't take her long to figure out how to keep the peace, both at school and at home. Of course, she dutifully put them on before leaving home, and very quickly reversed the process by the time she arrived at school, only to repeat the same procedure in the evening. Movies and certain parties were off limits, especially the Bohemian Hall. Later, Daddy let Monita start driving to help him deliver milk to town. She was about 14 years old. All was going very well until daddy saw one of his friends in town one morning, who asked him if he knew his new Whippet was turning corners on two wheels? He said, "Tom, by golly, she is right good at it. Only thing it is a bit dangerous." It turned out to be not only the screeching tires, but too many friends in the car as well.

My dad was overly concerned that his family be above reproach as they called it. By the time daddy took the driving privileges away, rebellion had already put down roots. Someone has said that rules and regulations without a loving relationship creates rebellion. There were several years of battling for control. Dad says he made a mistake in giving her so much freedom at 14. From a very young point of view, the raised voices and spankings made me sense something wasn't right in the house.

In fact, it became so difficult to conform to all of the church's teachings (not God's) that my parents stopped going to church at all for about a year.

THAT PROVED TO BE COSTLY!

CHOOSING A LOVE THAT WILL LAST

CHAPTER 11

BELOVED JUNIOR, PRECIOUS JUNIOR

During the time my parents had decided to quit going to church, a woman by the name of Mrs. Stapp went to my dad and told him that if he didn't get back in church, or set a better example, that the thing he loved most would be taken from him. In checking with my mother recently, she said she did remember something about it and added rather solemnly, "We never thought much of that woman."

Anyway, some months later while my dad was plowing in the field north of the house he heard a terrible strange sound coming from the area of the highway in front of our home. We lived on the main street of the United States, which was US Highway 66. Dad told someone he knew who it was before he turned and headed south to see what had happened.

He found my dear 9-year old brother, Thomas Powell Taylor, Jr., had been hit by a car as he attempted to run across the street. The driver was apparently drunk and did not stop to render aid. He just sped off. A close friend of our family, Ruth Cox, had given Junior and 11-year old Monita a ride home from school. Junior was in a hurry to play with his new bag of marbles Grandpa Jack had given him and attempted to run across the street as soon as he got out of the car. Mother said that Junior lived a few hours and was gone.

My parents, I am told, were bereft and devastated! Mother was six months pregnant which didn't help. I was about three at the time, too young to remember much. However, I clearly remember sitting in our large dining room with the lights being low. Everything seemed to be so dark and ominous. Something very grave had happened, but I didn't know what it was. In discussing this with mother recently, she remarked I should have known since his body was brought home for viewing. Maybe I was too short to see inside the casket. In any event, I didn't know what it was all about, nor where Junior went. I just knew Junior was gone, and he wasn't there to play piggyback with me anymore. I have no memory of grieving over him, nor going to the funeral or to the cemetery. I thought he was in the cedar chest. I know this sounds preposterous, but every time someone got close to the big cedar chest in mother and daddy's bedroom, they all acted strange and started crying.

This bit of news was relayed to my mother by some visiting friends who had asked me about Junior, to which I informed them he was in the cedar chest. All those big people (from my viewpoint) were appalled to think I would say such a thing. My embarrassment was real when everyone started crying again.

Still they didn't tell me where he was. Much later I learned that that cedar chest held his things; his little Indian costume, cowboy outfit, books, notebooks and a big jumbo pencil holding smaller pencils. Also, there was a special little bound brown notebook that held all his elocution sayings and poems. Many times Junior had stood before the Lions and Kiwanis Clubs and in his special winsome way endeared himself to the audience. I still have the little faded torn yellow pages of that book.

Here is one of many of his favorites that he did so expressively with his large gray eyes dancing about as his black shiny curls fell down wrecklessly across his forehead into his eyes. He was a miniature of my Dad--plus the curly hair.

HAND-ME-DOWNS

Don't look at these pants, please,
I think it's a shame.
But I have to wear them
Though I'm not to blame.

My Dad owned them first hand

CHOOSING A LOVE THAT WILL LAST

But he got too fat.
And Ned had a turn next.
And still for all that,

They wore and they wore, till
They came down to me.
I guess I'm a sight for
The kids here to see.

Oh, I tried hard to balk, but
Ma said, "I'll allow
They'll do you to play in
A while anyhow."

Some day when I'm married
There won't be a chance
Of making my children
Wear hand-me-down pants!

Through the years as we all grew older, whenever Junior's name was brought up or someone asked about him, both Mother and Daddy would start tearing up, so I knew few details then.

Several years ago I mentioned to Mother that sometime I would like for her to tell me more about Junior if she felt she could. It had now been 50 some years since Junior's death. She looked uncomfortable and although she didn't cry; she couldn't recall or remember too much about the lady who had given them that awesome message. That proved to be true prophecy, I would say. In Scripture I notice where the people rejected the prophets. The people chided Jeremiah, "Well, Jeremiah what is the sad news from the Lord today?" Jer. 23:33. Seldom were the prophets welcomed then or now.

Anyway, Mother suggested I read the poems she had written about Junior. That was the most she could talk about. Thank goodness, Mother is now able to mention his name without

GLORY CHAPMAN

crying. Time is truly a healer. Here is one of the poems Mother wrote.

MEMORIES

Though your soul is far away,
Yet your spirit seems very near.
And in my lonely hours,
I seem to hear your footsteps clear.

Coming with your sweet, eager face,
So full of the joy of life,
And putting up your full, sweet lips,
With such adoring grace.

In memory now I can see you,
As you mischievously looked in my face,
I'd fancy I could see the man,
Who'd steal all hearts in the race.

No more we'll see that sunny face,
No more that curly head,
No more we'll hear your laugh so gay,
But only memories instead.

My darling when I think of you,
It makes me so lonely and sad,
If I had not God to sustain me,
I think I should go mad.

But someday I shall see your face,
And hold you in my arms,
In that land where death can't come,
Where love will reign and nothing harm.
     Alice James Taylor

CHOOSING A LOVE THAT WILL LAST

All in all, though, my parents were not to be the same again. Mother cried and went through the whole grieving process, but it was another matter for my dad. Without ever stating it in so many words, nonetheless true, my dad had a *mad on* with God. Nothing could assuage his grief. The deepest kind of sorrow hung onto him like a black cloud, obscuring any sunshine. It was hard to be a Christian. Too hard! He would walk the floor many nights.

Someone also told me that my parents went to the cemetery many nights and stayed for hours. Mother says now that they did go some, but doesn't remember how often.

There was one especially poignant story about how much Norlyne missed Junior. Little 5-year old Norlyne would sit in the bathtub and sing to the top of his lungs, "I want another brother. Please bring me a baby brother next time. I lost my great big Junior." On and on, making up words as he went along as to how much he missed playing with him. His song requests were answered with two more successive little girl babies.

My parents' grief knew no bounds and they suffered and suffered by Junior's going away. Grief, I am told, affects people of different ages in quite diverse depths. In my experience and having read some, it seems the ages of 11 to perhaps 16 are very tedious ages and they are affected more adversely than some other ages.

Monita was 11 when Junior went away. She and Junior were very close in age and to each other. They were almost always together. Monita's devastation was greater than anyone suspected at the time. To this day she cannot attend anyone's funeral. She just can't. She didn't even attend her own favorite daughter Patty's funeral, who died at the age of 32 from simple gallbladder surgery. Nor did she attend dad's funeral.

Several years ago someone wrote and told *Dear Abby* of her aversion to funerals. "I've tried to force myself to go to funerals, but I can't make myself do it. I've been dressed and practically out the door, but something stops me. I've tried therapy but it didn't work for me. Signed, 'Incurable'."

Abby told her not to worry about it. "The only funeral you really have to go to is your own."

Since that time, Mother has expressed with regret that perhaps she and Daddy were so distraught in their own loss they failed to help Monita work through her grief. Sometimes we are struck so motionless that we are unaware of the extent to which others are struggling to survive.

After Junior's death, my mother was finding it more and more difficult to keep her vow to have more babies. This vow would come close to costing her life when the eighth baby was born.

I was reared in a God-fearing home, but not necesarily a God-loving home. Certainly, I gained much knowledge on the wrath and judgments of God. I knew them all. Sometimes a church can emphasize more punishment than love and mercy--not balancing it with presenting the total personality of God. Could be we learn and remember the tragic easier. It seems I was not as aware of God's love, His unconditional love, as I was of His anger and wrath. In light of the way I learned of my brother's death, perhaps it was understandable. Being so young, it made an extraordinary impression on me.

> Webster puts it this way:
> PUNISH: Implies making a wrongdoer suffer for his wrongdoing by paying a penalty, usually, with no idea of reforming or correcting him--to punish a murderer by hanging him.
> DISCIPLINE: Suggests punishment that is intended to control the wrongdoer or to establish in him habits of self-control.
> CORRECT: Suggests punishment of a wrongdoer for the purpose of overcoming his faults.
> CHASTISE: Implies punishment, usually physical punishment, along with an attempt to correct the wrongdoer.

CHOOSING A LOVE THAT WILL LAST

But I have learned that God's tough love or total love is too wonderful and awesome for me to comprehend, even now. It is the goodness of God that draws men to repentance. I like that! GOD TAKES AN ETERNAL VIEW OF OUR LIVES AND BRINGS CIRCUMSTANCES TO CAUSE US TO TURN WHEN WE ARE INCAPABLE OF CHANGING.

There are many avenues by which we can come to God; scared, coerced, forced, by duty, tradition, by habit or by God's spirit drawing us. It seems to me that it is love which makes obedience possible. Let me repeat it again, love is not love unless it is free. God lets parents choose God if they like, and children should be given the same opportunity. We cannot inherit our second birth. Also, God has no grandchildren. Then obedience is the evidence of that love that drew us in. Not many of us are drawn to some tyrant or a set of rules and regulations. We are drawn to a person by love. Force against force usually produces rebellion, like a parent force-feeding a child. Very often it boomerangs! A relationship of rules and regulations without love creates rebellion. Love without discipline creates chaos.

An example of this love can be found in marriage. There are certain norms or rules in marriage, but when you are in-love, I dare say those rules are disguised. Whatever is required, lovers will confess that it's considered a pleasure to perform for the loved one. We flow out of love to honor, respect and obey our chosen beloved. Rules and demands do not help us love him, but love helps us volunteer our services and even to go on beyond the rules to become a love slave.

It is my thought that God doesn't want forced love anymore than a sweetheart does. Love flowing in a circle between two hearts creates a powerful desire to please each other.

But my parents didn't know this at the time of Junior's death. After about a year my parents did return to the church, though not very enthusiastically. Dad tried very hard, but his heart wasn't in it. He went along perfunctorily, possessing no feeling or inner strength to help him cope with that giant called *grief.* He could not wrestle free of it. It immobilized him emotionally. Fourteen years went by after my mother's rededication to God with daddy going along, assenting, as I said, to the gospel.

Just as I am about to write the next sequence of events, it dawns on me, it is another woman who is to play an important role in my dad's story. Women are important!

A lady evangelist, Sister MacAdoo, came to Yukon to conduct a revival meeting in our church. At the close of each service she would ask those who wanted prayer to come forward. My father needed and desired the Holy Spirit, instead of his woeful spirit. He wanted the joy and free spirit like my mother exhibited, so he often went forward. It was also what he thought the other members expected him to do--at least keep seeking till he found.

After faithfully going forward for four nights, Sister MacAdoo looked dad straight in the eye and solemnly asked, "Tom, do you *really* want to be filled with the Holy Spirit?" He told me later he realized this lady meant business. She wasn't preaching just to have something to do. She expounded and proclaimed the Word to create players not spectators.

Daddy was what some people called a chronic seeker. Seems he could never have the knowing others spoke about. And, too, he was not forgetting his bitterness and resentment. He had been dealt a death blow. Also, weren't there others in the church who were no closer to God than he? Not too difficult to come up with the winning ticket when we compare ourselves with each other. It's when we compare ourselves with God's outline that we get the true measure. II Cor. 10:12,13.

To Sister MacAdoo's question, Dad finally answered, "Yes, I do," in a firmer resolve than previously. With that she turned and walked away. Nothing more was said or prayed except the benediction, and everyone went home.

About four o'clock the next morning, my dad woke up laughing, uncontrollably so. He felt extremely happy, but why? Nothing had changed. He nudged mother, "Honey, Honey, wake up!

CHOOSING A LOVE THAT WILL LAST

What is the matter with me? I am laughing and can't stop." It had been a long time since he had laughed, perhaps not in a decade--not since Junior went away. Dad told me this went on for while longer, and with this joy came a great inner hunger and unquenchable desire to know God. It was intense! Compelling! He had no control over it.

After breakfast Dad told Mother that he was going to Grandma's house and wouldn't be back until he found this God real for himself--and knew this God in a personal way. Thank goodness, it's not this difficult for everyone to find God, but you have to understand how long my dad had nursed his hurt. It was bigger and more formidable than he was by now.

At Grandma's house, a small group gathered to pray with my dad, and only my dad. Of course, Sister MacAdoo and Grandma were there. This prayer time went on for three days. They only stopped to sleep and have services at church each night. Dad said that he wasn't hungry and didn't eat for three days.

At the end of three days, everyone was pretty worn out, but this little group never let up. What beautiful sacrifices were made for another human being. I hope Sister MacAdoo knows this.

Upon arriving for more prayer on the fourth morning, my dad recalled having a bad taste in his mouth. "Awhile later, an object came up into my chest and on out through my mouth," he said. When that object (whatever it was) left, such joy, lightness and freedom flooded dad's entire being. He was free and God's presence enveloped him like a cloak. He has remarked it was impossible to describe. Now he understood what all those ministers and others had been saying all those years.

None present at Grandma's house possibly knew much about evil spirits. However, after studying Scripture concerning evil spirits, I am convinced that something was perhaps a sorrowful spirit. Whenever that oppressive, depressive, or possessive spirit came out, it left my dad free! free! free! in his innermost being. Perhaps only a person who has experienced such a release could appreciate and adequately identify with that sensation.

Many different kinds of spirits are mentioned in the Bible. Evil spirits can have strongholds in our lives, but the Holy Spirit (who is God) can break their power over us.

Dad was enraptured and engulfed beyond himself into such overwhelming praise and worship to God and Jesus Christ. He astounded even himself, as well as our whole family, friends and church members. My dad was certainly not a hypocrite. He would never admit to any experience he never received. My dad was no longer the man with a downcast sorrowful look, and many commented on what a changed man he was. He was now an active, convincing cheerleader for Christ. Dad was indeed *born again* and filled with the Holy Spirit. Being a skeptic and a cynic for so long, it wasn't easy for my dad to give control of his life over to God. Seems he was helpless to change except through the deep intercessory prayers of others, especially Sister MacAdoo, who went home and started fasting and praying. Without her prayers transfusing him, he might never have been able to break through that impregnable wall between himself and God. Once she started praying, his hunger for God grew stronger than any other desire.

My dad insisted that all along he wanted to get in earnest with God and someday he would, but he didn't have time for spiritual matters, what with farmwork, employees, and mother having eight babies within 14 years, not to mention many other excuses. With this spiritual boost, my father was power-launched into an unstoppable quest with God that continued until the day he died many years later.

Reminds me of the story of the four friends who brought their crippled friend to Jesus on a stretcher to be healed. There was such a big crowd there, they couldn't get in so they tore a hole in the roof of this man's house to lift their sick friend down into the room near Jesus. They weren't disappointed. Jesus simply spoke to the sick man, "Son, thy sins be forgiven thee," and later, "Arise, and take up thy bed and walk." Mark 2:4 KJV. Perhaps we are like a piano or organ, we need more than one note for a

CHOOSING A LOVE THAT WILL LAST

concert. We need help and encouragement from others. We are all sick with sin at one time or another and need love and forgiveness. No man is an island!

Life was to be different in our home from then on. My dad and mom were in complete agreement concerning us kids, our upbringing, discipline and training.

A LITTLE CHILD SHALL LEAD THEM

A shepherd stands beside a stream,
With sheep on one side and water between.

He talks to them, he calls, he pleads,
To cross and in new pastures feed.

But they stand and shake their heads,
Refusing to go where they are led.

Then in sorrow he goes back again,
And picks up a lamb and takes with him.

He safely carried it over across.
And sets it down on the grass, so soft.

Then as the mother sees her treasure fair,
Carried across the stream over there.

She forgets her fear and plunges in,
In her great desire to go to him.

Then as the others see her loss,
They also plunge in and go across.

Oh, now I know why our boy so dear,
Was taken away from us down here.

GLORY CHAPMAN

We failed to follow where He led,
And were indifferent when He pled.

Jesus, the shepherd, took our darling beyond,
The one, of which, we were most fond.
                Alice James Taylor

    With mother's struggle and dilemma concerning her vow and all the many babies, she, too, would need much help from others.

CHOOSING A LOVE THAT WILL LAST

CHAPTER 12

CHILDREN ARE A BLESSING FROM GOD?

Psalms 127:3

Children are a blessing from the Lord? Mother was to question that verse many times. She wasn't always convinced of the blessings at certain junctures in her life. During the early years, she wondered how many more babies there would be. Was there no cessation to having so many children? No end to all the work?

Mother often mused and had long thoughts about her vow. Especially before and after each of our births. She was seriously ill with blood poisoning when Lahoma was born--baby number three. In fact, she was so sick she couldn't raise her head off the pillow for two months and was delirious much of the time. Our family doctor, R. Kuchar, an aging rotund dutchman whom we all loved, his nurse, Grandma James and my dad took turns heating huge tubs of water, dipping towels into it, and placing the very hot, hot towels on mother's abdomen every few minutes.

This poisoning caused mother to lose all her hair. She was very bald for awhile. Also, she had to learn how to walk all over again. At this time Dr. Kuchar advised her not to have any more children. Now mother was naturally somewhat fearful and hesitant to have more babies. However, her recent vow was very fresh in her memory. Vows are sometimes not easy to keep-- sometimes seemingly impossible. Would she carry through with her vow if it meant losing her life?

When mother made her vow, she was careful not to reveal the vow to anyone in her family, especially since she had been so gravely ill, and the family had rallied together to take care of the three babies she already had.

Grandma Taylor took Monita, Aunt Mary was given Junior and Aunt Maud Schnur bundled tiny newborn Lahoma off to

Oklahoma City with her to keep for six months. What would her family do if she told them she was pregnant again?

Wasn't long till mother was given that opportunity as she was suffering with that wretched morning sickness once more. This nausea usually lasted about three months with each baby, and being so tiny and thin, 5-foot, one inch and 90 to 100 pounds, she had few reserves. The vomiting seemed to wring out every ounce of energy left in her.

Mother has remarked several times how much she admired Dr. Kuchar. But it is difficult for me to believe in all those years of having eight babies so close together with Dr. Kuchar seeing her periodically that he never once suspected she might be anemic or needed something to strengthen or build her up after each birth. My mother was pale looking and tired for years.

Years later, she had her blood tested in Texas and got some iron and thyroid supplements. It's hard to realize she suffered so needlessly all those years. Now in her 90's she is a cricket, we say. She has excellent health, teaches music and out works all of us, including my brother. She has remarkably good health considering her earlier illnesses.

Twenty-three months after baby three came, Norlyne Royal arrived three weeks late, brow presentation, and had a blood sack on the side of his head, which had to be operated on. "Otherwise, he was healthy, happy and precious," Mother said.

Some ten months later she was so sick at her stomach with me she wanted to die. Mother said that she felt like a limberneck, and thinking about all the work that was piling up didn't help. Someone told her if you put your finger down your throat it would help to get rid of that awful sickish feeling. It worked. Worked so well that it was like an artesian well. Now mother couldn't stop upchucking even when she went down to 67 pounds and was three months pregnant with me. She had to go to bed for three weeks.

Being pregnant and trying to manage and care for four children, a husband and farm work wasn't her idea of fun and games. Yet

CHOOSING A LOVE THAT WILL LAST

it was her vow, not my dad's. However, it wasn't long after this episode that she regained her strength, and carried me without incident the remaining six months.

Gloria Joy arrived on time weighing nine pounds and all was well with both mother and baby. Might insert here that many people have asked me about my name exclaiming, "Your mother and dad must have really wanted you to give you such a joyous sounding name." Considering the circumstances, I'm not sure.

As it turned out, I wasn't to be the baby of the family. Alice Marilyn was born 18 months later, though not without the unwanted nausea. All of us were born at home with Dr. Kuchar and a nurse in attendance.

The unthinkable was about to happen when Mother was approximately six months pregnant again with baby seven. It was Junior's tragic accident. In much sorrow and heaviness of heart, another baby girl arrived three months later. The good news was there were no problems in delivering the tiny towhead cherub named Ramona Lou.

Mother now literally trotted from daylight to dark. Her little brood needed to be fed, clothed, bathed and trained. She wasn't only physically depleted but emotionally spent as well.

As far back as I can remember, mother was always dressed, hair fixed and in high heels and hose before she left her room early each morning. Some in the family wondered why she didn't wear low heels with all that work to do, but she has extremely high arches and can't wear low heels. Mother was very fastidious in her dress. She was ready for the demands of the day. In later years I discovered this to be one of the main secrets in managing a busy household and schedule. There are just a few little things to be added to that, such as:

Bathe and put on house dress.
Fix hair and face for the day (get yourself out of the way).
Throw the bed up as you get out of it first thing.
Pick up toys, papers, glasses, and junk on way to kitchen.

Put any dirty clothes in the laundry sorter and wash only the bin that's full. Get a 3-bin laundry sorter on wheels.
After breakfast, get the dishes out of sight.
Plan what you are going to have for the evening meal.
Plan to clean the house really well only once a week.
Put same sheets back on after washing to avoid folding.
Shop for groceries every two weeks or once a month.

This can add as much as two hours extra to your day. It is a *must* in a large household. Now you are ready for most any emergency that might present itself.

There is an important part of my parents' lives I have not touched upon. That is their very special and unique relationship with each other. Mother perhaps would not have survived without this uncommon love. We kids didn't realize how rare it was until we left home. My daddy idolized my mother. She in turn certainly gave her all to daddy, to homemaking and the many farm chores. They were kindred spirits.

Dad was perpetually verbal in his love for mother. It was constant, never lessening throughout their 54 years together. The favorite line I remember most was dad always commenting to us kids just out of earshot where mother could hear him, "Isn't that the prettiest woman you ever saw? Look at that little form, or would you believe that little woman has had eight babies?" On and on with many adjectives and accolades. Many times he would sneak up behind mother, grab her from the rear, lift up her curls and kiss her on the neck. He especially loved the two curls she always wore, which dad referred to as *his curls*. Mother relished every minute of the attention and love. Though sometimes I could hear her whispering, "Tom, don't, not here!" She would pull away when we kids were around.

That is what I thought all marriages were like. Perhaps all us kids thought every mom and dad loved each other that much and were each other's best friend.

Never shall I forget the bafflement I experienced when I learned that parents of my friend had separate bedrooms. For the life of me I couldn't figure out why. My parents' bedroom was their sanctuary.

Reminds me of the time I saw my dad lock their bedroom door from the outside, locking mother in. What I didn't know was daddy would often put mother down for a nap so she wouldn't work herself into utter exhaustion. Dad would come in and swoop her up in his arms and carry her off to bed. At four, I thought he was being mean to her, since napping was definitely a punishment to me. And to be locked up to do it? Wow! Just as soon as daddy left the house, I would quickly pull a straight chair over to the door, climb up and unlock the door so mother could get out!

It was possibly about this time when my dear Aunt Nelle Getty (who died in 1987 at the age of 98) put forth that it would be a travesty against God if Alice has anymore children. They knew she must know what was causing it, and her family was greatly puzzled as to why Alice and Tom seemed to be so oblivious to their straits. You have to remember none of her family was aware of her vow.

It wasn't long until the travesty happened. Mother was pregnant again with baby number eight, Ruth Naomi. It seems the blood poisoning set in again with even greater vengeance than before. Mother was rushed to General Hospital in Oklahoma City where she lay in critical condition for several weeks. It was touch and go. In all, she was there seven weeks.

Of course we four little girls had to be farmed out with relatives. Grandma Taylor was so blessed to have Alice and me; Aunt Mary got toddler number seven with Aunt Maud taking newborn Ruthie. Aunt Maud loved babies so. She lost her only baby in infancy, and later her husband, while still in her twenties. My two oldest sisters and brother batched on the farm with daddy.

The talk continued in the family, "Why would Alice want so many children since she can't take care of the ones she has?"

Good thing my mother didn't hear those remarks until later. Her life hung by a thread for days. The doctor told them that the least little thing would be critical. The whole family was encouraged to be very positive to help her want to get well. If not, they might be stuck with us kids for life! Dad even went out and bought her a whole set of Haviland china that she loved. It did give her a big boost to know so many people loved and cared about her. In the meantime, their debts were piling up and they had to borrow money. Dad could little afford such extravagance, but life without his Alice would be no life at all. Incidentally, mother's hospital bill exceeded my dad's wheat crop that year.

My dad was perhaps too generous and would spend when he really couldn't afford it, but his love was stronger than his managerial ability. Dad always managed, but many times it wasn't easy.

Six months later, my dad brought this unknown woman home with him. I didn't remember mother. Besides, this strange lady was wearing a red skull cap or turban. She looked so very different with a bald head, though she might have had some short fuzz by then.

Mother and Daddy were so happy and relieved to have all of us back together again under one roof with them.

Personally, I liked being with Grandma--just the three of us. Better still, Grandma let me help her. And a real treat, she let me brush her waist-length corn silk yellow hair while she read in her Bible. It was so quiet and serene at Grandma's. She even shared with me where she kept her money after explaining to me it was very important that I tell no one. I didn't tell a soul either.

After this last bad chapter in their lives, Dad said that he had not made any vow and took care of the reproduction problem, explaining to anyone who was interested that he needed a mother for his children. Mother was Dad's queen. He saw to it she got whatever she needed if it was within his power to get it. My dad could buy more becoming and beautiful clothes for mother than she could. He would describe to the sales clerk she was about

CHOOSING A LOVE THAT WILL LAST

five feet tall, brown curly hair, brown eyes with a fair complexion. It sounds somewhat archaic today, but mother never paid a single bill or wrote a check in all their 54 years together. My dad took care of everything. After his death in 1972, she learned fast, but it is such a chore for her. My daddy never tired of showing his love for mother. Dad even told my brother-in-law that he never wanted nor was tempted by any other woman. He was a one-woman man!

One of my strongest memories of mother during that period in our lives was on Sundays. All nine of us going to church, sitting together on one pew with mother holding my hand, all the while rubbing and patting it, not stopping until the benediction. The vivid part is of her deep sighing over and over. I felt sorry for her. She was so tired! She told me that she was too tired to breathe.

No wonder she was breathless! There all of us sat dressed in our best bibs and tuckers (fancy ruffled organdy dresses which mother had designed, made and ironed). Spic and span with hair and curls all freshly done by mother, of course.

Someone in the family asked me if they could ask me a personal question, to which I reluctantly agreed, "Did you make a vow like your mother to have so many children?" My answer was a simple, "No. All six were planned in sets with four years between each set."

NOW FOR THE GOOD NEWS! Almost forgot to tell the most important part of mother's story. These many years later and before, she cannot extol enough about how blessed she has been in obeying and keeping her vow, exulting that we children and dad were the best and greatest thing that ever happened to her. This, of course, is in retrospect, but she is totally convinced God does indeed know what is best for us. WE SEE THE BEGINNING AND THE DURING, BUT GOD SEES THE ENDING!

For sacrifice means the surrender of something prized or

desirable for the sake of something considered as having a higher or more pressing claim.

I AM TRYING TO LEARN THAT OBEDIENCE IS BETTER THAN SACRIFICE!

CHOOSING A LOVE THAT WILL LAST

CHAPTER 13

SCHOOL DAYS! SCHOOL DAYS! DEAR OLD GOLDEN RULE DAYS!

The magical day finally arrived--my first day of school! Everything about school was new and exciting until another first grader, namely John Edgar Wheatley, ran up and kissed me. Being so shy, I spent the rest of the day crying with my head down on an old initial carved desk.

While in Oklahoma, we Taylor kids were tardy a lot to school. It would have been fine with me except when I would finally arrive with violin case in tow, the entire orchestra class would sing, "You used to come at nine o'clock, now you come at noon." In spite of it all, I guess I managed to play passably well, winning an original Mickey Mouse watch, which I still have. However, the day was ruined for me since I couldn't hold back the tears as usual. Any attention focused on me would make me cry. Why did I cry so much?

But on the whole, school was a happy place with much happening to make learning fun. In fact, I wasn't aware of when I learned to read, spell and do division. Miss Towe, our sexy young fourth-grade teacher, had our parents come to school and race with us students on the blackboard doing multiplication tables. Boy, we really showed our stuff on those days!

Also, having so many cousins in the same school, some 10 to 15, was comforting to a newcomer. We all lived within a four-mile radius of Yukon which had its advantages and disadvantages. For one thing, I didn't have to be introduced at school--not formally. Of course not, I was Monita's, Junior's, Lahoma's and Norlyne's little sister. Not only that but three more sisters would be coming soon--at the rate of about one every other year. There were lots and lots of Taylor kids, what with my dad having four brothers and several sisters in that area.

Grandpa T. Jack Taylor and Lola Fisher were married in Missouri in 1885. The *Eighty-Niner's Run* was only a year old when they decided to hitch up their covered wagon and head south to Oklahoma with several small children. Grandma told me of the time they had to ford a river while riding in the covered wagon and thought they would all be drowned. They arrived in Canadian County on the outskirts of Yukon. Grandpa Jack was a horse trader, as well as a wheat farmer. At the time of his death in 1929, he owned eight large farms all surrounding the Yukon area. More than a dozen Taylor farms dotted the rural countryside. However, by the 1980's, there were no Taylor farms left; that is, not the size they were originally. Slowly each family moved away or died. Only a few cousins still own small tracts of the original farms, with the rest having all been subdivided and developed. The Chevrolet Dealer Agency is now located on our north forty.

One incident happened when I was in third grade that did cause a small crisis in the Yukon school system.

Lucky Ritter, my very *bestest* girlfriend, and I were very close and spent a lot of time together. Lucky was an adopted child, who was a doll with shiny brunette locks and round dark brown eyes. She was the only child of an older lady. No father. *Only* child always sounded so special to me. I wasn't sure at that time if I was special or not. However, there were some indications that I was pretty high on the list with several persons--Monita and Grandma Taylor.

Lucky wore such beautiful clothes. Especially do I remember her elegant white wool coat with matching white fur hat and muff. No way will I ever forget what happened one day when Lucky wore that gorgeous infamous coat! Only one thing spoiled her perfect appearance that day--Lucky's long handles had dropped below her coat. Her mother made her wear those long johns with a drop seat lest she take cold. The rest of us all wore short socks.

During recess as we were coming down the stairs, I noticed her

CHOOSING A LOVE THAT WILL LAST

drop flap was down. I sidled up real close and whispered in her ear that her drop seat was showing. She wheeled around and slugged me on the side of the head with her red satchel. There is nothing like a crisis to bring out one's true character. Without so much as blinking, I went into action, kicking her with my muddy red-dirt boot. My boot imprint landed smack in the center back of that precious white wool coat. It stood out as big as life and twice as natural. Looked like a firebrand.

Within minutes after Lucky got home, her mother was on the phone demanding that Miss Mae Chapman, my beautiful single third-grade teacher, spank me. She did not agree, so early the next morning, Mrs. Ritter appeared at school insisting I be punished. When Miss Chapman again refused, she took her case to the school board.

Now, my family would learn of my disgraceful escapade at school since my Uncle Ralph Taylor was on the school board. When we got into trouble at school we were very careful never to disclose any of this information at home. A spanking at school meant a repeat of the same at home, only harder. We kids all stuck together in protecting each other. Usually there was strength in our Taylor tribe. Hoped it would hold up now, this being my first (caught) offense.

It was sad Mrs. Ritter got so wired because Lucky and I were still friends, but not for long. When Lucky's mother couldn't persuade the school board to deal out any discipline, she withdrew Lucky from the school system and moved to Oklahoma City, some 21 miles away. That was the last time I saw Lucky until some ten years later. We were both interviewing for a job at the First National Bank in Oklahoma City. Our paths have not crossed since that time.

GHOST STORIES

Memories of the ghost stories my oldest sister told the rest of us still haunt me. Really, Monita could tell wilder and scarier ghost stories as the night progressed, especially if she was babysitting us. We would squeal and yell out in terror. Actually Lahoma would scream the loudest and most bloodcurdling.

One particular night when I was about five or six, I dreamed everyone had gone off and left me all alone in that big dark house. The nearest neighbors were my grandparents who lived a quarter of a mile west on Highway 66, which had a service station across the street from them.

This is what they tell me happened. One of the men working at the service station saw a little girl in a long white nightie walking along close to the edge of the highway about 11 p.m., heading towards town. Thinking he recognized me, he approached to ask where I was going. Getting no response, he put me in his car and took me home.

Going up to the front door and knocking, Daddy asked through the window, "Who is it and what do you want so late at night?"

The man answered, "Tom, this is Bobby Mannes and I have one of your girls here."

"Oh, no you don't. All of my girls are upstairs asleep," my father angrily protested.

"Well, I think you better come to the door and see."

Daddy turned on the light and there I was. Daddy was indignant and wanted to know how he had gotten me out of the house without his knowing. He told my dad he saw me walking along the highway. Knowing what a scaredy-cat I was that story was hard to believe. My dad was dumbfounded, though he finally apologized. Daddy took me upstairs and put me in bed.

The next morning they kept asking me how I got out of the house and down onto the highway. I didn't remember any of it. I had been walking in my sleep. Good thing I didn't awaken while out there in the dark!

I'M GONNA MAKE YOU AN OFFER YOU CAN'T REFUSE!

CHOOSING A LOVE THAT WILL LAST

Daddy was trying to get one of us to confess to some misdeed. None of us would budge, so finally he offered a quarter to the one who confessed and there would be no punishment. No one spoke up, so I thought, *Why not get the quarter?* and fessed up. They never knew if I did it, and I can't remember what offense was committed. That seemed to me to be an all-win situation. That should prove I'm not stupid! Greedy maybe, but not stupid.

On too many occasions to suit my sisters, Monita and Lahoma, we four little kids would race out the back door, unlatch the west gate and run down the driveway to greet their boyfriends when they came to pick them up for a date. We would jump up on the running board of the car and peer in at them before they had a chance to even get out of the car. One time, I remember Monita's boyfriend (later her husband) hooked the handle of his little yellow convertible roadster (complete with rumble seat) so it would shock us a little when we touched it. Wow! What a jolt! Both Monita and Lahoma would plead with mother to make us stop this gross and most embarrassing behavior. But our babbling remained unabated and we never discerned the boyfriends' displeasure. Sometimes they brought us candy--other times not. It is still clear in my memory that the more Monita and Lahoma objected, the more strength and pleasure it gave us.

VYING

As we got older, there was a lot of vying among us six girls. Who was the shortest, cutest, prettiest, tallest, smartest? I remember more than once Lahoma would describe me to someone who had never met me, as being so beautiful, using other outrageous adjectives. Of course, when those same people would meet me, they had this puzzled expression as if to say, "Her? No way." It was extremely embarrassing to me. It took me awhile to figure out how to get her to stop. I reversed the scenario on her and raved endlessly as to her beauty. Let me tell you one occasion was enough to cure that problem.

Mother and Dad complimented us girls beyond our abilities or accomplishments. In fact, they made us think we were more wonderful than we were. However, dad would always add, "But none of you compares to your mother, who is the real beauty."

I believe it was Ruth Carter Stapleton who said that her dad made her think she was the most beautiful, most intelligent and most important person in the world. All went well until she went away to college, only for her peers to let her know she was none of those things. She said that it took her two years to be able to handle life.

It would appear that too much praise or too little praise can have lasting influence. Surely there is a moderate way to help our kids feel good about themselves. Extremes are always hard to deal with. "And every man that striveth for the mastery is temperate in all things...." I Cor. 9:25 KJV.

FIRST CHRISTMAS IN TEXAS

The move to McAllen was traumatic for some of us kids. At school, they put me in the sixth grade. Since Texas had only 11 grades at the time, there was some confusion and I skipped a year. My parents visited the McAllen, Texas area with the Bentsen Land Company and fell in love with the tropical climate, citrus and palm trees.

McAllen is almost as far south as Miami Beach, Florida. It is near the southernmost tip of Texas on the Mexican border. Some of the students commuted from Mexico to attend the McAllen schools. This Texas was definitely different!

It was a little unnerving to have someone come up and start talking to me in a language I didn't understand. The school was probably 75 percent Spanish students. I certainly looked more Spanish than many of them, but somehow it was all so strange and different than Oklahoma.

I was born with the name of *Gloria* on my birth certificate, but after the way they pronounced it, *Glaw-dee-a*, I changed it to

CHOOSING A LOVE THAT WILL LAST

Glory. Also, I was appalled that many people named their children *Jesus*.

If it was easy for me to cry in my own hometown of Yukon, then this Texas was a watershed. It was our first Christmas in Texas and our sixth-grade class was having a Christmas play. It required a small crying angel.

Hands were going up to help our teacher, Miss Alley, a beautiful auburn-haired young woman, with the type-casting of characters. Before I knew what was happening, Jack Miller, now our former Postmaster in McAllen, shot his hand up and volunteered for all to hear that Glory Taylor would be perfect because she is the smallest girl in the class and because she cries all the time. All eyes were now on me, and I didn't disappoint any of them. The spigot burst open, and the water poured forth, much to my mortification. Perhaps crying so easily was physical; however, I was seldom sick or ever had a cold.

I was a late bloomer and was no outstanding student as a 15-year old senior. Neither did I have as many dates as I would have liked in high school. It seemed to me the boys went for girls who were very curvaceous, only to discover later in life and six subsequent children, they want willowy girls. The reverse was true of me--too thin at 15 and plenteous curves after six children.

Mother and Dad were in complete agreement concerning us kids. There was an hierarchy in our family--God first, mother second, kids third and work last. However, it seemed sometimes that order got reversed quite a lot. Anyway, we kids knew we had a kid's place period.

When I was in junior high, Mother's favorite candy was a Hershey bar with almonds. Knowing this, I would save half of mine from school lunch and bring it home to her. To see her eyes light up made me so happy. Only recently, I asked Mother if she remembered this. She couldn't recall it. To me, it was a momentous occasion--probably because it was one of my few magnanimous moments.

I was being trained little by little, and though it wasn't a perfect vehicle nor possibly the best at all times, it ultimately produced certain characteristics in me.

"In the end, we are all the sum total of our actions. Character cannot be counterfeited, nor can it be put on and cast off as a garment. Like the markings on wood which are ingrained in the very heart of the tree, character requires time and nurture for growth and development. Thus also, day by day, we write our own destiny." Madame Chiang Kai-shek.

"Character is not made in crisis--it is only exhibited." Robert Freeman.

If there is righteousness in the heart,
there will be beauty in the character.
If there be beauty in the character,
there will be harmony in the family home.
If there is harmony in the home,
there will be order in the nation.
When there is order in the nation,
there will be peace in the world.
          A Chinese Proverb

This was a short detour of my early life. Now on to the events as an adult and how I would fare in view of my upbringing. As much as we may want to deny it, we are products of our training, perhaps our earliest learnings.

CHOOSING A LOVE THAT WILL LAST

CHAPTER 14

RELATIONSHIPS

According to Catherine Marshall in *Something More*, "Every human being has problems of relationship with other people. The other positive side is that in interaction between people we learn most of life's needed lessons."[1] When I read this 20 years ago, I did not fully understand what Catherine was saying. I see now, the very essence of life turns on relationships. It's not what you collect or have around you in your environment, but it's the relationships we have with others that teach us how to live. If we cannot accept ourselves, we cannot relate to others.

Favoritism runs deep and strong in our Taylor heritage. Real tacky favoritism which hurts and leaves emotional scars for life. However, I am happy to say our generation is improving somewhat.

It is my belief that favoritism breeds much inferiority, as well as superiority, which translates into a poor self-image or pride.

On more than one occasion, I tried to get Grandma to say I was her favorite. However, she never gave in to partiality. Not once. Dear sweet Grandma loved everyone. I never ever heard her criticize a single person.

While we may not like or enjoy everything about a person, surely there are *some* things to applaud and praise.

Grandpa Jack played favorites among his grandchildren, choosing Junior over Monita. He wasn't shy about it either. Often Grandpa Jack would have a big bag of marbles or candy for Junior while he had nothing for Monita. Surprising to me that Monita adored Junior in spite of this injustice. Grandpa was a puzzle to Monita.

Also, Grandpa Jack would pay his grocery bill at the local store about every six months, or when the crops came in, and the grocer would give him a big sack of candy for his 11 kids. However, he would hand the bulging sack over to the baby of the family, Kathryn, who in turn would put every piece of candy between her toes so none of the other kids would want any. That family certainly needed a fair and just patriarch!

On the other hand, some years later my mother's parents lived in a house on our farm. Would you guess the special game of favoritism was repeated with Lahoma being the one to be set up for affirmation and queen bee? Yes, and with much flare and no apologies. My Grandma Belle adored Lahoma, letting her wear her silk dresses, jewelry, hats, anything she wanted. Grandma would even hide her in the closet when Daddy would come for her. I don't think this left any imprint on the four of us little kids. We learned about this mostly when we got older and were told about it.

Monita was an all-American next-door type of girl with brown thick straight hair and green eyes. She was well proportioned, tan and healthy. There was no problem until tiny little baby Lahoma, who was four years her junior, arrived with shiny raven colored curly hair, large round clear blue eyes, skin of an angel with natural rosy cheeks. Mother would be with both of them somewhere, and invariably, they would be approached by someone who would exclaim with great enthusiasm how extraordinarily beautiful 3-year old Lahoma was. Not so much as a word or glance towards Monita, who was seven. Of course, Monita has long ago figured it out, but back then she used to say she wished she could pull all those long black curls out, and then see what she would look like. Not only that, Monita had to share billing with Junior as well, who was very handsome and gifted in public speaking. His audiences loved him.

We four younger girls were all pretty much average, so there wasn't too much vying until we got older. One time a boy mentioned to me that if I wouldn't go out with him, then he would ask my sister. Oh boy, that was the end of him--forever.

Speaking of favoritism, Monita had her favorite in our family--

CHOOSING A LOVE THAT WILL LAST

me. I was her baby and pet even though I wasn't the baby of the family. Before we moved to Texas and before she married, it was my happy privilege to be able to sleep with her and rub her back. She always took up for me until one unhappy day I spilled a whole bottle of India ink on the new carpet in her bedroom. My fall from grace was sudden. Katy-bar-the-gate, did she ever get mad--at me! I tried putting that black gooey stuff back in the bottle or to hide the spot, but it was hopeless. Monita flew downstairs to tell mother she was spanking me herself. Usually she wouldn't let mother touch me. To tell you the truth, I don't remember Monita putting a hand on me. Her bark was always louder than her bite.

While in home economics class in high school, Monita made me a coordinated little ensemble complete with scarf, and presented me to her class as a model. I can still remember standing on a high table, turning and turning for everyone to see Skeet's (nickname for Monita) little 4-year old sister, Goldilocks. That was my nickname until my long blonde curls turned into toffee colored ones.

One of the highlights of every year was going to Grandpa and Grandma Taylor's home for Christmas Day where the entire Taylor clan met, bringing armloads of goodies to be shared with probably 50 to 60 relatives. The food was incredibly delicious with each family bringing its own specialty.

One Christmas I remember getting scolded very badly by an aunt for sticking my little fingers in the icing on a cake which was setting on the edge of the table, just barely above my head. It never dawned on me that was such a deplorable thing. Really! Were we not all going to eat it anyway? So what was the big deal?

After eating, all 10 to 15 cousins, depending on which year, would take off for the park nearby to run, swing, teeter-totter and climb. At one time the Yukon public schools possibly had more Taylors in attendance than any other single family.

My daddy and his brothers were all born practical jokers. Any occasion was enough reason to spark my dad's mischievousness, especially when he was younger. One time, he promised for months to take me Christmas shopping in Oklahoma City--just the two of us. That was always a treat. Anytime we could be treated as an *only* child, it made us feel very special, even at six.

Finally the day arrived and off we went shopping. All was going very well until I became so enchanted with all the toys and bright tinsel in the windows that I couldn't seem to stay up with my daddy. He warned me several times to hold his hand so he wouldn't lose me. Enthralled with F. W. Woolworth's display of temptations, I lingered longer than I should have, and when I looked around I couldn't see my father anywhere.

At first, I made quick glances in all directions, then I began running up and down the sidewalk, at first slowly then faster and faster with an alarming bewildered expression. He had absolutely disappeared. By this time, my tears were coming fast, which of course was no great feat for me, but nonetheless I was shrieking, "Daddy! Daddy!, where are you?"

Unbeknown to me, my daddy was hiding behind a parked car in front of Woolworth's where he could keep an eye on me. He later told the others when we got home that he wouldn't have come out so soon, but that woman in the parked car kept giving him very dirty looks because she saw how brokenhearted I was. Needless to say, I was glued to his side for the rest of the shopping spree, and the glitter of Christmas toys took a dim second place.

Another of my father's favorite tricks was hiding valuable things which we would carelessly leave around the house. Some of us kids would lay our rings, watches or bracelets on the window sill above the sink.

Well, it would be a week or so before he would place it in plain view again. We always knew he did it because of the prankish look on his face. The good news was we had found our gold, but the bad news was he kept it so long.

My dad had a temper and one easy way to tick it off was to be insincere or hypocritical. One of our favorite tricks for getting out of having to do the dishes in our own home, or when we were a guest in someone else's home, was to go on profusely about how delicious the food was. And of course we would love to help with the dishes but we were so very, very sorry we couldn't stay. We had to leave right away. Other times we would go to the bathroom and wait out the dishes.

Nothing would be said to us in front of the hostess, but let us get home. In fact, my dad would sizzle before we reached home and mimic in a sarcastic high-pitched voice, "Oh, the food was so-o-o-o delicious and it was so-o-o- sweet of her to ask you-- blah, blah, blah. You were doing so fine during the first part, why did you have to ruin it with all the phoniness about how you would love to do the dishes? You know you never intended to do those dishes in the first place. Please leave off all that sweetness and goodness when you don't mean a word of it."

Hopefully some of this training rubbed off on all of us. Like mother says she is so very proud of her children: none have been in jail and none have sprouted wings. In this day and age all parents are trying to figure out how to get kids to finish whatever they start. Incidentally, among kids who use drugs, a survey showed most were not finishers, whatever that means. None of us have been able to come up with what mother and daddy did to accomplish this in us. But to this day all of us are finishers, almost to a fault. We would like to know what it was so we could pass it on to our children.

To sum up this chapter on relationships, there is one observation I have watched throughout the years, and that is; I know of very few families who have remained close or intimate when they are grown.

There are some exceptions, but by and large, there are different views, values, jealousies and distance. Sometimes there is a facade, and they have family gatherings, but underneath it all there is no close, intimate, loving relationship.

There is so much to learn about relationships. It is a lifetime challenge. Isn't it exciting that we keep learning until the day we die? Although my family had a great influence on my life, you will see that the most profound influence came from a relationship I had with a friend.

CHOOSING A LOVE THAT WILL LAST

CHAPTER 15

PORT MANSFIELD, TEXAS

Several months after my divorce, a group of five girlfriends and I spent the weekend at Port Mansfield at Billy Baggett's cabin on the Laguna Madre off the South Texas coast, where fishing is the *mainest* thing.

It was early spring and the weather was gloriously cooperative. Thank goodness there were five joyous souls along. The water and colorful sunsets seemed to draw me like a magnet as I stood mute in solitude on the shore for long moments of time. It seemed I was but a tiny speck of sand in the total scheme of universal things. If I put my thimble into the water and filled it, it would make no difference.

There was much jovial conversation, kidding and clowning around those three days. It was a great breakaway time for all of us; from family responsibilities and the daily routine of life.

On the last day before packing up to leave, Barbara Johnson came over to where I was sitting at the game table. Placing her hands upon my head, she said these words very enthusiastically, "Wait awhile, my daughter, and I am going to give you a great treasure: bright, shiny, crystal clear, and there will be no regrets."

I heard the words very distinctly. Especially the last words. "Would it ever be possible to be rid of the regrets? Really?" I wondered. Then what about the words, *wait awhile*. Did that mean I shouldn't get more involved in any relationships for awhile? Whatever it meant, I was just beginning to get involved. I felt Jason Henderson was special--very special. It seemed we had met quite by chance on a business deal. It was glorious to have someone to talk to. Adult conversation--someone to listen to me, care about me. The children needed so much time and attention, there seemed little left over for me.

It was like coming up out of a very dark, damp musty cellar full of gloom into a grand staircase filled with music, bright lights and exciting fragrances. Like going from hell to heaven. My stomach churned. I was alive and feeling again. However one thought kept nagging, "Is Jason the *treasure*?" How would it be made clear to me if he was the one?

At the time Barbara said the word *treasure*, it meant a *person* to me, though that is not usually the meaning we use for that word. What I didn't know was *which* person. That would test my faith in what God had spoken to me to the painful limit.

It seemed to me *at the time* every bit as severe a test as Abraham's when God asked him to put his son on the altar and sacrifice him. Abraham had waited 20 years for the fulfillment of this promised baby from his wife of 90. The problem wasn't with Abraham, apparently, because after Sarah died, he remarried and had six other children after the age of 137.

Anyway, Abraham had to know it was God asking such a thing. He didn't ask as we do so many times, "I wonder if that is the devil talking to me."

I also conjecture that Abraham could have told God, "No, God, I know you would never ask a thing like that of me." He could have stated many reasons why he couldn't obey giving up the son God gave him so miraculously.

What we miss is that Abraham had total and absolute trust in God and did whatever God asked him to do. Abraham passed the test. He *knew* God, not just *about* Him. He communed with God. He knew God personally. It was not a one-sided relationship either.

Abraham figured that if God asked him to kill Isaac, God could raise him from the dead, if necessary. After all, God had created Isaac out of the dead womb of Sarah in the first place.

The story doesn't relate the struggle Abraham may have had during his three days' journey to Mount Moriah to carry out God's orders. It doesn't say he discussed it with his wife or anyone else. Perhaps he did not confer with any man after God spoke. It was between him and God. Sometimes it is better to keep very private the things between God and us. We should mull them over in our heart like Mary did about Jesus and the many perplexing happenings during his life here on earth.

It was 18 months later that I decided to get the dictionary down and mull over the specific meanings of *bright, shiny, clear, treasure and regret.* Here is what I found:

BRIGHT means full of light, sound, cheerful, mentally quick, clever, being filled with or reflecting light, happiness and favorable.

SHINY means bright, smoothly polished, glossy.

CLEAR means free from dowdiness, muddiness, blemish; transparent, easily seen, easily understood; obvious; unmistakable, certain, positive, free from guilt, innocent, absolute, complete; to rid of obstructions, entanglements or obstacles; open; to remove, get rid of; to free.

TREASURE means any *person* or thing that is considered very valuable; to value greatly; cherish; wealth in form of money, precious metal, jewels, etc. I jumped when I read that treasure does indeed mean a *person*. That confirmed my feeling.

And REGRET means to feel sorrow over, mourn for a person or thing gone or lost, feelings of sorrow over what has happened.

If I tell you what I remembered most about those words, it would reveal a great deal about myself. It was the last five words that were so unbelievable to me, *there will be no regrets.* Those were the hardest words to take in. Was I not eaten up with regrets? Counting back in time now, I would say it took about five years to not feel any regrets. Now there are none. In fact, it wasn't too long ago when I actually gave God many thanks for letting my life fall apart. It was worth it all.

"When one door closes, another opens; but we often look so long and so regretfully upon the closed door that we don't see the one which has opened for us."[1]

Actually there was no problem believing the words spoken to me for the future, but what was hard was knowing how to proceed on a daily basis and with what relationships.

The thought came to me more than once about love, *If it feels so right how can it be so wrong?* from Debbie Boone's song, *You Light Up My Life.*

I knew Jason only casually prior to his wife's death, which was ten months previous. At the time of Barbara's revelation, we were lost in the ecstasy of sharing our lives with each other.

I kept a complete diary of our beautiful times together. Each tiny detail and expression of love was recorded. Nothing seemed too minute to record. Love has a language all its own. To this day, I have not gone back to read any of that diary since that day in the spring years ago. I cannot!

Later on it was the heartbreak of not receiving an answer on whether to marry Jason, whom I had been seeing for over a year by this time. It was an agonizingly difficult and stressful time for me. Several times I tried to mention this search for an answer with Jason, but we didn't get too far into the subject.

Falling in-love is not something you choose to do. It either happens or it does not. You cannot go out and say, "Today, I am going to fall in-love." Besides, the decision was not mine to make since I had given that choice over to God. I was trying to have no mind of my own in the matter, believing that 'GOD GIVES THE BEST TO THOSE WHO LEAVE THE CHOICE TO HIM.'

And, too, sometimes it turns out that we are in love with a person who does not in fact exist. Possibly he is not who we thought he was when we fell in love. Fantasy and infatuation bypass our head and good judgment many times.

Thus the agony began when I heard Barbara saying the words, "Wait awhile and I am going to give you a great treasure." Nonetheless it was to be a year and a half later before Jason and I stopped seeing each other.

There is much misunderstanding about spiritual gifts today, what they are and how they operate. There have been questions like, "Why didn't God speak to you direct? Why would He need another person to tell you what He wanted you to know? How can you tell a true word from a false word? Wouldn't that be dangerous? Isn't everything you need to know written in the Bible?"

First, I ran references on how you can tell a true word from a false one. It seemed so clear and simple: In Jer. 28:9 it says that if the prophecy comes true, it is a true word. If it does not, it is false. Another way to distinguish between the two is if the person giving the prophecy denies that Jesus Christ came in the flesh, it is false. I John 4. One thing we have to keep in mind is that everything God has in His kingdom, Satan tries to duplicate in his kingdom. I knew Barbara did believe that Jesus Christ came in the flesh. Now, I would have to wait and see if it came to pass.

I ran across several passages where the Lord dealt with false prophets in different ways. Sometimes they were stoned and in the case of Hananiah the Lord said, "Listen, Hananiah, the Lord has not sent you, and the people are believing your lies. Therefore the Lord says you must die. This very year your life will end because you have rebelled against the Lord." Jer. 28:15. And sure enough, two months later Hananiah died as the Lord said.

In Isaiah 44:25 the Lord embarrassed the false prophets by saying, "I am the one who shows what liars all false prophets are, by causing something else to happen than the things they say. I make wise men give opposite advice to what they should, and make them into fools. But what my prophets say, I do."

As to being dangerous, there seemed to be no way I could try to make the prophecy come true--short of deceiving myself--pretending to have an answer when in fact I didn't have one from God--only my own. Deep and long suffering surely would have knocked self deception out of me by now. So there was nothing to do but wait and obey instructions given. In that vein there was a lot of security concerning future events in my life. Usually there is some small part we play. For instance, in the word given at Port Mansfield, I was to *wait awhile*. Just from those few words given to me, there came a desire borne of God, I was convinced now, to wait and see *when* God would bring to pass what was spoken.

While driving along one day, this came to me out of the blue. I remembered reading where God gave special gifts to each man. I Cor. 12:1-12.

If I didn't possess a particular spiritual gift and my friend did, would I deprive her the opportunity of sharing and giving to me? If I would not accept her gift of words of love and encouragement, then her gift could not be used or given. Both would be the poorer. For instance if I was very ill and refused to let someone with the gifts of healing pray for me, who would be the loser? We all have gifts but each a different gift. It is up to us to discover what our particular gift is. Most of us would not refuse a gift someone offered. However, what instantly comes to our mind is, "Why doesn't God tell *me*?"

The spirit part of us needs nourishment as much as our physical and mental parts. We can understand this. Wouldn't it be interesting if we could see our spirit on a cat scan? I know it's invisible, much as our brain knowledge is invisible, along with the hidden functions of our physical body. It appears the most temporary and visible part of the human anatomy houses our invisible permanent eternal part.

Sometimes things out of sight are out of mind. Perhaps we give priority to the more obvious and visible. The invisible spirit world is the eternal world. The world we see and know is the temporary one. Visible, tangible things seem the more important. Also, the invisible is mysterious somehow because it is not seen, explored or understood.

What if the children of Israel had not listened to Moses telling them what God told him to tell them through Aaron, his brother? That is second hand, I believe. Sometimes they resented it. Remember reading about Miriam and Aaron? Moses' own brother and sister criticized him because he married a Gentile who was an Ethiopian. Numbers 12. Miriam informed Moses she was a prophetess and could hear from God as well as he

CHOOSING A LOVE THAT WILL LAST

could. God struck her with leprosy instantly.

Consider the rebellion Korah, Dathan, Abiram and On, together with 250 leaders, incited against Moses. They went to Moses and Aaron and said, "You are no better than anyone else; everyone in Israel has been chosen of the Lord, and He is with all of us. What right do you have to put yourselves forward, claiming that we must obey you, and acting as though you were greater than anyone else among all these people of the Lord?" Numbers 16. Does this have a familiar ring today? Moses had all the people get away from them and said if God had chosen him to be their leader, then the ground would open up and swallow the rebellious ones. In a few moments that is what happened. Everything that belonged to them, as well as their wives, children and friends, went down into Sheol and the earth closed upon them screaming, and they perished. Then fire came forth from Jehovah and burned up the 250 men who were offering incense.

Negativism is a step away from rebellion. Super criticalness breaks the bonds of love and produces a lack of joy. This precise frame of mind blocks God's intervention on our behalf. Should not our steps be--from rebellion, to acceptance, to relinquishment, to praise, to God changing the situation?

It seems so clear to me that God does indeed have His spokesmen and leaders. Certainly Scripture reveals not everyone is equal in responsibility. Incidentally, I notice there were many slaves back then; in fact, the children of Israel were slaves too, escaping from Egypt. They assuredly should have understood authority and leadership structure, having been slaves for 70 years themselves. Really long remembered learning is hard.

What if David had not listened to Nathan, the prophet? Why didn't God speak directly to David? He had in times past. Why speak through Nathan and Gad? There are many such incidents listed throughout the Bible where someone delivered a word from the Lord to others.

One time God even used a jackass to speak to Baalam. That should teach us not to judge the message by the messenger. In fact, it seemed to be the norm for God to always use his prophets and apostles to speak his instructions to the people. There is a Scripture in Ephesians 4:11 where Jesus set in the church the five *ministry* gifts: apostles, prophets, evangelists, pastors and teachers. These ministry gifts for the church are different than the gifts of the Holy Spirit mentioned in I Cor. 12:8. We have the latter three ministries, but where are the first two? Somewhere along the line the democratic rule was instituted into the American church. We no longer let the prophets speak, or perhaps there are so few apostles and prophets today. Where are these missing ministry gifts for the church?

"But can you name even one of these prophets who lives close enough to God to hear what He is saying? Has even one of them cared enough to listen?" Jer. 23:18.

In researching this, I discovered that God, throughout the Bible, used the apostles and prophets to speak directions and the will of God. "In olden times God did not share this plan with his people, but now He has revealed it by the Holy Spirit to His apostles and prophets." Eph. 3:5.

"Do not smother the Holy Spirit. Do not scoff at those who prophesy, but test everything that is said to be sure it is true, and if it is, then accept it." I Thes. 5:20.

"We are to covet to prophesy." I Cor. 14:39

"But always, first of all, I warn you through my prophets." Amos 8:7.

Rev. Earl Paulk of Chapel Hill in Atlanta said that we must move from being chaplains of the world to being the prophetic leaders of the world for the future.

Now, as to the question, "Isn't everything written in the Bible that we need to know?" It is my belief, there are not some specifics. For instance, what if a girl marries a homosexual unknowingly? Is she required to stay with him or kill him as in Lev. 20:13? Neither does it say what to do if your husband abuses you repeatedly. Stay, divorce him, take him to a counsellor, have him arrested, hide out, what?

CHOOSING A LOVE THAT WILL LAST

However, the Bible sets forth clearly defined principles and general instructions by which to live, not listing specific problems that can and do arise. Those principles are administered and executed by a sovereign God with justice and mercy for all, but the individual must find specific guidance for his own life. General directions are just that. Specific directions are just that. That is why each man has to "...work out his own (specific) salvation with fear and trembling, for it is God at work." Phil. 2:12,13. KJV

When confronted with puzzling questions I had no answers for, I didn't move or act but simply waited--waited until it became discernible.

During this time, I remember very distinctly reaffirming to God about wanting his very best and FIRST choice for me. **I wanted to find a love that would last.** At the same time, I would have to be worthy of such a choice person. One of life's worst tortures would be making my own choice, only to spend the rest of my life wondering what His *first* choice would have been. No way! I was determined with a determination that was beyond myself.

Oswald Chambers calls this, "having no mind of our own in the matter."[2] Something in me wanted to see if God would indeed give the best to those who leave the choice to Him and hoped I would be wise enough to accept His decision.

Launching out on this quest in waiting for God's answer was exciting. It also helped to focus my attention away from my problems onto the solution and provision.

Somewhere deep inside of me, I felt more and more that God did indeed know me, and where I was. In the waiting for Him, I found deep security and contentment. The more I meditated upon the words spoken, the more strength and faith I gained. Again, I shared this with no one at this time, except Barbara. My family and friends knew nothing of this venture into faith. Man had not been capable of helping me when I needed it most. Now, I would place my total confidence in God. Still there were days when things seemed to go wrong. That is when I would get these words out and take them like one takes a medical prescription from a doctor--take three times a day and one at bedtime. It was very therapeutic.

I was on a secret mission and with it came renewed energy to keep me alive and strengthened to be able to grasp hope. Hope and despair are on opposite poles.

Frankly, there were words given to me I didn't understand or know what they meant. In that case, I filed them away and waited. Waited until it was made clear. The gifts of the Holy Spirit are not dangerous unless you undertake to make them come to pass on your own, or speak your own words and thoughts.

God cannot reveal to us everything before it happens. We would ruin it everytime. Master and student must walk a step at a time together. The student is but a babe concerning the ways of God. God's pace with us is probably governed by the student's willingness to learn.

Why is it that rebellion doesn't have to be learned while obedience has to be determinedly and deliberately learned? Getting Adam *out* and Christ *in* produces many a civil war. Have you ever wondered why it takes no teaching to learn the four-letter words and so laborious to learn the Ten Commandments? We are born with a sin nature, meaning evil comes natural to us. There is no antidote for change without Jesus Christ, who willingly gave His life to rid us of this evil nature. Our *spirit within* has to be *born again* if we are to have God's nature. We received satan's nature at our first birth. Here we have God overcoming satan again. The difference is; we have the choice of which master we will serve since we were given free wills.

Someone has described the conflict between good and evil within us as a black dog and a white dog constantly fighting. Which dog wins? THE ONE I FEED!

I didn't realize how much this inner conflict was affecting me until my bank called and wanted me to come in and give them another signature for my accounts. I told them they already had signature cards on me. "Yes, we do, but your signature is nothing like it used to be. It has changed totally and we can't use the old one anymore." After hanging up, I pulled out some old checks along with my recent ones and compared the signatures. I couldn't believe the difference.

MY SEARCH FOR GOD IS WARMING UP AND I RECEIVE ANOTHER PROPHECY!

GLORY CHAPMAN

CHAPTER 16

RUN BABY RUN!

During my struggle, I read the words of wisdom, words of knowledge and prophetical ones given to me over and over. Reading them produced a stamina, a strength I did not have within myself. That is why some wondered how I was able to manage as well as I did. They knew nothing of my secret source of encouragement and hope.

Then, the next January Barbara gave me these words.

"My daughter, seek ye first the Kingdom of God and walk in my ways. There is a great unrest that has settled over the world, not just among my people, but over the whole earth; turmoil, upheaval and restlessness, but I would speak or give you peace in the midst of the turmoil--a peace you don't understand.

"I have seen your tears in the night. Do not fear as long as you walk with me through the darkness and uncertainty of your life, and I will bring you to a place of happiness. Do not say within yourself and contemplate this alternative or that alternative. I will lead you naturally into the place I have before-time prepared for you. Do not say, 'Shall I take this road or path or the other' for I will naturally lead you into the place I have heretofore prepared for you. Nothing shall harm you and it is all good that I have for you. Trust me for it is all good. You shall have great happiness. I have planned it before this time for you.

"Do not look behind. Do not look behind like Lot's wife did. You have said in your heart, 'What shall become of me, what shall become of my children?' I will take care of you and I will take care of the children. Do not be troubled. Eventually, even you shall see the reason and the way I have led you."

But Barbara wasn't the only one with a message. It was weeks later that another friend, Daisy Wiltbanks, gave me these words:

CHOOSING A LOVE THAT WILL LAST

"My daughter, I have seen your tears and I would say unto you, I am coming to you out of all the tragedies of your life. Trust me for I am coming to you."

As these words were spoken to me, I wrote them down verbatim and placed them in a strong metal box because I knew I couldn't retain the exact wording and their meaning. They are among my most prized possessions, though certainly not above the inspired Scriptures.

Oswald Chambers says that we are never to worship our rare moments, but these words nursed me along to health. Therefore, they are priceless to me.

You have to realize that some of the persons giving me these words were not privy to my innermost thoughts at all. I am a very private person. These words flowed into my spirit continuously like an intravenous feeding. A sickness of the heart can't be reached somehow--food or drink will not placate it, travel won't quench it and parties can't drown it.

These words of life bathed over my sagging spirit much like a perfusionist bathes a person's heart during open heart surgery to keep it alive. This is the affect these words had on my inner being. Nothing had changed on the outside, but I was getting nourishment where I needed it most. It felt good. It felt peaceful. It felt like life pulsating back into my heart. I was beginning to learn how to lie back and let the love drip, drop by drop, into my spirit without fretting about all the tomorrows.

A part of me kept saying, "Get up and run. Run baby run!" But I was helpless in that it seemed I had no arms and no legs. I upbraided myself by saying, *Other people have worse problems. My problems are not all that bad. It isn't the end of the world. It is better than terminal cancer.* Only one problem; my spirit wouldn't buy it, and I lay wounded as if someone had stomped the life out of me and had left me for dead. My idealized kind of life was gone forever.

DEAR LORD, PICK ME UP AND CARRY ME!

CHAPTER 17

TURN IN THE ROAD

Although I was praying for a sign, for direction, I wasn't prepared for the number of things that would suddenly be revealed to me. It began one day when Barbara and I were out by the side of her pool in mid March that same year when she gave me these words.

"I am going to make a turn in the road for you. Another news day is coming. Things are progressing along as they should, even progressing faster than you know. I am holding your hand. Take a deep breath as we are going into higher, thinner air. I will be with you and I am holding your hand. I am going to wait awhile to put the missing piece in.

"There is going to be a news day about an important event."

Later as Barbara was explaining what she had said, she drew a little sketch of a cracked pitcher in red ink. I still have it attached to the words.

Still later these words were given in a small group as one of the gifts of the Holy Spirit.

"You think material things are real, but I am more real. But I am more real. How can the created say to the creator, 'I am more real.' Eternal things are the real."

The next year a few days after New Year's Day, Jennie Simmons, my beautiful inside-out friend, gave me this Scripture to look up in The Living Bible.

"Since Christ suffered and underwent pain, you must have the same attitude He did; you must be ready to suffer, too. For remember, when your body suffers, sin loses its power, and you won't be spending the rest of your life chasing after evil desires, but will be anxious to do the will of God." I Peter 4:1,2.

CHOOSING A LOVE THAT WILL LAST

A week later, the Holy Spirit spoke these words through Barbara.

"God is going to give you a new thing to work on. A project that your mind can get into and will absorb your interest and be very interesting to you. You are on the edge of something, but I don't know what it is. You are going to enjoy and love it and have much laughter.

"About editorializing, the Lord would say to you that you have often editorialized on the comments of others, but now the Lord is going to make comments through you directly, and it would be wise to have a tape recorder near at hand where you can easily turn it on because you are alone a great deal during the daytime. The Lord is going to begin to show you things about homey little illustrations.

"You will be amazed at the end of a few months at the thoughts He is going to give you that are original and yet so common in our experience. He will use these comments for they will be His comments. He will use them in written form, in conversational form and in teaching. Do not be tempted to explore your mind and do not be tempted to explore the minds of others along the line I am going to give you. Don't think the thoughts are going to come from your thoughts, but they will be my thoughts and my comments on daily life for I am the Master Teacher of the parable.

"Therefore, this is the pearl that I give to you in your own field to dig for, to find and to cherish. And it will be a contribution that you will make through me, through my Spirit, for I shall make a master teacher out of one who thought she really had no real education in spiritual matters, except through the hard knocks of life. You will be amazed at the things you will find, even things I know about you and about others that you know. Just as you have kept a diary for many, many days, so I shall use these truths that I shall teach you and they shall be as a diary unto you and of daily pearls which I shall give to you.

"Now I am going to give to you your calendar for the year.

May is going to be a very important month in your life. October is another very significant month. Around Thanksgiving your heart will be very full of thanksgiving for I shall add a richness and a luster to your life before this year is over, and there will be no strife. And as I add this new chapter of this year, you shall praise your Lord and thank him for this life."

Barbara added, "Your night of woe is over and past, and you are going to be settling into your new life at last."

A month or so later, Barbara came by my home and delivered these words.

"The stop-gap measure is worn out. Keep still a moment in your heart, and I will speak out against the very nature that is troubling you so and against those who lift up their hands against the Almighty God in rebellion and defiance for surely there has been a defiance or a fist shaking in my very face by those who would hurt you.

"There are those who have chosen to live close to me. Not that I choose one over another to live close to me, but those who look to me deserve to live next to my heart. Do I not allow them to? Others do not understand my ways and do not try to make sense out of my words. They do not live close to me but only pretend. Their show-of-pretense is down and out now, and all that you see in ruins and rubble is really something good for you because when there are no walls of pretense and no shields to hide behind, you can see clearly into the innermost heart of the matter.

"Yet out of the depths of death comes a resurrection life. Has not this always been my principle and always my way, saith God, that all things that are counterfeit and all fleshly nature must die. And you must enter into this death many times that the resurrection life may grow stronger. Therefore, rejoice, my daughter, for you have a life of beautiful proportion coming into its own for that which has been fleshly has died. You have mourned many times that which you once held in your hands, and the life you have built; and you have seen it go down to ashes. You have seen the very dearest thing destroyed, seemingly at the hand of man. But I am allowing you to look at the remains of something beautiful in the natural that you might recognize in the future the transparency of the natural, the failure of it and the disintegration process that takes hold of it so that you might place all of your treasures in that which cannot be corrupted and that which cannot be changed or shaken. And that you might be made into a pillar with strong foundations that will continually be a pillar in the temple of the Lord God so others might come and lean against, and nothing shall cause it to shudder, tremble or fall.

"Therefore, look up and rejoice, my daughter, for all the shambles that you see around about you are temporary. It shall pass speedily away, but what I have made in you is permanent, strong and unyielding to the pressure of man and is beautiful in my eyes.

"I shall use your experience, just frankly, in a book. You shall look out of this book with eyes that see into the very souls of other men and women, and they shall say, 'This is my story. This is my life. These are my feelings.' For you are not alone in your deepest need, but all humanity does cry aloud and groan in travail to be born into the peaceable Kingdom of God where all is peace and tranquil. But until then you must be by my side and let me lead you into green pastures and let me cause you to lie down by the bubbling brook and give you to drink that others might also find me and find the way out of their trouble. I have come out with you to another gate in your life, not a wall, not a barrier, and you shall enter into a new phase--a useful life, a life of joy and happiness.

"I cannot deny my promises to you, but neither could I circumvent the way that has led to the growth of your joy and understanding. Therefore, come, I am beckoning you forward. Come with me to another day, another field of labor, another experience of learning and growing, and you shall see and rejoice in what I have in store for you. It's in the oven, like a cake being prepared and it is baking."

There was no way I could express my feelings when those

words were given to me. They completely overwhelmed me inasmuch as I was no writer. At that moment, I don't think I completely believed I could or would write a book. However, it seemed I didn't have to rely on my own ability.

According to Elisabeth Elliot in *Loneliness*, "With what misgivings we turn over our lives to God, imagining somehow that we are about to lose everything that matters. Our hesitancy is like that of a tiny shell on the seashore, afraid to give up the teaspoon of water it holds lest there not be enough in the ocean to fill it again. 'Lose your life,' said Jesus, 'and you will find it. Give up and I will give you all.'"[1]

Somehow those words instilled in my heart more faith than fear. Previously, I would have reacted with a great deal of unbelief, but the way He spoke to me changed my thinking.

I sensed I was falling in love with God because of the loving gentle way He came to me. I was strengthened and encouraged by those words, but at the same time I sensed the need to change some of my preconceived ideas.

LORD, HELP ME TO TURN LOOSE OF MY LIFE AND SEE THINGS FROM YOUR PROSPECTIVE!

CHOOSING A LOVE THAT WILL LAST

CHAPTER 18

BAD THINGS DON'T HAPPEN TO GOOD PEOPLE

Having to put on paper some of the things I believed earlier seems a bit ridiculous to me now, but only in retrospect. At the time, I really did deep down believe that God wouldn't let anything bad happen to me or mine. Nothing bad. Not ever. And I could quote numerous Scriptures to back it up.

In fact, one evening as we were sitting on the banks of the Rio Grande River, watching several little busy beavers feverishly building their dams, Jason said, "You act as if you never thought you would ever have any problems." Would you believe I was surprised by that statement? He was absolutely right. I didn't ever plan on having any trouble. Perhaps that was why I was so ill equipped to handle it when it came.

Jason explained practically the same principle to me when one of his clients came in one day with some more bad news to which Jason informed him, "Isn't it good that you have had so many problems?"

The more a muscle is used, the stronger it becomes. My mother is such an advocate of keeping in shape by walking, working, and keeping active. Her favorite line is, "You lose what you don't use."

Hannah Smith in *The Christian's Secret of a Happy Life* writes, "If we do not accept the circumstances God's permissive will has allowed, then He permits the difficulties to heap up. For most of us that's the only way He can get our attention. We must see all of life as coming directly from God's hands."[1] This is known as the prayer of relinquishment as Catherine Marshall calls it. I should stop demanding anything and want only what He wants for me, whatever it is. Are not acceptance and relinquishment very close? Resignation is very divergent.

ACCEPTANCE

Only in acceptance lies peace, not in resignation
        nor in busyness.
Resignation is surrender to fate.
Acceptance is surrender to God.
Resignation lies down quietly in an empty universe.
Acceptance rises up to meet the God who
    fills that universe with purpose and destiny.
Resignation says, "I can't."
Acceptance says, "God can!"
Resignation says, "It's all over for me."
Acceptance asks, "Now that I am here, what's next, Lord?"
Resignation says, "What a waste."
Acceptance asks, "In what redemptive way will You
    use this mess, Lord?" [2]

Later I learned from Proverbs 24:10 which says, "You are a poor specimen if you can't stand the pressure of adversity."

Along the same line Robert Leighton wrote, "Adversity is the diamond dust Heaven polishes its jewels with."[3]

The real title of this chapter should read, *Bad Things Don't Happen to Good People Because God Won't Let It.* That was the reason I tried to be good--so bad things wouldn't happen to me or mine. Another thought comes to me right now, "Why do *good* things happen to *bad* people?"

Hence, this was another battle within to find out what went wrong. Where and how had I arrived at such an unrealistic conclusion? How was I so far off course, but didn't realize it at the time? "And we know that all that happens to us is working for our good if we love God and are fitting into his plans." Rom. 8:28. Bad things can and do happen, but the wondrous part of it all is that God eventually takes those bad things and turns them into good for us.

CHOOSING A LOVE THAT WILL LAST

Upon delving more deeply, I discovered I could quote many Scriptures that if taken out of context and by themselves would indeed prove my position. Quite convincing that we are in fact protected by God over evil or anything unpleasant touching us if we read only selected passages.

In playing Bible Trivia with Mother, I noticed that the followers of Jesus Christ were beheaded, flayed alive, sawed in half, boiled in oil, killed with knives, crucified, stoned to death, put in pits, burned at the stake, put in lions' dens, and had their eyes put out. The seven Maccabee sons had their tongues cut out, scalped, hands and toes cut off and fried, forcing their mother to watch. Each son made a remarkable and notable speech before his death. There were also other heinous deaths.

If I consider that Job was mentioned by God as being a perfect and upright man, and the apostles no slouches either, as not being spared suffering, then how do I reconcile the two views?

Consider what happened to Jesus Christ while he was here on earth. Now mix those words in with Job's experience. Job was shot out of his comfortable happy affluent existence into a very wretched suffering one, all in a day's time. And God was silent to Job for about a whole year. Only after the total stripping (all but his life) did God come to him. How puzzling to Job not to know *why* God allowed this to happen to him. I loathe where his friends accused him of many sins, but even in his depraved condition, he did not lie. He refused to lie for the honor of God. He still had his integrity intact. If he had not stolen anything from the poor or from widows, he spoke up and said he was innocent. I like that. Under some circumstances, you might confess to anything just to receive relief. In Job's silent time, he had many advisors--his four all-knowing and talkative friends, as well as his lovely wife, who suggested that he curse God and die.

Perhaps Job passed the final test when he confessed, "Though he slay me, yet will I trust him." I noticed with particular interest that Job longed to appear before God with his predicament. He wanted to argue his case. His focus seemed to be on himself. In the last chapter of Job, toward the end of that horrible and tragic year, he winds down to but one conclusion. Job confessed he did not know God like he thought he did. He said, "Who's to say how many of our perceptions about God are correct? I have heard of thee by the *hearing* of the ear; but now mine eye *seeth* thee." Job. 42:5. Job is now focusing on *God*.

I remember a minister being interviewed on the *700 Club* not too long ago. He used the phrase, "I have seen the invisible Christ." Hearing and seeing are two separate things.

I often wish I could have lived when Jesus was here on earth, could have seen His eyes and felt His compassion. Without some kind of personal encounter with Jesus or seeing Him with our spiritual eyes, it is hard to follow Him or obey His commandments from intellect or sheer willpower. To me, it is likened to a marriage of convenience. It's possible to perform and go through the motions but the real joy and fulfillment comes from falling in-love, then whatever is required is considered a privilege.

Another analogy would be reading about someone else *in-love*. It is certainly not the same as falling in-love yourself and experiencing all the sensations and emotions. The two sensations are distinctly different.

To think I would be exempt from any suffering is preposterous to me now, but only now. My thought is that God is after something in all of us. Perhaps getting us on a one-to-one basis with Himself. The sooner we are stripped of self and other helps the better, but it seems we cannot get there by ourselves. CERTAINLY, WE WOULD PREFER TO BE DELIVERED FROM SUFFERING OR ADVERSITY RATHER THAN TO BE SUSTAINED THROUGH IT.

More and more of my preconceived ideas about God were tumbling down one by one--ever so slowly.

Paul E. Billheimer quotes this poem from an unknown author in *Don't Waste Your Sorrows*:

CHOOSING A LOVE THAT WILL LAST

> " I walked a mile with Pleasure;
> She chattered all the way,
> But left me none the wiser
> For all she had to say.
>
> I walked a mile with Sorrow;
> And ne'er a word said she;
> But, oh, the things I learned from her
> When Sorrow walked with me." [4]

I realize now that my attitude toward sorrow and difficulty is not to ask that they be prevented, but to ask that I may preserve the self God created me to be through every fire of sorrow.

Oswald Chambers writes, "That there ought to be no sorrow, but there is sorrow, and we have to receive ourselves in its fires. Sin and sorrow and suffering are, and it is not for us to say that God has made a mistake in allowing them. Sorrow burns up a great deal of shallowness, but it does not always make a man better. Suffering and pain either give me myself or it destroys myself. We cannot receive ourselves in success, we lose our head; we cannot receive ourselves in monotony, we grouse. The way to find ourselves is in the fires of sorrow. YOU ALWAYS KNOW THE MAN WHO HAS BEEN THROUGH THE FIRES OF TRAGEDY AND RECEIVED HIMSELF. You are certain you can go to him in trouble and find that he has the deep capacity for identifying with you."[5]

He who suffers most has the most to give. Until one is broken, he is full of himself, his plans, his ambitions, his value judgments. One is often so full of self that there is little room for more of God.

One good thing that came out of a multitude of problems is that little things don't upset me anymore. ONCE THE WORST HAS HAPPENED, EVERYTHING ELSE IS LESS. It is incredible to observe the actions and reactions of others in crises. Usually the newly initiated into the fires of adversity are the most vocal and overwhelmed. Troubles can strengthen or weaken one; depends on one's adaptability to reverses.

"God enables us, through His grace, not to waste our sorrows. What happens when bad things happen to good people? Through God's grace, they become better people, and God turns their sufferings into servants for His glory."[6]

My aunts, Mary Helen Glass and Pauline Blessings from the Napa Valley in California both work in psychiatric hospitals. I asked what I thought was a complicated question, and didn't expect to receive such a simple answer to, "Is there one main reason why most of your patients end up on your floor?"

"Yes, sure," Pauline responded. "It is fairly easy to explain. Good and bad things happen to everyone in life--no exceptions. The ones who adapt and grow with the disappointments and adversities never end up here. The others who refuse to adjust and keep looking back, not forgetting nor forgiving, come here."

"Heavenly Father, give me serenity to accept what cannot be changed, courage to change what should be changed; and wisdom to know one from the other," Dr. Reinhold Niebuhr wrote.[7]

SEARCHING IS PROVING TO BE AN INTERESTING QUEST!

CHOOSING A LOVE THAT WILL LAST

CHAPTER 19

MY TRACK RECORD ON GOD

A few months later I received a letter from one of my dearest friends, Georgie Horner of Waco, Texas. In it she described the difference between faith and trust. She explained they are two different things. I had never thought about it before.

Georgie went on to say we all received a portion or deposit of faith at birth. Rom. 12:3 KJV. It is much like receiving little arms and legs when we are born. However, that is only the initial equipment and unless we exercise our tiny arms and legs, or our faith, they atrophy quickly, becoming useless when we need them most.

Faith can wither away as surely as our physical parts. We don't usually think of these two being synonymous because our faith is invisible while our body is visible. Therein lies the subtle deception of neglecting one more than the other.

Pat Robertson is his book, *The Secret Kingdom*, has a whole chapter on the 'Law of Use'. It is a must in reading. What you don't use, you indeed lose.

Pat uses the parable of the talents of money that Jesus taught. One servant was given five talents of money, another two and the last man only one talent. After some time, the lord returned and called the men to him to give an accounting. The one with five had traded and earned five more, and the man with two had done likewise. The poor man with only one talent of money hid it to protect and keep it safe and had earned nothing.

In handing out the rewards, the lord gives the man with the ten talents of money many more responsibilities. Also, the two talent man who had earned four was given much more. What stands out to me is what he did with the last man. The lord took away the only money he had, and guess what he did with it? He gave it to the man with the MOST, who now has 11 instead of five. Does that sound like socialism to you? No, it's to the man who uses well what God has given him that gains still more, and he shall have abundance. But from the man who is unfaithful, even what little responsibility he has shall be taken from him. Matt. 25:21-30.

"He who does not work, neither should he eat." II Thes. 3:10 KJV.

In other words, the more we use our faith, the stronger it becomes and brings more faith with it. The principle being to everyone who has and uses what he has, more shall be given, whether in muscles, faith or money, until one day we will hit the exponential curve.

The heroes of faith are mentioned in Hebrews 11. All of them persevered over every kind of obstacle imaginable. It is in the consistency of exercise that we develop strength. This 'Law of Use' can be applied to every area of the visible and invisible world.

Robertson writes, "You can take what you have, refuse to use it, and ultimately lose it. For instance, you could tape your hand to your side in such a way that you would be unable to move it. If you left it there, totally unused, for six months, the muscles would wither. Even what you had would have been taken away."[1]

Trust is another matter. Trust is the track record of the object of our faith--not in faith itself. To put it more simply, we have a friend whom we have faith in to do certain specified things. When, over a period of time, this friend does indeed carry through exemplarily, then trust begins to form between the two. The track record speaks for itself.

To a greater or smaller degree we all exhibit trust, though we may not be consciously aware of it in our postman, chef, pilot, captain, president, lawyer, doctor, pharmacist, minister, teacher, friend, parents, employer, mate and children.

It is certainly interesting to me to see how often and at what intervals these words came to me. The next words came from

CHOOSING A LOVE THAT WILL LAST

Barbara four months later.
"This is a good news day. You have been very perplexed and struggled in your mind about many things. Before now the tide has been going out and everything with it, but I say the tide is going to turn and it is already beginning to turn. It is going to come in and you shall observe and see that I am going to bring a treasure trove and lay it at your feet. I have many treasures for you, and you will say, 'God is so great and mighty and God is more than I can fathom.'

"I have put a fence around you, and you have not tried to break out of this fence. This, my daughter, has been good to me. I put that fence around you.

"There is one special gift I have for you which is above all of the other treasures. I will lay it at your feet and I will open it. You will not even have to unwrap it as I am going to open it for you. You shall see what a treasure it holds. You shall have a new home, new family relationships, a new life and you will say, 'I am so completely happy. How can it be so?'

"You have said within yourself and seen so many obstacles but don't think of the hurdles. You have thought there would be big hurdles, and what you would do if this or that came up. I am going to remove the hurdles and there will be no hurdles to jump.

"Will I not bring to pass everything I have told you, and am I not able to do it? Trust me. I am bringing you many treasures. You are to rest from all your imaginations and struggling and see it brought to pass. Wait and you shall see what I have for you. God will bring it to perfection if you will believe. Just rest.

"You will not have to plan, wish, hope and dream or long for the things you want in life. But they will become a reality and they will be yours. You will not need a telescope to see them. God is very pleased with you."

This message was reassuring and at the same time exhilarating because I had so much to look forward to. Hope creates terrific energy and strength. My faith and trust were rising along with my spirit, even though there was nothing I could do to bring any of this to pass. In fact, over and over I was told not to try to do anything. Just wait and trust Him.

On the back of one of my notepads were these words which I jotted down. God in His sovereignty can change the course of history, nations, streams, oceans, events, diseases, kingdoms, individuals, actions, thoughts, feelings, attitudes, habits, associations, relationships, denominations, churches, finances and governments.

Webster says *sovereignty* means: supreme power and right to exercise it; dominion; independent state.

Just trying to comprehend the magnitude, supremacy, authority and power of God certainly dwarfed all my learning. I must never judge God based on my limited experience.

Months later Barbara delivered this message to me. "I speak to you, my daughter, to reassure you. Have I not spoken and will I let my Word fail? I say unto you, I will bring to pass everything I have spoken to you. After a little while you will laugh. I say laugh and laugh greatly before your God and even dance and exclaim at the things God does and with great laughter. No more sorrow. You will laugh in the face of the devil when he says, 'Did God really say that?'

"You will say with great assurance and without hesitation, 'Yes, my God did, and I know it is true,' and laugh in his face. You shall not be shaken even through difficulties and hard places.

"After a little while you shall have great joy. I will chase away any enemies with a stick that would dare to rise against you, and I would cause them to be brought to naught."

It was as if I needed bolstering up some times more than other times. At this state of affairs in my life, it was almost comical to think I would ever truly laugh, much less laugh greatly, even dance with joy. However, it was jolting me out of old thought patterns, and that was good.

The last part came to pass rather soon inasmuch as when faced with difficulties and problems, the uneasiness and vulnerability seemed to be gone. I would soon be out of Intensive Care and

CHOOSING A LOVE THAT WILL LAST

could be sustained for longer periods of time on my own.

Psalms 32:7 says, "I will instruct you, says the Lord, and guide you along the best pathway for your life; I will advise you and watch your progress."

Then after church one Sunday, these words were given to me by a person I know but casually.

"I have seen your heart my child. I have seen your tears. You have been very alone. I have been developing a quiet and submissive spirit within you. I am very pleased with you. I am very pleased with you.

"I have seen your heart and you have tried to do right. You have said within yourself, 'What shall become of me?' I have a plan for your life and you will not need to ask others to tell you for the answer will be made very clear and plain to you, and it will be very soon."

These words brought tears to my eyes and healing to my heart. Also, these words were confirmation of the words previously spoken to me by others. At this point, I was wondering if my life would be governed by others always telling me what the Lord was saying through their particular gifts, which healed me. And I appreciated them, but at some point in time, I longed to *know* within myself the answer. This particular word gave me the assurance that I would know *within* the choices I should make. To me, that felt good and out of harm's way.

God uses many ways to communicate His directions. I had pondered over and over just how in the final conclusion I would receive this *knowing within*. And by what means would my knowing come? From the Bible I knew God used many different ways. Ultimately, I didn't guess it, and it never entered my mind the method He would use when the answer finally came. In the meantime, I must let God handle His part and I would exercise my faith and trust in Him.

Jennie Sirmons called me again in October, which was about two years or more from the first words of wisdom given to me. She had been reading the book, *Lord of the Valleys* by F. Bulle, and she gave me his words:

"Most of us have our reserve weapons stashed away which we think we can use if the Lord doesn't come through. But until we render up all our arms and our spirit, which would seek by any means its own deliverance and concede to 'being defenseless,' we tie God's hands."[2]

That was a warning because at that particular time I may have unconsciously been planning to do things my way--just in case.

Barbara's next words were perplexing and puzzling.

"This is a quiet time and I am going to give you quietness within. It is very near to your coronation day. You are a princess now, but you are going to be crowned queen. I have a beautiful crown for you. Many shall see it. You will have authority and reign and will be as a queen with your wishes and desires fulfilled. I have a crown for you in this life, not only in heaven.

"How can I show you heavenly things when you cannot understand earthly things? It has been so near and so far, and yet so far and so near. Think about what this means."

I was baffled by the terminology He used in the first part, and lost as to what 'so near yet so far, and so far yet so near' meant. Wow!

The Lord knows me so well. Those words spoke volumes to me inasmuch it seemed a long time since my wishes and desires had been considered. Also, the last part is a riddle. I love to try to figure out legal problems, Boggle, games, puzzles and repairs. God knew those words would take my mind off vintage things and help me to focus on something fresh and challenging. I loved that!

"I asked God for strength that I might achieve;
I was made weak that I might learn humbly to obey.
I asked for help that I might do greater things;
I was given infirmity that I might do better things.
I asked for riches that I might be happy;
I was given poverty that I might be wise.

CHOOSING A LOVE THAT WILL LAST

I asked for power that I might have the praise of men;
I was given weakness that I might feel the need of God.
I asked for all things that I might enjoy life;
I was given life that I might enjoy all things.

I got nothing that I asked for, but everything I hoped for.
Almost despite myself my unspoken prayers were answered.
I among all men am most richly blessed." Anonymous

WELL, MY TRACK RECORD ON GOD WAS BUILDING!

CHAPTER 20

PARTING

Someone has said life should consist of someone to love, something to do and something to look forward to.

Those three things comprise a big order!

My notes say that another friend asked me if I ever tried to write or liked to write, mentioning I should keep everything I put down, my diary, notes and everything.

This friend also said, "You are going to be sitting in that chair a year from now and you will not believe the great things that God can cause to happen."

My only reaction to that, I remember, was, "I can't wait."

This is the first recollection I have of this. In my memory, it was Barbara who said I would one day write a book. Now, I see it was at this previous time. What a surprise. Apparently it just went over my head. It was prophetic, but I missed it at the time. That's why the Lord has to come to us via many persons. Writing a book was the last thing in the world I thought I would ever attempt to undertake. I heard those words about writing a book and I filed it way back in my mind that perhaps someday I might. By nature, I write lots of notes. I have a daily calendar filled with events going back 20 years or more. That is just me. Also, through the years, any good and worthwhile articles that interested me, I put in a special file. I have several hundred articles, poems, news clippings, photos, and other papers. Strange, but as of this date, I have used none of these resources for this book. This file contains the best of what I have read during my adult lifetime. Maybe another book later!

On January of the next year, Barbara called to tell me these few words.

"The ultimate surprise is waiting!"

CHOOSING A LOVE THAT WILL LAST

What in all the world did that mean? My meditation time was really getting interesting, puzzling but interesting and exciting. What utter relief to have so many brand-new things to think about and anticipate.

Then in February, Barbara spoke these words of comfort to me.

"The Lord is near you, and the Holy Spirit is here to comfort you. His word has never failed and will not now. Don't let bitterness in your heart because it causes a hardness of heart. He will bring to pass everything He has spoken to you in times past, but just stand steadfast and wait yet a little while. He will bring only the things to pass He has bargained for with you.

"Don't try to analyze or reason this out. Don't rely on man's wisdom. God never fails. Just trust, wait and rest. He will be your Guide and Counselor."

Oswald Chambers writes in *My Utmost For His Highest*, "Our trust is in God up to a certain point, then we go back to the elementary panic prayers of those who do not know God. We get to our wits' end, showing that we have not the slightest confidence in Him and His government of the world; He seems to be asleep, and we see nothing but breakers ahead.

"There are stages in life when there is no storm, no crisis, when we do our human best; it is when a crisis arises that we instantly reveal upon whom we rely."[1]

I was again at the crossroads and seemingly still lost. Life had gone gray, colorless and tasteless. Grief is gray, I believe. Nothing stands out--it's all monotonous, meaningless and dull. I had hit another numbing low. In trying to read and reread the words given to me, they seemed lifeless. I couldn't seem to draw any strength from them now, or figure out what all they meant. It had been so long--too long.

In some strange way I didn't want to let go of grief. It seemed more preferable than *nothingness*. Nothingness has to be the barest of all landscapes. Could it be that a poor relationship is somehow better than no relationship--an impaired relationship chosen over no relationship?

"Dramatic and drastic change can be a crisis. We are comfortable with the familiar, there is security in the well-traveled path. Change requires adjustment, response, responsibility." [2]

Or could it be as Elisabeth Elliot explained it in, *Loneliness*, "I will not relinquish this misery, not right now. God has taken away what I most wanted. I have a right to feel sorry for myself. I have been wronged. I will refuse, for a while at least, any offer of comfort and healing. Don't speak to me of joy. You pour salt in my wounds. Let me lick them for a while." [3]

In all fairness, none of these messages from Barbara or others were shared with Jason. Several times we discussed God a little. Once, I even suggested that he try God and see what would happen. Give God a chance. He stated that he would need to be alone for two weeks to find God.

Even though he didn't know the quest I was on, I am sure he felt a reluctance on my part which made him feel very insecure. Things between us limped along. For more than a year, I couldn't bring myself to make a clean break with Jason. Our spirits were not meshing, and I felt that if anyone else would do, then he must take that option. Marriage should only be when you can't live without the other person.

Sometime later, I called Jason during office hours at his legal firm and asked him to come to the house. Sitting on the sofa in my little office, steeling myself, I very calmly told him that it was goodbye, and asked him to return all the letters I had written to him. He dropped his head and didn't say a word for several minutes. Looking very downcast, he said softly, "I wish you wouldn't do this." He asked if there was anyone else. I assured him there was no one else; that I loved him, as well as his children. The deal I made with God was still not shared. He held me close for a few minutes, then turned and quickly walked out the back door to his Mercedes.

Closing a door that was so precious to me was like cutting out my heart. I didn't dress, put on any make-up or comb my hair for several days. I was bereft.

I thought his coming into my life at such a time was providential, and that perhaps we were meant for each other. We had a little game we played called, "Edward and Wallis." The adorable way he explained just how he could add onto his home to make room for all of us--the trips we would take together--on and on. There were so many happy memories shared that would die hard. I went down to 109 pounds, which on my 5-foot 3-inch frame was thinner than I had been for some time. Food was repulsive and sleep impossible.

Happiness goes so swift and sorrow so painfully slow.

After Jason left, I called Barbara to come over. When she arrived neither of us said a word for about 30 minutes. Really! I was too distraught for words. "Sometimes words are inappropriate, an instrusion on the deepest and most sacred experiences of life."[2] Barbara knows me so well and waited for me to talk first. I have found that sitting quietly and lovingly is all one really needs to do. Words at such a critical time are useless.

Like my sister, Ruthie, expressed when she lost her husband and two small children when she was 21, even tears can't reach the depths of grief. She said tears would be a blessed relief. The deepest kind of loss and grief is beyond tears.

"The deeper the sorrow the less tongue it has." Talmud.

The doorbell rang and Barbara answered it. It was my sister, Ramona. She came on into the office and stood in the doorway.

After I didn't say a word, she turned to Barbara and asked, "What happened?"

Barbara replied, "I don't know. She hasn't said a word since I got here."

All I remember is my sister looking puzzled. Neither Barbara nor I answered her and she left.

Slowly I opened up. Dear Barbara stayed with me the whole afternoon. What love!

The next day was Lori's birthday, and a party had been planned in the playroom at our home. Someone took over, I don't remember who, and I stayed back in the bedroom the entire party. My precious little Lori!

Once again, I sought solace in the little church across the street, spending hours and tears there.

Little by little I was recovering and reaffirmed my will to do what God knew best. I had lost my footing temporarily.

During this time, I remember specific friends, too many to name individually, who imparted such love to me. It was immensely healing. **When one is so ill, it is of highest importance that only love be given.** My daughter, Shari sent me a black marble shard with the words, "Life is fragile, handle with prayer." I keep it by my lavatory where I can see it daily.

CHOOSING A LOVE THAT WILL LAST

CHAPTER 21

HIS NEEDS HER NEEDS

There was so much to learn about life, relationships and how to handle disappointments. Also, it was most important to me that I not repeat my same mistakes. I was recovering and reading more again. Along the way, different ones talked to me about the dangers of remarriage.

One such conversation was with my good and longtime friend, Anna McDonald. She felt the most important thing was that I marry a Christian.

"Anna," I questioned, "Which one? I thought you told me that a married deacon in your church ran off with some other woman last week. Okay, line up six Christian men and tell me which one will be compatible and will turn out to be noble after 30 years. How long will he live and what diseases will he contract?"

"Oh," she exclaimed, "I see what you mean."

Of course marriage is a risk at best--hence the need for someone to choose *who knows the future*--not only knows the future but knows what my purpose and place is in it from an eternal viewpoint.

There are people with many attributes that aren't compatible in disposition, personality, capabilities, spirituality, habits, desires, values, temperaments, intelligence or goals. Not any old Christian will do, after all.

This is explained in the book, *His Needs, Her Needs*,"[1] Dr. Willard F. Harley, Jr. lists the five top things a man and woman want from each other in marriage.

HIS NEEDS

Sexual fulfillment

GLORY CHAPMAN

Recreational companionship
An attractive spouse
Domestic support
Admiration

HER NEEDS

Affection
Conversation
Honesty and openness
Financial support
Family commitment.

Dr. Harley says that it is mostly in the order given. I highly recommend that you read this book. There are many differences between what a man wants and what a woman wants in marriage.

It has been said that men are the headlines, and women the details. Men the answers and women the questions.

One of the most tragic things in life is when two good people get married only to discover later they are unable to fulfill the needs of each other. They get along like two peeves in a pod and seem to bring out the worst in each other instead of the best.

Dr. Harley so graphically writes about the deposits and withdrawals of our *Love Bank Account*. If someone else fills one or more of our needs, we unconsciously deposit to their account instead of to our mate's.

For instance, here is an interesting letter to *Dear Abby* about how marriage can evolve into disaster.

"Dear Abby: I have been married for over 30 years, and when my husband never wanted to go out in the evening, I thought it was because he was so tired from working all day. He has the kind of job that doesn't require him to account for his time.

"Then I found out he was in the habit of picking up tramps when he was supposed to be on the job.

"You once explained why a man will treat a tramp better than

CHOOSING A LOVE THAT WILL LAST

he treats his wife. I remembered that explanation, and it helped me to feel better. I need to read it again, but I can't find it. Can you?" Hurting in Oklahoma.

"Dear Hurting: Yes. And here it is: A man picks up a tramp because he wants a female companion who is no better than he is. In her company, he doesn't feel inferior. He rewards her by treating her like a lady.

"He treats his wife (who is a lady) like a tramp because he feels that by degrading her he will bring her down to his level. This makes him feel guilty. So in order to get even with his wife for making him feel guilty, he keeps right on punishing her."[2]

How could this wife have known he would turn out this way? Which prompts me to ask, "How can I make an intelligent and wise judgment without having all the facts?" There are too many unknown variables. Also, I don't know what the future holds. "How grateful I am that God's greatness transcends my ability to know and understand. For if my finite mind could grasp the infinite God, then it would bring God down to my human level."[1] My judgment is flawed and has big gaps in it. My friend's story illustrates my point.

Mona knew her husband for 11 years before she married him. He worked in her same office. She told me she used every measuring tool available. After a marriage that lasted less than a year, she told me that she could have put her hand in a paper bag, pulled out a name, and he couldn't have turned out worse. Choosing a mate is certainly one of life's riskiest ventures. It seems all of life is a risk unless we receive information from the One who has all knowledge. Ask Him to choose for you and then accept His choice. **God can be trusted to choose a love that will last.**

We need also to be aware of the passages or cycles of marriage:

1. Young love   1st & 2nd years
2. Realistic love   3 through 10 years
3. Comfortable years   11 through 25 years
4. Renewing years   26 through 35 years

GLORY CHAPMAN

5. Transcendant

    Intimacy   36 years through life.

    Retirement

I love how Erma Bombeck explains love and marriage. "We have gone through three wars, two miscarriages, five houses, three children, nine cars, 23 funerals, seven camping trips, 12 jobs, 19 banks and three credit unions. I had cut his hair, and turned 33,488 pieces of his underwear right side out. He had washed my feet when I was pregnant and couldn't see them and put his car seat back to its original position 18,675 times after I had used it. We had shared toothpaste, debts, closets and relatives. We had given one another honesty and trust.

He came over to where I was seatd and said, "I've got a present for you."

"What is it?" I asked excitedly.

"Close your eyes."

When I opened them, he was holding a cauliflower that comes packed in a pickle jar.

"I hid it from the kids," he said, "because I know how you like the cauliflower."

Maybe love was that simple."

"But what we learn in the time of trial is our treasure forever. Misfortune never leaves us where it finds us. More important than asking the question, "Why did this happen?" is to discover, "Where will it lead me?"[3]

God does not leave us without resources that will enable us to cope.

Though Jason left a big void in my life, and I felt disconnected somehow, I slowly recovered as I read and re-read what was coming--and soon. It seemed the Lord wouldn't mind if I cried

CHOOSING A LOVE THAT WILL LAST

when it hurt, but at the same time, I must not cry or rebel against God because of the turn of events in my life. After all, I did put God in charge of my decision making, did I not? Had I not asked God to give me FIRST choice? A deal is a deal, and I must have a stiff upper lip and not whimper when things haven't gone my way. I kept re-avowing to God that I wanted His best regardless of how much I cried or pled. *Glory, please grow up!* I told myself. It was not an easy assignment when my heart and mind weren't cooperating. NO MATTER, THE BEST IS YET TO BE!

I will leave my future in the hands of the master matchmaker who has planned every day of my life. I will follow His schedule--not mine. It is my belief there is none so wise as He! What strikes me as so paradoxical and fickle is that I am unsure of my own judgment, yet I fear MORE what God might choose for me. Oh, Lord, help my distrust of You.

None of this struggle would have been necessary had I known what was in store for me. I could have saved myself so much anguish. However, I was in need of a big repair job, but didn't know it.

IT SEEMS HARD TO TRUST WHERE I CANNOT SEE!

GLORY CHAPMAN

CHAPTER 22

ME A PHARISEE?

"O wad some Pow'r the giftie gie us to see oursels as ithers see us!" Robert Burns.

It was more than three years after my divorce when I received a telephone call from Dale Chapman, a man from Baltimore, Maryland, whom I knew was getting a divorce. He had recently moved to McAllen. There were three children involved, and I wanted nothing to do with anyone's divorce problems. I had enough problems of my own. He called to ask me a question about how to get in touch with Barbara. I told him very curtly, "Don't you call me!" I felt that any two Christians should be able to work out their marriage and that there should be no divorce. I blurted all this out without knowing any facts. Wise, right?

Very clearly and distinctly, I heard inside myself these words, *If you cannot have any compassion for others in their problems, neither will I work out your life.* Those thoughts jolted me to a sudden change of heart because I certainly was most interested in getting my life in order. Only then did I listen. He wanted to know where Barbara Johnson was. I was civil, though not overly kind, and hung up.

I was short on compassion, and here is what Jess Moody had to say on the subject, "Compassion is not a snob gone slumming. Anybody can salve his conscience by an occasional foray into knitting for the Red Cross. Did you ever take a real trip down inside the broken heart of a friend? To feel the sob of the soul-- the raw, red crucible of emotional agony? To have this become almost as much yours as that of your soul-crushed friend? Then, to sit down with him--and silently weep? This is the beginning of compassion."[1]

CHOOSING A LOVE THAT WILL LAST

Someone once said, "Pity weeps and runs away--compassion comes to help and stay."

Even though I was divorced, I didn't want much to do with any man who was divorced. About a week prior to this call, Jennie Sirmons had told me over the phone how she and Bennie (her husband) would gladly suffer persecution for this man. They knew by the Spirit certain things which I did not. Whenever there is trouble, any kind of trouble, whether personal or between my friends or family, I disappear. I avoid controversies like the plague, partly because the Bible says not to judge and maybe because I heard so much discussion at home while growing up about such matters. I don't know, but I am nowhere to be found.

After Jennie hung up the phone, I thought about what she had said, "She and Bennie would gladly suffer persecution because of Dale." I wondered what that meant. Had I ever been called upon to suffer for a friend, to hold up for a friend to the loss of other friends? No incident came to mind. Don't know if I had the opportunity and failed, or if I ever was presented with that choice. Jennie's words came instantly to mind when I said, "Don't you call me." I was more civil, but I still didn't want to be near problems, especially divorce problems. Perhaps God wanted me to learn some things from this man before he would send the right person into my life. There was no doubt I needed to learn much more. On that basis and that alone was I able to handle our friendship.

I was not curious as to why Dale wanted to call Barbara because I knew how much she counseled and prayed for people with overwhelming problems.

There was much discussion about complex problems that happen in life and how to handle them. It seemed to me there were no easy answers, and prayer was the best avenue for solutions.

It's my opinion, the less you talk with other people the better, and the more you talk to God the wiser. Barbara was the link that perhaps saved Dale's life, literally. He was planning to commit suicide because it seemed there was no other way out. When a person is in deep agony, it is crucial to throw out a rope of hope. Losing hope is the last straw before despair sets in to destroy a person.

Later, Barbara called on the phone to give me these words of wisdom.

"Be still and know that I am thy God, the Lord of your choices. Be not dismayed nor fooled by any tricks of the enemy. I will keep your heart and mind in peace."

By then it was summer. School was out and the four youngest children and I were going to spend the entire summer in Cripple Creek, Colorado, where we had friends who had a small cottage which we could rent. I had met Jim and Ann Tolbert through mutual friends, Bill and Peggy Nix, while they were visiting Texas. Later they were guests at our ranch in Mexico. They invited us to spend some time in Colorado next summer. In the meantime, my two oldest children, Herby and Shari, had married.

Just getting out of the Valley (McAllen) sounded like an ideal getaway and would be a welcomed change. All I wanted to do was rest and try not to think of anything. Peace and quiet was what I craved. No more getting up early, cooking meals or doing homework. What sheer ecstasy to do nothing and to think about nothing in particular--just rest and read.

We were not out of McAllen 20 miles when the bombshell of thoughts dropped into my mind. The children were all comfortably nestled down in the car with their color books and reading when these words zoomed into my consciousness, *What a Pharisee you are!* Where in the world did those thoughts come from? *Me a Pharisee? What is a Pharisee?* I thought. What instantly came to my mind was that Jesus never talked nice to them. I supposed a Pharisee was someone who was super religious and prayed on the street, had a lot of rules and regulations, pious, argumentative, legalistic, someone with a holier-than-thou-attitude, unteachable with preconceived ideas about God and His plan for man. Wow! It seemed I had a good understanding of what a Pharisee was. Not only that, but as I pursued each aspect of a Pharisee, it became clear to me I was truly a bonafide one. What a complete surprise!

I can honestly say, the thought of being a Pharisee had never entered my mind before this time. Never. The Holy Spirit must have brought it to my attention. The Bible says the Holy Spirit will be our helper, guide, teacher, comforter and lead us into all truth. The truth about myself was startling. Previously, I had no idea I was a Pharisee. You cannot repent of something of which you are unaware. My indictment was as clear in my spirit as if the words had been written for my eyes to see in giant print. There is no sound or audio needed between spirits. Spirit to spirit language is different from the spoken audible language.

The rest of the drive to Colorado was spent in dealing with this pharisaical attitude. I prayed for release from this demoniacal spirit. Strange how clear it was to me. If someone else had tried to convince me I was a Pharisee, it would have been a grapple. The Holy Spirit was so gentle and kind not to embarrass me when I needed convicting and correcting. It was as if I was a bird in a cage and the Holy Spirit came and opened the door and said, "Fly away, fly away little one." As I left the cage of prejudice, judgmentalism, argumentative doctrine along with my pet beliefs, there came a freedom within to sing, rejoice, and worship. That little cage was so confining and so very limiting. Now my spirit could soar to greater heights of love, compassion, and a closer relationship with God than I had ever known before. I was free to fly within the confines of God's big wide world of liberating truth. Jesus said, "You shall know the truth and the truth will set you free." John 8:32 I became a free person that day. All those bonds were broken within my spirit, and I could truly worship my Father in spirit and in truth. John 4:23. Don't ask me how that happened. I just know it did. It released me from studying doctrine as such, and propelled me into developing a loving relationship with my Father, listening to His voice and following where He led. Never again will I return to that cage. I felt freeborn and uncaged by the time we drove into Cripple Creek.

It was the second evening when we arrived at Jim and Ann Tolbert's two-story comfortable, 100-year-old stone home at 9,000-feet altitude. We were so excited about getting settled in our little cabin two doors from theirs. Well, Jim had told me over the phone not to worry about anything, just pack up and get there. I kept asking about the cabin. He assured me everything was fine and to come on, not really answering me. Sensing that something wasn't quite right, I called a second time asking about the cabin. "Don't worry about a thing. Everything is fine and will be taken care of," he repeated.

Jim and Ann were glad to see us and after all the greetings, I approached the subject of the little cabin and how anxious we were to get all settled in. He looked sheepish and said that their tenant had decided not to move after all, but that they had moved his brother, Frank, and their nephew, Scott, to the house next door which they called a library.

All five of us were to move into their second floor, which was very adequate and comfortable. I could tell they had gone to a lot of trouble for us. However, as we were all unloading and carrying the suitcases upstairs, Jim motioned to Ann not to carry anything heavy.

"Ann, is your heart worse?" I ventured. She said she had been having quite a lot of distress with her heart and had not been able to sleep very well.

Can you imagine my stress when my four little Indians were running and jumping around above her bedroom? The floors squeaked fairly loud, and of course Tom and Lori had to go to the bathroom several times a night. We would tiptoe and open the door as gently as possible, but then the polished oak floor would creak. *What if she has a heart attack while we are here?* I speculated. Having that many house guests is a strain at best. I was furious at Jim for not telling me the cabin was unavailable.

After several days, I faced him with it and Ann's health, and could he please get us some place to stay in Cripple Creek. He told me there was nothing else available because of the summer season. I couldn't believe it! Our summer plans shot to pieces. Besides I wasn't getting any sleep because I was staying awake lest one of the children wet the bed and I hadn't brought any plastic. We were traipsing back and forth to the bathroom every few hours.

What now? A whole summer ahead of us and this. To top it all off, Tari had started crying a lot, saying she wanted to go home. It got worse by the day--homesickness--she said for her friends.

Without appearing to be upset and as diplomatically as I could, I told Jim and Ann we were leaving sooner than we had planned. They had entertained us royally, going to all the sights around, the Royal Gorge, packing a picnic lunch, driving to a private hunters' lodge, and taking me to a show at the Broadmoor Hotel in Colorado Springs. The kids loved going down into the old gold mine shafts, as well as swimming at the local Country Club.

Tami was in no hurry to return home as she was smitten with 17-year old Scott and his guitar. He played and sang to us a lot. It appeared he had eyes for her too.

Tom and Lori were in their heyday and were as good as angels.

We said our goodbyes and headed toward Colorado Springs and stayed at the Broadmoor a short time. Tari kept crying to leave so we headed on toward Amarillo, Texas, where my special Aunt Cleo and Uncle Grover Forbes live. It had been several years since I had seen them, so I called and a man's voice answered.

"Is this you, Uncle Grover?" I questioned.

"No, did you want him?"

"Yes, is he there? This is Glory. The kids and I are in Amarillo and would like to drive out and see all of you tomorrow if that is possible."

"Oh, Glory, this is Bill. You must not know. Have you been gone from home for awhile? Dad passed away two days ago and we had his funeral this afternoon."

Oh Wow! Bill put Aunt Cleo on the phone, and she insisted we come on by anyway. I don't know who was more forlorn, all of them, or all of us.

We talked and talked about times past and what a wonderful visit we had with Bill, Donna, his wife, and their three sons, as well as Aunt Cleo. All the while if anyone looked at Tari Alice, she would tear up and no one knew why. She was a chip off the old block! She still wanted to go home, even if no one was at home.

Next we headed toward Waco to see Georgie Horner and her family for a few days, much to Tari's chagrin. However, Georgie and Bo's two teenagers were there--Nancy and Judy. That helped and we all had a great time picnicking on Lake Waco, eating and goofing off.

We stayed in a house nearby. It was relaxing and we could spread out with all our stuff without being in anyone's way. There was one fly in the ointment though, and that was I couldn't sleep because I was afraid. The house was sort of a scary big old house and it made a lot of strange noises at night. Of course, I was careful not to mention this to the children, but about daybreak I would fall into an exhausted sleep.

A few days later, we finally headed south to McAllen and arrived home on July 3. So much for a leisure summer away in the mountains!

Home looked good to the children and they were happy as can be. They had their playroom, television and friends. Barbara Johnson was thrilled we were home so soon and invited all five of us out to their home for a July 4th barbecue and swim party, saying lots of people would be there.

This is a blow-by-blow account of the evening as I remember it. We arrived and the first person I saw at the party was Mrs. Iris Chapman, Dale's mother. She had come with Dale. Mrs. Chapman was sitting on the sofa and smiled so big at me and motioned for me to sit on the sofa beside her. We chatted for

CHOOSING A LOVE THAT WILL LAST

awhile, everyone wanting to know about our trip.

Most of the guests were outside around the pool and some were in the pool. After eating, more of us went for a swim.

Everyone was having a good time and ducking each other. I remember Dale coming over and ducking me. Let me say that is not one of my favorite things. I never learned to hold my breath under water, and I sort of sputtered but didn't say much. Everyone was in a jovial mood. All of a sudden I saw Barbara with a camera, and she took a snapshot just as I surfaced spewing and gasping.

Later I heard that Dale's mother told him, "Glory is adorable."

CHAPTER 23

THE GREAT DEBATE

The next day, Dale called to apologize for dunking me in the pool and asked if we could go out to dinner. We went to the Executive Club. We talked about the trip to Colorado, my children and his children. He told me he was busy building a Christian book store in El Centro Mall. It was supposed to open around the first part of August. Previously, Dale had a small chain of bookstores in the east. He said some of his most rewarding ministry has been through the Christian bookstores, as well as teaching, which he loves.

Dale was pretty down, I could see, from the divorce and problems he faced. It kept coming to me that if I couldn't help someone through their difficulties, how would the Lord help me through mine. There were many inner struggles.

Dale was very intelligent and said many things which helped me, but back in the back of my mind, I wondered why he couldn't heal his own marriage. The pharisaical part of me said, *Physician heal thyself.* I believe that is what was said to Jesus as He hung there dying on the cross for all mankind. What bad timing that poor soul used, and I used. Remember when someone is in extreme pain or suffering, only love should be administered.

Also, Dale kept saying that he was usually such a strong person. I thought, *He thinks that's strong?* Moreover, going with a divorced man, any divorced man, wasn't in my plans. However, I began dating one because I knew I needed to learn and mature as much as possible. Dale was an excellent teacher and he didn't hesitate to tell me when my thinking wasn't right. In fact, as we saw each other more and more, we began to have many heavy discussions, later developing into debates, especially on the topic of how to find God's will. That was the doozy!

CHOOSING A LOVE THAT WILL LAST

Between Barbara and him, I read probably six to eight books on the subject. He wasn't timid about telling me he didn't think I knew how to find God's will. One time it would be my stubbornness that was perhaps in the way. Another time it would be my hardheadedness. This would go on when we were out together, and many of our phone conversations were heated discussions on various topics. I found this stimulating.

I might add, there was no loss of words on my part either to point out some of his shortcomings. We were very open and brutally honest with each other. Why not lay all the cards on the table? What did we have to lose? Were we not learning much about ourselves?

Gradually, I started calling Dale, *Chappy* because he said that Chappy was his dad's nickname. It seemed to fit him better than Dale, though he didn't much like me changing his name.

Then one day, Barbara came to my office and gave me these words.

"I have a plan for a new lifestyle for you. Parts of this plan are as though you have been planning all your life, but never quite achieved, and yet other parts will be brand new to you.

"If you had a nine-to-five job and a career of your own, you would have known a certain amount of success, but I have not planned for you to have this type of success.

"In fact, if you had yielded to me at the beginning of your life, you would have amounted to a certain stardom by now.

"However, in the twinkling of an eye a new career will come zooming in upon you. If you had fallen on your face at first, it would have been better. The Lord would have rebuilt your life earlier.

"From the course you have taken from your youth, this is the proper time, and the Lord is going to build a new life, a new career in a sense, and a new household.

"There will be many folds and stresses that will wrinkle your brow at times, because the field will be new to you so that you will have to walk by faith rather than from your past experience.

"I am a dependable business partner. I am a dependable partner in all areas of your undertaking. If you will depend upon me and seek me and continue to seek me, you will find the unfolding of these opportunities."

The first part of this message made me feel extremely sad because I had missed God's direction and choice early in my life. As to a new career, there was no way I could interpret that. Its meaning was obscure to me. There was nothing to do but wait for its unfolding.

Then in mid-summer, this encouraging word came through Barbara.

"I have the authority and I can shut the mouths of the evil gossipers and the gainsayers. The tongue is such a small instrument but has such power to do evil. It can be so cruel and can be used to put lashes on the back. It can cause channels and divisions in the body. Also, it can be used for great comfort and can speak the mighty works of God and consolation to those in need.

"If you will let me control your tongue and speak only that which is good, that which is kind and comforting, I will bless you in many ways. I will bless you in many areas of your life if you will let me control your tongue all the time.

"I am going to shut their mouths and not only that but change their attitudes. You will see the ones that have caused division and laid the whip-lashes on the backs, and their attitudes will be changed."

On August 17, I received an unsigned postcard with the word, *LOVE* written real big across it. I learned later it was from Jason and it upset me.

The next day my accomplished longtime friend, Florence Veale, and I flew to Dallas to hear Kathryn Kuhlman speak. We had read and heard a lot about her, so we decided to go and hear her for ourselves.

Florence is my friend who drops by at the needed moments, and says and does the right things. This happens so often that at one time I thought she must have a peephole into my heart. She rescued me more than once.

The Kathryn Kuhlman meeting was unusual. Minutes before Mrs. Kuhlman entered the stage, the air was electrified--dead silence--but you sensed a holy atmosphere in the big ballroom auditorium. I never felt this before or since, but I started weeping. Many people were helped and some healed.

However, one of the saddest and most heartbreaking things to see was the look of total hopelessness on the faces of those who were on stretchers and in wheelchairs. This was their last chance and they weren't healed. At the end of each service before Kathryn left the auditorium, she repeated how distressing it was for her to see those people disappointed. She said that it was going to be her very first question when she got to heaven, "Why was not everyone healed?" Kathryn went on to state that many times some agnostic or unbeliever would receive healing while some who were considered pillars of the church and saints were not. It was all a mystery to her, she explained.

It seems to me that divorce and healing are somewhat similar in that some marriages and bodies are healed while others are not. It is indeed a dilemma!

Barbara called me near Labor Day and said,

"Last year's avenues were closed and barricaded to you and the traffic stopped. There was a detour. This year's avenues are open and the traffic will flow. Last year's jokes were this year's miseries. There will be joy this year. Do not turn your face into your pillow and cry anymore. There will be joy. Do not fear."

Barbara added these words of her own. "You are going to win out. I see you with a garland of flowers around your neck like the winning horse!"

Three weeks later at a meeting at Barbara's home, Gayle Gardner told me not to make any hasty decisions concerning big matters in my life.

On a Monday late in September, these words were given to me by Barbara.

"There is going to be a new stream of thought going through you. I am going to show you a new way out of these difficulties.

"Do not rush. It is a process to slow down this journey. Do not go headlong into anything. This road goes up and arches over into a stream and then onto many different experiences and will meet many other lives. There will be new streams and new avenues."

In the meantime, Chappy and I were spending more time together, getting to know more about each other, our values and goals. He was getting acquainted with my children, spending time with them, listening to their concerns and taking Tommy (only boy at home) fishing and throwing the ball. Only then did he ask me to marry him. He seemed very sure, but I told him I was waiting for God to give me His choice. It was God's choice--not mine to make. Up to this point, it seemed I hadn't received a clue as to whom I should marry, or if I should remarry. Of course, Chappy thought I was whistling in the dark and should make my own decision after prayer. He found this pact I had made with God a bit uncommon.

In November, Jennie Sirmons told me after church, "Do you remember one Sunday morning before your trip to Colorado you came up and kissed me?"

"No," I said. She continued, "When you did that I knew your mourning days were over. That it wouldn't be long."

After Thanksgiving, Martin Hirshberger gave me the following words from the Lord when I was at another meeting at Barbara and Harry's home. Chappy was not with me for some reason.

"My daughter, do not think of the hurts any longer. Do not look back as I have healed the hurts. Do not look back or you could fall into another trap.

"I would speak to you from *within* yourself. Even in the presumption of your own mind or your own way, I have led you to teach you. Some people will tell you one thing and others another thing, but I am going to lead you from *within* and you will know clearly what I have for you."

CHOOSING A LOVE THAT WILL LAST

Martin added, "You have been in much frustration and it's hard to find God's leading in frustration. Therefore, wait for the Lord and when your frustration ends, you will know what you are to do. IN PEACE THE LORD SHALL DIRECT YOU."

Barbara spoke the only words that came to her.

"Do not worry about a thing."

She also added that she saw a pearl necklace and a blank space at the end, indicating the need for some more time. Pearls represent wisdom and knowledge. He was teaching me more.

"Man is so made that he can carry the weight of 24 hours--no more... I have promised to help you with the burden of today only, the past I have taken from you and if you choose to gather again that burden and bear it, then, indeed, you mock Me to expect Me to share it. A man on a march on earth carries only what he needs for that march. Would you pity him if you saw him bearing too the overwhelming weight of the worn out shoes and uniforms of past marches and years? And yet, in the mental and spiritual life, man does these things. Small wonder My poor world is heartsick and weary."[1]

It was close to Christmas when in my home around the den game table, Barbara gave me these words.

"For I have broken the outer shell of your being, beneath the circumstances, beneath the people involved and all other aspects of your life. I am the One who broke the outer surface of your being.

"Not that they may look upon it to say, 'Isn't that ugly and look what happened to her, or how strange that it should be like that,' but I smashed you that the life that is within might ooze, seep and pour, even vaporize out to others. As a broken pitcher that has been smashed, I have put all the pieces back together. It is a thing of beauty, except there is one piece missing. Like people poking or putting their finger in the hole and picking at it or seeing the missing piece of your life and wondering at the incompletion and at the missing part.

"Your vessel is a thing of beauty, not like a lot of cheap brass pitchers coming off an assembly line. I have put each piece back together and there are many crevices, cracks and fissures, but I am going to give it a high polish and complete it. This broken pitcher will be a thing of beauty and will pour out to others."

Those words were unusual, but at the same time they did express how I felt. I felt incomplete. One of the main things on my mind was how to discipline the children. I was not equal to exerting much authority over the two oldest children. I needed someone loving and strong to head up our home. In my experience, I have never seen a woman who could adequately take a man's place in disciplining and rearing children, especially teenagers. I knew in my spirit someone was coming, but I didn't know *what* person. Instructions given me were that I was to quit trying to figure it out, wait and rest. Sounds simple, right? NO!

No doubt there are countless people walking around looking fairly normal and healthy physically while their spirit is truly almost lifeless. Perhaps that is what is meant when someone says, "I am not living. I am only existing." A part is missing, an obscure part, a part that is not easily understood or studied very much, a part that sometimes is not given much attention--the spirit part of us.

We can be fully developed in one area, only to be lacking in another. As adults, we need to be a total, complete and mature person in all three parts: body, mind and spirit.

"Spiritual maturity is sharing the affections of God and discerning His voice. **It is loving what God loves and hating what He hates.**"[2]

But if we have an affluent lifestyle, friends and achievement, it is easy to overlook the hidden silent gnawing inside. Also, it is quieted temporarily with things and busyness of everyday life.

"God's ways are as mysterious as the pathway of the wind, and as the manner in which a human spirit is infused into the little body of a baby while it is yet in its mother's womb." Ecc. 11:5.

CHOOSING A LOVE THAT WILL LAST

"Be *still* and know that I am God." Psalms 46:10 KJV.

In many of the words given me, I notice much admonition is given concerning my frustration, my contemplating the different alternatives and my struggling. I discovered that hearing from God was not baby work. It was mature hard work.

THIS SEARCH IS LEADING DOWN UNPREDICTABLE PATHS, BUT I AM LEARNING TO TRUST MY TEACHER MORE AND MORE!

GLORY CHAPMAN

CHAPTER 24

A KNIGHT

Approximately four years from the time the first words were spoken, Barbara turned to me while sitting on the sofa in the den and said, "I am afraid to say it, but this is what the Lord has to say today." My mood was somewhat somber.

"Glory, I have found the man who pleases us both the most. I have found him not to be faultless, but to be perfectly pleasing to my eyes because he tries to be led of my spirit in all things. I have found him to be a good student of my spirit, to be teachable and to be flexible and malleable to my touch. I have found him to be honest, true and loyal, not only to me, but to you also.

"I have made him available to you at your disposal for much learning, for pleasurable moments of companionship and as a teacher in the kingdom things of God. The love light or light of his eyes is for you, and do I condemn him for this? No, I will not condemn him for this. God placed him at your feet. I have put him at your disposal and he is like a knight that God has knighted and here is his princess.

"Continue in his love and make plans for the future if you desire for surely I will bless this house, and I will bless you out of the abundance of my heart for it will be a true treasure house where I will reign supreme and much happiness will flow from here, saith the Lord."

I had tears streaming down both my cheeks. I knew who the Lord was speaking about. It was Chappy. My own preconceived notion would be if God was in the two of us getting married, why didn't he make everyone else assent to it as well. Why was my family so opposed and vehement about me marrying a divorced man with three girls? Their feelings were much like mine in the beginning--why couldn't two Christians work their marriage out?

CHOOSING A LOVE THAT WILL LAST

Was it possible to be persecuted within a Christian family?

Then the thought of Mary, the mother of Jesus, came to my mind, along with Moses, David and others. It seemed I was still clinging to my age-old theory of bad things or opposition doesn't happen if you are following God's will.

The memory of James and Peter, the disciples, flashed into my mind. Were not both of them imprisoned about the same time? Yes, but not both of them were delivered. Peter was released in answer to prayer, but they took James out and killed him with a sword. Acts 12. Did they not pray for James also? Did James' wife feel let down? Why were they both not spared? Stephen was not kept from being stoned to death while he preached under the anointing of the Holy Spirit. Was he not in the center of God's will?

But what about Psalms 91:7 which says, "A thousand may fall at your side, ten thousand at your right hand, but it will not come near you." Verse 11. "For he will command his angels concerning you to guard you in all your ways."

What I missed and didn't discern at the time was the angels do take charge, whether their orders are to give us longer life in this world or to take us home to heaven. There has to be a time to die. Also, God uses his sovereign judgment, knowing the present, past and future of our lives. Death presents no fear for me anymore. If in this life we are working to reach that beautiful other life, then why are we resisting so? The book, *Angels On Assignment* by Frances and Charles Hunter, changed my whole concept of what heaven is like.

I didn't mention to Chappy this last prophetic word given to me. There still was no way that I had the knowing *inside* me yet. In fact, I was still very frustrated concerning marriage to anyone at this point. It all seemed too complicated. Marriage is practically impossible with just your husband and own children. What about Chappy's three girls, how would they feel, plus all the problems that would be involved with ex-mates?

The last thing in the world I ever wanted to be was a *step* mother. It was always such a dreaded word to me. When have you ever read, seen a movie or play about a wonderful, loving stepmother? Oh yes, *Sound of Music* is possibly the only one. At my age, did I think marriage was only possible to someone who had never been married? That was highly unlikely, and then wouldn't he be a stepfather?

My dear next door neighbor for 15 years, Arlene Seibring, often commented to me (before my divorce) how in the world did people divorce, remarry and merge two sets of children, expressing life was so tedious with just the original set. I couldn't imagine either how it would all ever work out.

In fact, in McAllen, there was a family in this situation that we both knew. Jack and Ann Thomason tried very hard to get his and her children to like each other. It didn't work so they tried letting his children live in one house and hers in another several blocks away. The parents rotated between the two homes. Even that failed and eventually while still caring a great deal about one another, they divorced. It was just too much to cope with.

Over the years since my divorce, several people have asked why I was waiting to get married. I explained that marriage was serious and was my last chance at happiness. There can be no mistake this time, especially now with so many children. It is going to take a miracle!

Chappy and I were seeing a lot of each other, and the kids and I often had him over for dinner in the evenings. Tom and Lori especially loved him. He would ride them piggyback throughout the house. They had known little male attention and they were loving it.

Chappy was so good with all of them, particularly in discussing anything they had on their minds. He was a good listener, very caring and unselfish. One thing stood out about him and that was his deep capacity for love. I observed this often. Some men may want to love deeply, but their capacity is small.

Discussions between Chappy and me ended up being repercussions many times. It seemed his teaching, my reading and other helps had not produced enough knowledge for me to know God's will for my life yet. Sometimes it appeared he understood my honesty and quest to know, but at other times he was doubtful as to my ability to hear and receive an answer. He even told me once in exasperation (or perhaps in total honesty), "You are not the prettiest girl I have ever seen." I was crestfallen, not because I wasn't the most beautiful girl in the world but I thought he should think so anyway. You know, through eyes of love. However, he quickly added, "It's the real you that I love--your spirit." He added that perhaps I was in the top ten in beauty as well. He said he was impressed with my intelligence--at times. But to have been a Christian for so many years, surely I should have been able to discover God's will by now.

A few weeks later this word was delivered by Barbara.

"You are going to have a meeting with someone, and when this meeting takes place she will feel like a steamroller has run over her. But the Lord says, 'Don't let that concern you because she will recover. Let God speak through you and use you however you feel led by the Spirit.' You will see her reaction is like she has been steamrolled. It is all right and God will lift her up again. It's in the Lord's will because He has to do something strong.

"There will be an unpleasant part that will have to be shared and differing views will come out. It might seem harsh, but still God is in all this. Like a meat grinder and dough coming out all ground up. It is going into a loaf of bread. Just leave the results to God. It is going to be good."

Within minutes of three days' time, I received a phone call from a friend whom I had loved for many years, whom I will call Stephanie Davis. She called to apologize for the things she had said about Chappy and me. We talked awhile and to this day, I can't remember the entire conversation (not in my notes), or all that was said. Anyway, she hung up.

In about ten minutes she called back, and I could tell she was completely steamrolled and had been crying. However, the word given about someone being steamrolled still didn't come to my mind. She was upset but very sweet and reconciliatory and said she wanted to apologize for her daughter also, to which I replied, "No, don't. Only she can do that. Leave it alone, and the Holy Spirit can impress upon her whatever she needs to do about her part." I told her how very much she had meant to me over the years and that I loved her, her husband and daughters very much.

As I am now typing and going over these words with a closer look than I have for 19 years, some are amazing as to the fulfillment and the clarity I see from a retrospective viewpoint.

MY KNIGHT WAS WAITING!

CHOOSING A LOVE THAT WILL LAST

CHAPTER 25

OUR LAST SUPPER

On May 8, late at night, Barbara called and had these words for me.

"The only word I have is by the middle of the month your heaviness of heart will be lifting, and by the end of the month you will be dancing and happy."

Almost immediately after receiving these words, Chappy had had it with me, my indecision, and my not knowing in the least what I thought God's will was. There seemed to be no encouragement, and he even blurted out, "I don't think you know how to find God's will and you never will. I can just see you at age 80 rocking in a little rocking chair (he pantomimed it out, using a high-pitched voice) still saying, 'I don't know. I am still waiting on God.' If you don't know now, you never will and I want out. I can't take it any longer, and when I back out, I back out, not to change my mind."

He was right. It had been too long and I still didn't know. I defended by saying, "Do you want me to pretend I have an answer when I don't?" Of course, he said he didn't, indicating that I might be incapable of receiving an answer because I was probably expecting God to write the answer in big neon letters in the sky, and that God doesn't do that.

Repeatedly, I kept reassuring him that I was open to any method God might choose. Surely by whatever method I would receive the message, I would have the *knowing* beyond any doubt. Those few words carried a big emphasis on the word *knowing within* myself.

Fine to advise and counsel others as to whom they should marry, but quite another matter to be the *one* to have to live out all those 50 or more years. It is very dangerous, I believe, to do much of this sort of counseling. Unless the persons involved have the knowing, I doubt if your having it for them will abolish their doubts and indecision, enabling them to live with each other in all the years to follow.

A good motto in any situation is--if in doubt, don't. Chappy has said that the meaning of love for him is being unable to live without that person. Otherwise, do not marry.

Well, it was the first part of May and we were breaking up. That didn't seem to make my heart happy nor did I dance as was in the word given to me. Very quickly, I had to review my covenant with God and my relationship with Chappy. My conclusion was I had gone too far now to abandon my agreement with God and go off on my own when I could possibly be so close to the real thing. The counterfeit often comes just before the real. Also, God would know what a person would be like in 20 and 30 years. He could see every day for the rest of my life. I would trust His judgment--veto mine.

We agreed to part as friends. There was no need to be enemies and he wished me much happiness and love. That same week, we went out to dinner. We called it *Our Last Supper*. We went to the Executive Club again and sat in the back against the brick wall at a table for two. I had little to say. The thought I might truly be an old woman in a rocking chair at age 80 still saying, "I am waiting for God," did indeed terrify me, but not enough to give up waiting for Him. I was sort of numb, filled with fear, realizing no one I knew had done it this way. "Should I obey God or man?" kept running by me, too. Some of my family were very vociferous (to put it mildly), and it seemed a dozen voices clambered within me.

"You have no answer until you receive a genuine answer," held me firmly together in spite of all the outer happenings. I look back and realize God gave me this kind of faith when I needed it. I had given Him carte blanche for all my major decisions. They actually were not mine to make anymore inasmuch as I had given that right away. **If marriage was His best, then He would**

CHOOSING A LOVE THAT WILL LAST

choose a love that would last. In that sense, I felt peaceful, though numb. That's the nearest I can describe my feelings at that particular time.

As I said, our last supper ended with each wishing the other the best.

SOMETIMES SEARCHING HURTS!

CHAPTER 26

A REAL ANGEL

The next days were filled with long and good thoughts about our relationship, and how much I had learned and appreciated about Chappy. It was tough but I held my feelings in check. Giving my heart away again without knowing the person to be chosen would be disastrous for me emotionally. It's not to say my emotions didn't become involved, but I managed to keep a tight rein on them.

Ten days later while sitting in church with the children, Brother Oliviero from Waco, Texas, the speaker for the morning service, asked anyone with needs to come forward and stand for prayer.

There were about 15 who went forward, and I was one of them. I stood there, but didn't say or pray one word. In a loud, clear distinct voice, Brother Oliviero said, "God says to give up your preconceived ideas. Give up your preconceived ideas." No one needed to tell me, I knew those words were meant for me. I don't know how I knew, but they were unmistakably meant for me. However, I honestly couldn't put my finger on just what preconceived ideas I had that should be given up. I was much too close to the forest to see the trees. Change is impossible without the knowledge of what it is that needs to be changed.

In a few moments everyone filed out of the church and left.

The church is about eight blocks from my home, and as the children and I backed out of the parking lot and headed north, an angel, a real live angel, came near and just above my car and said these inaudible words to me, "Today you will tell him." I knew immediately who and what that meant.

Let me explain, the angel wasn't visible to my natural eyes, but most clearly seen with the eyes of my spirit. Don't ask me to explain how that works. I just know that it does. I saw the angel

CHOOSING A LOVE THAT WILL LAST

so clearly and there was only one. Like Dwight L. Moody described his angel visitation, "It was the loudest silent voice I ever heard." God's voice is not always expressed in words. Sometimes it is made known as a heart-consciousness.

To me, the angel's voice wasn't coercive or demanding. It was as if this was the perfect time, and I knew exactly who and what it meant. There was no need for further instructions. Spirit to spirit operates without sound, as I have said before.

Have you ever had a SUDDENLY happen to you? Somehow after waiting for five years, this seemed too sudden for me, and I pleaded with the angel to please give me one week; that I was tired and I needed to talk to the children. Very frankly, I was catatonic and emotionally exhausted. I had just that week told Olma and R. T. Sparks, neighbors down the street who stopped by the front yard to chat, that I had decided that I wasn't ever going to remarry. It was entirely too chancy.

First, I was awed (I guess that's the right word) that God would send an angel with the answer. In fact, I was completely blown away by what the angel told me to do, and it had to be done that day. It was all so sudden--like a thunderbolt. I thought I was open to any method God might choose to come, but AN ANGEL? I never guessed an angel would deliver the answer. NEVER! I was in shock and speechless. Maybe it could be described by saying I was in awe and amazement like those people who saw Jesus heal the blind man. This stunned me because of what the angel told me to do, "Today you will tell him," and the day was half over already.

Being such a slow deliberate person, it was shocking to have to act so fast. The children of Israel, who had been slaves in Egypt for 70 years and wanted to leave, prayed they would be liberated, but when Moses told them they were leaving at midnight *that* night, it was too *suddenly* for them.

We pray and think we believe and yet when the answer comes, we are truly shocked. Reminds me of the people praying for Peter's release from prison, and when he knocked on the door of his home, they said that it couldn't be Peter. He was in prison. We are too human and so little divine.

Some asked me later about what the angel looked like, or if I quizzed him. I was far too caught up with the SUDDENLY to think to ask questions.

No matter. The angel proceeded to go along as the car moved without another word said.

When we reached home, I fixed lunch for the children and afterwards quickly went into my bedroom to rest. I was bone tired physically and emotionally. The angel stayed, saying nothing, but I was conscious of his presence. Probably an hour later the phone rang and it was Chappy. He asked if he could come over and get his bike. We were returning the gifts we had given each other. I had given him a bike for Christmas, and he had given me one. Both were at my home.

About an hour later Chappy came over, and asked me, "Have you decided what you are going to do?" I replied, "Yes." He rather reluctantly inquired if I was going to marry someone else, to which I suggested, "Let's take a drive."

Knowing that I must tell him today, I wanted a minute to plan what I would say and how. Certainly I didn't want it to be in my little office at the house since we had fought over so many subjects there. It should be an appropriate setting--quiet, peaceful and romantic. It was May 18 and a very hot, humid day in the Lower Rio Grande Valley. Where in the world could I find a cool place at 4 p.m.?

Not knowing where we were headed when we started out, Chappy asked, "Where are we going?"

"Just drive south on Tenth," I said. When we approached Highway 83, I asked him to turn right, still not knowing where a good place would be.

"Ah, I know where we are going. We are headed to the La Posada Coffee Shop," Chap exclaimed knowingly.

When we reached that intersection, "I said to just keep going west." I was mysterious and secretive.

CHOOSING A LOVE THAT WILL LAST

Probably a half a mile later, with the angel following closely overhead, I thought about the *Valley Botanical Gardens*. It was a beautiful palm-lined drive with many tropical plants lining a big canal full of water. It was a passable setting. It wasn't cool, but the slight lazy breeze made the heat bearable at that time of day.

Never shall I forget Chappy's old green car turning in through the gates and the angel right up with us. After parking, we found a semiprivate spot of grass near some mesquite trees. Chappy got out and laid on the ground face-up toward the sky, and I was sitting on my legs on the ground facing him. He knew I was going to say something, but he had no idea what.

At this time, I didn't mention the angel. I had been busy rehearsing to myself what I would say at this most important time. Something to preface all our good times together, then about this angel and other loving and heartfelt words.

When I leaned over closer to tell him, I found these words tumbling out of me, shocking even myself, "I am going to marry *you*." Oh no, that ruins it, so curt and matter of fact, I thought.

Chappy turned as white as his guayabera shirt--as if I had hit him in the face. His reaction surprised me. He just lay there, not saying a word for about five full minutes. I was thinking, *No matter, if this is of God, it will be all right.*

As soon as I said those words, "I am going to marry you," the angel disappeared and was gone. He came about 12:15 pm and it was 4:30 by now. It was incredible that the angel would have stayed that long. Perhaps he was given the mission with instructions not to return until he knew it was completed.

Incidentally, or not so incidentally, there are millions of angels who do nothing but God's bidding. They are God's workforce. There are also many different classifications of angels mentioned in the Bible--worship, death, messenger, ministering, destroying and warrior angels.

Finally, Chappy found his voice, enough to murmur weakly, "I don't know. I will have to think about it." That sobered me somewhat.

Of course, I told him that he could have all the time he wanted. He took me home, saying I would hear from him later. I did take special note that he didn't take his bike with him!

Sunday night passed, all day Monday, Monday night and all day Tuesday. On Tuesday evening, Chappy called to see if he could come over.

Meanwhile on Monday, Barbara came over and spent several hours. I teased her a bit first, "Barb, guess what happened yesterday?" I had her keep guessing until she could guess no more. Since she and Chappy had chided me on how the answer would come, I wanted her to guess every possible method till she couldn't. After enough torture, I related to her about the angel and what I had told Chappy and his great comment, "I don't know. I will have to think about it."

Barbara was wearing slacks and she let out a war whoop and did a half somersault onto the bed. Her emotions run true. If she is sad, she cries and if a long awaited answer arrives, she goes bananas. We laughed and danced for joy. She was so totally happy and relieved. Barbara's track record on God was building too.

Very early on that same Sunday this is what happened to Chappy, which he shared with me later. As he was leaving his apartment to go to church (not mine), the words came to him very clearly, "Today I am going to change the course of your life." There was no angel, only these words. He had no idea what those words meant.

I was calmer than calm although the days passed very slowly from Sunday to Tuesday evening. God and I were talking pretty close. Under my breath, I kept confessing, *If this is your number one choice, then nothing can stop it. Also, if I have in any way misinterpreted what is happening, then you are still in control, whichever way it goes.*

Chappy eventually got around to saying he believed that he and God would say, "Yes." But I could sense some reservations of his own. Remember I didn't tell him what changed my mind. It

CHOOSING A LOVE THAT WILL LAST

was months before I told him of the angel's visitation. I don't know why I waited to tell him. Maybe because he wouldn't believe a real angel came just for me. It was very sacred to me. It still is and I hesitate to tell it for fear it will be misunderstood. Anything unknown, unfamiliar and beyond our experience can create weird remarks.

For instance, calculus terrifies me because I am unfamiliar with its mathematical symbols. I might make a lot of stupid remarks because of my ignorance. Calculus remains undisputed. I am the one lost to its operation. When I first began to learn about the computer, everything about its criterions were foreign to me and I asked many elementary and dumb questions.

Sheldon Vanauken in *A Severe Mercy* says, "Most of the people who reject Christianity know almost nothing of what they are rejecting: those who condemn what they do not understand are, surely, little men."[1]

Will Rogers said, "We are all ignorant, but in different subjects."[2]

May 18 will always be special to me, very special. PERHAPS IT WAS AT THAT MOMENT I KNEW OF WHAT MARTYRS WERE MADE. It is when you know that you know that you know within yourself, that you are ready to die for that truth. It is the most secure position that I have ever experienced. A security beyond reason--beyond intellectual reasoning.

Whether we live on earth or in heaven--it makes little difference. It's all gain either way. I like what Elisabeth Elliot had to say in *The Savage My Kinsman*. Someone asked her, "Aren't you afraid to take your little blonde daughter, Valerie, back into the Auca Indian territory in Ecuador?"[3] Earlier the Aucas had murdered her husband along with four other missionaries. She answered that it made no difference from where she left this world to enter the next. Her part was to follow where He led her. It was in God's hands, not hers. However, it was doubly hard for Chappy to make this decision, knowing how indecisive I had been. He wondered what brought about the change, and would it last.

"I wanted to make it as hard on God and as easy as possible on myself," the words of Harald Bredesen. He explains that if nothing is too hard for God, then relax and let him prove it. God even invites us to take a turn at proving him. Harald is the one who also gives his *tool kit* to everyone he meets. If they aren't ready or interested in God now, Harald gives them the kit which contains information as to how to reach God when their time of emergency or crisis comes.

Well, this search had produced more than I ever dreamed--a real live angelic visitation with the answer I had waited for for so long. I was astounded and overcome by God's personal interest in my affairs. Not in my wildest dreams did I ever guess he would use a messenger angel. It was a very humbling and life changing experience.

This is the way God chose to help me this time. However, we have no say as to how God does things. His ways are not our ways. God seldom does anything the same way twice. He is so creative and unlimited. In healing people, I notice in Scripture Jesus used various methods--touch, spittle, word, called evil spirits to come out, forgave their sin first and then healed them.

MY SEARCH HAS ME AWESTRUCK!

CHOOSING A LOVE THAT WILL LAST

CHAPTER 27

SPECIAL GIFTS

Usually at some time or another there comes into every life some crisis too heavy to bear alone. It is at those times we need private duty nursing to assist us back to health, whether it be physical, mental or spiritual.

Looking back, I see how very fortunate I was to have a friend like Barbara. She listened to me for hours on end. I used her as my lifeline. She was one of several friends who contributed toward my well being. The gifts God gave Barbara; words of wisdom, words of knowledge and prophecy, are to be used as beautiful gifts to encourage, comfort and teach others. These gifts are not to be underestimated. They bring hope, life and faith, and those were the gifts she gave to me.

Since that time, I have taken people out to Barbara's home whenever they came to me in desperate need, and I was unable to speak words to help them. Some seemed to revive under our very eyes when the Word of the Lord was given. We witnessed the buoying up of their spirits immediately. Words spoken through her were life giving. The whole chapter 12 of I Corinthians talks about these special gifts that the Holy Spirit gives to believers, dividing to every man severally as God wills: the word of wisdom, word of knowledge, faith, gifts of healing, working of miracles, prophecy, discerning of spirits, diverse (unlearned languages) tongues and interpretation of tongues.

Jesus told his disciples, "Oh, there is so much more I want to tell you, but you can't understand it now. When the Holy Spirit, who is truth, comes, he shall guide you into all truth---he will tell you about the future." John 16:12,13. The Holy Spirit is the third PERSON of the Trinity, who lives in us when we invite Him in.

"Touch not these chosen ones of mine, he (God) warned, and do not hurt my prophets." Psalms 135:6.

The gifts of the Holy Spirit as listed above are not to be confused with mediums, channelers, fortunetellers, soothsayers or necromancers, which are spoken of often in Scripture as being evil and counterfeit. God dispenses His Holy Spirit to His believers, and the devil gives his evil unholy spirit to his followers.

"There are two equal and opposite errors into which our race can fall about the devils. One is to disbelieve in their existence. The other is to believe, and to feel an excessive and unhealthy interest in them."[1]

It is comforting to know that the devil is not omnipresent (present everywhere), omnipotent (having unlimited or universal power and authority), nor is he omniscient (having total knowledge; knowing everything). Remember the devil can only be present at one place at a time, but he does have his demons tormenting, forcing, afflicting, possessing, demonizing, oppressing and depressing a person.

Regardless, Satan will never give up trying to vie with God for power, worship and dominion until he is finally put into a bottomless pit by Michael the arch angel upon instructions from God. In the end, God and good wins out. However, before Lucifer was cast down to earth, (Isaiah 14:5 and Revelations 12:9) he was so persuasive that he convinced one-third of the worship angels in heaven to leave with him. I wonder if those fallen angels would make that same choice again. It says in Jude 1:6 KJV that these fallen angels are reserved in everlasting chains under darkness unto the judgment of the great day." That prompts the thought, then from where do evil spirits come?

C. S. Lewis says in *Mere Christianity*, "Some people think the fall of man had something to do with sex, but that is a mistake. What Satan put into the heads of our remote ancestors was the idea that they could be like God, could set up on their own as if they had created themselves--be their own masters--invent some

CHOOSING A LOVE THAT WILL LAST

sort of happiness for themselves outside God, apart from God. And out of that hopeless attempt has come nearly all that we call human history, money, poverty, ambition, war, prostitution, classes, empires, slavery--the long terrible story of MAN TRYING TO FIND SOMETHING OTHER THAN GOD WHICH WILL MAKE HIM HAPPY. The reason why it can never succeed is this. God made us: invented us as a man invents a machine. A car is made to run on gasoline and it would not run properly on anything else. Now God designed the human machine to run on himself. He, himself, is the fuel our spirits were designed to burn, or the food our spirits were designed to feed on. There is no other. There is no true or lasting happiness apart from God."[1] Sound familiar these days? It's the same old rebellion with a new name, THE NEW AGE.

The war is still on--God from heaven and the devil from the earth. God is the original and true while Satan is the fallen and the false. God has his followers as does Satan. The devil is not a leader; he is a driver. He seeks to *control* our will. God, however, doesn't take over our will and drive us beyond our control. He may give motivation, but that is much different than compulsion. God calls us to exercise our own will to do His will. It's a choice. Satan is our adversary--adverse to our best interest. Many people are trapped in habits and activities that are killing them, but they are controlled by some force beyond themselves.

Of course, we are subject to the devil's subtle persuasion, especially in the weak areas of our life. Some people aren't aware that the devil has power. He does, but not as much as God. For instance, when Moses went to the Pharoah 17 times to request permission for the Hebrew people to leave Egypt, the magicians could do the miracles that Moses did, but only the first three. After that Satan couldn't compete.

It is imperative that we know the Scriptures so as not to be duped, and to know the difference between the two kingdoms. This is how clever Satan is. Throughout the Bible, God is referred to as the light of the world, and His kingdom is light.

John 8:12. In trying to appear as God, Satan masquerades as an angel of light, and his kingdom is always referred to as dark. II Cor. 11:14 NIV. An unlearned man may not know the difference. We are to study the Scriptures and know what they say. There was a time when God winked at ignorance, but not anymore. Acts 17:30 KJV.

In this connection, just a bit of information about IDOLS and things of the OCCULT. This seems to be a big area in which many, even Christians, are uninformed. The following are several scripture passages that I have found that address idols and the occult.

"You must never worship any other god, nor ever have an idol in your home." Psalms 81:9.

"Can your idol make such claims as these? Let them come and show what they can do!" says God, the King of Israel. "Let them try to tell us what occurred in years gone by, or what the future holds." Isaiah 41:21,22. Verse 24 says, "But no! You are less than nothing, and can do nothing at all. Anyone who chooses you needs to have his head examined!"

"Don't act like the people who make horoscopes and try to read their fate and future in the stars! Don't be frightened by predictions such as theirs, for it is all a pack of lies. Their ways are futile and foolish. They cut down a tree and carve an idol, and decorate it with gold and silver and fasten it securely in place with hammer and nails, so that it won't fall over, and there stands their god like a helpless scarecrow in a garden! It cannot speak, and it must be carried, for it cannot walk." Jeremiah 10:2-5.

"A sorceress shall be put to death." Exodus 22:18.

"You have advisors by the ton--your astrologers and stargazers, who try to tell you what the future holds. But they are as useless as dried grass burning in the fire." Isaiah 47:13,14.

"You are like an unfaithful wife who loves her husband's enemies. Don't you realize that making friends with God's enemies--makes you an enemy of God?" James 4:4.

"Burn their idols and do not touch the silver or gold they are

CHOOSING A LOVE THAT WILL LAST

made of. Do not take it, or it will be a snare to you, for it is horrible to the Lord your God. Do not bring an idol into your home and worship it, for then your doom is sealed. Utterly detest it, for it is a cursed thing." Deuteronomy 7:25,26.

"No Israeli may practice black magic, or call on the evil spirits for aid, or be a fortune teller, or be a serpent charmer, medium, or wizard, or call forth the spirits of the dead. Anyone doing these things is an object of horror and disgust to the Lord, and it is because the nations do these things that the Lord your God will displace them." Deuteronomy 18:10,11.

"He will send tuberculosis, fever, infections, plague, and war. He will blight your crops, covering them with mildew." Deuteronomy 28:22.

"He will send upon you Egyptian boils, tumors, scurvy, and itch, for none of which will there be a remedy. He will send madness, blindness, fear and panic upon you." Deuteronomy 28:27,28.

Remember in chapters 31 and 35 of Genesis that Rachel was cursed because she sat on some idols taken from her father's tent. She died two months later in childbirth when Benjamin was born.

When I first knew Chappy, he asked me if I had anything of the occult (representative of other gods) in my home. I didn't think so, but upon a closer look I found a horoscope on "Sagittarius," a book, *A Gift of Prophecy* by Jeanne Dixon, and a small brass Buddha for burning incense. I say they are nothing and I don't worship them. True, but that is not how God views them. He is a jealous God and He doesn't want reminders of His worst enemy around, anymore than your spouse wants a display in his home of your former boyfriends. God says we have to choose which man we want to the exclusion of the other.

"...For I, the Lord thy God, am a jealous God, visiting the iniquity of the fathers on the children to the third and fourth generations of those who hate Me, but showing mercy to thousands, to those who love Me and keep My commandments." Exodus 20:5,6.

There are two kinds of jealousies; one that protects while the other destroys.

So, I got rid of my occult symbols. In looking around the house, I also discovered a Zeus figurine and some dragons painted on a chest. They were also destroyed.

In the completion of all things, God will ultimately be the King of all Kings, bringing his Holy City, the New Jerusalem down from heaven and place it right on top of Satan's defeated kingdom in the old city of Jerusalem. Of course, God has to form a new earth and a new sky first. Then this Holy City will be the home of God and He will now live *among men forever*. Revelations 21:1-5.

In the meantime, we are to pray like it says in the Lord's Prayer, "Thy Kingdom come. Thy will be done on earth as it is in heaven."

The battle is finally over. God wins and the Garden of Eden is regained. I would dare say some people aren't aware of these two kingdoms, or at least to the extent we must choose which kingdom we will ultimately live in *forever*. We will all live forever, but *where*? THE CHOICE IS OURS!

Even though I thought I was free of Satan's influence, when I looked I found his presence in my home and life. It wasn't until I rid my life of satanic symbols that I was able to hear God's message more clearly. Things changed quickly soon after.

CHOOSING A LOVE THAT WILL LAST

CHAPTER 28

MAMA'S WEDDING GOWN

One day, Chappy asked, "When would you like to get married? A year from now?"

I questioned, "Why wait a year when we know?"

In discussing different dates, we discovered my children wanted to spend several weeks with their dad, and Chappy's children wouldn't be coming till later in June, so we decided to go ahead and get married before my children left.

The date of Wednesday, June 4, 1975 was set, which was only three weeks away. However, not long after we set the date, the Christian Book Store was flooded due to the roof leaking, and my bedroom flooded due to heavy rains backing up in the patio because we hadn't cleaned out the rain gutters. Only several hours before the ceremony was to begin, did we get both places cleaned up and back in order. It was two a.m. when Chappy finally finished his store.

Our wedding at St. John's Episcopal Church was beautiful in every detail. My blue beaded wedding gown was the one I had worn at Herby's wedding, as well as to Shari's, and now it was *Mama's* wedding gown.

My two sons, Herby and Tom, gave me away. When the minister asked, "Who gives this woman to be this man's wife?"

All the children said in unison, "We do." There was muffled laughter. I was so proud of them.

As we stood facing each other silhouetted before the altar, Chappy sang to me in his deep rich baritone voice the song, *Because*. He looked taller than his usual 5-foot-10 inches. We exchanged gold wedding bands. It was a sacred moment to remember forever.

At the lovely reception in the Paul Veale home, co-hosted by the

Bill Nixes, Tommy came up to Chappy, hugged him and said, "Hi, Daddy."

After the reception, Bennie and Jennie Sirmons drove us to our hotel for the night. The next morning, they were going to drive us to the airport in Reynosa to depart for Mexico City. The next morning, they sent a mutual friend instead, and we supposed something must be wrong. We knew we couldn't leave until we learned if they were all right.

Well, it seems Bennie hadn't felt well during the wedding or reception, but was jovial and no one suspected he wasn't feeling great. He didn't want to put a damper on the festivities and happiness. They didn't rush us, and it was probably about 10 p.m. or more when they dropped us off at the hotel. We detected nothing wrong from their behavior. What we didn't know was Bennie's throat was closing up on him. It was some sort of allergy from working out in their yard. As soon as they delivered us to the hotel, they immediately sped to the emergency room at the McAllen Municipal Hospital, where he just made it in time. Some kind of friends!

Our honeymoon was idyllic. Since man began, he has dreamed of faraway exotically beautiful places. Such a place is Ixtapan de la Sal, Mexico, which is located about an hour's drive out of Mexico City in the Sierra Madre Mountains.

Nestled down in a valley among acres of green foliage and flowers too numerous to mention sits Hotel Ixtapan. It is a present-day Garden of Eden. The lush unbelievable gardens seem so fresh. It is as if each plant was potted and replaced daily if it shows any sign of deterioration.

The cuisine is French to compliment the architecture. We relished reading each evening's menu! Parisienne grapefruit, Madrilenian Consumme, Cream St. Germain, Quiche Lorraine, Fish Filet Veracruz style, Chicken Cuernavaca style, Quince Jelly with cheese, Pinon Nut Cake, Special Ixtapan Cake. Chappy noticed with some amazement and amusement that I had two desserts each evening!

CHOOSING A LOVE THAT WILL LAST

At night, we were lulled to sleep by the singing of tropical birds and the sounds of a mariache band. Glancing over from the golf course, I noticed there was a little red train with several cars hooked on, winding its way in and around the curves of the mountains. "Oh, Chappy, could we take a ride on that little red train after lunch?" Of course, that's what happens on a honeymoon--everything is, "Certainly sweetheart. Anything you wish or want," was Chappy's happy reply. *Silver Streak* was playing at the in-house theatre, and Chappy couldn't wait to share it with me that night.

However, there was one game Chappy wasn't interested in playing anymore after he lost four games of caddied tennis to me. His ego mended a bit though when he beat me at every single game of pool.

Ixtapan is known for its world famous spa, and when I returned from a session with a mud pack still on my face, I clowned around a bit when I came into our chalet called *La Fantasia*. Chappy looked up somewhat startled and said, "What on earth is that dirt doing on your face?"

I rolled my eyes in a dramatic way and said, "It's to make me beautiful."

"It's wasted, all wasted, because you are already beautiful inside and out," remarked Chappy, looking at me with love-filled eyes.

It was interesting--as we dressed every evening for dinner--our clothes blended so well. Considering we bought very few clothes for our wedding, it was a happy coincidence. Living in McAllen's warm climate, we hadn't worn some of these particular clothes while dating. Our photos show we are remarkably coordinated.

One day Chappy and I were in the pool, wrapped around each other when a New Yorker asked us how many children we had. Quickly, I added them all up and replied, "Nine." Their mouths fell open and didn't close until we swam away, no doubt thinking number ten would soon be on the way!

The only thing that marred our carefree too-good-to-be-true

days was the thought of having to leave this paradise.

Reluctantly packing on the last morning, we looked at each other longing to capture every ounce of pleasure spent at Ixtapan de la Sal. We felt it would last a lifetime in our memory, and it has.

When the driver turned down the last long lane to take us to Mexico City and to our plane, Chappy and I looked out the rear window of the limo as if to indelibly recall every tiny detail of the resort.

It was a good thing we had such a marvelous honeymoon because when we returned home, there were some confrontations which were very painful.

CHOOSING A LOVE THAT WILL LAST

CHAPTER 29

CONFRONTATIONS

By the time I married Chappy, he had developed a good relationship with my four youngest children, who were then 10, 11, 15 and 17 years old. But it didn't just happen. It wasn't long after Chappy and I had started going together that Herby went to Chappy's office at El Centro Mall. Herby, who was a confused young married adult at 22, was livid with anger and didn't hesitate to give Chappy a piece of his mind. I can just visualize the encounter with Herby's large black eyes snapping all the while his face turning redder and redder!

It seems his dad had heard I was going with Chappy and assumed we would get married. At that time, it wasn't even close. Herby was stirred up about financial matters. Chappy took him on for over an hour to settle him down. There is no way any woman is a match for such problems. After this confrontation, he and Chappy have been very close, and respect each other a great deal. There is nothing they won't do for each other. They love taking hunting trips together now.

A child or for that matter an adult doesn't always know who is lying to them. I feel so sorry for children of divorce. However, it is even sadder for children who have to live their entire lives in homes where they will never know what a normal home is all about. Of course, not all homes are abnormal where divorce occurs.

But in my judgment, sometimes the greater damage can be done where abnormal home situations exist, passing maladjusted behavorial patterns down from generation to generation, than damage from divorce if a good, stable and loving home is provided for them after the divorce. At least, these children will recognize abnormality and realize the need for change in their own homes when they marry.

Statistics keep coming out about abusive fathers being victims of child abuse. There are generational sins according to Marilyn Hickey. For instance, not only sins but other things can be passed down, such as certain phobias--fear of high places, fear of bridges, fear of airplanes or fear of insects. Usually, if you ask the victims if their grandmothers or grandfathers had this same fear, they will answer in the affirmative, even going back several generations. Prayer can break the power of these generational sins.

Soon after our marriage, Chappy and I tried to establish a whole new family unit to get everyone to be loyal. If it was discovered any of them weren't, then we had a family council. They were confronted with the issue. Disloyalty from any member of the family is not tolerated.

For instance in our family, if someone makes a remark about another member who isn't present, Chappy will wait until later and call out, "Tami, come on in, Lee Ann has something she would like to say to your face." Usually, it is confronted, both sides heard and it is worked through without going any farther. We are all well aware that none of us is perfect and it is normal and natural to have to get some things off our chests, but not behind an absent member's back.

Our reasoning is that if they think things aren't right and won't confront or bring it out in the open, then they need help to confront. That's why a patriarch is of utmost importance and of highest priority in any home. This cannot be overstated. The men are the protectors. It takes force to meet force.

There have been times when Chappy and I have heard some remarks which were disloyal, and it was dealt with. We encourage the children to love both parents, and that it isn't necessary to put one down or to choose sides. Perhaps this isn't always the case from the other side.

I remember one time, Kimberley Christine did something deceitful. We were all eating dinner and afterwards, Chappy

CHOOSING A LOVE THAT WILL LAST

asked her to go get the dictionary and read aloud to everyone what *deceitful* means. Kim came back from the library with the big old dictionary and read, "Deceitful means to imply a deliberate telling of lies or acting dishonestly, usually by one who expects to gain something for himself; to mislead, to cause to follow the wrong course or do the wrong thing, although not always on purpose; to delude is to fool someone so completely that he accepts as true or real something that is false; betray implies a breaking of faith while seeming to be loyal, true, or friendly."

It was very embarrassing and difficult to see her suffering, but it was like surgically removing a big old festering carbuncle in order that it might heal from the inside out.

Then what? All eyes were downcast and teary. Chappy then asked her to please read it again. So between blubbers, she repeated the meaning of deceitful. Some might say, "Isn't that a bit harsh?" If you could witness the results of that terrible moment, you would indeed be very pleased, even though there is still a need to help all of us in this area. However, it made a great impact on all of us. Hopefully, we all benefitted from that lesson.

It has been said that reputation is what people *think* you are, and character is what you *are* in the dark.

This confronting business was painful for me since we seldom confronted in our family when I was growing up. That's one thing I asked my dad about while he was in the hospital about a month before he died. Why didn't he stop all the disloyalty in the family? He replied rather sadly that he should have but didn't. Now he was too ill. It was confusing to me since he was such a loving and good father. He was strong and excelled as a man in so many areas of life.

Here is a poem my Shari wrote in 1972 which expresses so well what all the grandchildren felt about my dad.

GLORY CHAPMAN

MY GRANDPA

There is one person in my world
That I can truly respect.
Being a man advanced in age
Grandpa, my mother's father,
Commands my admiration.
His proud, green eyes
Constant, confident talk
Speak wisdom, thoughtfulness
And determination to me.
A keen sense of humor
In an elderly man is rare
Yet Grandpa possesses that
Funny, light side, manifested
Mostly by an upturned mouth
And eye twinkling gaze.
Slightly stoop shouldered
He still leaves an erect impression.

Grandpa's honest, caring heart
Radiates a warmth I wish to bask in.
His love for his young looking
Wife, children and grandchildren
And great grandchildren is touching
A religiously right gentleman,
Grandpa does not push his point
But is a convincing example
Of one who has lived well
And wisely with the help of God.
His fine everyday conduct
Convinces me he is truly good.
Thus I do respect, like
And love this gentleman.

CHOOSING A LOVE THAT WILL LAST

When God set up the order of the family unit, placing men as the spiritual leaders, it was for a very good reason. For whatever it is worth, I believe the world's present dilemma can be traced to the lack of leaders in each home. Men, as a rule, are not leading out, training their children, or showing by example the worth of a woman and her valuable place beside him, loving her like his own body. That produces strong, healthy and vigorous offspring instead of the reverse. Strong women leaders in the home with subdued or passive men will not produce *normies*.

Since my marriage to Chappy, relationships between all of the children and us have improved a great deal, and I give Chappy credit for leading out where few men dare to tread. In fact, there is so much love and loyalty among all of us now. None of us want to be confronted with mutiny. It's too painful.

We let no known enemy into our camp. If they have bitten once, they aren't allowed in again to hurt until there are some visible signs of changing or of repentance. "But I will not allow those who deceive and lie to stay in my house." Psalm 101:7.

We felt it was better to forego some family gatherings until things were cleared up rather than pretending all was well when it wasn't. If there is no reconciliatory spirit, sometimes it is better to wait and let things level out. The buck stops here. What I can't understand is why the disloyal ones want in if they are so critical. Disloyalty must be dealt with and forgiven so love can flow freely again!

When I was growing up, we had some problems in my family because some of the others thought Mother was partial to me. Partiality can happen, but often it is misunderstood since some children show their parents more respect, love and confide in them more. They come up close. Seems one of the words of wisdom given me addressed this very issue. It's not that God has any favorites, but some come up closer and choose to be close to Him.

A mother's love is never less for any of her children, but her appreciation of one can be greater perhaps. It is very difficult to have a lot of gratitude for a child who shows little love, gives still less of herself, and you hear rumblings of her disloyalty behind your back. No mother can or should appreciate these things. This has to make a difference. How much, I don't know.

Chappy and I both feel that loyalty should be rewarded, even if it isn't always equal, basing our belief on God's reward system based on deeds. It seems very peculiar to me that some parents leave their estate equally divided in their wills even though some of their children have been disloyal or haven't spoken to them for years. God does not judge this way. His rewards are based on quality of deserving well or ill.

Let me expand this just a bit. By not being left any inheritance or money doesn't mean the child is out of the family any more than a child of God who goes to heaven, but he has little or no reward. Some believers will just barely make it into heaven, the Bible says. However, his deeds will not entitle him to any rewards after he gets there. I Cor. 3:15.

Let me make it clear we aren't born into the kingdom by good works; it is by believing that Jesus gave his life so that we might have eternal life through Him. But certainly after becoming God's child, we want to be obedient, and our good deeds should follow. The gift of redemption is a gift given by Jesus to us.

"For by grace are ye saved through faith; and that not of yourselves: it is the gift of God: Not of works, lest any man should boast." Ephesians 2:8,9 KJV.

David said in Psalms 37:18, "Day by day the Lord observes the good deeds done by godly men, and gives them eternal rewards."

"For we must all stand before Christ to be judged and for our lives laid bare--before him. Each of us will receive whatever he deserves for the good or bad things he has done in his earthly body." II Cor. 5:10.

"I saw the dead, great and small, standing before God; and The Books were opened, including the Book of Life. And the dead were judged according to the things written in The Books, each according to the deeds he had done. And if anyone's name was not found recorded in the Book of life, he was thrown into the Lake of Fire." Rev. 20:12,15.

"See, I am coming soon, and my reward is with me, to repay everyone according to the deeds he has done." Rev. 22:12.

In the same way, a parent recognizes his own by the fact he is mentioned in his will, but the reward he receives is based on his quality of deserving well or ill as he has lived his life. The parent's love is unconditional, but the rewards aren't equal any more than God's rewards are. This is important for all of us to learn. Unconsciously, we may believe we will all be treated the same by God because that is what our parents did. Very subtle misguidance.

This is another good reason why a dad is of great importance in every home. With a just and fair patriarch, confronting can produce much harmony and unity within a family.

Have you noticed that any problem seems to shrink when it is shared with someone who truly understands us and the problem? Sharing reduces its weight and size.

"REVERENCE FOR GOD GIVES A MAN DEEP STRENGTH; HIS CHILDREN HAVE A PLACE OF REFUGE AND SECURITY." Psalms 14:26.

GLORY CHAPMAN

CHAPTER 30

A TRIBUTE TO GEORGIA MARIE

"The day one dies is better than the day he is born. It is better to spend your time at funerals than at festivals. For you are going to die and it is a good thing to think about it while there is still time. Sorrow is better than laughter, for sadness has a refining influence on us. Yes, a wise man thinks much of death, while a fool thinks only of having a good time now." Ecc. 7:1-4.

Is this what we do? I think it is the reverse. Death is something that happens to our loved ones and eventually will happen to us. We are all terminal! Death should be a welcomed friend, except in some instances, of course. When people are too young, or leave small children behind, death isn't easy to accept. Death is an uncomfortable subject to discuss for most of us.

When Nancy called from Waco to say that her mother, Georgie, was gone, I couldn't seem to grasp the finality of it all or that I would never see her again on this earth. My world seemed to go right on as if nothing had happened and yet she was gone. She was here yesterday but is gone today.

It has been said if we have two true friends during our lifetime, we are indeed fortunate. Georgie was one such friend. She was one of my closest friends for over 30 years. When she and Bo, her husband, moved to McAllen, we met when I was first married. From the day we met to the day she died we remained tight loyal friends. We shared a great deal with each other.

One time, she told me about Mike, her oldest son, being spanked very hard by his dad for something he had done. Mike was probably about five at the time. Georgie, in trying to soothe him, told Mike that in heaven there would be no spankings, no crying and no sickness. Whereupon he suddenly dried his tears and looked up so hopefully into her face, "Oh, you mean daddy

CHOOSING A LOVE THAT WILL LAST

won't be there?" Another time when they were all in church, Mike was acting up so Georgie gave him a little pinch. He yelled out loudly for all to hear, "Stop pinching me!"

Personally, I used the *finger* method on my children in church. If they were sitting behind me, and I could hear them cutting up, I would hold up *one* finger. The second time it was *two* fingers, which sobered them up somewhat since the hand with *three fingers* meant a spanking at home later. Every once in a while we still use finger signals as an in-family joke.

All through the years, there was seldom a week went by that Georgie and I didn't either write or call each other about all the happenings in our lives, both the good times and the bad.

Since Georgie had cancer and her prognosis wasn't good, during the last six months of her life, all her friends wrote what she had meant to them in a special book. Nancy sent me what I had written in it since I didn't have a copy.

"Dearest Georgie:

Friendship is unlike other relationships in several ways. First, it's a free choice. I choose to be a friend. It is very special in that it isn't propelled by kin or blood. Love between friends flows from its own merits. The mutual constancy of giving and receiving is the pulsating force which nourishes our relationship.

Friendship signs no contracts nor does it respond to coercion or pressure. The love expressed between friends is the glue that bonds tight the friendship.

Georgie, time has proved our enduring friendship true, which spans more than 30 years.

"A friend is one who brings his faith...In time of need along to you...And like the sun that dries the rain...Can turn the heaven back to blue...A friend is one who holds your hand...And softly smiles into your eyes...When they are bathed in quiet tears...And in your heart a darkness lies...A friend is one who understands...When all the others are perpexed...And some in silence walk away...And those who stay around are vexed...A friend, indeed, is finer still...Who lifts his sword in your defense...Though there is danger that he falls...And loses all at your expense...How sad it is for all of us...That there are really very few...Among the many whom we know...Who care what we may say or do." Anonymous.

Close friends know all about each other, yet remain as a defense against any who would not see the highest and best in the other. Friends are not perfect, but bring out the best in each other.

I recall you mentioned a long time ago that I was opinionated. That helped me to work on that unwanted characteristic. "Faithful are the wounds of a friend." Proverbs 27:6. I'm a better person for having known you. It has been said that if we have two true friends throughout our lifetime, we are blessed indeed. So I am!

Your unselfish ways challenge me. The good in you isn't suspicious of the evil in me.

>I love you! Let me count the ways:
>
>Your sense of humor rates high.
>Your smile and laughter is in my memory always.
>Your kindness and tenderness warms me when I hurt.
>Praying to our Father with me in all the circum-
>   stances of our lives strengthens me.
>Your lack of jealousy and envy allows our love to
>   grow--and even to bloom.
>Your optimism about life encourages me. You
>   seeing the good in others blesses me.
>Your capacity to love with an understanding and
>   sensitive heart makes you, Georgia Marie Ashley
>   Horner, my dearest and rarest friend.

"So let the way wind up the hill or down; sometimes rough or

CHOOSING A LOVE THAT WILL LAST

smooth, the journey will be a joy, still striving for the things I sought in childhood: fond friendships, high adventure and a crown. I shall grow old, but never lose life's zest, because the last turn in the road will be the best." Anonymous.

Always loving you,
G + G = G G & G

Translated: Georgie plus Glory equals gobs of gab and giggles. Georgie gave me a gold charm with those G's on it many years ago.

Upon learning the dreaded disease cancer had taken her, I was deeply happy that her suffering had ended, but very brokenhearted for those she left behind. She has arrived *home*, to her magnificent permanent home. Her trip through life was but a summer's holiday compared to the time she will spend in her FOREVER HOME.

During her two-and-a-half-year illness, I went to see her several times. In between we stayed in touch by phone. Sometimes we would talk for an hour or more at a time. Perhaps the most outstanding characteristic about Georgie was her sense of humor and her capacity to love. Her antics could keep me in stitches. If any situation got too heavy, she could pull it out with one of her good ones, and it would break up everyone.

Toward the last when we knew she wouldn't be here much longer, she shared the day-by-day experience of what it was like to be dying. Georgie told me that 55 friends had been to the hospital to see her Monday and that 22 had come by noon on Tuesday.

I exclaimed, "Georgie, you are having some kind of going away party!" She really chuckled.

"Remember how we used to talk about what heaven would be like. Now you get to go before I do. I think I'm a little envious."

"Oh, Glory, I don't know if you're supposed to be envious.

Well, in this instance, maybe it is okay," she informed me. She went on to tell me she was getting excited. "If this is dying, then I don't want to go on living."

Earlier I said, "George, remember I will meet you at the Eastern gate. Don't forget to wait for me there."

To which she said, "If I'm not there, then look for me at the other place."

"Look at what other place?" I shot back instantly.

"Oh, I mean at the other gate," she quickly answered, laughing.

The last conversation was, "I'm so happy for you George, but I am crying for me. I will miss you. I love you so."

"Yes, I know Glory, and I love you very much. Don't ever forget how much your friendship has meant to me through the years. Also, don't forget I want my coffin open and I want everyone to cry a lot because they're going to miss me."

I got choked up and couldn't talk anymore!

Later, I asked George if she got a preview of what heaven was like, would she tell Bo, and he could relay it to me? She assured me she would. I thought she might have an experience like my dear fairylike 88-year old friend, Margaret Mann, had before she died. I still keep hearing echoes from the past of Margaret expressing, almost daily, "This is the happiest day of my life."

Little 90-pound Margaret had broken her hip and was in the hospital for the first time in her life. It was about two weeks later when she showed me her scar. It was perfectly healed. Chappy and I tried to get to the hospital every day to see her since she was a widow and had no children. She was quite alone in this world except for the myriad friends she had.

On Thursday evening, she told Chappy and me that some angels had appeared to her and stood at the foot of her bed. They told her, "We will come for you in three days." Chappy asked what they looked like? She said, "They were so beautiful, all in dazzling white."

"How many were here, Margaret?" Chappy queried. She held up her little frail hand and Chappy asked, "Five?"

CHOOSING A LOVE THAT WILL LAST

"Oh, no, there were two," folding down her other three fingers.

From then on she wasn't the same. She kept her eyes closed and was waiting expectantly as if she didn't want to miss her appointment with the angels.

When she told Peggy Nix about seeing the two angels, Peggy said, "Oh, no, Margaret, we still have a lot of things to do."

Very firm and adamant she explained to her, "No, Peggy, in three days the angels are coming for me."

Early Monday morning, around 6 am, the nurse called me to come right away. By the time I arrived, Margaret was gone. The nurse was somewhat perplexed in that she and Margaret had been chatting when she stepped out into the hall to get some clean linens. When she came back in, Margaret was gone. Just like that! She wasn't sick or delirious at all. She was getting ready to be dismissed from the hospital.

Ruthie Sidelnik, her neighbor and friend, had visited with her Sunday afternoon. Since Margaret had her eyes closed, Ruthie just sat down quietly in a chair close by, not saying anything to her. Ruthie heard her talking to her father and husband. Wow! In three days she did indeed leave with the angels.

At the last when Georgie got worse, they wanted to know if I wanted to come and see her. I just couldn't. I wanted to remember her as she used to be. She had lost 50 pounds through the two surgeries and several rounds of chemotherapy. However, she never lost her hair.

Georgie was witty and so loving to the end. Bo said that she went to sleep peacefully, not saying anything. Her life touched so many, as well as those in the hospital. Her joy was remarkable. Her goodbye with Bo and their four children was so complete in sharing and telling each of them how very much she loved them. It made the grieving process somewhat easier.

Her funeral had the connotation of, "Let's all celebrate Georgie's homegoing." That cemetery doesn't hold the real Georgie--only the shell that housed her spirit. That shell will decay, but she lives on in a better world. What she has done on earth is finished and her books closed.

I just say, "Thank you, Lord, for lending Georgie to us for awhile." Her life was not in vain. She left so much of herself in her husband and children: Mike, Pat, Nancy and Judy, also her many friends. She may not be visible, but she lives on in our hearts, as well as in the invisible kingdom of God.

My tribute to a great and faithful friend. "Goodbye for a little while Georgie," I whispered as I placed a single red rose in her hand.

CHOOSING A LOVE THAT WILL LAST

CHAPTER 31

LIVING AGAIN AFTER DIVORCE

Three days after Chappy and I arrived home from our honeymoon, his two girls came to live with us for the summer-- Kimberley, 13, and Lee Ann, 11. Knowing that Kim and Lee Ann were here, Tari, Tami, Tom and Lori couldn't wait to return home to be with them. All of them love each other. Really!

I would have to say that Lee had the toughest time adjusting and went through a very confused time, but don't think it bothered her relationship with the other kids.

There was no bickering over who would have which bedroom or bathroom. Of course, on more than one occasion the children, his and mine, tried to divide Chappy and me. However, we hung together no matter what we said to each other in private. It was all the kids against us if there was any choosing sides. That's what we preferred.

Kim and Lee didn't know what to call me. Chappy didn't want them calling me *Glory* or *Mrs. Chapman*. Soon after they arrived we all went to Mexico. I was reading to the full carload the book, *The Emancipation of Robert Sadler* by Marie Chapian. By the time we arrived at our place, *Isle of View* in Lazarillos de Abajo, a little village near Horsetail Falls, South of Monterrey, all the kids were chiming in with "Yessuh, Massuh Beal, Suh," changing to "Yessuh, Massuh Dale, Suh" whenever Chappy asked them to do something. If I talked to them, they countered with "Yessum, Ms. Glory." From then on I became *Ms. Glory*, not only to my children but also to their friends as well.

Later and at different times, Kim and Lee came to live with us and attended schools in McAllen. Tami and Kim are especially close, being two years apart in age, and love each other so much. One day at school one of Kim's friends asked about Tami, and

Kim made the remark how much she loved her. The friend shot back, "I thought she was your stepsister."

Kim lovingly informed her, "Yes, she is, and I love her very much."

Her friend looked puzzled and retorted, "I never heard of that!"

We don't use the word *step* in our vocabulary to explain our relationships. It is either, "This is my sister, or my special sister." Let them figure out who belongs to whom. As a group, they call themselves *The Chaplocks*--half of both their names. Of course, Chappy feels especially blessed to have two sons, having none of his own; however, his three girls could never be replaced in his heart. His oldest daughter, Linda, married before Chappy and I did, having lived with her dad and grandmother Iris for a year in McAllen, graduating from McAllen High School. Chappy asked Linda one day what she thought about him asking me out. She told him she thought that was a good choice.

Now comes the most painful part to write about and I shall attempt to open my heart a bit.

Years before, I remember Catherine Marshall telling about her marriage to Leonard LeSourd after being a widow for 11 years and taking his three young children to rear. She was so happy and full of hope and anticipation, and was going to write a whole book on being a stepmother, but first she had to live it. I couldn't wait to read this upcoming book and informed the Reviewers' Guild members I had dubs on that story.

Catherine is one of my favorite authors, and I waited with great expectation to read about how she managed the stepchildren. If anyone could, I felt she could. When at last the book appeared, *Something More*, I read a couple of chapters and she mentions nothing about this part of her life. Finally in the third chapter she devotes only a small part of it to stepmothering. I was disappointed. She said that it wasn't at all like she anticipated; she was not the kind of stepmother she thought she would be, and the children were not like she thought they would be. From reading that part, I would say the whole experience was too

CHOOSING A LOVE THAT WILL LAST

painful and disappointing to write much about. However, in later years as the children grew and matured, the whole picture changed.

Stepmothering is probably the most perplexing and tough role any woman can be called upon to fill. There is something about being a stepmother that I haven't been able to put my finger on. You want to be a good mother to these special children who have come into your life, but at the same time you don't want to take the place of their real mother. Also, I know it must be extremely painful to judge any other woman as being favored over your own mother. Remember they don't have all the facts like you do. Many times it is impossible or unwise to give them all the facts. Also, an injured parent may tell things in such a way so as to lead their children to believe something false. That further leads them to distrust either parent. You can see how easily the gun is loaded!

Neither does the child want you to be her peer. So I guess I am a mother-figure. Being a mother myself, I wouldn't want to deprive any mother of that same privilege.

Mostly, I just love them and let the position I fill fall where it may. I endeavor not to take myself or them too seriously. In most instances, I have found if I reverse the situation by putting myself in their shoes, I am able to discover how the problem should be resolved. Of course, my batting average isn't 1000. I also use this technique in our marriage. It helps to keep me on track!

Chappy explained it so well to my children before we married, sitting them all down to have a good long talk concerning our upcoming marriage. He pointed out that he wouldn't ever try to take their dad's place in their hearts since they already had a dad. But that he would fill the position of father-figure in the home to protect, provide, love and take care of them. That he would be the authority in the family and would be there for them, but that he would never replace their dad. Chappy has been true to his word, encouraging them to love, and even forgive their dad when needed.

When I asked Lori recently what her first impression was at the time Chappy talked to all of them, she said, "You remember I was crying, but what I didn't tell you then was why. I was crying because I was so happy. I loved Chappy and I was going to have a daddy." We asked Tom the same question, and he said that he wished his dad could be like Chappy since he was his dad. Tari said that she cried after going to bed, expressing she didn't want me to marry anyone. Tami related that it seemed there would be so many changes which would be strange and unknown.

It is my opinion that it is important for a special mother not to hold too much inside, or the hostilities are likely to explode when she least suspects it and threaten the marriage. Of course, now that they are more mature and some of them have children of their own, it has worked to make us all very appreciative of each other.

When they were younger, it seemed I could feel what they were feeling, and it made me so heavy-hearted I couldn't talk about it. One time when they were leaving on the plane from Brownsville, I can't express the melancholy that came over me. Like my heart was a big bag and it was about to get too full of hurts for them.

I know now, they perhaps weren't as sad as I thought they were. For example, it wasn't until this year that Tari shared with us why she looked so downcast in our family portrait. It was taken during the time of the divorce and she looked so very forlorn in it. Recently, while looking at that particular photograph, Tari volunteers to the whole family, "Do you all know why I looked so mad or sad in that picture? It was because the photographer didn't give me enough time to wash my hair, and my hair was all greasy and flat." I wanted to faint just to make all that worry worth the effort.

Strange what you can learn about your children after they are grown. On a recent trip to Florida, we were discussing where Tami had gotten her bad eyes since all the other children have such good eyesight. Tami said, "Well, Mother, when I was in grade school, the teacher took us all outside to see the eclipse, warning us to use a special paper viewer." Tami thought it would be okay not to use the special device, and it damaged her eyes. That was the first I learned of that!

Children, as a whole, are very resilient, flexible, adaptable and lovable. However, life can hand out some pretty confusing issues which have to be worked through. There should be no sorrows, at least not for children, but there is sorrow. Knowing that, then the next order of business is to try to help them the best way through it.

It is my hope this story will be told as honestly and lovingly as possible without hurting any of them. As I said before, there were no problems between the children that they couldn't handle. It was like having your best friends spend the night--one long slumber party. All except Tom, who was the only boy at home and his bedroom was on the west wing while all five girls were on the east wing. He buddied with them, but not in the same way. However, he was very special to Chappy and he had more time for him since he was the only boy and they did male things together.

From this vantage point, it's hard to remember where the first bit of rumbles came from, but I believe from the household duties they all had been assigned for the summer.

First, I wrote a list of things to do and assigned each one their portion. Some didn't like their assignments and would rather do other things, or thought they were being given more than the others.

So next I listed the duties on little slips of paper and let them draw. That was met with about the same result. Finally, they began trading with each other since Kim hated vacuuming while she didn't mind sweeping the big patio every morning. It was harder and more often, but she loved it. I believe Tom turned out to be the permanent garbage man. Tami and Tari usually ended up with KP (kitchen patrol) very often on their list.

Then there seemed to be a need to guide them as to how they were spending their allowances. They were saving zero, and one week, between them, I believe, they lost $29.00. Their allowances were based on how well they performed their work-- the reward system. Also, there needed to be some encouragement to get value for their money since much was going for junk. We tried to teach them to give some to God, save some, and then use the balance for value purchases. To this day, they are all very astute in their buying.

If they didn't do their particular chore, Chappy was to be told. Sometimes I would tell and sometimes I wouldn't. It put me in the position of tattling on them, which none of them liked, or liked me for doing. Once in a while I would wait too long to say something. Instead I would keep track of each time they did what on paper. In mentioning to Chap I was keeping a record to be sure the work was distributed evenly, he reacted rather strongly.

He told me, "Love never keeps score." So I abandoned that idea.

"Life is not fair and don't try to make it fair. Men are not created equal. A baby born blind, deaf, dumb or crippled cannot avail himself of the so-called equal opportunity."

The opportunities are there, but they aren't equal to everyone else. In the Bible, there were definitely chosen leaders, followers, helpers, angels, slaves, servants, women, rich, poor, gifted and anointed.

We felt the ideal way to handle any situation was to sit down and talk the whole matter out, except in our case it didn't always seem too wise to let our children know everything that was going on with the other parents. We did discuss, I believe, most everything that was happening in our household. But there were other voices being fed into their minds that we didn't always know about. Hard to combat what you don't know. Sometimes what you don't know can hurt you. Poor kids trying to be friends with both parents and sometimes parents won't let them be neutral. They want to be loyal to both their mother and father, but at times the situation seems to demand otherwise.

When the girls borrowed and wore each other's clothes, shoes, ribbons, as well as many other items, they usually worked that out among themselves. Now and again there was one who would borrow a blouse or skirt and wouldn't hang it up, or see that it got laundered. It seemed the children all got along better with their special sisters and brother than they did with their own real sisters and brother. Occasionally there was a good fight but always with their blood sister. That certainly kept down favoritism and bickering about who was in the wrong. They settled it between themselves and forgot it.

Chappy was a wonderful disciplinarian, I thought. He gave much, loved much and cared much. However, the children thought he was too strict sometimes and would buck his authority, but usually not for long. We had a couple of runaways which were painful times for them and us. One time it was over doing her duties on time. She didn't mind doing them, she said, but only when she got around to them--usually mouthing off in the stalling process. Well, doing that many dishes late could be disastrous for the next big meal coming up.

The other runaway was caused by grounding her for six weeks for sneaking the pick-up truck out after midnight and driving around town for several hours (she said). It certainly couldn't be overlooked, but six weeks is much too long, I believe. She said we shortened it some and her phone privileges were restored after a while.

In editing this, she informed me that she was grounded six months (I can't believe that) and that she took Lori with her which we never knew until now, and Lori, of course, was never punished. From time to time, parents can get a little too carried away and have to repent also.

Oh, the things parents learn after their children are grown! I told her she will be able to understand how worried a parent can be when her own children try the same thing on her. In listening to newscasts, if anything bad happens, chances are it is after midnight.

Another time Chappy and I arrived home just in time to witness

Tami trying to break down a door with an axe because Tari pretended to be reading her love letters. Don't know who was worse; the one teasing and egging her on, or the one with the axe. You need the patience of Job and the wisdom of Solomon to know how to rear children.

Sharing the work was easier when they were younger. When the children returned home after being away at college, they didn't want to be told to do certain chores. Incidentally, one year Chappy and I had four in college and two in private schools. Having adults living back home creates a different set of relationships as to running the home. They don't want to be treated as children, possibly guests, but not children. Neither do they want to be adults and assume much responsibility. We stress it is never right for any member of the family not to carry his own weight. There are no *no pays* here. Everyone chips in, however small. We feel their self respect is involved and that is very important.

Chappy and I are willing to help, run alongside and teach, but ultimately each child must peddle his own bicycle. We didn't ask the children to make the other's bed or pick up after them, but we did expect each of them to take care of himself. Maybe we stressed this too much. They should also be taught to be givers, as well. None of our children are angels, neither have any been in jail. They are loved and we feel loved by them.

All nine of our children are a mixture of fascinating, fun loving kids. There are so many lessons to be taught and learned.

THERE IS LIFE AFTER DIVORCE!

CHOOSING A LOVE THAT WILL LAST

CHAPTER 32

NORMY, ABBY NORM AND SUBY NORM

When Chappy and I were first married, and I wanted his undivided attention, I would ask him if I could talk to him, but only if he would promise not to answer me for a whole day. Then he could share and I would keep quiet for a day. That has worked very well for us.

However, this does not work with the children, and a special mother has to make many allowances and see the whole picture instead of taking it all too serious and personal, especially, if you know you love each child equally. No doubt love is the key. Sure, there are opportunities special mothers can use if they desire and perhaps get away with for awhile. Don't be tempted. Children don't hold grudges or remember how much they hurt you.

In my opinion, lately, more is said about stepfathers being bad than stepmothers. However, it seems to me that stepfathers have the easier role inasmuch as they are only home a few hours each evening while the stepmother is usually there 24 hours and has to direct the crew. That's where the rub comes in. The stepchildren have to adjust to another way of doing things.

Since some of the children were dating, Chappy and I tried to teach them about the different types of human personalities: Normy, Abby Norm and Suby Norm, as we called them.

J. I. Rodale in Synonym Finders says that NORMAL is usual, ordinary, conventional, regular, accepted, approved, standard, average, medium, steady, even and typical. In psychology normal means adjusted, well-adjusted, in good shape, healthy, natural, reasonable, sane, all there. SUBNORMAL means inferior, low, under the required level, insufficient, inadequate, below par, below normal, less than average, not up to standards, not all there, deficient and maladjusted. ABNORMAL means irregular, not typical, not usual, not normal. So we used the short terms, *Norm, Abby Norm and Suby Norm* to explain our point of view in certain situations. We still use these expressions in-family. For instances if one of the children does something inferior, we address him or her with one of the normy adjectives.

I like what Pat and Shirley Boone did when their girls began dating. First, they invited the boys to their home for dinner and got to know them to see if they fit in with their family and their values.

Sex was a lively subject many evenings around our dinner table. Chappy would usually sum it all up this way: at 19 you think sex occupies 90 percent of your time in marriage. Actually, sex probably takes no more time than half of one percent of your life. So, it is of great consequence how you spend the other 99.5 percent. Of course, there's the mystery of physical attraction but beyond that its the things you share. That way you can create a dozen strands, great and small, that will link you together. And your trust in each other will not only be based on love and loyalty but on the fact of all the many sharings—a hundred strands twisted into something unbreakable.

Dating was certainly a broad subject. Joshua Harris explains in *I Kissed Dating Goodbye* that we need to practice smart love because it unlocks God's best for our lives. Joshua says that dating leads to intimacy but not necessarily to commitment.

Also, that dating tends to skip the *friendship* stage of a relationship. C. S. Lewis describes friendship as two people walking side by side toward a common goal. In dating, romantic attraction is often the relationship's cornerstone. The premise of friendship is that we're interested in the same things; let's enjoy these common interests together. If, after developing a friendship, romantic attractions forms, that's an added bonus.

Intimacy without commitment is defrauding. Intimacy without friendship is superficial. A relationship based only on physical attraction and romantic feelings will last only as long as the feeling last.

Joshua further explains that dating often mistakes a physical relationship for love. Just because two bodies are drawn to each other doesn't mean two people are right for each other. A physical relationship doesn't equal love.

Dating often isolates a couple from other vital relationships. They don't need anyone else. When we allow one relationship to crowd out others, we lose perspective and will probably make poor judgments.

Elisabeth Elliot says that unless a man is prepared to ask a woman to be his wife, what right has he to claim her body?

Because dating doesn't require commitment, the two people involved allow the needs and passions of the moment to take center stage. The couple doesn't look at each other as possible life partners or weigh the responsibilities of marriage. Instead, they focus on the demands of the present. And with that mindset, the couple's physical relationship can easily become the focus. If many people in dating relationships really examined the focus of their relationships, they'd probably discover that all they have in common is lust.

In friendship, they can practice the skills of relating, caring and sharing their lives with other people and can observe what they'll one day want in their mates.

Romance can thrill us to our core, but it's only a small part of true love. We've been playing in the sandbox and God wants to take us to the beach.

You've heard the line, "If you really loved me you'd do it." In other words, "I don't care about you, your convictions, or how this could damage you emotionally—meet *my* needs."

Remember guys struggle more with sex drives and girls struggle more with their emotions. Girls need to be more aware about playing games and leading boys on. They need to know how easily their actions and glances can stir up lust in a guy's mind.

Certainly when you fall in-love, you are in an altered state of mind. In early dating it is important to stay in groups and stay away from situations that place you alone for long periods of time. There are many ways to observe what a person is like by watching how they manage their life, relationships and time.

A relationship usually does not grow once sex is involved due to the change in focus.

Infatuation can cause problems for us because it is most often founded on illusion. We've substituted fantasy for all the information we lack about the person. As soon as we get to know that person's true identity and discover that our "perfect" man is human like everyone else, our dreams fade and we move on to a new crush. To break the pattern of infatuation, we must reject the idea that a human relationship can ever completely fulfill us.

Not to be overlooked is the difference in character defects and faults. If any character defects are present (like lying, cheating, stealing, immorality, murder, selfishness, abusive, jealous and controlling person) the marriage is doomed. Faults can include many annoying habits which can also strain the best marriage, some of which may not be tolerable to you.

We have heard it said, "Watch how a boy treats his mother." But I believe the better way to observe is to watch how his father treats his mother.

Another good thing might be to practice practical life skills and budgeting. Ask your parents to let you take over the maintenance of your house—including paying the bills, repairs, shopping, planning menus and cooking meals for a few months—you'll soon find out about financial responsibility.

Many evenings were spent in discussions and debates on various subjects concerning God, his plan for man, along with the part we play. One topic I recall was on the difference in forgiveness and reconciliation. We must always forgive but we are not always reconciled. Always be aware that you can't reconcile the irreconcilable! However forgiveness takes only one. A child can and must forgive a parent for abusing him, but he isn't reconciled to that parent to repeat the offense. He may remove himself until the parent is healed and repents.

Jesus was willing to forgive and reconcile the second thief dying on the cross beside him, but reconciliation takes two. Only one thief was forgiven and reconciled while the other one was not. He chose to use his free will not to accept, though love and pardon was available to both.

"Loving my enemies does not mean thinking them nice either. That is an enormous relief. For a good many people imagine that forgiving your enemies means making out that they are really not such bad fellows after all, when it is quite plain that they are. Wishing him good, not feeling fond of him nor saying he is nice when he is not. This is loving your neighbor as yourself. You may not always like yourself and what you do, but you do keep on loving yourself and wishing yourself the best."[1]

Let me, for emphasis, say how C. S. Lewis said the same thing in another way, "I remember that when Christian teachers told me long ago that I must hate bad man's actions but not the man, I used to think this a silly, straw-splitting distinction: how could you hate what a man did and not hate the man? But years later it occurred to me that there was one man to whom I had been doing this all my life--namely, myself."[2]

Another good topic we discussed was that self-centeredness can often be confused with selfishness. The two are poles apart. Self-centered persons focus on self as if they were the center of all happenings, attracting attention to themselves as opposed to others. A self-centered person can be a very generous person, whereas a selfish person is concerned unduly with personal profit or gain, lacking consideration for others--greedy. Have you ever had a conversation with a self-centered individual only to discover every subject ended up about herself, perhaps even glancing at herself in every mirror she passed?

Another interesting topic was the difference between jealousy and envy. Jealousy is when we see someone with something we want, we go out and get one like it. Envy is when we see someone with something we want, we go and take it away from him for our own enjoyment.

Christian psychiatrists Frank Minirth and Paul Meier believe that, without exception, all addictions are based on shame. What in adulthood becomes an addiction to substance or activity frequently can be traced to childhood shame. The pressure of hiding family secrets or our own perceived failure and inadequacies can be overwhelming. We certainly need to make our homes a place where discipline is administered with acceptance and love. Is there any job as difficult as rearing balanced and healthy children?

The subject of faith versus presumption was a delicate one to understand. This difference wasn't clear to us until we met the authors of the book *We Let Our Son Die.*[3] Larry and Lucky Parker told us their disturbing story at the Christian Booksellers National Convention in Anaheim, California.

They were new converts and were told to make a positive confession, take the Word, confess it, stand upon it, claim it, holding God responsible to fulfill it by healing their 11-year old son, Wesley, who had diabetes. Wesley died after three days of intense suffering without insulin which his parents withheld. They were devastated and were searching for answers as to where they went wrong. This is what they learned and passed on to us over lunch one day.

Someone explained to them that they applied faith unscripturally. "We tried to force God into healing Wesley, not realizing the difference between proving and tempting God."

When Jesus went to the pinnacle of the temple, the devil tempted him to prove God. "If you are the Son of God, cast yourself down for it is written He shall give his angels charge concerning you: and in their hands they shall bear you up..."

Jesus' response had been, "You shall not tempt the Lord your God."

Perhaps one cannot arbitrarily take a verse from the Bible and say, "I'm going to stand on it."

The promises of God must be given; that is, inspired by the

CHOOSING A LOVE THAT WILL LAST

Holy Spirit to a person for a specific need. Only when God speaks to us clearly can we stand, for it is then that God's gift of faith begins to flow on our behalf. Some passages are for general application. But not all verses necessarily will apply to our circumstances or God's plan for our lives.

Capriciously claiming the general promises of the Bible for specific needs opens the door to presumption. Sometimes spiritual insights can be transformed into formulas, which are not evil in themselves but can have heartbreaking consequences. One cannot live by another person's faith. Problems arise when a formula is presented as an absolute for others to follow. Too often it becomes a straight jacket of legalism. When the formula doesn't work, the individual is troubled with guilt and his faith weakened.

The Parkers explained to us that God didn't tell them to withhold Wesley's insulin to prove His faithfulness or their faith, as they had assumed. By taking Wesley off his insulin, they, in effect, were forcing God to heal their son. In relating this tragedy to us, they felt they prevented God's perfect method for Wesley's life.

Stubbornness is not faith either. Still, a balance exists somewhere. If we are the author, God isn't obligated to finish it. Hope sometimes can be mistaken for faith. The gift of faith can operate only within the program of its author.

The Parkers remarked they had acted presumptuously in trying to prove God and their faith, when all the while they were tempting the Lord instead. Also, withholding Wesley's insulin hindered healing, for God cannot answer faith that is rooted in presumption and which maneuvers Him into acting against His sovereign will.

Perhaps the story about Jesus asking Peter to walk on the water is a good illustration concerning presumption. If the other disciples presumed upon the same word, they would most likely have drowned. Christ's word to Peter was meant for him alone.

The Parkers summed up their tragedy by saying that a

Scripture was given to them by the Holy Spirit to comfort them. It was I Corinthians 13:13. And now abideth faith, hope and love, these three; but the greatest of these is love. "WE HAD PITTED FAITH AGAINST LOVE. Love had told us to give Wesley the insulin and end his agony. What we mistook for faith demanded that we resist the temptation to give insulin and continue to prove God. Any action we take that is contrary to love must be re-examined. Love is the controlling factor in faith that is authored by God. Our love should have overruled what we thought we were required to do."

LIVING, LEARNING AND LOVING IS PROVING TO BE CHALLENGING!

CHOOSING A LOVE THAT WILL LAST

CHAPTER 33

WHEN DOES A MOTHER RETIRE?

Surprisingly, there was a problem we hadn't taken into account with our large brood. It was sleep or rather the lack of sleep. There were three to five of our children dating at any one time. Finally, in desperation, Chappy asked that all of them gather on the front porch and ring the doorbell only once. That seldom happened. They were given a definite curfew. I wish I had had them place an alarm clock, setting it themselves for the curfew hour, and place it close to our bedroom door. That way they would have to hurry home in order to shut it off before it buzzed, waking us up. Well, so much for hindsight.

Someone has said that from the cradle to the grave there is little time for sleep. As an infant we have colic, in adolescence we fight sleep, later dating keeps us up late, new-love and marriage takes hours of time, then the new baby changes our entire lives, and their teenage years of dating causes a loss of still more sleep. Finally they marry and leave home. And what do you know? Just when we are anticipating a good night's sleep, either the Change of Life hits us or the mid-life crisis--with insomnia.

Chappy's father was his dearest and closest friend from birth until his father's death in 1972. The only problem between them was Chappy choosing a profession other than building boats on the Chesapeake Bay. He was an only son and his father taught him so many important things. In hindsight, Chappy really appreciates and realizes how very wise his father was. His father taught him it wasn't always the work itself that was utmost, but the attitude and tenacity it took to finish a job. Sometimes just keeping constructively busy was another lesson.

If my children amount to anything, it will be because of Chappy. He deserves and will receive all the credit. There is no substitute for a man who is a man in his home. I let him handle all the discipline while I manage the home, food and small matters. No woman should assume a sergeant's position in the home. It causes role reversals and the children are confused as to what the male and female roles are. Why won't women just let men be men? Could it be because some men are wimps?

The biggest clue to being a good stepmother is the stepfather. If a SF doesn't back up the SM in situations large and small, you can forget the rest. There must be solidarity between the two parents. If the SF insists on treating his children differently than yours, or the SM favors her own children above the SC, there can be no happiness and a family unit will not form. It is my opinion that the natural parent should discipline his/her own children for at least the first couple of years until bonding can take place with the stepparent.

Chappy was indeed a very strong person. Very strong! God knew I needed a husband of steel and velvet. It must be said here that beyond any doubt Chappy showed no favoritism between any of the children--ever. He truly took my six children deep into his heart as if they had been born to him--just as I did with his children. I can't imagine life without them.

Perhaps, that kind of love should happen before anyone decides to marry someone with children. If you can't love them like your own, maybe there should be no wedding performed because that marriage won't be happy or last, I dare say.

There are family situations where there are no children of one parent but are stepchildren of the other. In any case, there must be the total allegiance between the parents. Children are to be given a child's place. I believe that was the problem Catherine Marshall encountered with her oldest new daughter. After Leonard's first wife wasn't there, he unknowingly allowed Linda to take the place of her mother. Certainly, we all do things which have repercussions that we were unaware of at the time. Here Linda explains in her own words, "I thought I wanted a loving relationship with you when you married my dad, but resentment crowded in. The reason was that at a gut level I thought you were taking dad away from me. I would no longer be number one in his life."

Several years after Chappy and I were married, Lori came into his office to talk to him about changing her name to Chapman. She had been toying and talking with the other kids about the idea for some time. Lori is a bit timid and shy and didn't know how Chappy would feel about her having his name. Of course, Chappy was very pleased at the idea, but told Lori that he would have to speak to Kim and Lee to see how they felt before he could give her an answer.

Later, Kim and Lee came bounding down the stairs with little Lori tagging behind, exploding with joy and happiness that Lori would be a *Chapman*. There was much merriment over Lori's wish being granted. Of all the children, I believe Lori, baby of the family, loves Chappy the most. Okay! Linda, Kim and Lee, I am ready for my lashes!

Lori was the children's gofer, meaning go-for. "Lori, would you please go down and get the curlers out of my car? Lori, would you put these jeans in the dryer for five minutes? Lori, please press this blouse for me. I am running late. Lori, you French braid so beautifully. Would you mind doing mine NOW? We told Lori she didn't have to do all their errands if she didn't want. Well, it seems she did want and they let her in on all their secrets. And she never once divulged one of them to us. Lori says the reason she didn't buck the house rules was because she learned from the others the consequences weren't worth it.

It was so very fortunate for Tom that Chap came into our lives at such a crucial time. If it is true that a boy must make transference from his mother to his father between the ages of 9 and 14, then Tom was right there. If there is no father, perhaps other male role models can be drafted to fill in; such as scout leaders, boys club, church youth groups, summer camp, uncles or brothers.

Tom gave us little trouble except when he bottomed out two

vehicles of Chap's. Chap couldn't figure out what was happening until one day a man mentioned seeing Tom speeding on North 2nd Street on a slight incline and jumping the railroad tracks, flying about five or so feet in the air, only to land keplop on all fours. Another time, I believe he was looking at girlie magazines. Other than that Chap and Tom are tight friends and loyal to each other. Tom has learned much in the construction business, as well as in the Christian Book Shops. Tom is shifting into manhood.

When Tom was younger he had fluid in his middle ear. His tonsils and adenoids had become so enlarged they blocked his Eustachian tubes, causing fluid to build up in his middle ear. The symptoms were a fear of heights, and a hearing loss. However, it was several years before it was diagnosed. After we had his tonsils and adenoids removed, I looked out one morning three days later, and he was walking on top of our seven-foot high brick wall. I guess his plastic tubes popped out in the yard. We never found them. His hearing is perfect now. However, he lost five of the fastest learning years, and I would say it took 15 years for him to catch up.

Later, Tom wanted to live with his dad, which turned out to be a hurtful experience, and it took him a long time to get over the rejection. Ever since, he and Chap have been the best of friends.

One of the most agonizing problems for SM'S and SF'S is in trying to help a child forgive one or both of his parents. It's rough, but he must settle it within himself. It has to be dealt with. Otherwise it will poison his future relationships. Forgiveness creates a liberating force within.

No doubt, children are at times disappointed and depressed with the kind of parents they have. When their parents are less than what they believe them to be, or what they want them to be, they can become disillusioned.

Joyce Landorf in *Irregular People* sums up the entire dilemma with the answer being, "Love that person as they are, not what you wish they were."[1]

The younger the child the longer it takes to get it all in

CHOOSING A LOVE THAT WILL LAST

perspective. As I explained to all the kids once; we are not perfect parents and neither are you perfect kids. The children must forgive their parents as surely as the parents have to forgive their children. Parents can also wish they had other and better kids.

It is still my deep contention that if the patriarch of the family doesn't function, no amount of substitution will make it a normal, healthy, loving family! The man is the head of each home. That way everyone is taken care of. If every man in the world would take care of his own son or sons, whether in training or financing, there would be need for few welfare programs in our country. It's that simple. Each man takes care of his own. Then as each son matures, he in turn takes care of his sons. "But if any provide not for his own, and especially for those of his own house, he hath denied the faith and is worse than an infidel." I Tim. 5:8 KJV.

Several incidents during the children's teenage years come to mind. One of them was the afternoon I picked Tami up from school. I was humming some tune. She said in disgust, "Oh, Mother, don't sing."

I slowed the car down and told her, "Get out, please." She walked all the way home. That was the last I heard of my melodious voice. Dear Tami!

There were many happy times together, especially around our big old octagon-shaped table at dinnertime. Also on trips. I remember reading various stimulating and interesting books as we traveled because it kept down the noise level in the car.

On one occasion, while driving home after dark (couldn't read) from a football game in Austin, University of Texas vs Texas A & M, and visiting Tari Alice, the kids were laughing, talking too loud and in general horsing around. It seemed like hours of this with Chappy reminding them several times to quiet down, only to begin again within minutes. Without warning, Chappy stopped the car and said very calmly and ever so softly (not his usual tone), "Okay, everybody out." Reminds me of the Godfather who said, "I'm going to make you an offer you can't refuse." Anyway, we drove off leaving all five of them beside the road South of Falfurrias at nighttime. Chappy and I drove on until we were out of their sight. What pure delight the quiet before turning around to pick them up. They thought it was a lark! They loved being abandoned by their parents so they could enjoy the noise before their parents returned.

We never were lonely with this bunch and there were always many happenings in a day. It seemed there was no end to what we should teach the children. Retirement seemed far away.

CHOOSING A LOVE THAT WILL LAST

CHAPTER 34

ISLE OF VIEW

Our ranch in Mexico, *Isle of View*, holds countless memories for our entire family. The old damned-up creeks, the Tarzan swing tied on a limb high in the pecan trees, the watermelons floating and chilling in the crystal clear cool water.

One time we put a big card table in the center of the creek and ate in our bathing suits while the water bubbled and gurgled on by us, splashing the rocky bottom. Also, we could always tell when the leeches appeared in the water because we could hear the kids' screams all the way up to the house. How they detested those leeches!

Our friends, Bill and Peggy Nix, had the Lower Hilton while we were perched atop the Upper Hilton, a distance of several hundred yards. Whenever they would leave for the U.S., we would run around to the other side of our mountain and ring and clang the old church bell my dad had installed near his cabin, and we would all sing to the Nixes below, "Vaya Con Dios." Our voices would echo throughout the whole Sierra Madre Mountain range.

One particular summer we spent a lot of time at *Isle of View*. It seemed to take four days to wash the city out of us. By then we were communing with nature and the natives. The sky was devastatingly beautiful since it was so dark--no city lights. The contrast made the millions of brilliant stars even brighter, being splattered unevenly across the black velvety dome encircling the earth.

In rearing children, my dad taught me it was important not to force your children to lie. For instance, when the children come in from a date not to ask, "Where did you go?" Instead, "Did you have a good time?" The children are more apt to open up and tell you all about the evening. Of course, if you have taught them well over the growing-up years, surely by now they should be able to make some good decisions on their own.

There is a world of difference between authority and domination. Authority sets the guidelines, guides, teaches and lets the child make some decisions along the way. Domination says here are the rules and you will obey them because I say so, or the church says so, without any participation on the child's part in making any decisions. Domination seeks to *control* another person's will. That is witchcraft.

Authority creates love, trust and protection while domination creates rebellion and prodigals. Prodigals because they go wild and out of bounds when they leave home. They haven't learned how to make any decisions of their own. Even God gives us a choice. While they are under our authority when young, they may make some wrong choices, but we are there to guide and encourage them to make better decisions the next time, or perhaps help them see the consequences of their choices. We are to train up a child in the way he should go and when he is old, he will not depart from it. Proverbs 22:6 KJV.

Every time I see a too fancy lady on TV, it is my guess that she is the end result of domination when young. Now that she is grown and out on her own, she can't get enough of the forbidden or restricted things. Represents breaking out of bondage. Dolly Parton said that her family was so poor, she was denied all the pretty things. Now she loves all those razzle-dazzle wigs, clothes and jewelry. Also, it seems to be more acceptable in certain religious circles than previously since some of the TV personalities are coming out. I dare say few of them were given many choices while growing up. Later it seems to cause an over-emphasis.

There is another cardinal rule that Chappy and I regard as pertinent in rearing children. Do not let them use you. For example, after they are grown and on their own, it is important not to let them use you in any way, except in exceptional circumstances. My dad used to say to any of us asking to borrow money from him, "Since you are going to pay it back, then why not go to the bank and sign a note? I won't co-sign, but if you can't pay the interest, I will." That was the last time my dad was in trouble with loans. Proverbs advises us not to co-sign anyone's note. (22:26).

There are several heartbreaking stories I heard only recently concerning parents lending their children money. Randall Pettit (not his real name) wanted to borrow $40,000.00 to clear up all his small debts and he would pay his parents back each month. Very soon afterwards, Randall bought a home and informed his parents he couldn't afford to pay them back, saying that he should have more at his age because his brothers have more than he does. Jolly O! The whole family has been affected and is estranged because of this loan. The parents were out the $40,000.00 and the love of their son, as well. The better part of wisdom would be to keep the 40 grand and have the love of the entire family.

Another story told to my mother was of Lydia Crockett (not her real name), who was in a rest home in McAllen. Lydia had two sons who wanted to borrow $100,000.00 so they could go into business. Of course, when the business got on its feet and was making a lot of money, they would pay her back. This was her life's savings which her doctor husband had left to take care of her. That was the last she ever saw of her money or her two sons. Unbelievable!

Don't distribute your wealth till death unless you are very wealthy, someone has advised.

Something for nothing, makes one greedy. Glory Chapman.

Of course, a parent may lend to a son if they have sufficient funds which they don't need for their old age, and have it understood it is to be deducted from their portion of their inheritance later on. And, too, every so often it might be good to give to them if you feel so led. Extenuating circumstances always have to be considered.

I saw Dr. Kevin Leman, author of the book *Birth Order*, on

television the other night and he remarked that as long as the parents keep doling out to the baby (or other children) of the family, the baby doesn't usually grow up. His suggestion was to let the baby hit bottom. It would do him good. Interesting!

Every once in a while Chappy and I would have fun with the children, usually at the dinner table. First, we would nudge each other discreetly, then move our eyes in a certain way, and whisper, "Shall we tell them?"

They would exclaim, "Tell us what?" They would go wild and guess it right away. "Are you going to have a baby, Ms. Glory?" In unison they would all turn green with envy and with many dramatic gestures yell, "Oh no, we can just see him now, M-R. P-E-R-F-E-C-T."

"Really, How can you say that? You would love him," we would counter teasingly.

"Yeah, but he would be special because he would belong to both of you."

Their reactions were comical to watch. They got extremely verbal and when we said, "Well, not yet but it would be nice, wouldn't it to have a little baby in the house?" They never agreed and were most resistant to even discussing it. It was hilarious to us!

There was a problem with food when we first merged our two families. I usually shopped once a month for all the staples, freezing all the milk and bread. Only lettuce, cabbage, tomatoes and some fresh fruits had to be purchased more often.

At the beginning of the month the pantry, frig and deep freeze would be stuffed with food. The kids would eat everything in sight. I would go to fix a casserole, a salad or whatever, only to discover the chips, bell peppers, nuts and fruits had all been eaten. I explained, "Hey gang, all the food is for you kids so please let me cook it first." No one liked going to the grocery store, including me.

Finally, we had a system. If I put the fruit next to the refrigerator, it could be eaten any time, but if it was placed next

CHOOSING A LOVE THAT WILL LAST

to the ovens, then it wasn't to be touched and was for mealtime. That worked some of the time. In fact, later Chappy even put a lock on the pantry door. It worked until Lori saw Chap open the door with a butter knife once. She showed the others how easy it was to open.

Understandably, all of them were famished when they came in after school, so we had a deal where they could eat all they wanted of celery, carrot sticks and juices, but nothing else till dinnertime. "Why?" they whined.

Chappy expounded, "Because you will all be full and there will be no one to eat what Ms. Glory goes to all the trouble to fix."

Six-thirty was the dinner hour at our house--the only dinner hour unless there was an emergency. All the kids made plans around that time. They could go back later, but they had to be at the dinner table with the whole pack. And, too, it made only one clean-up necessary, to say nothing of getting to see each other and catch up on the day's happenings. I would suggest if you can't do anything else, do have a dinnertime all together. It's number one priority on our list of rearing children. Number one!

Tari and Tami often thought the Chapman girls were too talkative and sometimes wired, and would interject, "Hey, let us talk once in a while." Whereupon we would all roar with laughter.

There was some trouble with our girls talking to boys at the curb in front of our home. We never knew for sure if they were flagging the boys down, or just waving to attract them. Anyhow, we wanted them to invite the boys on in instead of carrying on out in the street.

Taking baths had to be managed as well. My children were used to a large family, but I had to explain to Kim and Lee that all the rules change in a household of eight to ten and aren't the same as in a smaller family. For instance, not all of them could take baths at once. One reason being the two hotwater heaters couldn't supply enough hot water and bedtime got to be too late for the last ones. We suggested half of them bathe at night and the other half in the morning. Well, it seemed they all wanted to bathe in the morning. Some lamented they had never bathed at night and that they would feel yucky in the morning dressing and going to school without bathing, emphasizing their point by very pained expressions. I had no idea it would matter so much. Well, they adjusted, took turns and traded and we were careful not to notice who did what when.

Next was the laundry problem. Of course, having live-in help for over 20 years, I wasn't fully aware of just how many towels and linens we used everyday. You have to realize we lived on the Mexican border and domestic help was in abundance. I did realize we had to buy a washer and dryer every four years whereas my friends commented they bought them only about every eight years. Anyway, now that I was the laundress, I was appalled by as many as 18 dirty towels a day, not to mention other items. Realizing there was only an average of about seven to ten persons living there at a time, I couldn't figure out for the life of me how they could use that many towels if they tried. "Oh, Ms. Glory, we use one for our hair and one for our bodies." That was going to be more difficult than I had surmised. Whereupon, I prevailed upon Chappy to kindly install a long towel rod for each child. In no time at all we had enough bars so they could spread out all their towels to dry between uses.

They were receptive to this idea and usually used their same towels for about three days. However, from time to time there were some overtones of one of them grabbing the other's towel because it was closer to the shower door. Since we got firmer and louder than they did, they seldom bothered us with such trivia. On occasion, we could hear some running overhead and wondered who was chasing whom and for why!

Along with all this domestic training, we stressed the need to put more than one item in the dryer at a time, and if possible to steam press more than one article at a time. If you hang up your clothes, they won't need so many fluffing ups and pressings.

There were also the everyday adjustments that needed to be

made to make the household run smoother, and Chappy was super about helping to implement the changes.

Chappy started a tradition that made all of us very happy. On my birthday, he came bounding into our bedroom with my favorite breakfast on a tray, complete with a single red rose, singing to the top of his voice, "Happy Birthday to Baby." So thereafter everyone got the same treatment complete with photo included, despite their objections of how gross they looked in the morning. The others would jump out of bed and join in the chorus. For dinner, they chose the menu, kind of cake and friends.

As each child got older, I taught them to cook; first a single dish, salad or dessert. Later, they were to put a complete meal on the table with the salad being cold and the main course hot. Our goal was for all to be able to sit down at once and no one have to get up for a single item during the entire meal. It was a challenge! I would see them checking out loud to themselves: napkins, salt, pepper, lemons, butter, sauces, spoons in each serving dish, etc. Usually the younger ones would chime in when asked to start learning to cook, "Oh, I already know how to cook."

"Yes, my dear, your spaghetti and chocolate chip cookies are delicious, but we want a whole meal."

Honest to goodness, I never cared that much about eating until Kim and Lee came to live with us. When I would pick them up from school, they would run to the car and be all breathless, asking, "Ms. Glory, what are we having for dinner tonight? I am starved. I can't wait." They used other gestures and would moan and look so pitiful that by the time we reached the house the aroma of the food cooking caused more outcries. I am very sure that is when I got psyched out on food.

Actually, by the time I got it on the table, I, too, was shoveling it in as fast as they. I thought, "My mother should see me now," because I was the worst eater of her entire eight children. I am still overeating which makes me unhappy, but once psyched, always psyched!

GLORY CHAPMAN

In the food connection, one of the most fun times we have all shared was at the condo on South Padre Island, some 70 miles from McAllen. Some were married by this time, and ten of us were there this particular time and shared in the cooking. It worked like this: each two formed a couple and were responsible for one day's meals--brunch and dinner--complete with bringing all the groceries to prepare their gourmet menus.

It was deeply satisfying as parents, and fun to watch each set perform. Nothing was to be said to them. What each pair was planning was to be a surprise, but you should have seen the rest of us peering over the high snack bar the first day, observing Kim and Jim Skaines' (her husband) every move. It turned out they loved all the attention. It would make me nervous with that many eyes glued on my preparations. They used the large island cutting board to painstakingly chop, measure and assemble their kabobs until they presented us with their version of bon appetit.

Tari and Tami formed a team. We kept missing Tami, who we discovered was making numerous trips to the supermarket to be sure her fresh fruit salad contained every fruit available. It was perfect, though a little over stirred. Tari prepared a new special recipe of curried chicken and rice. We observed that none was left.

Each couple outdid the previous one, it seemed, until Chappy and I were feeling concerned that the last twosome couldn't match the outstanding and delicious cuisine of the previous days.

We shouldn't have worried our aging heads because Lee Ann and Ted Burns (her husband) came up with succulent handpicked Idaho baked potatoes, individual T-bones barbecued on the grill over mesquite wood, a mouth-watering tossed green salad and dressing, together with large black olives with whole wheat buttered bread. We breathed a sigh of relief! There were many oohs and aahs! The salad was chilled and the bones were hot.

Tom and Lori served as a support team--setting the tables, cleaning up and handling the garbage.

They keep expressing that they want to repeat the performance

CHOOSING A LOVE THAT WILL LAST

soon since they enjoyed it so much. Their real fulfillment, I believe, came in being appreciated for their efforts, and their self worth got a big shot in the arm. They did indeed deserve the applause. This band does not hand out *Trade Lasts* easily.

Years before when Shari was learning to cook, she made some oatmeal cookies while I was shopping. Miss Independence wanted to do it all on her own to surprise me. Great! Oh, the tempting odor that wafted throughout the house when I returned was tantalizing! After dinner, Shari proudly presented her creation to eager participants.

Tami was the first to take a big bite of the cookie, only to look at it strangely. One by one we all sampled her dainties. Almost in unison we all said, "What did you put in these cookies?" You could see her disappointment mounting as she informed us she had gone by the recipe. Several had thought they tasted very salty. Shari went to get the cookbook and inquired, "Hey, Mom, what is a tsp? I didn't know so I just put in a cup."

She has not been able to live that one down--"Hey, Shari, what's a tsp?"

The strong emphasis Chappy and I have tried to impart to the children is that physical beauty is something unearned for the most part. It's what we add to any beauty we may have that counts when beauty and youth fades. Of course, beauty never hurts and helps a lot. Like, money isn't everything, but name one thing you can do without it.

An incident happened that Kim couldn't quite figure out. I was getting ready to leave for a party. Kim looked up with a startled expression. "What's the matter, Kim?" I queried.

"Well, I don't know if I should say this, but Ms. Glory, you don't look as pretty as usual," Kim replied a little reluctantly.

"I know, Kim, sometimes I want to go just as I am. After all, it is the real me I want them to love, not what I wear. However, I realize it is important to try to look my best most of the time."

Kim looked puzzled and asserted, "I never heard of that."

I remember Jason saying one time, "You sure don't try to

impress me." It was when I had worn a pair of tennis shoes with a small hole in one. Seeing me at my worst and seeing the real me was important somehow.

On the other hand, learning young to achieve, develop other qualities like academic prowess, athletic achievements and managerial ability can, in the long run, be more enduring and rewarding, creating a very healthy self worth that beauty alone can't accomplish. There have been some beauty queens who have withdrawn as they became older. Their product was beauty. Unless the physically beautiful woman develops something within her personality and spirit, it is possible her self esteem may deteriorate at the same rate her beauty fades. Isn't it fortunate our eyesight goes about the time we get wrinkles?

We feel the real beauty in any family is the one who makes others feel loved, accepted and important. If you have those attributes, believe me, the world is your oyster. It seems we are always so worried about how *we* look. Worry that much about how your mother, sister and friends look and you will be loved and cherished forever.

We play down any conversation in the family as to the personal physical traits: shortest, tallest, widest, fairest and ugliest, as well as intellectual or other prowess or the lack of it. Chappy has remarked over the years, "Isn't it fortunate that we have no ugly children?"

Each of them is a unique creation and we want them to be their own person. We don't need two of any of them. It is of great importance that each of them accepts himself.

I will never forget when I finally faced this challenge for myself. I settled it by saying to myself, *You are not the most beautiful girl in the world and neither are you the ugliest woman in the world. Just settle in and accept yourself for who you are, not who you wish you were.* Previously, I had been so self-centered because of my birdlegs and long nose. Remember other people cannot cure your insecurities. They may want to, but the insecure person has to deal with those problems within

CHOOSING A LOVE THAT WILL LAST

himself. Oh, the years I wanted to have my nose bobbed like Nanette Fabry. Twenty years later I saw her pug nose and was thankful I didn't have it done. My face is not shaped like hers.

Pretty Arlene Seibring, my next door neighbor, told me she had planned for years that her first paycheck after college would go to correct her slightly protruding front teeth. When the time came, her husband, Bart, asked her, "Who will love you anymore than they do now if you have your teeth fixed?" She couldn't think of anyone and never had the work done.

Someone has said that we begin to like another person the minute we detect some flaw, fault or imperfection in them.

A survey was made to ascertain at what age people were the happiest. It was determined by the poll that the age of 50 was the best. When asked why, the survey showed that at that age they feel they know who they are, have accepted themselves and can finally be their own person, saying *no* without apology.

We all have to overcome some handicap or obstacle in life. Peronally, I know of no one with a perfect life, and deduce there are few happy or perfect marriages.

How many people do you know who had perfect childhoods? That's a favorite line of mine when the children try to intimidate me by saying, "Everyone else's parents let them, or everyone else can stay out till two in the morning." First, I put forth that perhaps they could get themselves adopted to that generous and permissive family. Secondly, I ask them to name the friends with perfect parents and childhoods. Come on, call out their names!

Over the years, it has been my experience that most truly abused children say little or nothing about their parents. They are very protective and cover for them. Whereas, spoiled and pampered children are disrespectful and speak openly and disparagingly of their parents. The abused child tries to hide his parent's fault and show him love in spite of such harsh and uncivil treatment.

While a provisional in the Junior Service League, our small group was involved in some welfare training at the courthouse in nearby Edinburg. The counselor explained to us in detail about a 3-year old boy who had been placed on a red ant hill by his mother. Another time she put his little hands on a hot stove and burned him badly. Welfare, of course, wanted to take the little fella away from his mother. However, the little boy clung tightly to his mother and wanted to go home with her despite the torturous things she had done to him. The counselor tried, without success, to persuade him to go home with some nice people who would treat him kindly and lovingly. He sobbed wildly, "NO! NO! She is my Mama. NO! NO! NO! She is my Mama. I belong to her. I want to go home with my Mama. I belong to my Mama. I don't belong to those other people."

Just an observation in passing. We have discovered in rearing children that their rebellion subsides at about the same rate their own self-worth is realized and their lives are fulfilled.

Criticism is something we all meet at one time or another in our lives. This is the advice we passed on to our children about taking themselves or criticism too seriously. Never take to heart any criticism without first considering the source. But at the same time, there could be times when we should heed the critics.

Uncle Bud Robinson was a tongue-tied preacher in the early 1900's. After the services one Sunday, as he was walking along the path to his home, he overheard some members commenting that his sermon was extremely uplifting and edifying. Uncle Bud prayed, "Oh Lord, helps me not to get too puffed up."

As he neared his home, his ears caught the word from a nearby porch, "If I couldn't preach any better than that I wouldn't even try."

Poor ole Uncle Bud looked downcast and prayed, "Oh Lord, don't lets me get too puffed down."

It was some years ago that my sister, Ruthie, and her husband, Charles, told me about being out with a couple for the evening. During the entire time, the husband kept making derogatory remarks about his wife, using sarcastic and demeaning words and gestures. This went on unabated as the night progressed without

CHOOSING A LOVE THAT WILL LAST

his wife once offering any defense. Finally, in total disgust at the husband's insensitive behavior, Charles turned to the wife pleadingly, "Are all of those things true of you?"

With poise and quiet dignity, she acknowledged, "Yes, they are. That's why I couldn't marry anyone more intelligent."

There is much required of parents, especially stepparents. That role is one of life's greatest challenges, but ONCE THE WORST HAS HAPPENED TO YOU, EVERYTHING ELSE IS LESS. Before, little things would bother me, but not now. Also, knowing that I am in the center of God's will gives me great strength and security to endure much. This is the secret. Remember, too, Chappy is sharing this load with me. Life shared is half as heavy and twice as light.

Also, I am well aware of what is involved in rearing children. It is my belief that most parents experience some disappointing and heartbreaking times, as well as many joys and rewards. There are no perfect children and no perfect parents. So what else is new?

Some days I am sure they would rather have that adoptive permissive mother, and other times I feel loved through and through.

There are a few special things that transpire in being a mother--like prayers, sweat, talk, tears, patience, work and love. Just writing about all of them makes my heart beat wild with emotion and love, including our Godsend sons-in-law and Nancy and Margie, our beloved daughters-in-law. It also makes me wish I was a much better mother.

It has been 20 years since we merged and blended our families, and I would have to say God did a beautiful thing--not to be misconstrued there were no problems--but all of us are wiser, kinder and more appreciative of each other, remembering that relationships not only go on for a lifetime here, but in the next world also.

Here is a poem Shari wrote on December 3, 1982.

GLORY CHAPMAN

MOTHER

Your day.
Happy, happy birthday.
Happy, happy, happy day.
Mother, in each and every way
This greeting comes to you
With much love and appreciation
For the emotion and steadfast devotion,
The patience of a Latter Day saint
(Hardly a murmur or a complaint),
The sensible advice; Ann Landers would be jealous
Of one so scrupulously conscientious and zealous,
You could have made a good politician's wife
Yet still you lead an interesting life.
Are you sure you weren't born of nobility?
Because "Joan of Arc" you could be.

I admire your confidence and composure
It is characteristic of a 'domestic queen,'
Consistently kind, never mean,
True grit; able to master the futile fight
Ne'er turn tail and run in frenzied flight
Conquer we must, in God is our trust
Else we wither and turn into dust."

We thought we had our hands full and couldn't handle any more children, but that was before the doorbell rang!

CHOOSING A LOVE THAT WILL LAST

CHAPTER 35

YOURS, MINE PLUS THREE MAKES TWELVE

One day while I was alone, the doorbell rang and there stood Mary Robles, a girl whom Chappy had been teaching in a group in evening classes. I could see she was in great distress. Her aunt was with her and asked if Mary could come and stay with us.

Mary came in and her aunt left. It was awhile before Mary was able to open up and tell me what had happened. She began recalling the past first. Her mother had died two years earlier and things at home were intolerable for her because of her father's abuse, as well as for Sylvia and Mark, her sister and brother. "Could they all please come and live with us too?" Mary wanted to know.

Chappy and I talked it over and without knowing exactly what would be involved or for how long, we asked all three to move in with us. They were 19, 17 and 14 years old.

The other kids were so supportive and helpful with making them feel at home. There were days when it was tedious inasmuch as we had to help them with legal problems, as well as hiding them out during one period of time. At first, all three of them were very jittery and uptight.

If anyone would have told me earlier that I would take in three more children, I wouldn't have believed them. I assure you that if Mary had knocked on your door, you, too, would have taken them in. They are beautiful, warm and loving kids.

Not sensing or expecting that I would learn why these precious kids came to us, I discovered later we were the beneficiaries.

Sylvia would come in from working at the bank, put her arms around me while I was cooking dinner and say, "Oh, Ms. Glory, I have been thinking about you all day. I bet you don't like doing so much cooking." It was a new experience for me (not the cooking). Our children are dear and do memorable things, but not in this way. It touched me deeply.

Another time, I overheard Sylvia and Mary explaining how much they missed their mother, and how important a mother was. Our children reacted as if, "Oh Mother, she is always here. What's so special about a mother?"

Also, Tom had a brother, Mark, to share the west wing with. Mark was a well mannered and helpful young boy.

It was of utmost importance that we help these three children understand what happened and to forgive their dad. It was made easier when they understood they wouldn't have to go back and live with him. We stressed forgiving him, getting him help, but that they wouldn't have to tolerate his abuse any longer. When they fully realized that forgiveness didn't involve their returning, they felt safe and protected and it was easier to start forgiving.

"To forgive is to set a prisoner free and discover that the prisoner was you."[1]

It was indeed a joyless day for all of us when the three of them moved into an apartment with their grandparents. However, that trio is a part of our family and always will be. We dearly love them, and I might add all three are fine, having homes of their own.

In having lunch recently with Sylvia, she expressed again to me how very grateful she was to have been given the privilege to live in a normal and loving family. Otherwise, she would not have known what a home should be like. Sylvia brought me this article published by the Dallas Morning News on February 3, 1986, written by Joyce Maynard.

"...the only home worth having is the kind that makes you strong enough to venture forth. Nothing is worth much that comes without risk. Giving someone your heart. Having a child. They all leave us open to danger and loss. The more you risk, maybe, the more you have to gain. The more you have, the more you have to lose. And still, it's for all of us to press on, not shrink back..."

CHOOSING A LOVE THAT WILL LAST

It hurt to see them move out, and I told Sylvia that I wished they could have stayed longer. Now, to see all three of them maturing and adjusting, having mastered some of life's worst hurts, is a feeling beyond my ability to describe adequately. Sylvia and her husband, Robert, now have three adorable children.

Here is the letter Chappy received on Father's Day from Mary:

"Dear Chappy:

The Chaplocks nor Scurmans know what it's like to be miles away and yearning to be close to you. In fact, I doubt if they even realize how much they neglect you. Hee! Hee! We sure wish we could be closer. We asked the Lord for Dallas, but He gave us Columbus, Ohio. I guess that means you all have to come and visit us. There's only two of you and five of us. (Mary had three babies in one year. Twins and eleven months later another). What do you say?

"Don't you realize how much we need your special bearhugs, your warm smiles and especially those wonderful words of wisdom that you so beautifully possess? You've been a great inspiration to me, and I don't want you to forget it. You're a man acquainted with sorrow just like Christ, and like Christ you affect people around you just by being near them. When I think of you, I can't help but think of Jesus because to be in your presence is to feel Jesus' presence. There has been a purpose for all the pain in our lives and I thank God for you.

"Please give our love to Ms. Glory and all those blessed kids who get to be near you on such a special day as Father's Day."

Our love,
Mary and Paul

There were tears in Chappy's eyes when he finished reading that letter. And I was not neglected on Mother's Day either.

I often awake at 3 am every morning, and the things I have left undone that day for each child and others comes crowding in on me. Did I send that wedding gift, write that note, call my mother, plan to see Granny, how long since I did something special for our children and 14 grandchildren, plan a picnic, catch up on my photograph albums, have lunch with a friend, read books for my next book review and so on.

It certainly appears to me that I am far too busy to be the mother I envision myself to be. The days go jetting by me faster than the speed of light.

This little old lady in the shoe had so many children she didn't know what to do. Apparently!

Almost daily I tell the Lord how thankful I am that He gave me such a challenging and interesting life. Such a peaceful and fulfilling lifestyle, so full of love and trust. Perhaps the indicator would reveal that my nails have grown out, and probably I don't average a good cry once a year. This humpty-dumpty now feels whole, safe and loved along with her six big egglets.

If you can only know happiness to the degree you have known sorrow, then my cup runneth over.

"Sorrows remembered sweeten present joys. Joys are our wings; sorrow our spurs."[2]

This may surprise you, but whenever Chappy and I have a disagreement, I talk to God about it, reminding Him that He gave this man to me, so please have him apologize if he needs to. If not, for me to apologize to him. Usually it is settled forthwith. The judge of my Appellate Court is always in session, and I take my grievances there often. He speaks to all the parties involved and the differences are settled out of court.

This is not to say we don't have other problems, such as the tremendous economic downturn in the southern states. Certainly life has its ups and downs, but the big difference is we have someone who walks with us through them. They come to *pass*. Also, not to be overlooked is the fact Chappy and I have each other. "A joy shared is a double joy; a sorrow shared is only half a sorrow."[3]

We are still in training. We rely heavily upon our Father as His knowledge is invaluable on the unchartered courses of our lives, and He has the capability of changing the ebb and flow of the

CHOOSING A LOVE THAT WILL LAST

tides in our lives.

William Mathews says, "It cannot be too often repeated that it is not helps, but obstacles, not facilities, but difficulties that make men."[4]

When at last the nest was empty and all the children were gone, someone asked Chappy how it felt, to which he cheerily told them, "We cried for the first three minutes and have been laughing ever since. I've been trying to get Glory all to myself for ten years. I love it."

We now have 20 remarkable grandchildren who call us Gigi and Papa. They are *grand*. We have the best of both worlds--we love, spoil, tease and enjoy them without any of the responsibility of training. Each of them is precious and unique in his own way.

Children are indeed a reward from the Lord--priceless gifts loaned to us for a few years.

You may have also detected I have a short memory about some bad things. I let those go on down with the water under the bridge, keeping only the good memories for myself.

I like what C. S. Lewis said in *Mere Christianity*. "God asserts that every individual human being is going to live forever, and this must be either true or false. Now there are a good many things which would not be worth bothering about if we were going to live only 70 years, but which I had better bother about very seriously if I am going to live forever.

"The settled happiness and security which we all desire, God withholds from us by the very nature of the world: but joy, pleasure, and merriment, he has scattered broadcast. We are never safe, but we have plenty of fun, and some ecstasy. It is not hard to see why. The security we crave would teach us to rest our hearts in this world and oppose an obstacle to our return to God: a few moments of happy love, a landscape, a symphony, a merry meeting with our friends, a bath or a football match, have no such tendency. Our Father refreshes us on the journey with some pleasant inns, but will not encourage us to mistake them for home..."[5]

"If we will never live again after we die, then we might as well go and have ourselves a good time: let us eat, drink and be merry. What's the difference? For tomorrow we die, and that ends everything! Don't be fooled by those who say such things." I Cor. 15:32,33.

"There is a time, we know not when,
   A point we know not where,
That marks the destiny of men,
   For glory or despair.

There is a line, by us unseen,
   That crosses every path;
The hidden boundary between
   God's patience and His wrath."
         Joseph Addison Alexander

When at last this life on earth has ended, and we enter into our eternal and everlasting home, won't heaven be the grandest lifestyle? One so grand that we have not been able to think how grand. That should be grand indeed!

"...Eye hath not seen, nor ear heard, neither have entered into the heart of man, the things which God hath prepared for *those that love Him.*" I Cor. 2:9 KJV.

Our Father has a happy surprise awaiting our homecoming. We should be greatly heartened in old age looking forward to our Utopia--our forever home. Our senior years should be filled with eagerness and contented anticipation, knowing we will not only have the home of our dreams, but we will be with all those whom we have ever loved and we shall not run out of time. **TIME WILL BE NO MORE!**

"Only one life to live
T'will soon be past
Only what we do

CHOOSING A LOVE THAT WILL LAST

For Christ will last."

"To everything there is a season, and a time to every purpose under the heaven:
A time to be born, and
A time to die;
A time to plant, and
A time to pluck up that which is planted.
A time to kill, and
A time to heal;
A time to break down, and
A time to build up;
A time to weep, and
A time to laugh;
A time to mourn, and
A time to dance;
A time to cast away stones, and
A time to gather stones;
A time to embrace, and
A time to refrain from embracing;
A time to get, and
A time to lose;
A time to keep, and
A time to cast away;
A time to rend, and
A time to sew;
A time to keep silence, and
A time to speak;
A time to love, and
A time to hate;
A time of war, and
A time of peace." Ecc. 3:1-8 KJV

EVERYTHING IS APPROPRIATE IN ITS OWN TIME!

EPILOGUE

If you would like to let God make your choices, and choose a love that will last, but you don't know how to get started, here are some pointers.

1. **BE DESPERATE.** Many times we have to be desperate and hit bottom before we are capable of turning to God with our WHOLE heart.

2. **DRAW CLOSE** to God and He will draw close to you. **THINK** about God, **TALK** to God, express your innermost desires. Let your day be filled with little **prayers** to Jesus and little turnings towards Him. Jesus longs to help, but He cannot until the call of the soul gives Him the right to act. Seek to find the reason for which you were created. Then follow instructions to fulfill your destiny. That's where the joy is.

3. **ASK** specific questions. Be honest, **REPENT** of any known sins that would block your prayers, then bear your heart to God fully. **FORGIVE** others and yourself, forget and go forward.

4. Frequently **WATCH** your **attitude, tongue and the meditation** of your heart. These FIVE phrases can change your life. Try saying, "PLEASE--THANK YOU--I'M SORRY--I LOVE YOU--I'LL PRAY FOR YOU."

5. **READ OFTEN** these words from the book *God Calling*, "Say often, 'God bless....' of any whom you find in disharmony with you, or whom you desire to help. Say it, willing that showers of blessings and joy and success may fall upon them.

"Leave to Me the necessary correcting or training; YOU must only desire joy and blessing for them. At present your prayers are that they should be taught and corrected.

"Oh, if My children would leave My work to Me and occupy themselves with the task I give them. LOVE, LOVE, LOVE. Love will break down all your difficulties. Love will build up all your successes.

"God the destroyer of evil, God the creator of good--is Love.

CHOOSING A LOVE THAT WILL LAST

Loving one another is to use God in your life. To use God in your life is to bring into manifestation all harmony, beauty, joy and happiness."[1]

6. **WAIT** and remain in expectant faith knowing God heard you.

7. Each day write down three things you are grateful for.

8. Memorize and put indelibly into your mind these four things if you hope to be best friends before and marriage:
- **DON'T COMPLAIN**
- **DON'T CHANGE OTHER PERSON**
- **DON'T CRITICIZE**
- **DON'T BLAME**

You can use these simple steps in any situation in life, not just in divorce BUT IN CHOOSING AGAIN A LOVE THAT WILL LAST.

There is no instant formula. It will take time to develop a relationship with God. You must learn, grow and mature. These are guidelines and helps. Each relationship between God and you is unique. **READ the Bible and PRAY everyday,** asking the **HOLY SPIRIT to teach and lead you into all truth, and reveal His will to you.**

Remember God gives the best to those who leave the choice to Him.

YOU WILL BE AMAZED AT WHAT WILL HAPPEN TO THE SPIRIT PART OF YOU AFTER A FEW MONTHS!

Tear this sheet out and place it where you can read it often.

FOOTNOTES

CHAPTER 1:
1. Oswald Chambers, *My Utmost For His Highest*, (Dodd, Mead & Company, 1935).

CHAPTER 2:
1. James Dillet Freeman poem.
2. C. S. Lewis, *Mere Christianity*, (MacMillan Pub., New York, 1943).
3. Roger Elwood, *Angelwalk*, (Crossway Book Co., Wheaton, Illinois).

CHAPTER 3:
1. Neil Clark Warren, *Finding The Love Of Your Life*, (Focus on the Family Pub., Colorado Springs, Co.) pages 161-162.
2. Sheldon Vanauken, *A Severe Mercy*, (Harper & Row Pub., San Francisco 1977)
3.. Alice Byram, *Healing in Broken Places*, (Fleming H. Revell Company, Old Tappan, N. J., 1988).
4. J. B. Phillips, *The New Testament in Modern English*, (MacMillan Company, 1958-1959-1960).
5. Hal Lindsay, *Combat Faith*, (Bantam Books, 1986), page 14.
6. *Footprints*, poem, Author Unknown.
7. Paul Pearsall, *The Ten Laws of Lasting Love*, (Simon & Schuster, Inc., 1230 Avenue of the Americas, New York, NY 10020).

CHAPTER 6:
1. Sir P. Sidney, *The New Dictionary of Thoughts*, (Old Book Co., 1891).

CHAPTER 7:
1. Harvard Business Review, *Quote Unquote*, compiled by Lloyd Cory, (Victor Books, 1977), page 178.
2. C. S. Lewis, *Mere Christianity*, (MacMillan Pub., New York, 1943).
3. Marjorie Holmes, *Two From Galilee*, (Baker Book House, Grand Rapids, Michigan, 49516).
4. Roberta R. Potts, *Daily Blessings*, (O. Roberts Publisher, Tulsa, OK).
5. Harold Willmington.

CHAPTER 8:
1. Two Listeners, *God Calling*, edited by A.J. Russell, (Spire Books, pub. by Fleming H.Revell Co., Old Tappan, N. J. 07675).

CHAPTER 9:
1. Two Listeners, *God Calling*, edited by A.J. Russell, (Spire Books, pub. by Fleming H. Revell Co., Old Tappan, N. J. 07675).
2. *Ann Landers Column*, (Valley Morning Star Newspaper, Harlingen, TX 78550).
3. Orison Marden, *Quote Unquote*, (Victor Books, 1977), page 155.

CHAPTER 14:

1. Catherine Marshall, *Something More*, (McGraw-Hill Book Co., 1974).
CHAPTER 15:
1. Alexander Graham Bell, *Quote Unquote*, (Victor Books, 1977), pg.224.
2. Oswald Chambers, *My Utmost For His Highest*, (Dodd, Mead & Company, 1935).
CHAPTER 17:
1. Elisabeth Elliot, *Loneliness*, (Thos. Nelson Publishers, Nashville, Tn., 1982).
CHAPTER 18:
1. Hannah W. Smith, *The Christian's Secret of a Happy Life*, (Barbour & Company, Inc., Westwood, N.J., 07675, 1985).
2. Creath Davis, *Lord, If I Ever Needed You, It's Now!* (Baker Book, Grand Rapids, Michigan, 1981), page 88.
3. Robert Leighton, *The New Dictionary of Thoughts*, (Old Book Co. ,1891).
4. Paul E. Billheimer, *Don't Waste Your Sorrows*, (Bethany House Pub. Minneapolis, Mn. 55438, 1977).
5. Oswald Chambers, *My Utmost For His Highest*, (Dodd, Mead & Co., 1935).
6. Henry Gariepy, *Portraits of Perserverance*, (Victor Books, 1989), Pg 212.
7. Dr. Reinhold Niebuhr, *The New Dictionary of Thoughts* (Old Book Company, 1891).
CHAPTER 19:
1. Pat Robertson, *The Secret Kingdom*, (Thos. Nelson Pub., Nashville, 1982).
2. F. Bulle, *Lord of the Valleys*, (Logos Intl., Plainfield, N. J., 1972), page 160.
CHAPTER 20:
1. Oswald Chambers, *My Utmost For His Highest*, (Dodd, Mead & Co., 1935).
2. Henry Gariepy, *Portraits of Perserverance*, (Victor Books, 1989).
3. Elisabeth Elliot, *Loneliness*, (Thos. Nelson Pub., Nashville, Tn., 1982).
CHAPTER 21:
1. Willard F. Harley, Jr., *His Needs, Her Needs*, (Fleming H. Revell, 1988).
2. Abigail Van Buren, *Dear Abby Column*, (The Monitor newspaper, McAllen, Texas, 1-14-74).
3. Henry Gariepy, *Portraits of Perserverance*, (Victor Books, 1989).
CHAPTER 22:
1. Jess Moody, *Quote Unquote*, (Victor Books, 1977).
CHAPTER 23:
1. The Two Listeners, *God Calling*, (Fleming H.Revell Co., Old Tappan, N. J., 1988).
2. Jack Deere, *Surprised by the Power of the Spirit*, (Zondervan Pub. , 1993).
CHAPTER 26:

2. Jack Deere, *Surprised by the Power of the Spirit*, (Zondervan Pub., 1993).

CHAPTER 26:
1. Sheldon Vanauken, *A Severe Mercy*, (Harper & Row Pub., San Fr., 1977).
2. Will Rogers, *Quote Unquote*, (Victor Books, 1977), page 161.
3. Elisabeth Elliot, *The Savage My Kinsman*, (Harper & Bros., N.Y., 1961).

CHAPTER 27:
1. C. S. Lewis, *Mere Christianity*, (MacMillan Pub., New York, 1943).

CHAPTER 32:
1. C. S. Lewis, *Mere Christianity*, (MacMillan Pub., New York, 1943).
2. C. S. Lewis, *Quote Unquote*, (Victor Books, 1977, compiled by Lloyd Cory), page 147.
3. Larry & Lucky Parker, *We Let Our Son Die*, (Harvest House, Irvine, CA).

CHAPTER 33:
1. Joyce Landorf, *Irregular People*, (Word, Inc., Dallas, Texas, 1982).

CHAPTER 35:
1. Lewis Smedes, *Forgive and Forget*, (Navpress, Colo. Springs, Co., 80934, 1988), page 41.
2. Jean Paul Richter, 1763-1826, German Humorist, *The New Dictionary of Thoughts*, (Standard Book Company, 1891).
3. Henry Gariepy, *Portraits of Perserverance*, (Victor Books, 1989).
4. Williams Mathews, *The New Dictionary of Thoughts*, (Standard Book Company, 1891).
5. C. S. Lewis, *Mere Christianity*, (MacMillan Pub., New York, 1943).

LES MYSTÈRES DU FAR WEST

LES TROIS DESPERADOS

CAROLINE LAWRENCE

LES MYSTÈRES DU FAR WEST

1

LES TROIS DESPERADOS

Traduit de l'anglais (Royaume-Uni)
par Christophe Rosson

hachette

L'édition originale de cet ouvrage a paru chez Orion Children's Books,
a division of the Orion Publishing Group Ltd,
an Hachette UK company,
sous le titre :

THE WESTERN MYSTERIES
BOOK 1
THE CASE OF THE DEADLY DESPERADOS

Text copyright © Roman Mysteries Limited 2011.
Cartes, couverture et illustrations
copyright © Richard Russell Lawrence 2011.
Conception graphique : Lorette Mayon.

The right of Caroline Lawrence to be identified as
the author of this work has been asserted.

All rights reserved.

Traduit de l'anglais (Royaume-Uni)
par Christophe Rosson.

© Hachette Livre, 2013, pour la traduction française.
Hachette Livre, 43 quai de Grenelle, 75015 Paris.

À ma chère amie Penny,
qui m'a lancée sur cette piste poussiéreuse
le jour où elle m'a offert le True Grit de Charles Portis.

Virginia City en 1862

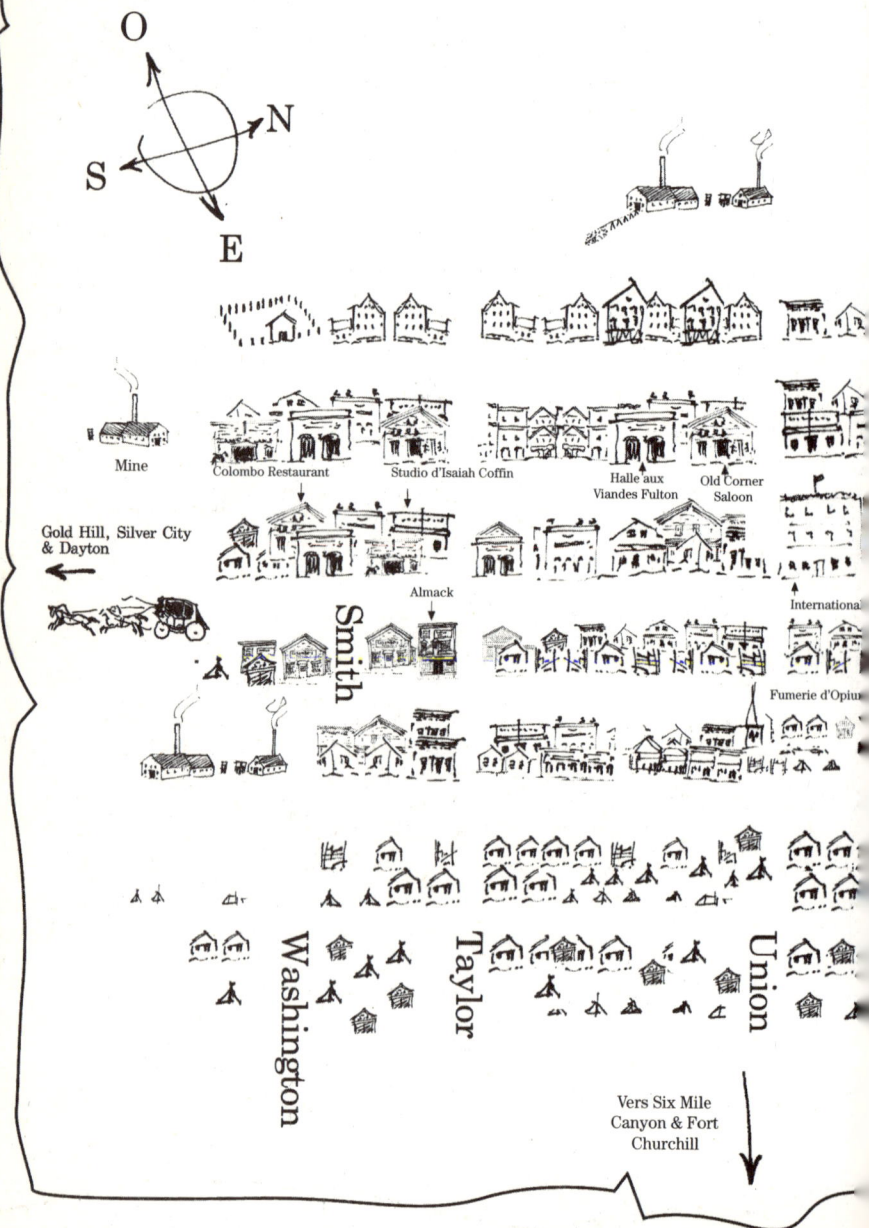

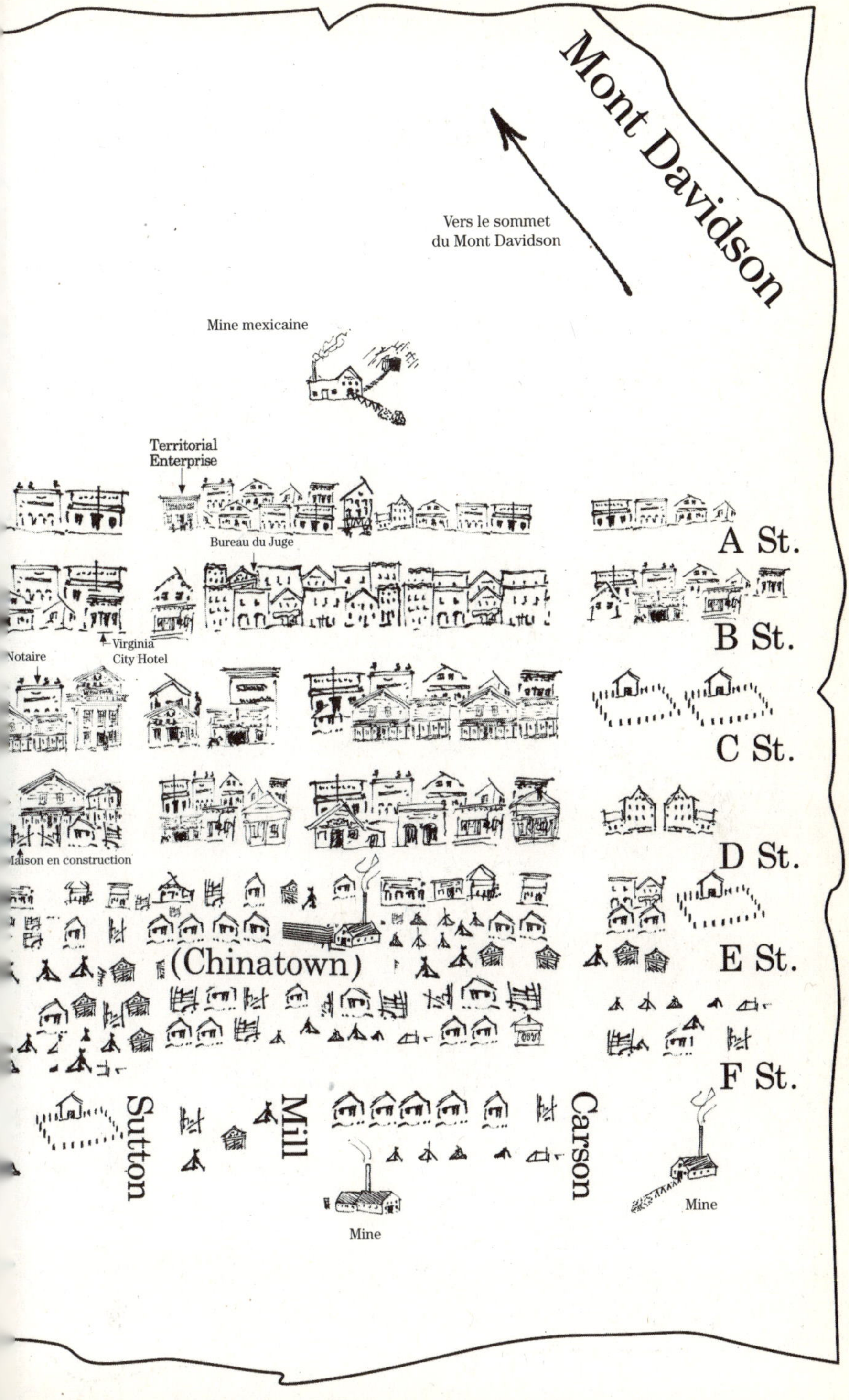

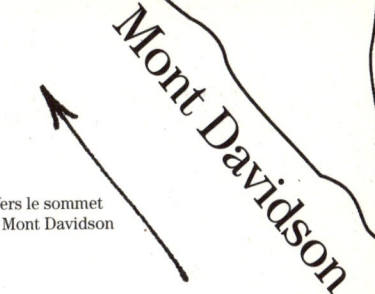

Mont Davidson

Vers le sommet
du Mont Davidson

Mine mexicaine

Territorial
Enterprise

Bureau du Juge

A St.

Notaire   Virginia
City Hotel

B St.

C St.

Maison en construction

D St.

(Chinatown)

E St.

F St.

Sutton   Mill   Carson

Mine   Mine

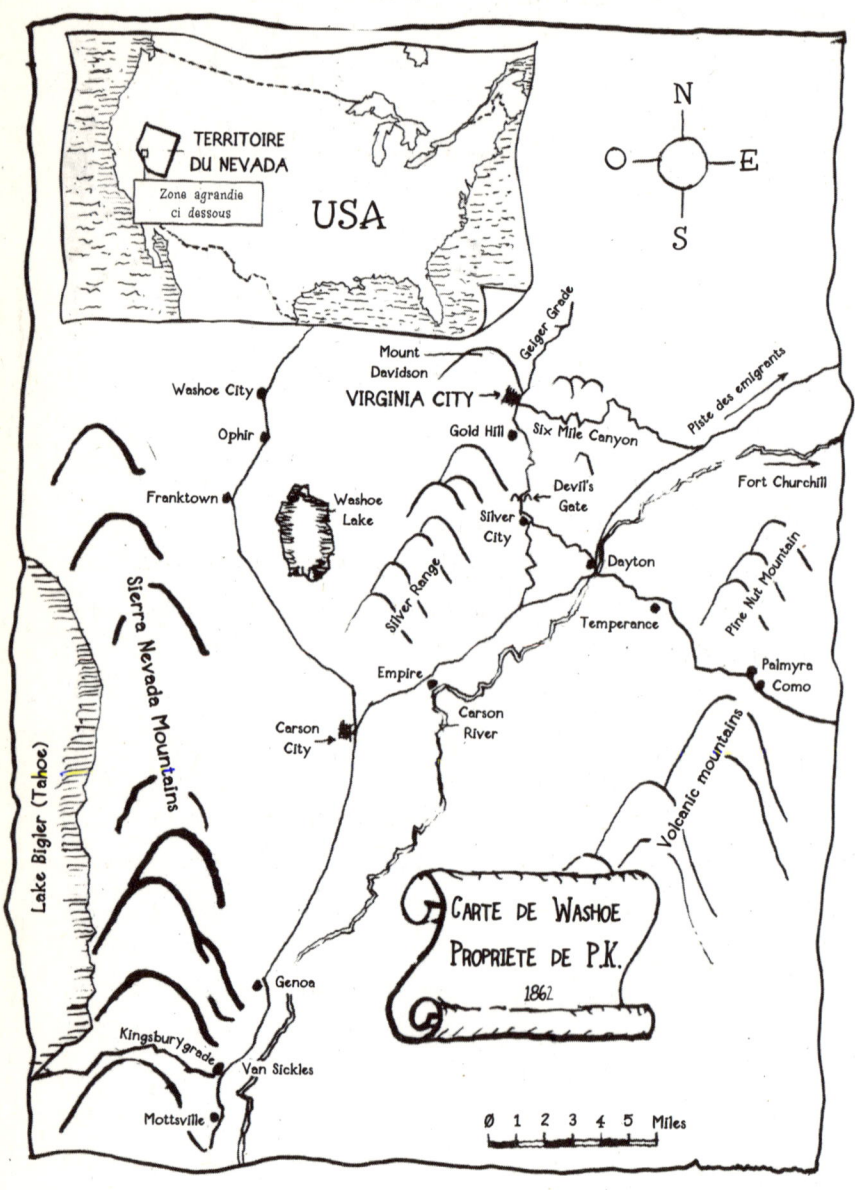

AVANT-PROPOS

Mon arrière-grand-mère, Gertrude Corinne Prince, est née à Battle Mountain, dans le Nevada, en 1877, au sein d'une fratrie de six enfants. Son père conduisait des attelages de mules, ce qui poussa bientôt la famille à s'installer à Sutro, toujours dans le Nevada : une ville proche des grandes mines d'argent de Comstock. Corinne travailla un temps pour la Monnaie de Carson City, avant de partir vivre, avec les siens, à Olympia, dans l'État du Washington. Par la suite, elle s'est mariée et a fini ses jours dans le sud de la Californie. À sa mort, à l'âge respectable de 99 ans, on a retrouvé des livres de comptes dans un coin de son grenier.

Lors d'un récent séjour en Californie, j'aidais ma mère à faire du rangement lorsque nous sommes tombées par hasard sur ces fameux livres — encore ficelés avec du ruban bleu délavé. Avant de les mettre à la poubelle, nous avons décidé d'y jeter un œil. Quelle n'a pas été notre surprise de constater qu'ils ne contenaient pas des données financières, mais les récits passionnants des aventures d'un jeune détective de douze ans. Il y évoquait ses enquêtes à Virginia City, aux premières heures de l'exploitation de l'argent. Ma mère ignorait d'où sa grand-mère tenait ces documents ; ils ne concernent en rien notre famille, et ont apparemment été rédigés quinze ans avant la naissance de Corinne Prince. En dépit du mystère qui entoure leurs origines, j'ai décidé de publier ces récits. Ils offrent un portrait de la vie au Far West, au temps de la guerre de Sécession – il y a de cela cent cinquante ans.

J'ai retouché le moins possible les textes, et me suis contentée de remplacer les termes susceptibles de heurter les lecteurs modernes. J'ai corrigé quelques fautes d'orthographe, mais j'ai conservé les majuscules, les abréviations, les « & », etc. Comme certains mots d'argot ou termes techniques peuvent être difficiles à comprendre, j'ai inclus un glossaire en fin d'ouvrage. On trouvera également une carte de Virginia City telle qu'elle devait être en septembre 1862.

En ce début des années 1860, les journaux des Territoires de l'Ouest n'hésitaient pas à publier comme vraies des histoires créées de toutes pièces. L'un des reporters qui commirent ces indélicatesses fut un dénommé Sam Clemens – lui aussi, nous allons le croiser dans cet ouvrage. Certains de ses articles étaient des mystifications grossières, mais ils lui valurent quelques ennuis de la part d'individus un peu trop crédules. Clemens finira tout de même par devoir quitter le Nevada... Du temps où il officiait à Virginia City, il avait utilisé plusieurs noms de plume, avant de se décider pour celui de Mark Twain.

Je ne suis pas certaine que le récit que vous allez lire soit authentique en tout point ; il s'agit peut-être d'une histoire à dormir debout inventée par Mark Twain. Je vous en laisse juge.

Caroline Lawrence
Londres, Angleterre, 2011

FEUILLE DE COMPTES 1

Mon nom est P.K. Pinkerton, et avant la fin de cette journée je serai mort.

Je me suis réfugié au fond de la mine de Comstock parce que j'ai trois desperados à mes trousses.

Là, je suis coincé, alors le temps qu'ils me retrouvent, je vais écrire mon histoire sur ces feuilles de comptes. En me dépêchant & en écrivant petit, je devrais pouvoir expliquer comment je me suis retrouvé ici, avant de n'avoir plus de bougies. Comme ça, ceux qui découvriront mon cadavre sauront tout ce qui m'est arrivé.

Et qui punir.

Sur ma pierre tombale, je veux qu'on grave :

P.K. PINKERTON
CALAMITY, 26 SEPT. 1850
VIRGINIA CITY, 28 SEPT. 1862
« DANS LE CHRIST JÉSUS,
VOUS NE FAITES QU'UN » GAL. 3:28
R.I.P.

Ma mère adoptive, Ma Evangeline, disait toujours que, quand Dieu vous octroie un Don, il vous plante en même temps une Épine dans les côtes pour vous apprendre l'humilité.

Mon Don, à moi, c'est d'être super fortiche pour certains trucs.

Par exemple, je sais lire & écrire, et je suis un crack en calcul mental. Je parle l'américain & le lakota, et aussi deux, trois mots de chinois & d'espagnol. Je sais tirer au pistolet & monter à cheval avec ou sans selle. Je sais pister, abattre & dépecer n'importe quelle bête, et même la faire cuire sur un feu que j'allume sans allumettes. Je sais quelles herbes font passer la migraine.

J'arrive à entendre les cris d'un bébé caille dans un buisson d'armoise ou une souris qui court dans un placard.

Je sais dire ce qu'un cheval a mangé rien qu'en reniflant son crottin.

Je peux distinguer toutes les feuilles d'un peuplier.

Après, mon Problème, c'est que je ne sais jamais dire si une personne est sincère ou pas quand elle sourit. Je ne reconnais que trois émotions : le bonheur, la peur & la colère. Et encore, des fois je me trompe.

Des fois, même, je n'arrive pas à reconnaître une personne que j'ai déjà vue. Pour peu qu'elle ait changé de coiffure, ou que l'homme se soit laissé pousser la barbe, ça me perd.

C'est ça, mon Épine : les gens m'embrouillent.

Et aujourd'hui, cette Épine va causer ma mort.

FEUILLE DE COMPTES 2

Tout a commencé avant-hier, le 26 septembre. En rentrant de l'école, j'ai trouvé notre cabane sens dessus dessous. Ça sentait le lait chaud. J'ai refermé la porte derrière moi & me suis avancé. C'est là que j'ai découvert mes parents adoptifs par terre dans une mare de sang.

On les avait scalpés & ils avaient l'air morts.

Je me suis précipité vers ma mère d'abord. Elle tenait dans une main son grand poêlon en fer. Comme il y avait du sang et des cheveux dessus, j'ai pensé qu'elle avait dû s'en servir pour se défendre.

J'étais là à la regarder quand ses paupières se sont entrouvertes. Elle a dit : « Pinky ? » C'est comme ça qu'elle m'appelait : Pinky pour Pinkerton.

Je me suis mis à genoux.

— Je suis là, M'man.

— Emmet est vivant ?

J'ai regardé papa. Il ne respirait plus. Il avait les yeux fermés & un sourire paisible aux lèvres. Il avait aussi une hachette plantée dans la poitrine. Ça m'a fait mal.

— Non, M'man.

— C'était un homme bon. Je vais bientôt le retrouver au Ciel.

— Dis pas ça. Je file chercher Doc Finley à Dayton.

— Non. (Sa voix était faible.) Pas le temps. Je meurs. Ton sac-médecine. Celui que ton autre mère t'a donné.

— J'ai rien dedans qui puisse t'aider, M'man.

— Non... Ce sac... c'est ça qu'ils voulaient.

Elle a soupiré, j'ai cru qu'elle était morte. Puis elle a rouvert les yeux & m'a pris par une main.

— Il contient ta Destinée. Tu te rappelles ma cachette secrète ?

— La latte déclouée derrière le poêle ?

Elle a fait oui de la tête.

— Tu es un malin, Pinky. Tu sauras te débrouiller. Prends ton sac-médecine et file. Avant qu'ils reviennent.

Sur le coup, je n'ai pas compris ce qu'elle voulait dire. Et puis si.

— Les Indiens qui ont fait ça vont revenir ?

— C'étaient pas des Indiens. (Sa voix était presque un murmure & sa peau avait blanchi.) L'un d'eux avait les yeux bleus. Il sentait la lotion pour cheveux Bay Rum. Les Indiens utilisent pas de lotion pour cheveux.

J'ai humé l'air. Ma Evangeline avait raison. En plus des odeurs de sang, de lait chaud et de gâteau sorti du four, ça sentait le clou de girofle : la lotion Bay Rum. J'ai aussi flairé une pointe d'aisselles moites.

Les assassins venaient de partir & ils pouvaient revenir à tout moment. Mon instinct me disait de décamper, mais je ne voulais pas laisser ma mère mourir seule.

— Va-t'en, Pinky. Trouve ton sac-médecine et disparais avant qu'ils reviennent.

Je me suis relevé & l'ai regardée. Dans une minute elle serait morte. J'ai serré les poings.

— Je vais retrouver ces hommes, ai-je dit, et te venger.

— Non. (Une pause.) Pinky ?

Je l'entendais à peine, il m'a fallu m'accroupir.

— Oui, M'man ?

— Promets-moi que tu ne tueras jamais. Même pas ceux qui m'ont tuée. Tu dois pardonner. C'est ce que Notre-Seigneur nous enseigne.

— Je peux pas promettre ça, M'man.

Ma vue se troublait. J'ai cligné des yeux & c'est passé.

— C'est mon vœu de mourante, tu dois promettre.

— Alors je promets.

Elle a fermé les yeux & murmuré :

— Promets que tu ne joueras pas aux jeux d'argent et que tu ne boiras pas d'alcool.

— Je promets.

Mais là, elle ne m'a pas entendu.

Je me suis relevé, j'ai regardé les corps de mes parents adoptifs. Ils étaient allongés côte à côte et la mare de sang continuait de s'étendre.

Je me suis dirigé vers le poêle en évitant de marcher sur toutes les affaires qui avaient été renversées. Une boîte de farine en fer-blanc s'était déversée par terre. J'ai bien fait attention à ne pas marcher dedans, pour ne pas y laisser d'empreintes.

J'ai retiré le lait du feu, il commençait à brûler. Puis je me suis agenouillé près du poêle & j'ai cherché la fameuse latte avec un petit trou. J'y ai glissé un doigt pour la soulever. J'ai récupéré mon sac-médecine & l'ai passé autour de mon cou. J'ai aussi trouvé dans la cachette une pièce en or de 20 $ que Ma Evangeline gardait pour les coups durs. Elle n'en aurait plus besoin, donc je l'ai prise. Je l'ai glissée dans mon sac-médecine avec le reste. Après j'ai remis la latte en place.

Soudain, j'ai entendu des hommes parler à voix basse à l'extérieur. Une marche du perron a craqué.

Je savais que c'étaient eux. Les tueurs qui revenaient.

J'ai cherché un endroit où me cacher mais, dans notre petite cabane, il n'y en avait pas tant que ça.

Il n'y en avait même qu'un.

FEUILLE DE COMPTES 3

Adossé au mur du fond, le grand buffet en pin de Ma Evangeline débordait de livres et de vaisselle.

Je l'ai escaladé plus vite qu'un écureuil dont la queue aurait pris feu. À proximité du haut du meuble, je me suis tourné pour grimper sur un des deux gros chevrons du plafond. Je suis peut-être petit pour mon âge, mais je suis agile.

Je m'étais calé sur le chevron avant même que la poignée de la porte d'entrée ait commencé à tourner mais, dans ma précipitation, j'avais fait tanguer le buffet. Quand la porte s'est ouverte, il y avait une grande assiette bleue & blanche qui allait dégringoler du meuble.

Elle a ralenti, hésité, puis s'est arrêtée juste au bord.

J'ai poussé un soupir de soulagement & me suis aussitôt figé en entendant un homme demander d'une voix peureuse :

— Ça craint rien ?

— Nan, ça va, lui a répondu une voix plus grave. Sont toujours morts. Entre, gros pétochard.

— Je suis pas un pétochard, a rétorqué l'homme à la voix peureuse. C'est que la bonne femme m'a pas raté avec son poêlon. J'ai morflé.

J'ai jeté un coup d'œil en contrebas : il y avait trois hommes dans la cabane. À leurs voix, c'étaient des Blancs, mais ils ressemblaient à des Indiens. En regardant mieux, j'ai vu que c'étaient des Blancs habillés en Indiens. Leurs pantalons étaient en toile et pas en daim, et leurs mocassins étaient des pauvres sandales en peau de bison. Ils s'étaient fait des peintures de guerre & avaient piqué des plumes de dinde dans leurs cheveux graisseux. L'un de ces hommes empestait la lotion Bay Rum. De là où j'étais, je n'arrivais pas à dire lequel c'était, mais je penchais pour celui avec les trois plumes de dinde. Les deux autres le suivaient.

Bien cramponné au chevron, j'ai essayé une ruse que ma mère indienne m'avait apprise : la Ruse du Buisson. Si on se cache derrière un buisson et qu'on imagine être soi-même ce buisson, alors on devient invisible. J'ai créé la Ruse du Chevron : faire semblant d'être une partie du chevron. Je me suis concentré à fond & j'ai prié pour que ma mère indienne ne se soit pas trompée.

— Je vous avais bien dit qu'ils allaient pas le cacher dans la remise, a fait le chef. Maintenant qu'ils sont morts, y a plus rien à en tirer.

Là-dessus, il s'est approché de mon père, l'a regardé en face & a dit :

— Rien n'est plus beau que la mort.

Et puis il a rigolé & s'est mis à tirer sur la hachette pour la récupérer. Ça a fait un bruit de ventouse quand elle est sortie de la poitrine de Pa Emmet.

— Fichons le camp, Walt, a dit Le Peureux. Je me sens pas trop bien.

— Il a raison, Walt, a ajouté le troisième homme, un grand avec une voix râpeuse. Je sais pas ce que tu cherches, mais tu le trouveras pas ici.

— Purin ! s'est écrié Walt (sauf que lui, son *r* sonnait comme un *t*).

Il a craché un jet de salive & de jus de tabac par terre.

— C'est forcément là, a-t-il repris. Faut juste trouver où.

Nouvelle pause. Le silence était tel que je me disais qu'ils devaient entendre les battements de mon cœur. Et puis Walt a repéré quelque chose :

— Mais visez donc un peu ça…

Je me suis avancé comme j'ai pu & ai découvert un détail qui m'avait échappé. Sur la table, il y avait un gâteau d'anniversaire, avec glaçage au chocolat et JOYEUX 12ᴱ ANNIVERSAIRE PINKY écrit en lettres de réglisse. C'était un gâteau fourré : mon préféré. Ma Evangeline avait dû payer une fortune pour se faire livrer du chocolat au beau milieu du désert du Nevada.

— Ils ont un gosse ? a demandé Le Peureux.

Du haut de mon chevron, je voyais la tache rouge que lui avait faite le coup de poêlon de ma mère.

— 'videmment, crétin, a répondu Walt. C'est la vraie mère du petit qui avait ce qu'on cherche.

— Du coup, le gosse a pu le récupérer… a fait Voix Râpeuse.

— Pinky, c'est un prénom de fille ou de garçon ? s'est interrogé Le Peureux.

— De garçon, l'a assuré Voix Râpeuse. J'ai connu un Pinky à Pendville. Pinky O'Malley, un vrai albinos avec les cheveux blancs et les yeux roses.

— Mais t'as aussi le Pinky's Saloon, à Esmeralda, s'est rappelé Le Peureux. C'est une femme qui le tient. Une Française, non ?

Walt venait de sortir de son étui un énorme Couteau de Chasse avec lequel il se découpait un morceau de tabac à chiquer. Il a dit :

— Bouclez-la, vous deux. J'essaie de réfléchir.

Il a enfourné sa chique à même la lame & s'est mis à mâcher. Au bout d'un moment, il a demandé :

— Il y a une école dans ce trou paumé ?

— À Dayton, je crois bien, lui a indiqué Voix Râpeuse. Cela dit, j'ai repéré des gamins près de l'église quand on est arrivés.

— Allons-y voir, a décidé Walt. Faut absolument mettre la main sur ce petit.

Il se dirigeait vers la porte & j'en étais presque à me croire sauvé. Mais là il s'est arrêté & est retourné tout doucement vers le poêle.

— 'ttendez voir, a-t-il fait. Il me semble qu'il y a eu du passage depuis qu'on a tué le pasteur et sa dame.

— Qu'est-ce que tu veux dire ? a demandé Le Peureux en tripotant la tache de sang qu'il avait à la tête.

— Il y a un truc de changé… Quelqu'un a retiré le lait du feu. Et je parie que ce quelqu'un est encore là.

FEUILLE DE COMPTES 4

Walt inspectait la maison, à la recherche de la personne qui avait retiré le lait du feu. Moi, je restais en apnée & les yeux fermés. Je faisais semblant d'être le chevron. Le sang battait dans mes veines.

C'est là que j'ai entendu Le Peureux dire :

— Je crois bien que c'est peut-être moi, Walt.

— T'en es sûr ?

— Mouais. Y a personne dans cette cabane. Venez, on décampe. On se fera lyncher si les gens de ce patelin nous trouvent déguisés en Indiens à côté des cadavres de leur pasteur & de sa dame.

Walt a craché par terre.

— Cette ville est qu'une chiure de mouche, je suis sûr qu'on est plus nombreux que les habitants. Et il faut qu'on retrouve le gosse. Essayons l'église.

J'ai entendu leurs pas s'éloigner, mais pas la porte se refermer. Au bout d'un moment, j'ai rouvert les yeux. Après un autre moment, j'ai rampé jusqu'au mur & j'ai pris appui sur le châssis de la fenêtre pour redescendre.

Walt avait raison. Temperance est une chiure de mouche dans le Territoire du Nevada. Cette ville est plantée dans la brousse au pied des Pine Nut Mountains, entre Palmyra & Dayton. En dehors de notre cabane & de trois ou quatre maisonnettes en bois, il y a une mercerie, une écurie de louage & une petite église avec un clocher en construction. Mais ni saloon ni boutique qui vende du whisky – d'où le nom de Temperance.

C'est le Rév. Emmet Jones, mon père adoptif, qui a fondé cette ville après une journée entière de prière & de jeûne. Il voulait un endroit où rien n'inciterait au péché. Il disait que comme ça il aurait moins de travail. C'était mal connaître la nature humaine. À l'heure où j'écris ces lignes, Pa Emmet doit être dans son cercueil, avec un trou en forme de hachette dans la poitrine.

Mon père espérait que Temperance serait une Oasis de Sainteté dans un Désert de Péché. Sauf que Temperance n'est pas une oasis. C'est un échec. La diligence ne s'y arrête que si quelqu'un agite les bras au milieu de la piste. Et la plupart du temps, elle ne s'arrête que s'il y a de la place à l'intérieur, ou si la personne qui fait signe est riche ou jolie. On est à 3 kilomètres de Dayton, d'où la diligence rejoint Virginia City par la route à péage. Virginia City et ses grosses mines d'argent qui exploitent le filon de Comstock.

La diligence de 16 heures n'allait plus tarder, et je comptais bien la prendre.

Mieux valait que je ne m'éternise pas à Temperance.

Ce jour-là, le jour où mes parents adoptifs ont été tués, le premier endroit où je suis allé en sortant de la maison, c'est les cabinets. J'espérais que Walt & ses hommes ne se trouveraient pas à proximité parce que j'avais franchement besoin. Quand j'ai eu terminé, je suis sorti accroupi & me suis jeté à plat ventre par terre. J'ai rampé de buisson d'armoise en buisson d'armoise jusqu'à la sortie ouest de la ville. Il n'y avait qu'une demi-douzaine de maisons, j'ai fait ça en moins de deux.

En général, pour l'école on met un pantalon noir qui gratte, une chemise blanche bien amidonnée & des gros souliers. Mais ce jour-là, vu que c'était mon anniversaire, Ma Evangeline m'avait permis de porter mes nouveaux habits : un ensemble en peau de daim à franges qu'elle m'avait cousu. La couleur des habits se confondait avec la poussière, et je passais inaperçu. Je me suis dirigé vers un bosquet d'armoise près de la piste.

Le bosquet empestait la mort et j'ai repéré une charogne de coyote noyée sous les mouches. Ça m'a fait reculer & j'ai failli aller attendre plus loin. Sauf qu'il n'y avait nulle part ailleurs où se cacher & que la diligence de 16 heures serait bientôt là. J'ai donc fourré la charogne sous le bosquet & suis resté tapi, le cœur qui cognait fort & le ventre un peu malade.

J'ai prié.

En relevant la tête, j'ai avisé deux chevaux et une mule qui attendaient devant la Mercerie du père Gould. Je ne les avais jamais vus avant. Il y avait un hongre bleu-rouan et une jument baie. La mule avait une robe blanche sale.

« Sûrement les montures de Walt et de ses hommes », je me suis dit.

J'ai aussi pensé : « Elle fabrique quoi, cette diligence ? »

Et enfin : « Qu'est-ce qu'il renferme de si précieux, mon sac-médecine ? »

Je me suis redressé sur mes coudes pour retirer le sac de sous ma chemise en daim. C'était un sac en peau de bison, décoré de perles rouges et bleues disposées en forme de flèche. Il était aussi gros que ma main droite, les doigts écartés. Ma mère indienne me l'avait donné avant qu'on ne parte pour l'Ouest avec le convoi de chariots. Je l'avais autour du cou pendant le massacre, mais je ne l'avais plus revu depuis que mes parents adoptifs l'avaient rangé dans la cachette sous le plancher. Je me rappelais à peu près ce qu'il contenait, mais j'ai préféré vérifier, alors j'ai soulevé le rabat & tout vidé par terre. En plus de la pièce d'or, il y avait trois choses : le couteau en silex de ma mère indienne, une feuille de papier pliée en quatre & un bouton de cuivre qui appartenait à mon vrai père.

Mon vrai père, il s'appelait Robert Pinkerton. Il vivait avec nous quand je suis né, et puis il est parti travailler comme Détective du Chemin de Fer et il n'est jamais revenu. J'avais 7 ans quand ma mère a appris qu'il était mort en défendant un train contre des bandits. Moi, je ne l'ai pas revu depuis mes 2 ans alors je ne sais pas à quoi il ressemble. Tout ce qu'il m'a laissé, c'est ce fameux bouton de cuivre. Ma mère m'a raconté qu'il l'avait perdu le jour où ils s'étaient rencontrés & qu'elle avait toujours voulu le recoudre. Sauf qu'elle n'en avait jamais pris le temps.

Ma mère chrétienne, Evangeline, adorait les romans de Détectives. Quand Pa Emmet et elle m'ont accueilli & que je leur ai dit que mon vrai père, Robert Pinkerton, était Détective du Chemin de Fer, elle a sauté au plafond. D'après elle, mon vrai père devait être le frère d'Allan Pinkerton, le fondateur d'une célèbre Agence de Détectives de Chicago. Celle qui a un logo en forme d'œil. Du coup, cet Allan Pinkerton devait être mon oncle.

Ma Evangeline m'a expliqué qu'un Détective c'est quelqu'un qui découvre la Vérité & apporte la Justice.

Elle m'a dit que les Détectives du Chemin de Fer sont chargés de défendre les passagers & leurs affaires contre les bandits.

Elle m'a dit qu'Allan Pinkerton était un grand défenseur des Nègres & qu'il employait des femmes aussi bien que des hommes. D'après elle, un Original comme Allan Pinkerton serait sûrement ravi d'avoir de mes nouvelles.

Alors Ma Evangeline lui a écrit, à Chicago, pour savoir s'il n'aurait pas un frère mort qui aurait eu un enfant avec une squaw lakota vers 1850. On a attendu sa réponse avec impatience, mais en vain. On habitait près de Salt Lake City, dans le Territoire de l'Utah, à l'époque.

L'an dernier, quand les journaux ont raconté comment mon oncle avait sauvé la vie à Abraham Lincoln, Ma Evangeline lui a de nouveau écrit, lui demandant s'il avait entendu parler de moi. Mais quelques jours après, on partait pour le Territoire du Nevada. Si Allan Pinkerton a répondu, sa lettre ne nous a jamais trouvés.

Couché dans la poussière brûlante de la piste, à côté du bosquet d'armoise, je serrais le bouton en cuivre de mon père pour la première fois depuis deux ans. Entretemps, j'avais appris à lire & j'ai donc vu qu'il y avait une inscription sur le bouton. Sur le haut, en arrondi, il y avait marqué **PINKERTON**. En bas, arrondi dans l'autre sens : **RAIL ROAD** – pour « chemin de fer ». Et entre les deux : **DETECTIVE**.

J'ai glissé ce bouton dans ma poche. Il avait une grande valeur à mes yeux, mais ça m'aurait étonné que Walt et ses hommes en aient eu après lui.

Le couteau en silex, il était bon pour écorcher les lapins, mais on peut s'en procurer n'importe où. Des fois, même, on en trouve par terre.

Je me suis dit que ça devait être le papier qui les intéressait.

Ça m'a rappelé qu'il était déjà dans mon sac-médecine quand ma mère indienne me l'avait donné. Mais bon, à l'époque, je ne savais pas lire.

J'ai donc déplié le papier & l'ai examiné.

C'était une lettre adressée à « Qui Cela Concerne ». Elle promettait au « Porteur » plusieurs hectares près de Pleasant Town, sur le pic du Soleil, entre la Butte & le Ruisseau. Et aussi « la cabane en pierre sur Grizzly Hill & tous les biens qu'elle contient ». Elle était signée U.N. Tel. – le nom de famille était illisible. Ça commençait peut-être par un O ou un G, voire un D. Je ne savais pas où se trouvait Pleasant Town, ni ce que désignaient la Butte & le Ruisseau.

Et puis j'ai vu la signature du témoin : Rbt Pinkerton. Le tout daté du 21 novembre 1857. J'avais tout juste 7 ans à l'époque, mais je n'avais pas revu mon père depuis des années. Je pense qu'il a dû se faire tuer peu de temps après s'être porté témoin pour la Lettre, parce qu'on a appris sa mort à Noël la même année.

J'ai replié le papier soigneusement & l'ai rangé dans mon sac-médecine avec le couteau de ma mère & la pièce de 20 $. Le Bouton, par contre, je l'ai glissé dans ma poche.

Je me disais que la diligence n'allait plus tarder. J'ai collé mon oreille à la piste & ai entendu un bruit de cavalcade qui approchait.

J'ai pensé : « Si je reste invisible encore quelques minutes, tout ira bien. »

J'ai essayé la Ruse du Buisson.

Mais c'était pas évident de se concentrer, avec la charogne du coyote qui me rappelait mes parents morts.

Il y avait autre chose qui me turlupinait.

Cette espèce de pressentiment que j'ai des fois, quand on m'observe.

C'est là que j'ai entendu quelqu'un crier : « Il est là ! Chopez-le, les gars ! »

FEUILLE DE COMPTES 5

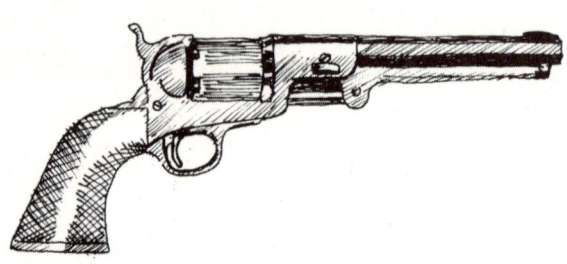

Je me suis levé d'un bond & j'ai détalé comme un lapin, mais un type m'a fait un croche-patte & je me suis cassé la figure. Ça m'a coupé le souffle & j'avais de la terre plein la bouche. J'ai craché. Le type qui m'avait eu m'a retourné & s'est assis sur mon ventre.

Heureusement, ce n'était qu'Olaf, une des trois terreurs de l'école. Ils habitaient tous à Temperance & étaient méchants comme des teignes, mais Olaf était le pire. Il a fait signe à ses copains. Abe m'a écrasé le poignet gauche sous son pied, et Charlie le droit. Contrairement à moi, ils ne portaient pas des mocassins souples, mais bien leurs gros souliers d'école.

Toujours assis sur mon ventre à m'empêcher de respirer, Olaf a gentiment demandé :

— Pourquoi tu t'enfuis comme ça ? Tu te disais qu'on n'allait pas te tabasser aujourd'hui ? C'est ton anniversaire, pas vrai ?

J'ai fait signe que oui.

Olaf s'est relevé et a dit à Abe & Charlie :

— On lui donne son cadeau ?

Les autres ont répondu ouais en me relâchant.

Un sourire aux lèvres, Olaf a demandé :

— T'aimes bien les marrons, toi, P.K. ?

Je ne sais jamais interpréter les sourires.

Ma Evangeline m'a expliqué qu'il fallait observer la figure des gens pour savoir ce qu'ils pensaient. Elle m'a appris à rechercher cinq Expressions.

1. Si la personne fait un sourire en forme de U & plisse les yeux, c'est un Vrai Sourire.

2. Si le sourire est en forme de trait, & que les yeux ne se plissent pas, c'est un Faux Sourire.

3. Si les lèvres de la personne sont en forme de cloche & qu'elle fronce le nez, elle est dégoûtée.

4. Si la personne ouvre les yeux en grand, elle est surprise ou effrayée.

5. Si elle plisse juste les yeux, c'est qu'elle en a après vous, ou bien qu'elle réfléchit, ou qu'elle soupçonne quelque chose.

J'étais quasi sûr qu'Olaf avait l'Expression n° **2** – le Faux Sourire. En même temps, il était à contre-jour & j'avais de la poussière dans les yeux, alors je ne distinguais pas assez son visage.

Il a répété :

— Les marrons, est-ce que t'aimes ça ?

Je préfère manger des marrons que de me faire taper dessus, c'est sûr. Alors j'ai fait oui de la tête, même si je me doutais qu'il y avait un piège.

J'avais raison. C'était un piège.

Olaf s'est tourné vers ses copains :

— Eh ben on va lui en filer douze, des marrons, à cet Accident de la Nature. Douze marrons pour ses 12 ans. Ha, ha, ha.

Et aussitôt ils se sont penchés sur moi & se sont mis à me frapper. Je me suis recroquevillé comme un asticot.

Mais d'un coup, ils se sont arrêtés & Olaf a dit :

— Gaffe, les gars. Voilà le reste de sa tribu qui vient à sa rescousse.

— Moi, je trouve pas qu'ils ressemblent à des Indiens, a fait Abe.

— C'est du sang, qu'il a sur son tomahawk, celui de devant ? a demandé Charlie d'une voix tremblotante.

— Et des scalps à sa ceinture ? s'est étouffé Abe.

J'ai entrouvert les yeux & ai tourné la tête pour voir de quoi ils parlaient.

Walt & ses deux acolytes approchaient à pied. Walt tenait à la main la hachette avec laquelle il avait tué mon père. On voyait encore du sang sur la lame. Ils se dirigeaient droit sur nous, d'un pas déterminé.

— Purin ! s'est écrié Olaf. On décampe !

Il ouvrait des yeux tout ronds : il devait être ou surpris ou effrayé, voire les deux.

Lui & les autres ont couru se cacher dans un petit bois de pins à environ 500 mètres de là. Ça n'était pas bien malin. Si vous croisez un ours & que vous décampez, l'ours vous court après. Là, pareil, dès qu'Olaf et ses copains se sont mis à courir, Walt & ses hommes les ont pris en chasse. L'un des complices de Walt a dégainé son pistolet & s'est mis à tirer. Au bruit, c'était sûrement un revolver Colt Navy. Olaf et les autres ont encore accéléré en entendant les détonations. Je les entendais japper comme des coyotes poursuivis par un ours.

Allez savoir pourquoi, toujours est-il que Walt & ses hommes ne m'ont pas repéré. Sans doute que, avec mes habits en daim, je devais ressembler à un monticule de terre. Et aussi, je me dis qu'ils étaient trop occupés à courir après Olaf, Charlie & Abe. Eux trois portaient des pantalons noirs & des chemises blanches : on les distinguait très bien dans le paysage.

Et c'est à ce moment-là que la diligence est arrivée. Elle traversait la ville en soulevant un panache de poussière jaune.

Je savais qu'elle ne s'arrêterait jamais pour un gosse à la peau marron & habillé en daim.

Moi, ça m'allait.

Si elle s'arrêtait, ça risquait d'attirer l'attention de Walt & de ses sbires.

Tout ce que je voulais, c'était qu'elle ralentisse.

Je suis donc retourné près du bosquet d'armoise, j'ai attrapé la charogne du coyote par une patte arrière & l'ai jetée en plein milieu de la route – pile là où les chevaux allaient passer. La charogne avait un peu la même couleur que la poussière de la piste, et j'espérais que le cocher ne la repérerait pas trop vite.

Les chevaux n'aiment pas marcher sur quelque chose. Le meilleur cocher du monde n'arrivera jamais à les faire écraser une personne ou un animal. Ce jour-là, le cocher a fait ce qu'il fallait. Quand il a vu la charogne au milieu de la route, il a tiré sur les rênes pour faire ralentir l'attelage puis il lui a fait contourner l'obstacle. La diligence est passée juste devant mon bosquet d'armoise & j'ai pu sauter sur la malle du courrier accrochée à l'arrière.

Je m'y suis agrippé comme une tique à un chien & j'ai prié pour que Walt et ses compères ne me remarquent pas.

FEUILLE DE COMPTES 6

À l'arrière de la diligence, il y avait un grand sac en cuir pour ranger les bagages. Je me suis cramponné à ses lanières de toile en espérant que le nuage de poussière me rendrait invisible.

Quand il m'a semblé qu'on devait être loin de Temperance, j'ai escaladé le grand sac en cuir pour aller me coucher sur le toit de la diligence. Certaines ont des caisses ou des bagages mais, sur la mienne, il y avait juste deux, trois sacs légers ficelés à la rambarde de fer qui faisait le tour du toit sur trois côtés. Pour ne pas me faire éjecter, je me suis accroché à cette rambarde, au-dessus du cocher – de l'autre côté, il n'y en avait pas. Là, je me suis aplati comme un timbre-poste sur une enveloppe.

Une ou deux fois, j'ai tourné la tête pour voir si Walt & ses hommes ne nous suivaient pas, mais la poussière était trop épaisse. J'ai bien essayé de tendre l'oreille, mais on n'entendait que les sabots des chevaux frappant la piste, leurs harnais qui cliquetaient & les essieux de la diligence qui grinçaient.

On roulait comme ça depuis une dizaine de minutes quand j'ai entendu le cocher crier « whooo ! » & j'ai senti la diligence qui ralentissait.

J'ai prié pour qu'on ne s'arrête pas.

Je fermais les yeux à les faire éclater, mais le cocher a quand même crié :

— Descends de là ! Et que ça saute !

J'ai rouvert les yeux. Le bonhomme s'était retourné et me dévisageait. Il brandissait son fouet en disant :

— Pas d'Indiens dans ma diligence ! Pas de Sauvages, toi comprendre ?

J'ai levé la tête pour répondre :

— Pitié, monsieur. N'arrêtez pas la diligence. Je suis en danger de mort. Je ne suis pas un Sauvage. Je suis méthodiste. Et je peux vous payer.

Le cocher a plissé les yeux.

— T'es le petit que le Révérend a adopté ?

— Oui, monsieur.

Il a craché du jus de tabac puis a décidé :

— C'est bon, je t'emmène, mais tu bouges pas de là-haut. Je veux pas d'Indiens sur mes banquettes.

Ma Evangeline disait toujours que c'est une marque d'ignorance de mépriser les gens en fonction de leur couleur de peau, vu que notre sang à tous il a la même couleur. Je sais qu'elle avait raison – du sang, j'en ai vu suffisamment pour être sûr –, mais ça n'empêchait pas que je me sentais différent d'elle et de Pa Emmet. Et pas juste d'eux, d'ailleurs, différent de tout le monde. J'ai fait oui de la tête au cocher.

Il a donné un coup de fouet & les chevaux ont accéléré.

Comme on soulevait moins de poussière, je me suis retourné pour voir si Walt nous suivait. Derrière nous, il n'y avait que le désert et des buissons d'armoise. J'ai poussé un gros ouf de soulagement.

Je restais agrippé à la rambarde & aplati contre le toit laqué de la diligence. Il faisait si chaud, sur la route de Dayton, que j'avais l'impression de griller comme un steak au barbecue. J'ai voulu fermer les yeux, mais chaque fois je revoyais mes parents dans leur mare de sang. J'ai préféré tourner la tête & regarder la plaine qui défilait.

La voiture n'a pas tardé à ralentir un peu et j'ai compris, au bruit, qu'on passait sur le pont de bois qui enjambe la rivière Carson. J'ai relevé la tête juste à temps pour voir fuser la pièce que le cocher avait jetée au gardien du péage. Là-dessus, il a de nouveau fait claquer son fouet, les chevaux ont accéléré & on est arrivés à Dayton en un rien de temps.

C'est dans cette ville que je vais à l'école, mais je n'avais jamais fait la route en diligence.

Dayton, avant, on l'appelait « Chinatown » à cause de tous les Chinois qui y vivaient. Aujourd'hui, la plupart se sont installés à Virginia City, ou sont partis travailler sur le nouveau chemin de fer de l'Est. Du coup, Dayton s'appelle Dayton. Pa Emmet m'avait expliqué que c'est la plus ancienne ville du Territoire – un titre de gloire que Mormon Station revendique elle aussi. Les deux ont été bâties en 1849, elles ont donc treize ans, un de plus que moi. Par contre, je suis plus vieux que Virginia City, qui a été fondée il y a trois ou quatre ans à peine.

Quand la diligence s'est arrêtée devant le Nevada Hotel, dans la grand-rue de Dayton, j'ai relevé la tête un tout petit poil. Tout était si calme. J'entendais des chevaux qui reniflaient & s'ébrouaient, des hommes qui discutaient & des femmes qui riaient. La voiture a un peu secoué quand un passager est monté dedans ou en est descendu. Je n'aurais pas su dire & je n'avais pas envie de trahir ma présence en me penchant pour regarder.

J'entendais un chant d'oiseau & voyais la rangée de peupliers qui suivaient le lit de la rivière. Je me suis mis à penser à notre institutrice, Miss Marlowe, une vieille fille qui s'était toujours montrée gentille envers moi. Ça me démangeait d'aller lui demander de me cacher chez elle. Ça aurait peut-être mieux valu.

Mais là, je voulais surtout m'éloigner le plus possible de Walt et de ses hommes & j'ai commis l'erreur de rester sur le toit de cette diligence.

FEUILLE DE COMPTES 7

La diligence avait à peine quitté Dayton qu'on s'est retrouvés sur la nouvelle route à péage qui passe par Gold Canyon. On slalomait entre les peupliers & les rochers. Au début, on avait le soleil en face de nous, vu que c'était la fin d'après-midi & qu'on filait vers l'ouest, mais ensuite on l'a eu de côté parce qu'on avait bifurqué plein nord. La route était tellement récente qu'il n'y avait presque pas de cahots. Par contre, on grimpait une pente sacrément raide & j'avais intérêt à bien m'accrocher à la rambarde pour ne pas tomber.

Au bout d'une demi-heure, on s'est arrêtés & le cocher a annoncé : « Silver City ! » Il a récupéré un des sacs ficelés sur le toit & l'a jeté par terre. Du coup, j'avais l'impression que tout le monde pouvait me voir, alors je n'ai pas risqué de lever la tête. Quelqu'un est monté dans la voiture. Et puis on est repartis.

Virginia City a beau n'être qu'à quelques kilomètres de Dayton, je n'y avais jamais mis les pieds. Ma Evangeline aurait bien voulu y faire un petit tour, quand on est arrivés dans le Territoire, mais Pa Emmet le lui a interdit. Virginia City, il l'appelait « le Terrain de Jeu du Diable ».

Il disait que cette ville était la plus infâme de toute la terre – plus encore que San Francisco. Les vingt-sept premiers hommes à y avoir été enterrés avaient tous été assassinés. D'après lui, à Virginia City, on n'est rien tant qu'on n'a pas « buté un gars ». Et l'homme le plus respecté de la ville n'est pas le pasteur ou le shérif, mais le patron du saloon, qui porte un gros diamant au revers de son veston.

Pa Emmet nous a encore raconté qu'une rue entière était réservée aux « Colombes de Suie ». Je ne connaissais pas l'expression, alors il m'a expliqué qu'une Colombe de Suie est « une pauvresse qui attise les hommes pour de l'argent ». Selon lui, elles se reconnaissent à leurs robes aux couleurs voyantes ornées de dentelle noire, et aussi au fait qu'elles ne portent pas de corset. Quand je lui ai demandé ce que ça voulait dire, « attiser », il m'a répondu « faire des bisous & des câlins ». Il allait m'en dire plus, mais Ma Evangeline l'a fait taire.

D'après Pa Emmet, Virginia City regorgeait de Chinois, de Mexicains, d'Indiens, d'Irlandais, de Mineurs, de Desperados, de Joueurs, de Tueurs & d'Avocats. Et pour lui, c'étaient les Avocats les plus dangereux. Il les appelait les « Suppôts de Satan ». Il disait qu'avec leurs belles paroles, ces escrocs pouvaient vous obliger à donner tout ce que vous possédiez. Lui, il aurait préféré dîner avec une Colombe de Suie ou un Joueur de Poker plutôt qu'avec un Avocat.

— La Porte du Diable ! a crié le cocher.

J'ai aussitôt relevé la tête & vu qu'on allait passer entre deux gigantesques rochers en forme de démon. Là encore, il a fallu ralentir et payer un Péage. J'en ai profité pour me retourner : aucun cavalier à l'horizon. Tout se passait bien, à quoi bon descendre ? Mais je n'ai pas eu le temps de décider – le cocher lançait une pièce au gardien & fouettait ses chevaux.

Plus question de faire demi-tour.

À mesure que la voiture grimpait, j'avais une drôle de douleur dans les oreilles. Et puis ça a fait « pop », j'ai eu la tête comme creuse & j'entendais mieux qu'avant. C'est là que j'ai perçu la musique de Virginia City pour la première fois.

Au début, c'était très faible, mais après j'arrivais à l'entendre même avec les bruits de la diligence : ça faisait comme un chant funèbre, grave et profond. Mélangé aux sabots des chevaux et au cliquetis des harnais, ça finissait par faire une espèce de chanson. N'importe quel bruit me fait de l'effet, du moment qu'il vient avec un rythme lent et puissant. Ça m'apaise & j'ai l'impression de flotter, le temps se dissout. Plus la diligence montait, plus la musique de la montagne devenait forte & moi, j'étais comme en transe. Je ne sais pas si ça a duré quelques minutes ou quelques heures, toujours est-il que l'arrêt de l'attelage et un coup de sifflet en provenance de la mine m'ont ramené sur terre.

— Gold Hill ! a annoncé le cocher. Prochain arrêt : Virginia City !

Je me sentais comme un nageur qui remonte à la surface après être descendu très profond. On faisait halte devant un hôtel situé juste à côté des mines : des espèces de gigantesques fourmilières qui luisaient d'orange, de jaune & d'or dans le soleil brûlant.

Je voyais aussi des bâtiments, un peu plus haut sur la pente, & j'ai compris que les coups sourds qu'on entendait provenaient de tous les Concasseurs de Quartz qui se trouvaient à l'intérieur. Il y en avait même un à l'extérieur d'un bâtiment. Il avait une structure en forme de porte, deux fois plus grande que la diligence, et était équipé de huit tiges métalliques qui pompaient de bas en haut & de haut en bas. Les mineurs l'alimentaient en cailloux que la machine pulvérisait, et le quartz partait ensuite dans les bâtiments pour être transformé en argent. C'est Miss Marlowe qui nous avait expliqué tout ça, mais je n'avais alors pas compris. Il devait y en avoir au moins mille, de ces concasseurs, à Virginia City, pour que ça fasse trembler la terre comme ça.

Et puis la diligence est repartie, mais plus lentement. La route montait toujours & ça épuisait les chevaux. Quand enfin on est arrivés en haut de la côte, j'ai vu le sommet désertique d'une montagne qui mangeait la moitié du ciel. Six ou sept rues en descendaient, comme des escaliers bien pentus. Des escaliers dont le pied se trouvait à ma droite, et le haut à ma gauche. Bordant chacune de ces rues, il y avait des maisons en brique ou en bois & même deux ou trois tentes. On roulait derrière des charrettes de foin, l'allure avait sacrément ralenti. On s'est arrêtés à l'entrée de la ville.

Le cocher a lancé :

— C. Street, Virginia ! La diligence continue jusqu'à l'International Hotel, mais si vous voulez descendre ici, vous pouvez.

Je l'ai entendu ajouter dans sa barbe :

— Vous serez sûrement rendus avant nous…

En dessous de moi, une portière s'est ouverte & j'ai senti que ça tanguait un peu. J'ai regardé en contrebas & ai vu passer une ombrelle rose & noire. Un dernier coup d'œil pour être sûr que Walt n'était pas dans le coin. La voie était libre, je me suis rassis sur le toit & ai tapoté l'épaule du cocher. Il s'est retourné, je lui ai tendu ma pièce d'or.

— File, a-t-il dit en crachant une giclée de tabac par terre. J'ai pas la monnaie sur 20 $. Tu me paieras la prochaine fois. Puis tu demanderas à ton révérend de père qu'il dise du bien de moi au Bon Dieu. J'm'appelle Jas Woorstell. Avec deux O et deux L.

J'ai fait signe que oui, puis j'ai fermé les yeux & j'ai prié en silence : « Seigneur, mon père est mort alors c'est moi qui vous le demande : bénissez, s'il vous plaît, Jas Woorstell. Avec deux O et deux L – pour sa bonté chrétienne. » Là-dessus, je me suis laissé glisser sur l'arrière de la diligence & me suis retrouvé debout par terre.

Une calèche vide s'était arrêtée derrière nous & il y avait une longue file après.

Je me suis dit : « C. Street, ça doit être la Grand-Rue. »

Puis j'ai pensé : « Faudrait pas traîner dans le coin, des fois que Walt et ses hommes m'auraient suivi. »

J'avais du mal à respirer & ma tête tournait. Je me suis engagé comme j'ai pu dans une rue qui montait, entre des buissons d'armoise, des cabanes & un Bâtiment de la Mine. Ensuite j'ai pris à gauche : la rue était poudreuse mais plate, alors j'ai foncé sur quelques mètres, la tête dans les épaules.

De temps en temps, je me disais : « Te voilà dans le Terrain de Jeu du Diable. Dépêche-toi de prendre tes marques. »

J'ai fini par m'arrêter, pour regarder autour de moi.

À Dayton, il y a deux blanchisseries tenues par des Chinois, mais là j'avais apparemment devant moi toute une rue de blanchisseries, avec aussi un dépôt de bois, un brasseur & deux, trois autres boutiques. Les toits en bois crachaient de la vapeur & de la fumée. Ça sentait la lessive et l'amidon. Le linge étendu se balançait dans la brise & on voyait même des draps sur les toits des cabanes. La rue grouillait de Chinois, mais en dehors de quelques enseignes écrites en lettres de chez eux, tout le reste était en américain. Ça disait : **XI YUP, LESSIVE & REPASSAGE** ou bien **SAM SING & AH HOP, LESSIVE**

J'ai repéré une pompe à eau devant une des blanchisseries. J'étais couvert de poussière après mon voyage sur le toit de la diligence, alors je suis allé me rincer la figure. Après ça, j'ai encore pompé un peu & j'ai penché la tête pour boire. C'est là qu'une voix de femme a crié :

— Stop ! Ne bois pas ! C'est du poison !

FEUILLE DE COMPTES 8

La femme a encore crié :
— Stop ! Toi pas boire !
Je me suis retourné, c'était la dame à l'ombrelle. Celle de la diligence. Elle avait des cheveux bruns, sur lesquels elle portait un petit chapeau à plumes. Comme habits, une robe bouffante rouge et rose.
Elle m'a dit :
— Toi pas boire. Eau mauvaise.
J'ai répondu :
— Pardon, madame ?
— Ah... Tu parles notre langue. Je t'avais pris pour un Indien. Je voulais te prévenir : l'eau d'ici n'est pas potable. Elle est polluée à l'arsenic, à la plombagine et au cuivre.
Je ne connaissais aucun de ces mots, mais ça faisait peur.
— Alors ils boivent quoi, les gens ? lui ai-je demandé.
— Du whisky, surtout.
Elle m'a dit ça avec un petit sourire : le n° 1 ou le n° 2, je n'aurais pas pu dire.

J'ai bien étudié sa silhouette. Sous la ceinture, sa robe était bouffante, mais au-dessus c'est tout juste s'il y avait un peu de tissu. Le tout avec des dentelles noires plutôt défraîchies. L'ombrelle était assortie à la robe. Cette dame tenait aussi à la main un éventail nacré & un joli petit sac orné de perles. Elle a dit :

— Il était pas chou, ce cocher, de te laisser ta pièce en or de 20 $?

Je lui ai demandé :

— Êtes-vous une Colombe de Suie ?

Elle a ouvert des yeux tout ronds. Ils étaient aussi bleus que le ciel.

J'ai ajouté :

— Si je vous le demande, c'est parce que mon père qui est mort disait toujours qu'une femme qui porte des habits rouges avec de la dentelle noire c'est souvent une Colombe de Suie. Mais vous, je vois que vous avez mis un corset, alors j'ai un doute.

— Ma foi, oui, a-t-elle répondu en agitant son éventail devant sa figure. On peut dire que je suis une Colombe de Suie, sauf que ça n'est pas une chose bien polie à dire à une dame. Je préfère qu'on me dise « Actrice ».

— Je suis navré, m'dame. Je ne voulais pas vous offenser.

— Alors tu ne m'as pas offensée.

Là, elle m'a regardé de haut en bas, puis elle m'a demandé :

— Tu peux m'expliquer pourquoi tu es habillé en Indien alors que tu parles notre langue ?

— C'est que je suis à moitié blanc, m'dame. Je m'appelle P.K. Pinkerton.

— Enchantée, P.K. Moi, c'est Belle Donne.

Elle m'a tendu la main, que je lui ai serrée. Ses gants noirs étaient poussiéreux. Elle sentait l'huile essentielle de rose et le whisky.

— Je reviens de Como, a-t-elle dit, où j'ai rendu visite à un gentleman de ma connaissance. Sinon, j'habite ici, à Virginia, dans une crèche sur D. Street.

— Comment vous faites, pour vivre dans une crèche ? C'est pas la maison du petit Jésus, ça ?

— Si, mais à Virginia une crèche, c'est aussi un tout petit logement. Tu es nouveau par ici, toi, pas vrai ?

— Oui, m'dame. Ça fait à peine quatre mois qu'on est venus vivre à Dayton.

Elle souriait toujours.

— Tu aimerais que je te fasse visiter ? m'a-t-elle proposé.

J'ai fait signe que oui. Ça me plaisait bien, qu'une habitante de la ville me fasse visiter, même si cette habitante était une pauvresse qui attisait parfois les hommes pour de l'argent.

Belle indiquait la rue avec son éventail :

— Ici, c'est F. Street. On l'appelle aussi Chinatown. Il y a pas mal de gens qui méprisent les Chinetoques et qui ne tolèrent leur présence que parce que ce sont d'excellents blanchisseurs. Moi, je les aime bien. Je trouve qu'ils sont toujours d'humeur égale. J'habite dans D. Street, mais je compte bien m'installer dans A. Street sitôt que j'aurai épousé un riche banquier ou un courtier. Tu vois, là-haut ? (Avec son éventail, elle montrait la montagne.) Les plus belles maisons sont situées sur les hauteurs. Dans ces quartiers-là, il n'y a presque jamais de fusillades.

— Des fusillades ?

— Oui. Ça arrive souvent que des messieurs se tirent dessus en pleine rue. En général, c'est juste qu'ils forcent trop sur la boisson, et vu que tout le monde a un pistolet sur soi…

— Vous en avez un, vous ? ai-je voulu savoir.

— Pardi !

Elle a glissé une main dans son décolleté & en a ressorti un tout petit Deringer avec canon gravé et crosse en noyer.

Ça m'a fait un choc. Mon père m'avait bien mis en garde contre Virginia City. Et là, je n'étais pas arrivé depuis cinq minutes que déjà je discutais avec une Colombe de Suie armée d'un pistolet & qui me parlait de fusillades entre ivrognes dans les rues.

Elle a précisé :

— Il n'est pas énorme, mais il fait des dégâts.

Elle a remis son Deringer à sa place, puis m'a sorti :

— Carson monte sur un train sans wagons.

— De quoi ?

On se dirigeait vers le nord, les montagnes à notre gauche. Belle Donne m'a expliqué :

— Quand j'ai emménagé à Virginia, il y a de ça trois mois, j'ai mis au point une astuce pour retenir les noms des rues. Celles qui sont désignées par une lettre sont orientées nord-sud, elles sont toutes plates. Mais les rues qui les coupent, c'est autre chose : elles sont pentues et portent des vrais noms pas faciles à se rappeler. Du coup, j'ai inventé une petite phrase dont chaque mot commence par la même lettre que ces rues-là : Carson Monte Sur Un Train Sans Wagons

– pour Carson Street, Mill Street, Sutton, Union, Taylor, Smith & Washington.

— Carson Monte Sur Un Train Sans Wagons, ai-je répété. C'est bien vu. C'est laquelle, la rue qui fait l'angle, là ?

— Celle-là, c'est Mill Street. On va la prendre pour rejoindre D. Street. Ma crèche est à deux pas mais, comme tu vois, entre Chinatown, la pente de la colline, le dépôt de bois et les bâtiments des mines, ça nous complique le chemin.

Elle avait raison. Je voyais la rue d'à côté, qui nous surplombait, mais c'était un vrai labyrinthe pour y arriver.

— Qu'es-tu venu faire à Virginia, P.K. ? m'a demandé Belle, chemin faisant.

J'avais toujours la tête qui tournait, alors j'ai pris une grande inspiration avant de répondre :

— Trois desperados déguisés en Indiens viennent de tuer mes parents adoptifs. Ils en ont après moi. J'ai pu leur échapper parce que moi aussi, je porte des habits d'Indiens. Ils n'avaient sûrement pas prévu ça.

— Oh. (Elle a posé une main sur sa gorge & s'est arrêtée de marcher.) Mais pourquoi ont-ils tué tes parents adoptifs ? Et pourquoi en ont-ils après toi ?

On parlait devant l'entrée d'une blanchisserie. L'enseigne était écrite en chinois, avec la traduction dessous : **HONG WO, LESSIVE**. Dans la petite cour de devant, il y avait un garçon de mon âge, ou un peu plus vieux. Il étendait des draps, nous tournant le dos. Il portait une chemise bleue sans col & délavée, un pantalon bleu dans lequel il flottait & une calotte noire toute poussiéreuse. Ses cheveux noirs étaient coiffés en une longue natte.

Belle m'a regardé ; je l'ai regardée.

— Je ne suis pas sûr de pouvoir vous faire confiance, ai-je dit. La diligence nous a déposés dans C. Street et vous habitez dans D. Street, alors qu'est-ce que vous faites dans F. Street ? Si ça se trouve, vous m'avez suivi.

Ça l'a fait rigoler.

— Si je suis venue dans F. Street, c'est pour récupérer du linge chez M. Yup, sauf qu'il n'était pas prêt. Ensuite, quand j'ai vu que tu allais boire de l'eau empoisonnée, j'ai pensé que mon devoir de Chrétienne m'imposait de te prévenir. (Elle m'a souri et s'est donné un peu d'air avec son éventail.) Alors, dis-moi, pourquoi ces hommes en ont-ils après toi ?

Son sourire était si doux que je l'ai pris pour une Expression n° 1 : le Vrai Sourire.

— Je crois qu'ils veulent récupérer ce truc, ai-je dit en retirant la fameuse Lettre de mon sac-médecine.

Je la lui ai tendue. Elle l'a prise, l'a dépliée puis a fait la grimace.

— J'ai l'air d'une institutrice ?

J'ai repensé à Miss Marlowe, de Dayton – elle portait toujours des habits sombres à longues manches et boutonnés jusqu'au cou.

— Non, m'dame, ai-je répondu. Vous ne ressemblez pas à une institutrice.

Elle a soupiré en roulant les yeux.

— Je ne sais pas lire ce genre d'écriture. Dis-moi ce qu'il y a de marqué.

Je lui ai lu la Lettre.

— Mazette, P.K. Cette Lettre m'a tout l'air d'être une espèce de Testament. Je n'ai jamais entendu parler de Pleasant Town ni du pic du Soleil, mais ce sont peut-être des noms de la région, vu que ça parle de la Butte.

— C'est quoi, la Butte ?

Indiquant une direction à l'aide de son éventail, Belle m'a expliqué :

— Cette bosse dans la montagne, là où les chevaux de la diligence avaient tellement de mal à avancer. Elle est située entre Virginia et Gold Hill.

— Vous croyez qu'elle vaut des sous, cette Lettre ?

À ce moment-là, j'ai remarqué que le petit Chinois s'était interrompu & qu'il nous observait.

— Sûrement, m'a répondu Belle, les yeux luisants. Si trois desperados sont prêts à tuer pour la récupérer, elle doit valoir au minimum un millier de dollars. Tu devrais la montrer à un Juge. Ou à un Avocat.

— Les Avocats sont des Suppôts de Satan. Je ne veux pas avoir affaire à eux.

J'ai replié la lettre & l'ai rangée dans mon sac-médecine.

— Où se trouve le Bureau du Juge ?

— Il y en a un dans A. Street, près de l'angle de Sutton Street, en face du Journal. Je crois qu'il y en a un autre à Gold Hill, de l'autre côté de la Butte.

— A. Street, près de l'angle de Sutton, ai-je répété. Carson Monte Sur Un Train Sans Wagons.

Belle regardait le chemin qu'on venait de parcourir. Elle avait les yeux grands ouverts & une main de nouveau appuyée contre sa gorge.

— P.K., a-t-elle fait. Tu m'as bien dit qu'ils étaient trois, les desperados qui en ont après toi et ta Lettre ?

— Oui.

— Ils ont deux chevaux et une mule ?

— Oui, m'dame.

— Cache-toi derrière moi, P.K. Je les vois qui viennent vers nous.

FEUILLE DE COMPTES 9

Walt & ses deux sbires, sur leurs montures, descendaient F. Street au pas, en surveillant les deux côtés de la rue.

Ils n'avaient pas l'air des plus excités & comme ils ne changeaient pas d'allure je me suis dit qu'ils ne m'avaient pas repéré. Mais ils risquaient de me voir à tout moment. J'ai cherché du regard un endroit où me cacher.

— P.K., a murmuré Belle Donne. Passe sous mon jupon.

C'était bizarre, comme proposition, mais j'ai tout de suite compris qu'elle avait vu juste. À moins qu'un Chinetoque ne m'ouvre sa porte sur-le-champ, je n'avais pas d'autre cachette à disposition. Plus rapide qu'un télégramme, je me suis jeté sous sa robe.

Ça me faisait comme une tente rose, sauf qu'à la place du poteau central il y avait les jambes minces de Belle Donne. J'ai pu voir qu'elle portait une culotte bouffante blanche, des bas blancs & des bottines noires avec une bonne dizaine de crochets de chaque côté.

J'étais bien protégé du soleil, là-dessous, mais pas de la poussière. Ça me picotait dans les narines.

Je me suis accroupi en attendant. J'avais la bouche sèche. Je sentais les vibrations de la montagne, & j'entendais les braiments d'un âne & les cris des Chinetoques qui s'engueulaient dans leur langue. Il y avait des cailles dans les buissons d'armoise & je les entendais qui faisaient : « Chicago ! Chi-ca-go ! » Il y a eu aussi des sabots de chevaux qui approchaient. Quand ce bruit a cessé, j'ai entendu le cliquetis d'une bride & la voix de Walt qui demandait :

— Pardon, m'dame, vous ne seriez pas venue par la diligence de Como ?

— Mais si, monsieur.

Toute la poussière qui flottait sous la robe de Belle Donne me chatouillait les narines comme c'est pas permis. J'ai étouffé un éternuement en me pinçant le nez.

— Est-ce que vous vous rappelez s'il y avait un garçon à bord ? Un petit d'une douzaine d'années. Il s'est enfui de Temperance et ses parents nous ont envoyés le chercher.

— Je ne me rappelle pas avoir vu de garçon à bord, vous m'en voyez désolée.

Je l'ignorais à ce moment-là, mais l'air de Virginia est très raréfié, ce qui fait qu'on a vite la tête qui tourne & mal au ventre, les premiers temps. J'étais justement en train de ressentir ces effets : la terre s'est mise à pencher de côté. Pour ne pas tomber, je me suis agrippé aux genoux de Belle Donne.

Elle a fait :

— Ooooh !

— Un problème, m'dame ? a dit Walt.

— Oui, je… je dois avoir une puce dans mon corset, ça m'a fait sursauter.

— Moi je serais bien ravi de vous en débarrasser, a rigolé Voix Râpeuse.

Cramponné comme je l'étais aux jambes de Belle, je sentais qu'elle tremblait.

— Pas maintenant, Dub, est intervenu Walt. On a d'autres chats à fouetter.

J'ai entendu une selle qui craquait, puis le « poc-poc » des sabots par terre. Les trois desperados partaient.

C'est là que j'ai fait la dernière chose à faire : j'ai éternué un grand coup.

Une pause. Un déluge de lumière. La voix de Belle qui criait : « Fiche le camp, P.K. ! Cours vite ! »

J'étais à moitié aveuglé par le soleil, après la pénombre rose dans laquelle j'étais resté caché, si bien que je n'ai fait qu'entrevoir les trois hommes qui nous dévisageaient depuis leurs montures. Je n'ai pas distingué leurs traits, je sais juste qu'ils portaient des chapeaux et de longs cache-poussière. Au même moment, j'ai senti Belle qui m'attrapait par la main pour m'entraîner vers une ruelle entre deux blanchisseries. En passant, on a contourné le jeune Chinois qui restait là, bouche bée.

En général, je n'aime pas qu'on me touche, mais cette fois je n'ai rien dit. J'ai suivi Belle au milieu des draps étendus qui nous fouettaient la figure. J'ai lâché sa main quand on s'est engouffrés dans la ruelle. Des deux côtés, les murs des cabanes étaient si proches que la robe de Belle frottait contre. J'étais obligé de rester un mètre en arrière. Belle me guidait dans un vrai labyrinthe de ruelles et de draps humides qui sentaient fort la lessive. Le tout sous le regard interloqué des Chinetoques.

— Rentre là-dedans ! a-t-elle dit, tout essoufflée, en me poussant à l'intérieur d'une blanchisserie.

Une série de slaloms entre des grandes cuves en bois pleines d'eau savonneuse & des Chinetoques interloqués & on s'est retrouvés dans une autre ruelle. Belle regardait de tous les côtés, comme folle. Ensuite elle m'a fait entrer dans une cabane pleine de vapeur & qui empestait l'amidon. Il y avait là cinq Chinois occupés à repasser du linge sur des tables. Ils ont relevé la tête – les joues pareilles à celles de hamsters – quand on est entrés puis se sont remis à repasser comme s'ils voyaient une Colombe de Suie et un Indien débouler dans leur atelier toutes les cinq minutes. Au milieu de la pièce, se trouvaient deux petites tables en bois sur lesquelles étaient empilés les draps propres à repasser. Certains retombaient sur les côtés des tables. Belle a tiré dessus pour faire une espèce de tente.

Je m'apprêtais à la rejoindre mais elle m'a repoussé.

— Toi, tu vas sous celle-là, m'a-t-elle dit. Y a pas la place pour deux sous la mienne.

Je me suis donc calé sous l'autre table, en rabattant les draps pour me cacher. Quand tout a été en place, j'ai légèrement écarté deux draps, histoire de voir ce qui se passait. La porte par laquelle on était entrés, c'était en fait juste un rideau qui laissait échapper la vapeur.

À force de regarder les Chinetoques travailler, j'ai compris pourquoi ils avaient des joues de hamsters : ils gardaient de l'eau en bouche & la crachaient sur les draps juste avant de passer le fer.

Du côté de Belle, on voyait un bout de sa robe rose qui dépassait d'un des draps. Mais dès qu'elle arrivait à planquer un côté, ça ressortait de l'autre. Ensuite j'ai entendu des cliquetis d'éperons & je me suis mis à me faire du mouron.

J'ai bien cru que mon cœur s'était arrêté quand le rideau de la porte a volé en l'air & qu'un homme est apparu au milieu de la vapeur. Il portait un chapeau mou à large bord et un cache-poussière couleur biscuit.

Je savais que c'était Walt ou un de ses acolytes.

Il était là à inspecter la pièce quand le bas de la robe de Belle a surgi de sous les draps.

— Te voilà ! s'est écrié Le Peureux en se dirigeant vers elle d'un pas décidé.

FEUILLE DE COMPTES 10

Voyant le desperado à la voix peureuse et au chapeau noir approcher de la cachette de Belle, j'ai pris les choses en main. Je me suis faufilé jusqu'à une autre table sur laquelle j'ai attrapé un fer froid que j'ai jeté sur Le Peureux.

Ça l'a fait hurler & bondir, puis il a porté une main à sa figure. Il saignait du nez.

Sitôt que les Chinetoques ont vu que Le Peureux risquait de salir tous leurs beaux draps bien propres, ils se sont mis en action. Trois d'entre eux l'ont expulsé de la cabane, un autre m'a pris par les épaules et le dernier est allé tirer Belle de sa cachette. En moins de temps qu'il n'en faut pour le dire, ils nous avaient tous éjectés dans la ruelle & nous criaient dessus en chinois.

— Purin de toi ! s'exclama Le Peureux en se dégageant des Chinetoques pour s'approcher de moi. Tu m'as cassé le nez ! Je vais vous buter tous les deux !

Là-dessus, il a sorti un revolver Colt Navy de son cache-poussière, l'a armé & l'a pointé sur moi. Mais il n'a pas eu le temps d'appuyer sur la détente qu'une détonation a retenti : Belle, avec son Pistolet de Poche. La balle a dû toucher le desperado à la main ou au poignet, vu qu'il a lâché son revolver comme s'il le brûlait. Alors que son Colt retombait par terre, un coup est parti & le bonhomme a jappé :

— J'ai pris une balle !

Il se tenait un pied & on a vu que le talon de sa botte avait sauté.

— Une balle de mon propre flingue !

Il a levé sa main ensanglantée.

— Et toi, tu m'as bousillé le pouce, salope !

— Plus un geste, l'a coupé Belle en inclinant légèrement le canon de son Pistolet, ou je tire dans tes Parties Intimes. Les mains en l'air !

— T'avais qu'une balle à tirer, ricanait Le Peureux.

— Pas avec un Double Deringer, a expliqué Belle. Comme tu vois, il n'y a qu'un canon mais deux chiens. Il y a donc une autre balle de calibre .41 là-dedans qui t'attend.

Le bonhomme a hurlé « Sale Purin ! », ce qui ne l'a pas empêché de lever les mains.

Son nez saignait toujours & un de ses yeux ne regardait pas droit. Avec le coup de poêlon qu'il avait reçu de Ma Evangeline, il n'était pas gâté.

Belle l'a fouillé & a trouvé sur lui quelques pièces en argent et deux, trois billets. Elle a fourré le tout dans son décolleté avant de crier au type :

— Ferme les yeux et compte jusqu'à cent, espèce de Vermine !

Comme Le Peureux obéissait, Belle m'a pris par la main & on est partis. Les Chinetoques ne gueulaient plus, ils nous observaient avec intérêt.

J'ai lâché la main de Belle presque immédiatement et l'ai suivie dans un corral. Elle a dérapé sur du fumier et a poussé un juron que je ne peux pas écrire ici. Je l'ai aidée à se relever, puis on est ressortis du corral, direction une ruelle pentue entre un dépôt de bois et l'arrière d'une brasserie.

Arrivés au bout de la ruelle, Belle a relevé le bas de sa robe et s'est mise à courir. Sa coiffure se défaisait & son chapeau à plumes ballottait comme un oiseau mort.

On s'était engagés dans une rue toute plate, flanquée de minuscules cabanes en bois, d'une poignée de maisons en brique & d'une ou deux tentes. Certaines cabanes avaient une lanterne bleue ou rouge à la fenêtre. Il y avait pas mal de maisons en construction & même des terrains à vendre.

Après le labyrinthe de ruelles de Chinatown, cette nouvelle rue était assez large pour des voitures. J'ai vu des chariots, des carrioles tractées par des mules & la charrette d'un laitier. Les gros chevaux qui tiraient cette charrette ont bronché quand Belle les a frôlés, si bien que leur cocher a dû les calmer.

Un boghei noir rutilant s'approchait de nous et, au moment où on s'est croisés, on a entendu :

— Tu as l'air pressée, Belle. Je peux te déposer ?

La dame qui avait dit ça conduisait le boghei. Elle portait une robe citron vaporeuse & un bonnet assorti. Sans même attendre une réponse, elle a éclaté de rire et tapoté le dos de ses chevaux blancs avec son fouet.

Belle a marmonné quelque chose comme « Purin de Sally la Bêcheuse » puis elle a traversé la rue & a pénétré dans une maison en construction. Les murs étaient montés, mais il n'y avait encore ni portes ni fenêtres, et même pas de toit. On s'est assis contre un mur, sous une ouverture de fenêtre. Pas encore habitué à l'air de la ville, j'étais comme essoufflé. Puisqu'il n'y avait pas de toit, je voyais passer les nuages dans le ciel. Ils étaient roses & dorés dans le soleil couchant.

De la rue nous parvenait le bruit rassurant de la circulation. J'ai l'ouïe très fine, et je ne détectais pas le moindre cliquetis d'éperons qui nous pourchasseraient.

Belle tripotait son chapeau pour le remettre en place. Le souffle encore un peu court, elle pestait :

— Ce qu'il me faudrait, c'est un joli petit boghei comme à Sally. Et deux chevaux. Je les mettrais à dormir dans l'écurie Flora Temple.

Sur ce, elle a donné une dernière petite tape à son chapeau, qui était à présent presque droit.

Je me suis appuyé au rebord de l'ouverture de fenêtre pour regarder dehors.

— La voie a l'air libre, ai-je dit en me retournant vers Belle.

Elle avait vidé le contenu de son sac sur le plancher. Il y avait là un sachet de poudre, un refouloir & quelques capsules fulminantes en cuivre. Elle rechargeait son drôle de pistolet à canon unique et double chien. J'ai pu voir qu'il projetait des balles grosses comme des pois chiches. Belle a dû remarquer que je m'intéressais :

— C'est un Double Deringer, m'a-t-elle expliqué. Inventé par un certain M. Lindsay après que son frère s'était fait attaquer par deux Indiens en n'ayant qu'une seule balle dans son pistolet.

— Je peux le prendre ?

— Je crains bien que non, a-t-elle répondu en enfonçant la seconde capsule.

Là-dessus, elle a braqué son Deringer sur moi en disant :

— Je vais te demander de me remettre ta pièce en or de 20 $. Et aussi ta Lettre à Mille Dollars.

FEUILLE DE COMPTES 11

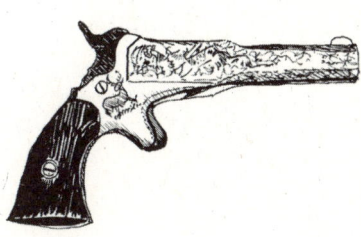

Je fixais Belle sans y croire.

Ses yeux bleus luisaient et ses joues rosissaient.

— Tu t'y feras vite, m'a-t-elle dit. C'est chacun pour soi à Virginia. Les hommes comme les femmes. Aboule tes trucs.

Je me suis dit : « Encore mon Épine... »

Un coup d'œil alentour pour trouver de quoi me défendre. Il n'y avait même pas une planche qui traînait. En plus, j'avais encore la tête qui tournait.

Belle a armé les deux chiens de son drôle de pistolet.

— N'y pense même pas, a-t-elle fait. Donne ce que je te demande.

J'ai sorti la pièce en or et la Lettre de mon sac-médecine et les lui ai tendues. Son regard rivé au mien, elle a ouvert son petit sac et y a fourré le tout.

Puis elle a braqué son arme sur mon sac-médecine en disant :

— T'as quoi d'autre, là-dedans ?

— Rien. Juste le couteau en silex de ma mère indienne et le Bouton de Détective de mon père.

— C'est quoi, un Bouton de Détective ?

Je n'ai pas répondu.

— Parle, ou je te descends.

J'ai sorti le bouton de ma poche et le lui ai montré.

— C'est un bouton de la veste de mon père qui est mort, ai-je expliqué. C'est tout ce qui me reste de lui. Il était Détective du Chemin de Fer.

Une grimace, puis :

— C'est quoi, ça, un Détective ?

— Un Détective, c'est une personne qui résout des crimes en suivant des indices. Comme M. Bucket dans *La Maison d'Âpre-Vent*. Les Détectives du Chemin de Fer, eux, ils protègent les voyageurs et leurs bagages.

— Ton M. Bucket, là, c'est qui ? Et qu'est-ce que t'appelles une maison d'Âpre-Machin ?

— M. Bucket est un personnage d'un livre de Charles Dickens. Vous ne connaissez pas Dickens ?

Au lieu de me répondre, elle a dit :

— Il a de la valeur, le bouton ?

— Pour moi, oui. Une valeur sentimentale.

— Tu ne m'as pourtant pas l'air d'être un sentimental, toi. Tu dois être quelqu'un de froid pour parler de la mort de tes parents sans aucune émotion.

— C'est mon Épine. Je ne sais jamais bien exprimer mes émotions. Ni les lire chez les autres, d'ailleurs. Par contre, mes parents me manquent beaucoup.

Belle m'a demandé :

— Ils te battaient, des fois ?

— Non.

— Tu peux dire que tu as de la chance.

— Ça je sais. Ils ont toujours été très bons envers moi. Ma Evangeline m'a appris à lire et à écrire, et Pa Emmet m'a enseigné la Parole de Dieu.

Là, Belle Donne m'a fait :

— Tourne-toi et assieds-toi en tailleur.

J'ai obéi.

Je sentais qu'elle me ligotait les poignets dans le dos. Après j'ai vu qu'elle s'était servie d'un ruban rouge.

— C'est mal, ce que vous faites, lui ai-je dit.

— Ta pièce, j'en ai plus besoin que toi, P.K. J'ai une sale habitude.

— Moi, tout ce que je veux, c'est pouvoir me payer un billet de train pour Chicago.

— Couche-toi sur le côté et plie les jambes, pour que j'attache tes chevilles à tes poignets.

Tout en me ficelant, elle a demandé :

— Pourquoi Chicago ?

— Parce que mon oncle Allan Pinkerton y dirige l'Agence nationale des Détectives. Il a des tas de Détectives sous ses ordres, y compris des femmes.

— Tiens donc ?

— Oui. Comme femmes, il y a par exemple Miss Kate Warne. Elle se déguise pour se faire passer pour ce qu'elle n'est pas.

Là-dessus, je lui ai cité un article de journal que Ma Evangeline m'avait fait lire :

— « Cet ingénieux déguisement a permis à Miss Kate Warne d'obtenir les aveux des coupables. » Des fois, même, elle « file » des gens. C'est-à-dire qu'elle les suit.

— D'où tu sais ça ? m'a demandé Belle sans s'arrêter de me lier les chevilles et les poignets.

— D'un journal. (J'essayais de la voir par-dessus mon épaule.) Je me dis que, si mon oncle emploie des femmes comme Détectives, il fait peut-être aussi travailler des enfants. Surtout s'ils sont de sa famille. Si je pouvais aller à Chicago, je suis sûr que mon oncle m'embaucherait dans son Agence de Détectives comme Privé. À condition que je me débarrasse de mon Épine.

— C'est quoi, un Privé ?

— Une sorte d'espion qu'on paie pour qu'il découvre la Vérité.

— Eh bien je te souhaite de réussir, a-t-elle dit en finissant de nouer le ruban. Sauf que là, j'ai besoin de ta pièce et de ta Lettre.

— Je vous ai sauvé la vie tout à l'heure, quand j'ai frappé le compère de Walt.

Ça l'a soufflée.

— Le compère de *qui*, tu dis ?

— De Walt. Du moins c'est comme ça qu'ils l'appellent.

Belle est venue se mettre face à moi.

— Ton bonhomme, là, c'était Walt-Les-Copeaux ?

D'un coup sa figure est devenue toute blanche, et elle avait le souffle court.

— Pas celui sur qui vous avez tiré, l'autre. Celui qui vous parlait quand j'étais caché sous votre robe.

— C'était Walt-Les-Copeaux ?

— Je ne connais pas son nom en entier. Juste que les deux autres l'appellent Walt.

— Grand Dieu… a-t-elle dit en enfouissant sa figure dans ses mains. Oh, mon Dieu, non !

— Qu'est-ce qu'il y a ?

— Walt-Les-Copeaux est le hors-la-loi le plus redouté de notre Territoire. (Je l'entendais à peine, vu qu'elle parlait dans ses gants.) Tu sais un peu pourquoi on l'appelle comme ça ?

— Non.

Belle a relevé la tête, et son visage exprimait une des rares expressions que je sais reconnaître : la Peur.

— On l'appelle Walt-Les-Copeaux parce qu'il découpe ses victimes vivantes.

FEUILLE DE COMPTES 12

Belle avait pris la poudre d'escampette avant que j'aie pu lui demander d'autres détails sur le desperado qui en avait après moi.

La première personne que j'avais rencontrée à Virginia City m'avait dépouillé et ligoté. Mes poignets et mes chevilles étaient ficelés ensemble, et j'étais couché à même le plancher. Encore heureux que Belle ne m'ait pas bâillonné. La nuit commençait à tomber.

Je ne voyais qu'une chose à faire : appeler à l'aide.

Mais bon, je n'aime pas ça.

Je préfère me débrouiller seul.

Il faisait de plus en plus noir.

J'entendais des cailles dans un buisson d'armoise : « Chicago ! Chicago ! » On aurait dit qu'elles voulaient me rappeler mon objectif.

Ensuite, ça a été des cris de coyotes dans le canyon. Les coyotes, ça mange tout et n'importe quoi : y compris un petit garçon moitié sioux, moitié blanc – ils ne regardent pas à ça. C'est ça qui m'a décidé : pas question de me faire dévorer vivant par des coyotes.

— Au secours ! ai-je crié. Venez m'aider ! On m'a dépouillé et je suis ligoté dans la crèche en chantier. Je veux pas me faire manger par des coyotes !

J'avais à peine lancé trois, quatre appels que j'ai entendu des pas devant la maison. J'ai tout de suite compris que les seules personnes qui cherchaient à me retrouver, c'étaient Walt-Les-Copeaux et ses deux acolytes.

Mes cris les avaient-ils alertés ?

Sur le moment, je crois que j'aurais préféré avoir à affronter une meute de coyotes affamés plutôt que Walt et son Couteau de Chasse.

J'ai fermé les yeux et essayé la Ruse de la Maison en Construction. Pour ça, il faut faire semblant d'être une Maison en construction et se fondre dans le chantier.

Ça n'a pas marché.

J'ai senti dans l'air une odeur de lessive et de produit chimique que je ne connaissais pas. Quand j'ai rouvert les yeux, j'avais une paire de sandales à semelles de bois devant moi. Au-dessus, un pantalon bleu délavé dans lequel son propriétaire nageait, et au-dessus encore une chemise bleue d'où sortait une tête de Chinois qui m'observait. Impossible de déchiffrer son expression.

Il s'est accroupi et a soufflé :

— Tais-toi, Crétin ! Je crois homme qui te poursuit pas loin !

Il s'est mis à triturer le ruban qui me liait les chevilles et les poignets. Il cherchait à me détacher.

— Dans le sac-médecine accroché à mon cou, j'ai un couteau en silex, ai-je indiqué.

Le jeune Chinois a récupéré le sac et sorti le couteau. Quelques entailles et j'étais libre.

— Viens ! a-t-il dit alors en me tendant le couteau et les restes du ruban rouge. Vite-vite !

Et il m'entraîna vers une ouverture pratiquée dans le mur, donnant sur l'arrière de la maison.

Mes poignets me faisaient mal, et j'avais des fourmis dans les chevilles, mais j'ai malgré tout réussi à le suivre sur la pente poussiéreuse. On s'accrochait aux buissons d'armoise pour avoir moins de mal à grimper. Du coup, on a fait fuir la famille de cailles qui me rappelait de partir pour Chicago tout à l'heure.

La pente était si raide que les bâtiments reposaient à moitié sur des pilotis. Le jeune Chinetoque m'a fait passer sous une de ces structures, où on ne nous verrait pas. Il s'est arrêté et a regardé si la voie était libre. Puis on s'est remis à grimper jusqu'à une espèce de ruelle qui passait entre deux bâtiments en bois. Je ne suis ni gros ni musclé, mais quand même, je passais juste. Le Chinois, lui, il était plus grand et un peu plus maigre que moi. Il devait manger moins bien.

Et puis on a fini par déboucher sur une rue flanquée de trottoirs bondés. Je n'avais jamais vu autant de monde dans un même endroit. J'entendais des rires de femmes, des cris d'hommes & de la musique. Le bruit était amplifié à cause de tous les balcons des immeubles qui formaient comme un toit & renvoyaient les sons. Il y avait des constructions en bois, d'autres en brique & à l'angle de la rue, sur notre droite, s'élevait un hôtel particulier à six côtés, en pierre grise. La rue grouillait de calèches et de chariots qui soulevaient des nuages de poussière.

— Jupon ! a lancé le Chinetoque. Arrête regarder. Suis-moi.

— De quoi, « jupon » ?

— Je t'ai vu caché sous jupon de méchante femme. Je t'ai suivi.

C'est là que je l'ai reconnu : le jeune qui étendait des draps devant chez « Hong Wo, Lessive ».

Je lui ai dit :

— C'est toi qui étendais des draps devant chez « Hong Wo, Lessive ». Je m'appelle P.K. Pinkerton. Merci de m'avoir sauvé.

— Moi, Ping. Maintenant tais-toi et suis-moi. Vite-vite ! Je t'emmène où tu pourras changer affaires. Là, on te voit comme criquet sur bol de riz.

Je n'avais pas d'autre choix que de le suivre en espérant qu'il n'essaierait pas de me dépouiller & de me tuer comme Belle. Tout en suivant Ping à travers la foule qui faisait craquer le trottoir, je remarquais que tous les hommes ou presque étaient des mineurs. Ça se voyait à leurs chemises de flanelle, à leurs pantalons, à leurs bottes hautes & à leurs barbes épaisses. Il y avait à peu près dix hommes pour une femme.

J'ai aussi noté qu'un bâtiment sur deux était un saloon ou un tripot à musique. Ça se reconnaissait aux chansons qu'on entendait de la rue : « Camptown Races », surtout. En plus des saloons, il y avait une Mercerie, un Laboratoire des Essais des Monnaies, une Banque Wells Fargo, etc. Et aussi une Blanchisserie chinoise, tenez.

Les gens me dévisageaient, et il y a même une femme qui m'a attrapé par le bras. Elle portait des anglaises blondes et un tout minuscule bustier rose.

— Voyez-vous ça... a-t-elle fait. Un joli petit Indien en habits de daim à franges. Est-y pas chou ?

L'homme qui se tenait à côté d'elle a craché du jus de tabac à 10 centimètres de mes pieds.

Ping avait raison : on me voyait comme un criquet sur un bol de riz.

Là-dessus, Ping m'a fait signe de m'engager dans la Grand-Rue. Lui, il a traversé entre deux charrettes qui transportaient du bois.

Au moment où je m'élançais à sa suite, j'ai repéré un grand immeuble en brique, de l'autre côté de la rue, le plus beau que j'aie jamais vu : deux étages, des boutiques au rez-de-chaussée, un balcon panoramique soutenu par des colonnes & auquel on accédait par de grandes fenêtres en arche. Une gigantesque enseigne accrochée sous le toit proclamait : **INTERNATIONAL HOTEL**. Sur un des angles, il y en avait une autre qui disait **AGENCE DILIGENCES CALIF**. J'ai pensé que ça devait être l'arrêt de la diligence pour Chicago.

Un claquement de fouet et un gros juron m'ont ramené sur terre, et je me suis écarté juste à temps pour ne pas me faire ratatiner par un attelage de bœufs. J'ai regardé des deux côtés puis ai foncé pour rattraper Ping. Lui était déjà sur le trottoir d'en face, à parler avec un Chinois habillé comme un banquier. Je les ai rejoints.

Ils avaient l'air de discuter d'un truc sérieux, alors j'en ai profité pour aller lire la notice placardée devant l'International Hotel. Moi, je lis un texte une fois, je ne l'oublie jamais. La pancarte disait :

RÉOUVERTURE !

INTERNATIONAL HOTEL

Propriétaires A.S. Paul & I. Bateman

❦ _Meilleur hôtel du territoire_ ❦

☞ Avec Petit Salon de 5,5 mètres sur 6 & 10 chambres pouvant être reliées & arrangées en chambres & petits salons pour les familles.

☞ Du toit de l'hôtel, ceint d'un mur pare-feu d'un mètre, découvrez une vue imprenable sur Virginia City & la campagne environnante.

☞ Un mât d'une hauteur de 12 mètres est également installé sur le toit.

☞ Le bâtiment est entièrement ignifugé.

☞ La ferronnerie de l'hôtel, à elle seule, a coûté plus de 4 000 dollars. Les frais de construction de ce nouvel édifice, mobilier non compris, se sont élevés à 14 000 dollars.

(L'ancien bâtiment, dans B. Street, accueille encore les visiteurs & sera remplacé à court terme, après agrandissement du nouvel hôtel.)

☞ Un service de _DILIGENCES_ relie l'**INTERNATIONAL HOTEL** tous les jours aux centres importants de la Californie & du Territoire du Nevada.

☞ Le _BAR_ vous propose les meilleurs VINS, ALCOOLS ET CIGARES.

Enfin, nous ne manquons jamais d'intégrer les dernières innovations du confort moderne à ce qu'il n'est pas vain d'appeler LE GRAND HÔTEL DU TERRITOIRE.

Après avoir lu cette pancarte, je suis allé regarder dans la vitrine du Wasserman's Emporium. Il y avait une statue en plâtre coloré d'un homme devant un Stand de Tir.

Puisque Ping discutait toujours, j'ai filé jusqu'à l'Agence des Diligences, en vérifiant du coin de l'œil que je n'apercevais pas Walt & ses sbires, ou même Belle.

Arrivé à l'angle de la rue, j'ai vu un panneau mal peint annonçant que je me trouvais à l'intersection de C. Street & d'Union. C. Street était toute plate ; par contre, Union avait une pente pas possible. À tel point que l'International Hotel avait l'air d'une part de gâteau posée sur la tranche, avec le glaçage devant.

C'est là que j'ai trouvé ce que je cherchais. Sur la façade de l'Agence des Diligences Calif., il y avait la liste des destinations & des tarifs. J'ai suivi avec mon doigt pour trouver le prix d'un Virginia City-Chicago.

100 $.

Autant dire une Grosse Fortune.

Il fallait donc que je retrouve Belle et que je récupère ma Lettre. Après ça, je pourrais m'acheter un billet pour Chicago et quitter cette ville où les hommes et les bêtes cherchaient à me tuer.

Au moment où je me retournais pour voir si Ping arrivait, j'ai entendu un coup de feu, et vu un homme qui se précipitait vers moi.

FEUILLE DE COMPTES 13

Il y avait un gros tonneau en bois devant l'Agence des Diligences Calif. Je me suis caché derrière pour que le bonhomme ne me voie pas. Il était blond, avait la figure rasée et tirait en l'air avec un vieux revolver Colt Dragoon. Ça faisait un boucan monstre et pas mal de fumée. Il a tiré encore quatre fois avant de continuer à presser la détente alors que le barillet était vide. Puis il s'est écroulé sur le trottoir, presque à mes pieds. Une femme a crié & un cheval s'est cabré, mais sinon la plupart des gens ça les faisait rigoler.

Pour moi, ça ne pouvait pas être Walt ou un de ses sbires, mais j'ai quand même reniflé l'air, au cas où. Pas une trace de lotion capillaire Bay Rum. Du whisky, par contre.

Des gens s'agglutinaient autour de l'homme.

— Il est mort ? a demandé un mineur barbu.

— Nan, juste bourré, lui a répondu un autre, qui a ensuite saisi le revolver de l'ivrogne en disant : Et moi, j'ai gagné un flingue. Yii haaa !

Sur ce, il a glissé le Colt déchargé sous sa ceinture & a déguerpi en poussant de nouveau des cris de joie.

J'ai senti qu'on me prenait par le bras. Très fort. Ça faisait mal. C'était Ping.

— Vite-vite ! a-t-il dit. Je t'emmène à l'abri.

Je me suis laissé guider dans Union Street, une rue transversale en pente, puis on a pris à gauche. Ça devait être B. Street, une des rues plates.

On avait beau marcher sur le bord du trottoir, les gens n'arrêtaient quand même pas de nous bousculer. Sûrement parce qu'on était chinois et indien. À un moment donné, on a dû se faufiler parmi un groupe d'hommes en redingote & chapeau en tuyau de poêle. Ils étaient gras, ils fumaient des gros cigares & se tenaient là comme si la rue leur appartenait. Des Avocats, à tous les coups. On est encore passés devant deux Saloons, un Restaurant et un Sellier.

Devant nous, il y avait un croisement & j'ai pensé : « Carson Monte Sur Un Train Sans Wagons ; Train égale Taylor. »

Bingo, le panneau accroché à la façade d'un immeuble indiquait TAYLOR STREET.

On a laissé passer un chariot avant de traverser.

— Tu m'emmènes où ? ai-je demandé à Ping.

— Juste là.

Il s'était arrêté devant une boutique de B. Street, côté est. Il a voulu ouvrir la porte. C'était fermé. Le temps qu'il sorte une clé de sa poche, j'en ai profité pour reculer d'un pas et regarder l'enseigne de la boutique : **ISAIAH COFFIN – AMBROTYPES & PHOTOGRAPHIES**.

Et juste là, j'ai senti une odeur familière, celle de la pipe de Pa Emmet. Je me suis retourné, une fille de mon âge sortait de la boutique d'à côté : **BLOOMFIELD TABAC**.

La fille avait des cheveux marron bouclés et des grands yeux marron aussi. Plus elle me regardait, plus on aurait dit que ses yeux s'agrandissaient. C'était quoi ? L'Expression n° 4 : la Surprise ? Ça me faisait râler de ne pas savoir lire sur les visages. Là, je me demandais si elle allait vouloir me tuer, elle aussi.

Mais elle n'a pas eu le temps de sortir un six-coups et de me truffer de plomb, car Ping avait ouvert la porte de chez le Photographe & m'attirait à l'intérieur.

Une clochette a tinté quand la porte s'est refermée.

Il faisait sombre, dans la boutique, & on sentait des odeurs chimiques bizarroïdes. Sur la gauche, il y avait un comptoir en bois avec une fenêtre panoramique à côté. Sur la droite, on avait installé une toile qui représentait un Troupeau de Bisons & un Convoi de Chariots dans les Grandes Plaines. Le peintre avait même dessiné des Tipis dans l'arrière-plan avec des nuages et des montagnes. Ça me rappelait des souvenirs tristes.

Et devant ce décor, un canapé recouvert d'une peau de bison & une chaise avec accoudoirs à franges de chaque côté. Il y avait aussi une espèce d'accordéon noir, terminé à chaque bout par une pièce de bois et de cuivre. L'objet était attaché à un support en noyer avec pieds en fonte.

— C'est studio d'Isaiah Coffin, m'a expliqué Ping. Meilleur photographe à l'ouest Rocheuses. Je travaille pour lui des fois. Il est pas là maintenant. Toi, attends. Dors dans peau de bison. Ici, il y a beaucoup costumes. Isaiah les garde pour ami de théâtre. Clients mettent des fois costumes pour photographies. C'est plus cher.

Indiquant l'accordéon noir en bois, j'ai demandé :

— Et ça, c'est l'appareil photographique ?

Ping a continué comme s'il n'avait pas entendu ma question :

— Mets autres habits ! Je dois partir. Je t'amène demain à *Journal Territorial Enterprise*. Oncle Joe travaille à journal. Son patron t'aidera pour retrouver Dame et Lettre à Mille Dollars.

— Qui t'a parlé de ma Lettre ?

— J'ai entendu, tu parlais à la dame.

— Et pourquoi tu fais tout ça ?

Il a croisé les bras, puis annoncé :

— Pour argent. Je veux moitié. 500 $. OK ?

Je commençais à comprendre Virginia City. Ici, personne n'agissait jamais par pure bonté chrétienne. Mieux valait que je ne m'éternise pas dans le coin.

— OK ? a répété Ping.

À voir la grimace qu'il faisait, même moi j'ai compris qu'il était en colère.

J'ai répondu :

— On m'avait raconté que tous les Chinetoques étaient calmes & d'humeur égale.

Ça l'a fait grimacer encore plus.

— OK ? 500 $?

— C'est d'accord. Mais seulement si je récupère des sous en échange de la Lettre. OK ?

— OK.

Il m'a tendu la main et je la lui ai serrée – Dieu sait pourtant que je n'aime pas toucher les gens.

Puis Ping m'a dit :

— Tu restes ici. Je te vois demain tôt. Touche rien. Isaiah doit pas te voir, sinon colère. (Il m'a passé sa clé.) Ferme derrière moi.

— Tu t'en vas ?

— Oncle va être colère. Autre oncle : Hong Wo, pas Oncle Joe. Je pars ou il me bat.

La clochette a tinté, la porte a claqué & mon samaritain grincheux avait filé.

Je regardais la porte. J'avais peur, j'avais faim, j'étais crevé. Mes parents adoptifs s'étaient fait tuer & scalper à cause de moi. Je ne possédais rien à part un couteau en silex, un Bouton de Détective et des habits qui me faisaient repérer comme un criquet sur un bol de riz. Sans compter les trois desperados qui voulaient me faire la peau.

J'en étais à me demander si les choses pouvaient empirer.

(Vu que j'écris ces lignes au fond d'une mine, à 60 mètres sous le sol, et que les desperados sont toujours sur ma piste, vous vous doutez que, oui, ça a pas mal empiré depuis.)

FEUILLE DE COMPTES 14

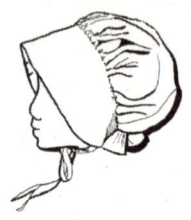

Dès que Ping a été sorti, j'ai fait comme il avait dit, j'ai refermé la porte à clé.

Puis je suis allé fouiller le grand placard aux costumes. Ça sentait la laine, la naphtaline & la lavande. Je n'avais jamais vu autant d'habits dans un même endroit.

Il y avait des costumes de velours avec collerette comme dans la pièce de Shakespeare que Ma Evangeline m'avait emmené voir. Et aussi des habits d'aujourd'hui, comme cette tenue de mineur avec bottes hautes, pantalon en toile, chemise de flanelle rouge, etc. Un costume de Banquier, un Uniforme de Pompier, des vêtements de Dame avec corsets & cerceaux à mettre sous la jupe.

L'Ami de Théâtre d'Isaiah Coffin devait aimer jouer des pièces de maintenant et d'autres du passé.

Il y avait même toute une série d'habits de Mexicain, de Chinois & d'Indien. Les costumes d'Indien n'étaient pas mal : encore plus de franges que sur ma tenue & même une coiffe à plumes.

J'ai encore repéré un pardessus bleu marine d'officier nordiste & son pantalon assorti. Un revolver Colt

Baby Dragoon était accroché à une patère : le même que ma mère indienne possédait, sauf que celui-là avait une crosse en ivoire. Je me disais que ça pouvait être utile de l'avoir sur moi. J'ai vérifié qu'il n'était pas chargé puis l'ai essayé – le chien était cassé, pas moyen de tirer. Je l'ai raccroché à la patère.

Je pensais : « J'aimerais bien voir une pièce de théâtre avec tous ces personnages dedans. »

Et c'est là que, derrière une rangée d'habits, j'ai trouvé ce qu'il me fallait : des vêtements pour enfants.

Je les ai passés en revue, et l'une des tenues m'a donné une idée. C'était une robe à manches longues en calicot rouge parsemé de petites fleurs blanches. De loin, on l'aurait dite rose. Elle avait des volants de dentelle blanche autour du col & des poignets. Sur le même cintre étaient accrochés un bonnet assorti, des socquettes & une culotte bouffante blanches ainsi que des bottines – les mêmes que Belle Donne, mais blanches. Et pour finir, deux petites perruques : une à anglaises blondes, l'autre à anglaises brunes.

Je me suis passé la main dans les cheveux. Ils sont raides et noirs. Courts, aussi, parce que j'ai eu des lentes le mois dernier & que Ma Evangeline a dû me raser la tête, vu que le shampooing à la térébenthine n'avait pas fait partir toutes les lentes.

J'ai donc mis la perruque blonde & me suis regardé dans un grand miroir étroit appuyé contre le mur. Les boucles blondes allaient mal avec ma peau cireuse & mes yeux foncés. Avec la noire, par contre, j'étais carrément quelqu'un d'autre.

J'ai retiré mes habits en daim pour passer les socquettes, la culotte bouffante, le chemisier, le jupon blanc & par-dessus tout ça la robe en calicot. Les dentelles me chatouillaient. Ensuite, j'ai enfilé les bottines. Pile ma taille. J'ai mis deux heures à crocheter tous les petits boutons. Et pour finir, le bonnet. M'habiller en fille, ça m'avait pris un temps fou et une énergie pas possible, mais le résultat en valait la peine. Mes deux mères elles-mêmes auraient eu du mal à me reconnaître.

J'étais « Déguisé », comme tous les Détectives dont j'avais lu les aventures.

Ping m'avait recommandé de rester là, mais j'étais trop excité pour dormir, alors j'ai réfléchi à ce que je pourrais faire.

Le Chinetoque avait parlé d'un de ses oncles qui travaillait dans un Journal dont le patron pourrait m'aider. Et Belle m'avait expliqué que le Bureau du Juge dans A. Street se trouvait en face d'un Journal. Qui sait ? peut-être que le patron aurait des dossiers et des cartes dans son bureau. Il connaîtrait peut-être Belle Donne. Comme ça, je pourrais récupérer ma Lettre & l'apporter au Bureau du Juge pour toucher ma fortune.

Après, je n'aurais qu'à acheter un billet de diligence pour Chicago & devenir Détective comme mon père.

C'était mon plan.

J'ai passé mon sac-médecine autour de mon cou et l'ai glissé sous la robe. La clochette a tinté au moment où je poussais la porte. Je l'ai refermée derrière moi, ai fourré la clé dans mon sac puis me suis dirigé vers le nord. Il faisait nuit, le ciel avait la couleur des soirs d'orage. J'avais froid et il y avait dans l'air comme une odeur de neige, alors qu'on n'était même pas en octobre. J'ai eu envie de retourner prendre un châle mais ça m'aurait fait perdre du temps. J'ai traversé Taylor Street sans encombre, direction le nord *via* B. Street.

Les saloons crachaient une musique entraînante. Je m'efforçais de ne pas me laisser entraîner. Comme j'approchais d'un saloon, les portes battantes se sont ouvertes & j'ai failli m'en prendre une en pleine figure. J'ai reculé, craignant des coups de feu, mais c'étaient juste deux types qui quittaient les lieux, le cigare aux lèvres. Ils sont partis côté sud. J'ai profité de ce que les portes du saloon battaient encore pour jeter un œil à l'intérieur. À la lueur des lampes à huile, je distinguais tout un tas de bonshommes accoudés au bar, avec des crachoirs tous les quatre ou cinq. Il y avait des femmes, aussi. Elles portaient des jolies robes décolletées. Sûrement des Colombes de Suie ou des Danseuses.

Je me suis engagé dans une rue transversale, Union, au bout de laquelle j'ai rejoint A. Street. J'ai pris à droite, en observant bien tous les bâtiments que je voyais de part et d'autre. Il faisait franchement sombre, dans cette rue : la seule lumière venait de torches plantées à même le sol.

— Je peux t'aider, petite ? a demandé une grosse femme en noir.

Elle tenait sous le bras un paquet enveloppé dans du papier journal. Du poisson, à l'odeur.

— S'il vous plaît, m'dame, lui ai-je demandé d'une voix de fillette, je cherche le Journal qui se trouve en face du Bureau du Juge.

— Le *Territorial Enterprise* est situé juste là-bas, à l'angle de Sutton. C'est le bâtiment avec les drapeaux.

Une petite tape sur mon bonnet, et elle est repartie.

Les torches me permettaient d'apercevoir un immeuble orné de deux pauvres drapeaux à l'angle de A. Street et de Sutton. Une construction en bois, pas très solide et sans étage. En m'approchant, j'ai pu lire l'enseigne qui indiquait : **BUREAU TERRITORIAL ENTERPRISE**. Accolé à un des murs, il y avait une espèce de cabanon recouvert d'un toit en pente, avec de la lumière à sa fenêtre.

Cette lumière m'attirait, alors je suis allé jeter un coup d'œil. À l'intérieur, des hommes en bras de chemise mangeaient autour d'une longue table. Il y avait des couchettes de chaque côté. Pour moi, ça ressemblait plus à une pension qu'à un journal, alors je suis retourné voir le bâtiment principal.

Sur la porte il était écrit **PONY EXPRESS EXTRA** en grosses lettres noires. La porte aurait eu besoin d'être repeinte, vu que ça faisait près d'un an que le Pony Express ne distribuait plus le courrier, depuis l'arrivée du télégraphe.

J'ai tourné la poignée et la porte s'est ouverte.

Une pièce unique était éclairée par des lampes à huile et chauffée par un poêle installé au fond. Sur une longue table en bois était installée la presse. (Je l'ai su parce qu'il y avait **PRESSE TYPOGRAPHIQUE, WASHINGTON** marqué dessus.) À l'autre bout de la salle, des bureaux à cylindre étaient contre le mur.

Un homme était assis à un de ces bureaux, il me tournait le dos. Un autre était debout, occupé à ranger des petits cubes sur une espèce de plateau métallique. Le premier ne s'est pas retourné ; l'autre a levé les yeux. Il avait les cheveux & la barbe couleur renard, le tout saupoudré de jaune pâle : la poussière d'alcali. Pareil pour sa chemise en laine bleue. Sa pipe empestait comme si une petite bête était allée mourir dedans. Le bonhomme, lui, ressemblait plus à un prospecteur ou à un mineur qu'à un reporter. (Je n'avais encore jamais vu de reporter en vrai, mais je les imaginais binoclards et tout tachés d'encre.)

Quand le barbu m'a vu, il a retiré sa pipe de sa bouche & m'a dit :

— J'ai bien peur que vous fassiez erreur, miss. Le saloon, c'est deux portes à côté.

Son collègue assis a jeté un coup d'œil par-dessus son épaule. Voyant ce qu'il croyait être une petite fille avec un bonnet rose, il a gloussé. Lui, il avait la figure allongée & les oreilles décollées. Sa moustache et son bouc noirs étaient bien entretenus. Il correspondait plus à l'image que je me faisais d'un reporter que l'autre avec sa pipe répugnante.

— Je ne cherche pas le saloon, ai-je répondu. Je voudrais voir votre patron. J'ai un gros Problème – une question de Vie ou de Mort.

— Et ce problème, dites-moi, est-ce que c'est un scoop ? m'a demandé le fumeur. Je suis le nouveau Local & j'ai besoin d'un Scoop pour demain.

— Qu'est-ce que c'est, un Local & un Scoop ?

— Un Local, c'est un reporter qui publie les infos locales.

— Et un Scoop ?

— Une info inédite et renversante.

— Dans ce cas, oui, je crois bien que j'ai un Scoop.

— Alors assieds-toi, miss, je t'en prie.

Il s'est approché & a retiré une chaise de sous un bureau. Elle était montée sur des petites roulettes & avait un coussin vert sur son siège en noyer.

— Je m'appelle Sam Clemens, a-t-il annoncé. Et ce monsieur, là-bas, c'est Dan De Quille, le rédacteur en chef de notre journal. Ne fais pas attention à lui. Moi, par contre, je peux t'aider. Si toi, de ton côté, tu veux bien m'aider.

FEUILLE DE COMPTES 15

Sam Clemens, le reporter aux faux airs de prospecteur, s'est assis face à moi.

— Alors dis-moi, petite. Ton Scoop, cette histoire de Vie ou de Mort, c'est quoi ?

Je me suis assis & ai croisé les chevilles comme une fillette bien élevée, puis j'ai répondu :

— Mes parents se sont fait tuer et scalper, moi je suis poursuivi par une bande de desperados. Là, je suis déguisé.

L'homme qui s'appelait Dan De Quille a toussoté avant de faire pivoter sa chaise. Sam Clemens & lui me regardaient avec des grands yeux. J'étais sûr & certain que c'était l'Expression n° 4 : la Surprise. Ils étaient bouche bée, aussi. Ensuite, Sam Clemens s'est penché vers moi pour m'enlever mon bonnet. La perruque est venue avec.

— Purin d'histoire ! s'est-il exclamé. C'est pourtant vrai que tu es déguisé. Et tu n'es même pas une fille, tu es un garçon. À moitié apache, on dirait.

— Sioux, ai-je précisé. À moitié sioux.

Ça a encore fait pouffer Dan De Quille, à son bureau. Sam Clemens l'a regardé d'un air soupçonneux.

— C'est une blague ou quoi, Dan ? lui a-t-il demandé.

Mais l'autre a juste haussé les épaules et dit :

— Je ne suis au courant de rien.

Sam Clemens s'est alors retourné vers moi :

— Qui t'a demandé de venir me raconter ça ? C'est Dan ?

— Je ne vois pas ce que vous voulez dire, l'ai-je assuré. Je me suis déguisé parce que c'était plus sûr. Je suis pourchassé par une bande de desperados.

Dan De Quille a encore pouffé, puis s'est remis à écrire.

Sam Clemens, lui, il est resté sérieux. Il me fixait, les yeux plissés. Expression n° 5. Il devait être furieux contre moi, ou en train de réfléchir ou de me soupçonner. Peut-être bien les trois.

— Je ne suis pas d'humeur à rigoler, a-t-il annoncé. Je viens d'arriver dans cette ville. Tout ce que je sais de Virginia City, c'est que les rues sont désignées par des lettres, et que l'air est si rare qu'on a en permanence le nez qui saigne.

— C'est juste « Virginia », Sam, l'a coupé Dan De Quille. Personne ne dit jamais « Virginia City ».

Sam Clemens l'a ignoré.

— Je viens de faire plus de cent bornes à pied sans rencontrer la moindre habitation.

— M'étonnerait, a fait, sans se retourner, son patron. Je parie que tu as fait route avec un convoi de mules.

— Ça fait six mois que je ne bois que de l'eau polluée à l'alcali et ne mange que de la couenne sèche. (Il a dit ça en se tapant la poitrine, ce qui a soulevé un nuage de poussière jaune pâle.) Et comme tu l'auras remarqué à mon odeur, j'ai eu tout juste assez d'eau pour boire.

— On m'avait parlé de café noir et de viande de bœuf, a marmonné Dan dans sa barbe. Par contre, je veux bien croire que tu ne t'es pas lavé depuis six mois.

— J'étais quasi millionnaire, s'est emporté Sam Clemens en frappant la table. Ma bêtise m'a tout fait perdre.

— Enfin un peu d'honnêteté, a ricané Dan.

— Je n'ai pas de temps à perdre à des balivernes. Il me faut un Scoop, faute de quoi je devrai imprimer cette histoire de charrettes de foin.

Il a coincé sa pipe entre ses dents.

— Mon histoire c'est pas des balivernes, ai-je dit. Cet après-midi, mes parents adoptifs se sont fait tuer et scalper. Quand j'ai découvert leurs corps, ma mère était encore en vie, mais elle est morte peu après.

Là encore, Dan De Quille a fait pivoter sa chaise & m'a dévisagé, les yeux tout ronds.

Ceux de son collègue étaient toujours plissés. Expression n° 5.

— Tu n'as pas l'air d'un gosse qui vient de voir ses parents massacrés, a-t-il dit. Tu es trop calme.

— C'est mon Épine.

— Ton quoi ? a fait Sam Clemens.

— Je ne sais pas bien exprimer mes émotions. Ni les lire chez les gens.

Dan De Quille s'est levé.

— Tu es un Sauvage ou un Croyant ? m'a-t-il demandé.

— Je suis méthodiste. Mon père adoptif était un pasteur méthodiste et j'ai embrassé sa foi.

Je leur ai cité l'Évangile selon Matthieu, chapitre 10, verset 32 :

— « Quiconque se sera déclaré pour moi devant les hommes, à mon tour je me déclarerai pour lui devant mon Père qui est dans les cieux. »

Dan De Quille a fait oui de la tête puis a pris un livre noir couvert de poussière sur une étagère :

— Jure sur cette bible que tu ne te paies pas notre tête.

J'ai posé la main droite sur la bible.

— Je jure et Dieu m'est Témoin que mes parents ont été tués et scalpés.

Les deux hommes se sont regardés.

Le patron a demandé :

— Donc, ce que tu dis, c'est que les Indiens païutes ont pris les armes ? C'est arrivé quand ?

— Il y a à peu près trois heures, vers 15 h 30. Mais ce n'étaient ni des Païutes ni des vrais Indiens. Par contre, les types qui ont tué mes parents adoptifs voulaient leur faire porter le chapeau. J'ai sur moi quelque chose qu'ils recherchent, c'est pour ça qu'ils me pourchassent et que je me suis déguisé.

J'ai remis mon bonnet.

Sam Clemens s'est penché vers moi, toujours avec l'Expression n° 5 – ses yeux bleu-vert plissés :

— Et les coupables, tu sais qui c'est ?

— Leur chef, on l'appelle Walt-Les-Copeaux. Je ne connais pas les noms de ses deux complices.

— Ha, ha, ha ! s'est esclaffé Sam Clemens. Un desperado qui s'appelle Walt-Les-Copeaux. La bonne blague. Faut que je la note, pour le cas où je voudrais écrire un roman à deux ¢.

Dan De Quille, lui, était blanc comme un linge.

— Qu'est-ce qu'il y a, Dan ? lui a demandé Clemens. Tu te sens mal ?

Sans prononcer un mot, Dan De Quille s'est levé & s'est dirigé vers une liasse de papiers posée sur une table à côté de la Presse Typographique. Il a pris deux feuilles et en a donné une à Clemens & une à moi.

— On a imprimé tout ça hier, a-t-il annoncé, à la demande du Marshal Bailey.

J'avais entre les mains une affiche **WANTED**, avec le portrait d'un homme. Sous le portrait, on lisait : **WALT DARMITAGE – ALIAS « WALT-LES-COPEAUX »**. Une ligne en dessous : **RECHERCHÉ MORT OU VIF**. Et puis : **RÉCOMPENSE 2 000 $**.

J'ai enfin pu voir le visage de l'homme qui cherchait à me tuer.

FEUILLE DE COMPTES 16

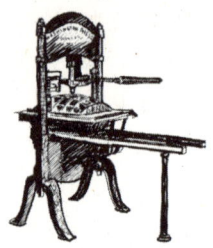

L'affiche **WANTED** montrait un sale type aux yeux pâles, le menton balafré & la moustache tombante.

Rien que de le regarder, ça me glaçait les sangs.

Après, j'ai remarqué des petites lettres écrites sous la récompense.

Ça disait :

Walt-Les-Copeaux se déplace souvent avec Dubois « Extra Dub » Donahue et Boswell « Boz » Burton. Une récompense de 200 $ est offerte pour chacun de ces deux hommes.

— C'est bien lui ? m'a demandé Dan De Quille. C'est l'homme qui a tué et scalpé tes parents ?

— Je ne l'ai vu que de dessus et de loin, mais je crois bien que oui.

— On l'appelle « Les Copeaux » parce qu'il découpe ses victimes avant de les tuer. Et aussi parce qu'il récite « Le Corbeau » d'Edgar Allan Poe quand il les charcute.

— Il récite un poème ?

— Tout à fait. C'est le desperado le plus redouté de tout le Territoire et il voudrait bien prendre le contrôle de notre ville. Ça lui ressemble tout à fait, de se faire passer pour un Païute juste pour semer la pagaille. Les gens sont encore nerveux, après tous les ennuis qu'on a eus avec les Indiens il y a de ça deux ans.

— Purin d'histoire ! s'est exclamé Sam Clemens en reposant son affiche **WANTED** sur la table. Walt-Les-Copeaux et ses acolytes qui s'attaquent à Virginia City. Virginia tout court, je veux dire. Ça c'est un Scoop, Dan. Rappelons les maquettistes, il faut refaire la une.

J'ai dit :

— Ça ne s'est pas passé à Virginia mais à Temperance.

— Temperance ? a fait Clemens en interrogeant De Quille du regard.

— Un petit bled dans la vallée de la rivière Carson, a expliqué le rédacteur en chef, pas loin de Dayton.

Il commençait à reprendre des couleurs, et s'est tourné vers moi :

— Raconte-nous ce qui s'est passé. Sois bref et précis.

Je leur ai tout dit.

Ils ont pris des notes & quand ça a été fini, Dan De Quille m'a demandé :

— Donc tu es l'unique témoin ?

— Oui, monsieur.

J'ai soigneusement plié l'affiche **WANTED** et l'ai rangée dans mon sac-médecine – pour le cas où je me retrouverais face à Walt et où j'aurais besoin de le reconnaître.

Dan De Quille continuait avec ses questions :

— Walt sait que tu l'as vu ?

— Non, monsieur. Il en a après une Lettre que mes parents m'ont léguée.

— Elle est où, cette Lettre ?

— Chez Belle Donne, la Colombe de Suie qui me l'a volée, avec aussi une pièce en or de 20 $ qui appartenait à ma mère.

Le rédacteur en chef a légèrement rougi.

— Je vois de qui tu parles. Elle crèche dans D. Street et, à l'heure qu'il est, on la voit souvent dîner au Colombo Restaurant.

Sam Clemens regardait Dan De Quille par en dessous.

— L'homme est le seul animal qui rougisse, a-t-il dit. Ou qui en éprouve le besoin.

Dan s'est éclairci la voix et a repris :

— Je ferais mieux d'aller raconter au Marshal ce qui s'est passé à Temperance. Si ça peut nous éviter une nouvelle guerre indienne…

Sur ce, il a récupéré son chapeau en tuyau de poêle et a lancé à Sam Clemens, qui était toujours occupé à arranger des petits caractères métalliques sur leur plateau :

— Et ne t'avise pas d'imprimer cette histoire.

— Comment ça ? a fait l'autre. On ne l'imprime pas ?

— Walt-Les-Copeaux est le desperado le plus sadique et le plus craint qu'on ait vu depuis longtemps. Amuse-toi seulement à raconter qu'il a un peu bousculé une vieille dame, et il te tranchera le nez. Tu imagines ce qu'il fera si tu l'accuses de meurtre. Si ça se trouve il nous découpera tous les deux !

— M'enfin, Dan, c'est un Scoop. Un Scoop en or massif, même.

Son patron m'a regardé.

— Comment t'appelles-tu ? m'a-t-il demandé.

— P.K. Mais ma mère adoptive m'appelait Pinky. Pinky pour Pinkerton.

— Tu es bien sûr que Walt ignore que tu as découvert sa supercherie ?

— Sûr & certain. Il me pourchasse pour récupérer la fameuse Lettre ; il doit se dire que je l'ai. Il ne sait pas que j'ai vu ce qu'il a fait, ni à quoi je ressemble. Par contre, il connaît mon surnom et il sait que j'ai 12 ans. D'où mon déguisement.

Dan De Quille s'est adressé à Sam Clemens :

— Si on imprime cet article, Walt saura que P.K. est un témoin. Autant signer tout de suite son arrêt de mort.

FEUILLE DE COMPTES 17

Dan De Quille a mis son chapeau et annoncé :

— Je vais dire au Marshal de se rendre à Temperance et d'expliquer aux gens de là-bas qu'ils ne doivent pas s'en prendre aux Païutes. Sam, tu veux bien rester ici avec P.K. ? Le Marshal voudra peut-être l'interroger avant de partir. Mais surtout, tu n'imprimes rien sans mon accord.

Là-dessus, il est parti en coup de vent.

J'ai regardé Sam Clemens ; il m'a regardé.

Puis il a poussé un profond soupir & s'est assis.

— Voilà-voilà, a-t-il dit. Mes rêves de Scoop viennent de se briser sur les écueils de la Prudence, alors autant essayer de sauver les meubles. Parle-moi de toi. Comment un petit Indien comme toi a-t-il pu se retrouver à vivre chez un pasteur méthodiste et sa femme ?

— Ma vraie mère était une Lakota – il y en a qui les appellent Sioux. Elle s'est fait exclure de sa tribu à 14 ans pour s'être liée à un trappeur. Après, elle a rencontré mon père. Elle aimait sa barbe et les boutons de sa veste. Elle est tombée enceinte de moi et, quand elle a senti que le moment arrivait, elle s'est accroupie derrière un buisson et je suis né. Ça s'est passé en bordure de la ville de Calamity, près des monts Disappointment dans les collines Noires. Et vu que, d'après elle, je me contentais de la regarder comme un asticot, sans sourire ni pleurer, elle m'a appelé Œil du Buisson.

Sam Clemens a pouffé.

— Œil du Buisson ? Pas mal, ça. Et ta mère, elle avait quoi comme nom ? Un truc romantique : Pocahontas ou Petite Biche ?

— Elle s'appelait Accroupie sur une Souche.

Sourire de Clemens.

— Et ton père ?

— Il s'appelait Pinkerton.

— Allan Pinkerton ? a-t-il demandé en retirant sa pipe répugnante de sa bouche. Ce ne serait pas l'homme qui a sauvé la vie du président Lincoln l'an dernier ?

J'ai fait signe que oui, et ajouté :

— Il tient une célèbre Agence de Détectives à Chicago.

— Et c'est ton père ?

J'ai fait non de la tête :

— Mon père, c'était son frère aîné, Robert. Lui aussi était détective.

Je lui ai montré le Bouton de Détective du Chemin de Fer.

Sam Clemens a remis sa pipe entre ses dents, a pris le bouton & l'a étudié.

— « Pinkerton Rail Road Detective », a-t-il lu avant de me le rendre. J'ignorais que Pinkerton avait un grand frère.

— Mon père est resté avec nous quelque temps, ensuite il a disparu. Je ne me rappelle même pas de quoi il a l'air. Après ça, ma mère a dû se débrouiller toute seule. L'été, on prenait des bêtes au piège ; l'hiver, on vivait en ville & elle préparait des remèdes indiens pour les gens qui tombent malades. Et puis un jour, il y a de ça deux ans, elle s'est mis en tête d'aller s'installer chez les Washoe. Je ne sais pas trop ce que c'est.

— C'est le nom d'une tribu d'Indiens qui vivent dans la vallée entre ici et la sierra Nevada. Donc ta mère voulait profiter des mines d'argent ?

— Je n'en suis pas certain. Elle était amie avec un monsieur qui s'appelait Tommy Three. Ma mère a vendu notre tente et nos chevaux, et nous a acheté des places dans un convoi de chariots qui partait pour l'Ouest. On traversait le Territoire de l'Utah quand notre chariot s'est retrouvé isolé des autres. Une bande d'Indiens Shoshone nous a attaqués deux jours plus tard, et a massacré ma mère, Tommy Three et Hang Sung, notre cuisinier.

Sam Clemens a levé les yeux de son carnet.

— Tous les trois ont été massacrés ?

— Oui, monsieur.

— Tu me fais marcher ?

— Non, monsieur.

— Pourquoi les Shoshone ne t'ont-ils pas tué aussi, si je peux me permettre ?

— Je n'en sais rien. Je ne me rappelle même pas ce qui s'est passé. Je me suis retrouvé à côté du chariot qui brûlait. Les Indiens avaient emporté nos provisions et nos chevaux. Par contre, ils m'avaient laissé là, vivant, avec les trois cadavres. Ce jour-là, je portais mes vieux habits en daim. Si ça se trouve, c'est à cause de ça.

— Tu es donc doublement orphelin ?

— Oui, monsieur.

Sam Clemens a retiré sa pipe de sa bouche pour l'examiner.

— Et ensuite ? a-t-il repris. Qu'est-il arrivé après le massacre ?

— Un autre convoi est arrivé deux jours plus tard, pendant que je creusais les tombes.

— C'était quand, déjà ?

— Il y a deux ans. À l'été 1860.

— Première année de la Ruée vers l'Argent... a fait Sam Clemens. Tu avais quel âge, à l'époque ?

— 9 ans. Presque 10.

Il a de nouveau enfourné sa pipe avant de demander :

— Et tu essayais d'enterrer tes morts tout seul ?

— Oui, monsieur. Ç'aurait été mal de laisser ma mère, Tommy Three et Hang Sung se faire dévorer par les coyotes et les vautours. Surtout ma mère.

Sam Clemens s'est mis à cligner des yeux très vite.

— Cochonnerie de poussière d'alcali, a-t-il dit. Ça pique les yeux.

Il a sorti un mouchoir & s'est essuyé la figure. Je ne voyais pas ce que ça pouvait arranger : le mouchoir était aussi poussiéreux que ses habits et son visage. Au bout d'un petit moment, il a recommencé avec ses questions :

— Et cet autre convoi t'a emmené ?

— Oui, monsieur. Le Révérend Emmet Jones et sa femme faisaient route avec les chariots. Ils ont eu pitié de moi et m'ont adopté. Ma Evangeline m'a expliqué que ça faisait plusieurs années qu'elle essayait d'avoir un bébé mais que le Seigneur n'avait jamais voulu lui en accorder un. Pa Emmet a dit que c'était la Volonté du Seigneur qui leur imposait de m'apporter amour et miséricorde. Ils ont été très bons envers moi.

» On s'est installés près de Salt Lake City, et mon père a essayé de devenir le pasteur des Mormons. Ma Evangeline m'a appris à lire et à écrire, Pa Emmet m'a enseigné les Écritures. Il y a de ça six mois, les Mormons ont demandé à mon père de partir. À la même époque ou à peu près, le Seigneur lui a demandé de fonder dans la région de Comstock une ville qui s'appellerait Temperance, et qui serait une Oasis de Sainteté dans un Désert de Péché. On est arrivés dans la région au printemps dernier et, maintenant qu'il est mort, ça m'étonnerait que Temperance survive longtemps sans lui. (J'ai baissé les yeux.) Pa Emmet disait toujours que Virginia City était le Terrain de Jeu du Diable. Et le Diable a fini par le tuer.

Sam Clemens hochait doucement la tête.

— Perdre ses deux parents, c'est une tragédie, a-t-il dit. En perdre quatre, c'est de la négligence.

Je ne savais pas quoi répondre.

Il me regardait en plissant les yeux. Ça faisait la quatrième fois qu'il affichait l'Expression n° 5.

— Tu sais, a-t-il commencé, ça n'est pas banal de voir ce qu'on prend pour une jolie petite fille vous raconter ces choses-là sans manifester la moindre émotion. Je ne suis pas certain de pouvoir te faire confiance.

— C'est mon Épine.

Il a tiré quelques bouffées de sa pipe. Puis il a déclaré :

— Tu es un drôle de petit gars, P.K.

Et là, sans rien ajouter, il s'est levé, a glissé une main dans la poche de son pantalon & en a ressorti un petit revolver.

FEUILLE DE COMPTES 18

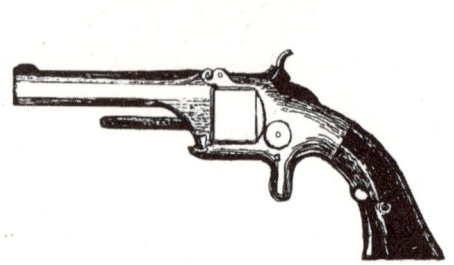

Voyant Sam Clemens brandir une arme, je me suis jeté sous la lourde table en bois aussi vite qu'une couleuvre dans une galerie de taupe.

— Sors donc de là, P.K., a-t-il dit. Je ne te veux aucun mal. Au contraire, j'ai un cadeau à te faire.

J'ai sorti ma tête de sous la table.

— Je ne crois pas à la violence, a-t-il annoncé. La seule fois de ma vie où j'ai tiré sur un homme, c'était au début de cette guerre entre nos propres États qui fait encore rage. J'ignore si c'est la balle que j'ai tirée ou une autre qui l'a tué, mais sa mort m'a gelé jusqu'à la moelle des os. C'est entre autres pour ça que je suis venu dans l'Ouest, pour échapper aux carnages de cette foutue Guerre. Néanmoins, je veux t'offrir ce présent qui pourrait bien te sauver la vie un jour. Tiens. Prends-le.

Et il m'a tendu son arme par la crosse.

Tout penaud, je me suis relevé et ai pris le revolver. C'était un petit modèle – le canon devait mesurer une dizaine de centimètres – mais assez lourd pour sa taille. La crosse était en noyer, je l'avais bien en main.

Sam Clemens a précisé :

— C'est un Smith & Wesson n° 1 à sept coups.

— J'en ai entendu parler. La balle, la charge et la capsule sont dans une seule et même cartouche.

— Exact. Ça s'appelle une cartouche à percussion annulaire. Et le petit bijou que tu as en main, c'est le dernier cri. Tu n'as qu'à armer & tirer.

— La détente, elle est où ?

— Elle se déploie lorsque tu armes.

J'ai rabattu le canon pour dégager le barillet : il contenait sept Cartouches à Percussion Annulaire. Je les ai retirées puis j'ai remis le barillet en place, replié le canon & armé le revolver. Ça a fait sortir la détente. Je l'ai pressée et ai répété l'opération plusieurs fois. Le mécanisme était un peu bizarre, mais ça fonctionnait.

— Bien vu, non ? a fait Sam Clemens.

Il a posé sur la table une poignée de cartouches supplémentaires qu'il avait dans sa poche.

Je savais que mes parents adoptifs n'auraient pas voulu que j'accepte ce cadeau. Mais ma mère indienne, si. Elle m'avait appris à me servir d'un fusil & d'un revolver. Mon père le Détective aussi, je crois que ça lui aurait fait plaisir.

Tout en rechargeant le barillet, j'ai demandé :

— C'est du calibre .22 ?

— Tout à fait. La balle est de la taille d'une granule homéopathique et, pour abattre un adulte, la dose prescrite c'est sept.

J'ignorais ce qu'était une granule homéopathique ; par contre le calibre .22 c'est le plus petit qui existe.

— L'autre souci, poursuivait Sam Clemens, c'est la précision. J'ai un ami qui avait essayé de tirer sur une vache avec un Smith & Wesson n° 1... tant que la vache ne bougeait pas, elle ne risquait rien.

J'ai terminé de charger le barillet, l'ai remis en place & me suis tourné vers le reporter :

— Si j'accepte ce cadeau, vous allez vous retrouver sans défense ?

Sam s'est rassis & a tiré quelques bouffées de sa pipe.

— J'ai un revolver Colt Navy dans ma couchette, à côté. Je crois que je vais le porter sur moi, pour ne pas me faire remarquer à me balader sans. Je te le donnerais bien, mais tu risquerais vraiment de blesser quelqu'un. Le sept-coups, là, ça va, il ne ferait pas de mal à une mouche. C'est juste pour dire que tu as une arme sur toi.

— Alors, si je visais ce tableau, accroché au mur... ?

— Je pense que tu le raterais. Et pour ce qui est des gens, disons que tu leur feras plus de peur que de mal – ça peut être utile.

J'allais pour glisser le revolver dans la poche droite de ma chemise en daim quand je me suis rappelé que je portais une robe. J'ai donc rangé l'arme et les cartouches dans mon sac-médecine. La crosse ressortait un peu. Ça me permettrait de dégainer plus vite. J'ai ensuite passé le tout sous ma robe. On voyait un peu le sac, mais pas tant que ça.

La porte s'est ouverte & un garçon de mon âge est entré, un pichet fumant à la main. Ça sentait le whisky, le lait, le miel & la muscade.

— Votre punch au lait, monsieur, a dit le garçon.

Il avait un épi dans ses cheveux brun clair, et des taches de rousseur sur le nez. Il a déposé son pichet, puis il m'a vu & a ouvert de grands yeux.

— Oh pardon, bonjour, miss, a-t-il fait en ôtant son chapeau et le pressant contre son cœur. On ne se connaît pas, je crois. (Petit sourire.) Vous êtes nouvelle par ici ? Je vous trouve très jolie. J'ai même très envie de vous voler un baiser…

— Tu es l'attrape-science de l'imprimeur, toi, pas vrai ? a demandé Sam Clemens tout en prenant un verre sur l'étagère.

— Oui, m'sieur.

— Et tu t'appelles comment ?

— Horace, m'sieur.

— Eh bien, mon cher Horace, je te suggère de remettre tes envies de bisous à un autre jour. (Là-dessus, il s'est servi une bonne rasade de punch.) Maintenant, file.

— Oui, m'sieur, a bégayé Horace.

Il s'est dirigé vers la porte mais, comme il ne me lâchait pas des yeux, il se l'est prise sur le coin de la figure. Ça l'a fait rougir et il a décampé.

— C'est quoi, un attrape-science ? ai-demandé.

— Une façon de dire « apprenti » chez les imprimeurs.

Clemens a bu une gorgée de punch puis a déclaré :

— Une des plus belles inventions de l'homme, ce punch.

Il a vidé son verre & quand il l'a reposé il avait du lait dans sa moustache poussiéreuse.

Clemens se resservait du punch quand la porte s'est de nouveau ouverte & Dan De Quille nous a rejoints.

— J'ai répété au Marshal ce qui est arrivé à tes parents, P.K., a-t-il annoncé en accrochant son chapeau au portemanteau. Son adjoint et lui sont en route pour Temperance. Je suis passé au Colombo Restaurant, mais Belle n'y était pas.

Il s'est assis sur une chaise & a poursuivi :

— Tu m'as bien dit que Belle t'avait pris ta lettre, celle que recherchent Walt et ses sbires ?

— Oui, m'sieur.

— Et tu te rappelles ce qu'elle disait, cette lettre ?

— Je m'en souviens parfaitement. Moi, quand on me montre un truc, je ne l'oublie jamais.

FEUILLE DE COMPTES 19

L'affiche **WANTED** que Sam Clemens avait reposée sur la table y était toujours. Dan De Quille l'a retournée puis m'a tendu un crayon.

— Marque tout ce dont tu te souviens, m'a-t-il dit. Nous devons déterminer pourquoi Walt veut à ce point mettre la main sur ce document. Sam, sers-moi donc une tasse de ton punch. Ça sera bienvenu.

Pendant que les deux reporters buvaient, j'ai retranscrit la Lettre aussi fidèlement que possible. J'ai même rajouté la signature illisible et celle de mon père. Après, je leur ai montré la feuille.

Dan De Quille et Sam Clemens l'ont lue très attentivement.

Au bout d'un moment, Dan m'a fait :

— Mon cher P.K., je ne peux rien affirmer, mais si ta lettre est authentique et si tu parviens à la récupérer, tu pourrais bien devenir propriétaire d'une partie du mont Davidson. Et donc de la moitié des mines de Virginia. Tu serais millionnaire.

Entendant ça, Sam Clemens a failli s'étouffer & il a recraché du lait par le nez. Son patron lui a tapé dans le dos. Ça a dégagé un nuage de poussière jaune pâle.

— Va donc prendre un bain, lui a-t-il conseillé. Pour aujourd'hui, on se contentera de ton histoire de foin, là.

— Un millionnaire ? répétait Clemens tout en s'épongeant la figure avec son mouchoir crasseux. Ce petit Indien en robe pourrait devenir millionnaire ?

— Les Bains Selfridge & Bach, dans B. Street, a insisté Dan De Quille. L'eau y est chaude, et ils la changent assez souvent. C'est ouvert jusqu'à minuit. Dis à Bach de brûler les habits que tu as sur toi.

Sam Clemens regardait ses manches couvertes de poussière. Puis il s'est gratté les aisselles.

— Tu as sans doute raison. Ça ne sera pas du luxe. Par contre, je n'ai pas d'habits de rechange. (Il s'est tourné vers moi.) À moins que notre petit millionnaire n'accepte de me prêter 1 $ ou 2 ?

Dan De Quille s'est levé en soupirant. Il a glissé une main dans sa poche & a lancé une pièce en or à son reporter :

— Voilà 20 $. Bach te donnera de quoi te vêtir. Tu me rembourseras sur ta première paie.

— Ça me va, a accepté Clemens.

Sur ce, il a remis sa pipe entre ses dents & s'est dirigé à grands pas vers la porte.

Mais au moment de sortir, il s'est retourné & m'a dit :

— J'espère que tout va bien se passer pour toi, P.K. Il n'est pas dans mes habitudes de prier, mais là je crois que je vais faire une exception.

— Merci, m'sieur, lui ai-je répondu. Et merci aussi pour le revolver.

Quand la porte s'est refermée sur lui, Dan De Quille m'a demandé :

— De quel revolver parlais-tu ?

— Du Smith & Wesson n° 1 à sept coups que M. Sam Clemens a eu la gentillesse de m'offrir. C'est le dernier cri, avec la balle, la charge et la capsule intégrées dans une cartouche métallique.

— Et tu sais te servir d'une arme à feu ?

— Oui, m'sieur.

— Sam a bien fait, alors. De toute façon, tout le monde porte une arme dans cette ville…

Disant cela, il tapotait le Colt Navy qu'il avait à sa ceinture. Puis il s'est rassis & a de nouveau étudié ma Lettre.

— As-tu déjà entendu parler d'un dénommé Grosh, P.K. ?

— Non, m'sieur, ai-je répondu.

Et tout à coup, une idée m'est venue :

— Vous croyez que c'est le nom de l'homme qui a signé la lettre ? Celui dont je n'ai pas réussi à déchiffrer la signature ?

— Je le pense, oui. Ce nom de Grosh est légendaire, dans notre bonne ville de Virginia. Hosea Ballou Grosh et son frère Ethan Allen Grosh étaient experts mineurs. Ils avaient fait leurs classes en Californie, du côté de Volcano, & sont venus ici il y a une dizaine d'années pour chercher de l'argent. De l'argent, tu m'entends ? Pas de l'or.

— De l'argent, ai-je répété.

— Voilà. Il se trouve qu'il y avait déjà quelques mineurs dans la région. Des hommes attirés par la Ruée vers l'Or de 1849. Ils exploitaient les rivières et ça leur rapportait peu. Quand ils ont creusé le sous-sol, ils n'ont découvert qu'une boue bleue et lourde qui ne les intéressait pas. Les frères Grosh, eux, ils ont compris que cette boue contenait de l'*argent*. Alors, en 1856, ils ont écrit à leur père, dans l'Est, qu'ils avaient trouvé de riches gisements d'argent dans Gold Canyon & que l'un d'eux était « monstrueux ».

— Et c'est bien, ça, « monstrueux » ?

— C'est même très bien. Les frères Grosh étaient sur le point de faire fortune. Hélas, ils sont morts avant d'avoir pu établir leurs droits.

À cet instant précis, la porte du journal s'est ouverte brusquement. Ça nous a fait bondir de nos chaises, Dan et moi.

Mais bon, ce n'était pas Walt-Les-Copeaux qui nous regardait, sourire aux lèvres, depuis l'embrasure de la porte, mais un Chinois habillé comme Ping.

— Salut, Joe, lui a fait Dan De Quille.

Puis il m'a expliqué :

— Le Vieux Joe est notre cuisinier. La plupart de mes employés mangent à côté, mais Joe vient parfois m'apporter un petit repas spécial.

Je l'ai salué d'un signe de tête. Ça devait être l'oncle de Ping.

— Salut, monsieur Dan, a dit le Vieux Joe. Vous faim ? Vous vouloir repas spécial ?

— Je meurs de faim. Je pourrais manger un bœuf entier – cornes comprises ! Qu'en dis-tu, P.K. ?

— Oui, c'est vrai, monsieur, moi aussi, je meurs de faim.

— Nous pas bœuf ce soir, a fait le Vieux Joe. Garçons mangé bœuf entier – cornes comprises.

Ça a fait sourire Dan.

— Va pour un de tes petits déjeuners du soir, alors. Puis, se tournant vers moi :

— Tu veux boire quoi ? Lait ? Bière ? Whisky ?

— J'ai un faible pour le café noir, ai-je répondu.

Il a acquiescé & a annoncé au Vieux Joe :

— Deux cafés & une assiette de pancakes avec du bacon & un pot de ton sirop d'érable. Et ne confonds pas avec le sirop de sorgho, cette fois, hein ?

Le Vieux Joe a incliné la tête & s'est tourné vers la porte. J'ai vu qu'il avait une natte grise qui lui descendait jusque sous la taille.

— Où en étais-je ? a repris Dan.

— Aux frères Grosh et à leur gisement monstrueux.

— Voilà. Donc, les Frères Grosh ont testé ce filon et l'ont trouvé pur. Par contre, pour en extraire l'argent, ils avaient besoin de fonds.

Il s'est calé contre le dossier de sa chaise avant de poursuivre :

— On a un proverbe dans la région qui dit : « Pour se payer une mine d'argent, il faut posséder une mine d'or. » Conclusion, les Frères Grosh ont décidé de retourner à Volcano, où ils avaient des soutiens financiers. Sauf que, avant le départ, Hosea s'est donné un coup de pioche dans le pied. La blessure s'est infectée, et il est mort au mois de septembre. Fou de douleur, son frère Ethan voulait tout laisser tomber. Puis il s'est remis & a décidé d'exploiter le fameux filon. Mais pas avant d'avoir enterré son frère.

J'ai fait oui de la tête – ça me rappelait mes parents adoptifs. J'espérais que le Marshal prendrait soin de leurs corps.

Le rédacteur en chef du journal continuait :

— Le temps qu'il rembourse les obsèques de son frère, on était déjà mi-novembre. Les montagnes de la sierra Nevada, on ne devrait jamais les franchir après octobre. Ethan Allen Grosh et son compagnon – un jeune Canadien répondant au nom de Bucke – ont quand même pris le risque… (Dan s'est mis à hocher la tête.)… et l'ont payé au prix fort.

Je me suis penché en avant. Je connaissais l'histoire d'une famille, les Donner, qui s'était fait surprendre par une tempête de neige dans ces mêmes montagnes. Il y en a qui étaient morts de faim & les autres avaient dû manger leurs cadavres gelés pour survivre.

— Il a gelé dans une tempête de neige et son compagnon l'a mangé ? ai-je voulu savoir.

— Non, mais il neigeait énormément, et ils ont été forcés de manger leur âne. Ils se sont débarrassés de toutes leurs affaires, y compris leurs cartes, leurs documents officiels et leurs échantillons. Quand enfin ils ont pu rallier le Campement de la Mine de la Dernière Chance, ils avaient les pieds tellement gelés qu'on a dû les leur amputer.

Ça m'a fait frémir. Amputer, je savais que ça voulait dire couper.

J'essayais de m'imaginer la vie sans pieds.

Pas moyen.

— Bucke a survécu, a conclu Dan De Quille, mais ce pauvre Ethan Allen est mort. Une rumeur prétend qu'il aurait rédigé un Contrat concernant le fameux filon monstrueux sur son lit de mort. Quand Bucke a été remis « sur pieds », il a cherché ce document, mais ne l'a jamais retrouvé. D'autres racontent qu'il y avait d'autres hommes au Campement de la Mine de la Dernière Chance. L'un d'eux a pu l'emporter. Par chez nous, le Contrat perdu d'Ethan Allen Grosh est un peu le Saint-Graal. Quiconque le trouvera et le présentera à un juge sera aussi riche que Crésus.

FEUILLE DE COMPTES 20

— C'est quoi, un Saint-Graal ? ai-je demandé. Et c'est qui, ce Crésus ?

— Un Saint-Graal est un Objet de Grand Désir. Quant à Crésus, c'était l'homme le plus riche qui ait jamais existé.

Dan De Quille s'est levé avant de poursuivre :

— Le document qu'on t'a volé fait peut-être de toi le propriétaire des terres situées au nord de la Butte et au sud du Ruisseau sur le pic du Soleil, près de Pleasant Town.

D'un doigt, il me montrait un tableau accroché au mur.

— Cette Vue panoramique de Virginia City a été réalisée il y a tout juste un an. Le pic du Soleil est l'ancien nom du mont Davidson – sur un flanc duquel est installée notre bonne ville.

— Et Pleasant Town ?

— Pleasant Town, c'est Virginia City. On l'a rebaptisée il y a de ça deux ans, en l'honneur d'un mineur ivre, Finney, dit « le père Virginny ». Ce Finney était tombé par terre et avait brisé une bouteille de whisky sur un caillou. Pour ne pas gâcher ce précieux liquide, il avait décidé de baptiser aussitôt l'endroit « Père Virginny ». Ça a bien plu à tout le monde, et le nom de Virginia est resté.

— C'est comme pour Dayton, alors, ai-je dit. Avant, la ville s'appelait Chinatown.

Dan a acquiescé.

— Le fait que ton document parle du « pic du Soleil » et de « Pleasant Town » au lieu de dire « mont Davidson » et « Virginia City » semble indiquer son authenticité.

— Ce serait quoi, sinon ?

— Un faux. Mais de qualité.

À ce moment-là, la porte s'est ouverte dans un grand fracas. Dan et moi, on a sursauté.

C'était le Vieux Joe qui nous apportait un plateau.

— Purin, Joe, a fait Dan, tu pourrais être plus délicat avec cette porte.

— Pardon, monsieur Dan, s'est excusé le Chinois.

Ensuite il a déposé son plateau sur la table & en a retiré 2 assiettes de pancakes, un pot de sirop & 2 tasses de café noir. Il y avait aussi une coupelle de beurre – moulé en forme de dragon – et des couverts.

— Tu me rapporteras de la crème pour mon café, Joe, lui a dit Dan alors que le Chinois s'en allait. Tu l'oublies à chaque fois.

— Vite-vite ! a répondu le Vieux Joe.

Puis Dan m'a fait :

— Régale-toi, P.K. Mais attention au beurre : Joe fait de jolis moulages, mais on trouve parfois des poils de souris, des bestioles ou d'autres cochonneries dedans.

J'avais vraiment faim & les pancakes étaient délicieux. Le beurre, ça allait, il n'était pas trop poilu.

— Ça me rappelle… a poursuivi Dan en versant du sirop d'érable sur ses pancakes. Le père Pancake lui-même s'était lié d'amitié avec les frères Grosh pour découvrir leur secret. D'aucuns racontent qu'ils s'étaient associés.

— C'est qui, votre père Pancake ?

— Henry Comstock. C'est lui qui a donné son nom au filon au-dessus duquel nous nous trouvons. Bon, certaines personnes prétendent qu'il n'y aurait pas qu'un seul filon, la chose reste à prouver. Toujours est-il que le père Pancake est allé trouver deux mineurs qui venaient de découvrir des traces intéressantes. Il avait fière allure dans son costume de confection, alors quand il est allé dire aux mineurs qu'il possédait la terre que ceux-ci exploitaient, ils l'ont cru. Et depuis, on a baptisé ce filon gigantesque de son nom.

— Pourquoi est-ce qu'on l'appelle « le père Pancake » ? ai-je demandé.

Dan a pouffé.

— La légende raconte qu'il était trop paresseux pour se préparer du pain, et qu'il se contentait de pancakes.

— Ou alors il est comme moi, il préfère les pancakes. Les jours de fête, Ma Evangeline prép…

J'ai baissé les yeux par terre sans finir ma phrase.

L'espace d'un instant, j'avais oublié que ma chère mère adoptive était morte. Je ne mangerai jamais plus de ses pancakes.

On a poursuivi le repas quelques minutes en silence, puis Dan a repris l'affiche **WANTED** au dos de laquelle j'avais recopié le texte de la lettre. Il faisait la grimace.

— Tu vois, P.K., il y a un truc qui me chiffonne, là-dedans.

— Qu'est-ce que c'est ?

— Je trouve bizarre qu'Ethan Allen Grosh ait légué toutes ses terres au « Porteur » de la lettre et non à son père dans l'Est, à un de ses partenaires à Volcano, ou même à Bucke, son compagnon.

J'ai répondu :

— Peut-être que mon père était un des hommes présents au Campement, et qu'Ethan Allen Grosh a voulu le remercier. Ou alors, mon père lui aura conseillé d'adresser le document au « Porteur » parce qu'il comptait nous l'envoyer, à ma mère et à moi, pour qu'on ne soit plus pauvres.

— Possible, a marmonné Dan en reposant l'affiche sur la table, côté **WANTED** dessus.

Puis, tout en sauçant son dernier morceau de pancake dans ce qui lui restait de sirop d'érable, il a conclu :

— N'empêche, la première personne qui se présentera au Bureau du Juge avec ce document risque bien de devenir propriétaire de notre montagne et de tout l'argent qu'elle recèle. Pas étonnant que Walt-Les-Copeaux soit prêt à tout pour mettre la main dessus.

— Et si c'est Belle qui apporte ma lettre au Juge ?

Dan a haussé les épaules.

— À elle la fortune.

— Mais cette Lettre m'appartient.

— Alors il vaudrait mieux que tu la récupères avant demain matin…

Pour la troisième fois de la soirée, la porte s'est ouverte dans un bruit de tonnerre.

Exaspéré, Dan De Quille a soupiré avant de dire :

— Joe, je t'ai demandé d'être plus doux avec cette porte.

Là-dessus, comme il regardait par-dessus mon épaule en direction de l'entrée, j'ai vu ses yeux qui s'écarquillaient. Je me suis retourné et mon sang n'a fait qu'un tour.

Cette fois, c'était bel & bien Walt-Les-Copeaux. Avec ses deux acolytes.

FEUILLE DE COMPTES 21

Walt-Les-Copeaux se tenait dans l'embrasure de la porte. J'ai pu voir son visage bien clairement pour la première fois. Il n'avait plus la moustache tombante comme sur l'affiche **WANTED**, mais je l'ai quand même reconnu : il empestait la lotion capillaire Bay Rum. Il avait les yeux bleu métallique, le nez cassé & une balafre au menton. Son cache-poussière couleur biscuit ne cachait pas vraiment son ceinturon à deux étuis : un pour son Revolver Colt Army à crosse en os, l'autre pour son gros Couteau de Chasse. Il me semblait voir deux scalps encore sanguinolents accrochés à sa ceinture.

Walt s'est avancé – ses éperons cliquetaient à chacun de ses pas. Ses sbires le suivaient. L'un était grand & maigre, avec une énorme pomme d'Adam – je n'en avais jamais vu de si grosse. J'ai appris par la suite qu'il s'agissait de Dubois « Extra Dub » Donahue. Le petit, avec un œil de travers & le nez défoncé, c'était Le Peureux : Boswell « Boz » Burton, l'ordure qui nous avait pourchassés, Belle & moi, dans Chinatown.

Allait-il me reconnaître, sous mon déguisement de petite fille modèle ?

J'ai regardé Dan : ses yeux faisaient la navette entre Walt et le portrait de l'affiche **WANTED**.

J'ai posé mon assiette sur cette affiche, de sorte que le desperado ne puisse pas la voir.

Visiblement, mon geste a comme réveillé Dan, car il s'est levé et a demandé :

— Je peux vous aider, les gars ?

Il parlait d'une voix calme, mais de là où j'étais j'entendais qu'il avait la gorge sèche.

— Mouais, a fait Walt, mâchant une chique. On est venus signaler un crime. Des Indiens qui ont tué le pasteur de Temperance. Et puis sa dame, aussi. Les ont même scalpés.

— Pour ça, vous devriez vous adresser au Bureau du Marshal, lui a renvoyé Dan De Quille.

Il s'appuyait du bout des doigts sur la table, & je voyais bien qu'il tremblait.

— Il est pas là, le Marshal, a repris Walt. Son adjoint non plus. Ils ont laissé un mot, comme quoi ils s'absentaient.

Et il a ponctué sa phrase d'un jet de salive et de jus de tabac.

— Essayez donc auprès du Shérif de Gold Hill, a proposé Dan.

— On aurait voulu commencer par faire publier cette tragique nouvelle. Ça vous intéresse pas ? Préférez qu'on aille trouver vos collègues de Carson ?

— Du tout, du tout. Évidemment que nous sommes intéressés. Entrez donc. (Puis, s'adressant à moi :) Maisie, tu devrais rentrer ou bien maman va s'inquiéter.

J'ai fait oui de la tête & me suis levé.

— En échange de c't' info, a repris Walt, on se disait que vous pourriez peut-être nous renseigner.

— Vous renseigner ?

Les mains tremblantes, Dan a posé son assiette sur la mienne & me les a données toutes les deux. Dessous, il tenait l'affiche **WANTED** comme un set de table.

— C'est qu'on cherche le gosse au pasteur, continuait le desperado. Un petit de 12 ans, à moitié indien et qui se fait appeler Pinky. Ça vous dit quelque chose ?

— Non, a réussi à répondre Dan. Un gamin de 12 ans à moitié indien qui s'appelle Pinky, ça ne me dit rien. (Se tournant vers moi :) Tu diras bien à maman que le repas était délicieux. Et maintenant file.

Pour accompagner ses paroles, il m'a donné une petite tape sur le bonnet.

Les assiettes & l'affiche en main, je me suis dirigé calmement vers Walt & ses hommes, mon bonnet bien enfoncé sur mon front.

— Ce gosse, est intervenu Boz, il a les yeux noirs, un regard froid et la peau couleur gadoue. M'a balancé un fer à repasser dans la tronche. En taille, il doit être à peu près comme votre fillette, là.

Je me suis figé.

Dan a dit d'une voix chevrotante :

— Je ne l'ai pas vu.

Je me suis remis à marcher. Les bords de mon bonnet me faisaient comme les œillères des chevaux : ça m'évitait de paniquer en voyant les regards des trois desperados qui me dévisageaient.

Je ne voyais que leurs jambes. Et je priais pour qu'ils déguerpissent vite fait. Sur ce, leurs jambes se sont bel et bien mises à bouger, pour me laisser passer.

Mais à la seconde même où je croyais m'en tirer, une botte s'est mise en travers de mon chemin. Et une voix peureuse a sorti :

— Minute, petite.

La botte, je savais qu'elle appartenait à Boz, celui à qui j'avais cassé le nez. Si par malheur je relevais la tête, il allait reconnaître mes « yeux noirs » et ma « peau couleur gadoue ».

J'ai préféré jeter les assiettes et partir en courant.

Quelqu'un a crié :

— Rattrapez-la, les gars !

Leurs bottes faisaient comme une fusillade sur le trottoir.

Mais là une balle a sifflé à mon oreille & j'ai compris que les bruits de fusillade ne provenaient pas de leurs bottes.

FEUILLE DE COMPTES 22

Même la nuit les rues de Virginia City grouillent de monde.

J'ai traversé Sutton Street sans regarder à droite ni à gauche, du coup j'ai failli me faire renverser par un boghei : les deux chevaux de l'attelage se sont cabrés, leurs sabots ont battu l'air à quelques centimètres de ma tête.

Moi, je ne pensais qu'à une chose : échapper aux balles qui fusaient.

J'ai pris à droite, direction le sud dans B. Street.

Dans le virage, j'ai vu une double porte ouverte et de la lumière qui s'en échappait.

Je me suis précipité à l'intérieur, ai grimpé un escalier tapissé puis me suis engouffré dans un couloir flanqué de portes numérotées.

« Ça doit être un hôtel », je me suis dit.

Dans mon dos, j'entendais des bottes à éperons qui fonçaient dans l'escalier, j'ai donc voulu me cacher dans une des chambres.

J'en ai trouvé une d'ouverte, il faisait noir dedans.

Du coin de l'œil, j'ai repéré une femme en robe bouffante verte et jaune, et un homme en gilet de brocart. Ils faisaient les foufous sur le lit. Ça n'aurait pas plu du tout à Ma Evangeline. Elle me gronde toujours quand je m'amuse à sauter comme un cabri sur mon matelas. Elle dit que ça abîme le sommier.

— Eh là ! a fait l'homme.

Et la femme s'est écriée :

— Oh, une petite fille !

Je les ai ignorés & me suis élancé vers une double porte vitrée. J'étais dans tous mes états mais j'ai quand même réussi à m'arrêter – un peu plus et je passais par-dessus la rambarde du balcon & m'écrasais sur le dos des chevaux attachés devant la porte de l'hôtel. J'ai reculé en titubant et ai regardé autour de moi. Sur ma droite, il y avait un autre balcon qui donnait sur l'immeuble d'à côté, avec un gouffre profond de 6 bons mètres entre les deux. Si je voulais échapper aux desperados, j'allais devoir franchir ce gouffre.

C'est là que j'ai franchement maudit mes bottines et ai regretté mes mocassins. Je suis monté sur la rambarde. Je chancelais un peu. Puis j'ai repris l'équilibre. Et j'ai sauté.

J'ai atterri sur le balcon d'en face comme j'ai pu, en me tordant légèrement la cheville droite.

— Purin ! me suis-je exclamé en boitillant.

Coup de chance, la porte-fenêtre n'était pas fermée à clé. Elle s'est ouverte sur une chambre sombre, à l'autre bout de laquelle passait un filet de lumière : le bas d'une porte. J'entendais les sons étouffés d'un orgue de Barbarie qui jouait « Aura Lee ». J'ai traversé la chambre au pas de course. Au moment où j'ouvrais la porte pour me faufiler dans le couloir, j'ai adressé une prière au Ciel : « Aidez-moi, Seigneur. Aidez-moi à échapper à ces desperados ! »

Je me suis engagé dans le couloir tout simple et en bois ; le son de l'orgue devenait plus fort à mesure de ma progression.

Ça sentait le whisky et la fumée de cigare. D'après ça et la musique guillerette, je devais me trouver dans un saloon.

Je me suis approché de la rambarde qui donnait sur une grande salle pleine de lumière. Des hommes jouaient aux cartes, assis à des tables rondes couvertes de nappes vertes. Le bar en acajou était installé à un bout de la salle, et à l'autre bout il y avait le nègre qui actionnait l'orgue de Barbarie et quelques dames à moitié nues.

Je suis resté là un moment, à chercher par où m'enfuir. Puis j'ai repéré l'escalier sur ma gauche.

J'allais m'y diriger quand j'ai vu Walt qui approchait.

J'ai voulu faire demi-tour mais une porte s'est ouverte & Extra Dub est apparu.

Les deux hommes avaient le sourire aux lèvres, ils prenaient leur temps.

Ils savaient que j'étais fait.

— Bien, bien, bien, disait Walt. Tu dois être Pinky. Je crois que t'as plus trop le choix : file-moi cette Lettre et on te fera pas de mal.

— Je ne l'ai plus, ai-je répondu. Une Colombe de Suie me l'a volée. Elle s'appelle Belle Donne.

Walt s'est penché pour me regarder bien en face.

— Essaie encore de nous embobiner, a-t-il fait, et je te transforme en passoire.

J'ai regardé par-dessus la rambarde, dans la salle en contrebas. Il y avait une table juste en dessous de là où j'étais. Les joueurs qui y étaient assis m'observaient. Il y avait un tas de pièces au milieu de la table, avec aussi des verres et des cartes.

À ma gauche, Walt-Les-Copeaux braquait son revolver sur moi ; à ma droite, Extra Dub me visait lui aussi.

Je n'avais pas franchement le choix.

Je ne voyais même qu'une seule chose à faire.

J'ai sauté par-dessus la rambarde.

Presque aussitôt, deux coups de feu ont retenti.

Je m'attendais à m'écraser sur la table, alors vous imaginez ma surprise quand je me suis retrouvé dans les bras d'un homme. Un des joueurs, qui s'était levé pour me rattraper. Grâce à ses réflexes, j'avais échappé aux balles et à une blessure.

Cet homme et moi, on s'est regardés une seconde. Il avait les yeux très foncés, presque noirs. Il ne montrait pas la moindre émotion.

Le joueur d'orgue de Barbarie ne bougeait plus, l'espace d'un instant il y a eu un grand silence – à part l'écho des coups de feu.

Puis tout à coup la voix de Walt a retenti :

— Dub, espèce de Crétin, t'as failli me buter ! Me vise donc pas ! Vise la gamine !

De nouveaux coups de feu ont éclaté, des femmes se sont mises à crier & je me suis retrouvé sur mes pieds car mon sauveur avait besoin de ses mains pour dégainer. Il a tiré en direction des deux desperados. Dans la seconde, tout le monde tirait dans tous les sens.

C'était la grosse pagaille.

Mais je ne suis pas resté pour voir comment ça tournait.

Plus rapide qu'un télégramme, j'ai filé en direction du bar et me suis faufilé derrière en me penchant. Ça me protégeait des balles.

Une fois à l'extrémité du comptoir, j'ai remis mon bonnet en place, pris une grande inspiration puis ai foncé vers les portes battantes – mes deux bras tendus bien raides devant moi.

Clin d'œil de la Providence, le battant gauche de la porte s'est écrasé contre la poire d'un bonhomme qui arrivait à toute allure. Il en est tombé à la renverse. À la lueur de la torche qui éclairait la façade du saloon, j'ai vu que c'était l'autre sbire de Walt : Boz, le poissard au nez en compote.

Deuxième fois de la journée que je lui cassais la figure.

Plus personne ou presque ne tirait dans le saloon, mais aucun ne s'était lancé à ma poursuite non plus. J'ai baissé la tête & me suis éloigné aussi vite que me le permettait ma cheville endolorie, tout en essayant de ne pas trop me faire remarquer.

Puis j'ai pris le côté ouest de B. Street, où l'ombre était plus profonde, et j'ai pu accélérer. Puis carrément courir. J'ai traversé une rue transversale sans même regarder à droite et à gauche avant.

J'ai eu de la chance de ne pas me faire renverser par une charrette ou un boghei. J'étais tellement troublé que, sans le faire exprès, j'ai marché sur la queue d'un vieux chien marron couché sur le trottoir juste après le Old Corner Saloon. Le chien a jappé un coup, s'est dressé sur ses pattes et s'est mis à aboyer. La pauvre bête était occupée à mâchonner un os devant la Halle aux Viandes.

Ses aboiements m'ont comme réveillé.

J'ai ralenti l'allure mais, au moment où je traversais une nouvelle rue en pente, je me suis dit que si je continuais comme ça je risquais de sortir de la ville. Et de me retrouver à découvert. Je me suis donc adossé à une palissade en bois pour me reposer & reprendre mes esprits. En plus, je tremblotais parce qu'il avait commencé à neiger. Je n'avais ni manteau ni veste sur ma robe fine.

Quelques heures plus tôt, je possédais une Lettre qui aurait pu faire de moi un Millionnaire. Là, je me trouvais au beau milieu d'une ville remplie de pêcheurs, avec trois desperados à mes trousses. Et comme si ça ne suffisait pas, je portais des bottines blanches, un bonnet, une robe rose et une culotte bouffante dessous.

— Pitié, Seigneur, aidez-moi, ai-je prié à haute voix.

Sur ce, j'ai levé les yeux au ciel et aussitôt 2 Solutions se sont présentées à moi.

De l'autre côté de la rue, j'ai en effet repéré une enseigne qui m'a fait l'effet d'une source fraîche en plein désert. Elle disait :

ISAIAH COFFIN – AMBROTYPES & PHOTOGRAPHIES.

J'avais la clé de ce Havre de Sécurité dans mon sac-médecine. J'ai repensé à la peau de bison toute chaude et au canapé moelleux. Je mourais d'envie de m'emmitoufler dans la peau & de me coucher sur le canapé.

Mais deux portes plus loin, il y avait une autre enseigne :

**COLOMBO RESTAURANT
TITUS JEPSON, PROPR.,
SALLE PRIVÉE POUR DAMES & ENFANTS.**

C'était là que Belle Donne prenait parfois ses repas.

J'avais le choix : ou j'utilisais ma clé pour me réfugier dans le studio d'Isaiah Coffin, ou je continuais à rechercher Belle Donne et ma Lettre.

J'ai décidé de me montrer courageux et de poursuivre ma Quête. Première étape : un détour par le studio de Coffin.

Pour retirer ces habits de fille.

FEUILLE DE COMPTES 23

Les lampes à huile posées sur les tables & accrochées aux murs de la salle du Colombo Restaurant faisaient une jolie lumière dorée. Ça sentait le chou, le rôti de porc & la fumée du poêle à bois en fonte qui chauffait dans un coin. Il y avait des tables partout & pas une chaise de libre. La plupart des hommes portaient la barbe. En entrant, le bruit des couverts m'a fait du bien, et puis tout de suite le silence s'est abattu. Les clients s'arrêtaient de manger pour me dévisager.

Il faut dire que je m'étais changé.

Je pensais : « Le Colombo Restaurant ne sert peut-être pas les gens habillés comme moi. »

Mes soupçons se sont confirmés quand un jeune serveur mexicain est venu se planter devant moi, tenant en main des assiettes.

— Fous le camp, m'a-t-il dit. Vite-vite ! T'as pas le droit d'entrer ici !

Et il a fait un signe du menton qui voulait dire « fous le camp ».

Moi je n'ai pas bougé et, d'une voix grave, j'ai demandé :

— Je cherche Belle Donne. J'ai un message important à lui remettre.

Le jeune serveur m'a dévisagé quatre secondes, a jeté un coup d'œil aux clients puis m'a fait comprendre que c'était OK.

— Suis-moi, a-t-il dit, on a une salle pour les femmes et les enfants. (Puis, à voix basse :) Prochaine fois, passe par l'entrée de service.

À l'autre bout de la salle principale, il y avait une porte qui donnait sur une deuxième pièce, plus petite, éclairée & chauffée comme la première. Une famille de six personnes mangeait à une table rectangulaire & une femme seule, habillée en noir, dînait à une petite table ronde.

Sans lâcher ses assiettes, le jeune serveur m'a conduit à une petite table carrée dans un coin, près d'une fenêtre sur le rebord de laquelle on avait installé une fougère. Il faisait bon & j'étais bien content de m'asseoir.

Il m'a dit :

— Attends ici. Je vais chercher le propriétaire, M. Titus Jepson.

Moins d'une minute plus tard, il revenait :

— M. Jepson dit que les amis de Belle sont ses amis. Tu veux manger quoi ?

— Je viens de dîner, ai-je répondu. Par contre, j'ai un faible pour le café noir.

Il a hoché la tête.

— Je t'en apporte un.

Ça m'a laissé le temps d'observer les autres clients. La famille de six, c'étaient tous des blonds et ils se parlaient dans une langue étrangère. À les voir & les écouter, ils me faisaient penser à Olaf, la petite terreur de Temperance. J'en ai conclu qu'ils devaient venir de Suède. Ils avaient tous une bonne carrure & la tête en forme de dé à jouer.

La femme seule me rappelait un peu mon institutrice de Dayton, Miss Marlowe. Sauf que Miss Marlowe, elle est jolie, alors que cette femme pas vraiment. Elle me regardait en retroussant le nez. Expression n° 3 : le Dégoût.

La porte de la cuisine s'est ouverte & un bonhomme roux a passé la tête dans notre salle. Il m'a observé deux, trois secondes. Puis il s'est retiré.

Quelques minutes plus tard, il réapparaissait, une bonne part de gâteau au chocolat dans une main et une grosse tasse de café noir dans l'autre. Il a posé le tout sur la table et s'est assis en face de moi.

— Je suis Titus Jepson, a-t-il annoncé. Le propriétaire de cet établissement.

Il avait le ventre bien rond & portait un tablier blanc tout taché de gras. J'en ai déduit qu'il était aussi le chef des cuisines.

— Gus m'a dit que tu étais américain, continuait-il, malgré les habits que tu portes. Et aussi que tu connaissais Belle.

J'ai fait signe que oui, les yeux braqués sur le gâteau au chocolat.

Il avait l'air bon.

Ça m'a rappelé celui que j'avais vu à la maison. Avec glaçage au chocolat et lettres de réglisse. Le gâteau d'anniversaire que Ma Evangeline avait préparé pour moi et que personne ne mangerait jamais. Les quatre dernières heures, j'avais assisté à la mort de mes parents adoptifs, voyagé sur le toit d'une diligence, je m'étais caché sous les jupons d'une Colombe de Suie, m'étais fait dévaliser & tirer dessus.

— Mange, te gêne pas, m'a dit Titus Jepson. C'est la maison qui régale. Comme je disais à Gus, les amis de Belle sont mes amis.

J'ai pris un morceau de gâteau et l'ai porté à ma bouche. Là, j'ai hésité.

Et si ce Titus Jepson était de mèche avec Walt et m'avait reconnu ?

Et si son gâteau était empoisonné ?

N'avais-je donc rien appris durant mes quatre premières heures passées sur le Terrain de Jeu du Diable ?

J'ai reposé ma fourchette.

— T'aimes pas le chocolat ? a fait Titus Jepson.

— Si, j'adore.

— Ben alors pourquoi tu ne manges pas ?

— J'ai peur qu'il soit empoisonné.

Titus Jepson a pouffé.

— Il y a pas de poison dans ce gâteau et je vais te le prouver. (Il s'en est pris une portion et l'a enfournée.) Je l'appelle le Comstock fourré : chocolat et couche de glaçage argenté. (Il a souri – j'ai vu qu'il lui manquait une incisive.) Bon, le glaçage c'est pas vraiment de l'argent, hein ? Juste du sucre glace parfumé à la vanille.

J'en ai pris une bouchée.

Un vrai bonheur.

Peut-être même meilleur que celui de Ma Evangeline.

— Le glaçage est censé représenter le gisement d'argent de notre montagne, m'a ensuite expliqué Jepson. Du coup, tu te doutes que je suis un monofiloniste.

— Un quoi ?

— Un monofiloniste est une personne qui croit en l'existence d'un filon unique.

— J'entends parler de « filon » à tout bout de champ, mais je ne vois pas de quoi il s'agit.

— Un filon, si tu veux, c'est comme une veine, mais plus proche de la nappe. Par chez nous, il y a des gens qui croient à la doctrine des filons multiples – comme un petit tas de pancakes qui se seraient écroulés. Mais la plupart d'entre nous, on pense qu'il n'y a qu'un seul filon sous cette ville – comme le glaçage dans ton gâteau.

Là-dessus, pointant un doigt boudiné vers ma part, il a fait :

— Tu permets ?

Je ne voyais pas trop ce qu'il voulait dire, alors j'ai répondu :

— Oui.

Là, Titus Jepson a serré le poing & aplati ma part de gâteau.

Je regardais le massacre d'un air dépité. Il était vraiment trop bon.

— Vous avez massacré mon gâteau, ai-je dit.

— Imagine que cette part, c'est le mont Davidson.

— Mais il était trop bon.

— T'es gentil. Bon, imagine que la couche vanillée soit un gros dépôt de minerai d'argent. (À l'aide du couteau à beurre, il a raclé le glaçage du dessus et l'a étalé sur le bord de l'assiette.) Je parle pas de ce glaçage-là, mais de celui de dedans. Le glaçage situé *entre* les couches. C'est ça, le filon. La Veine principale.

J'ai fait oui de la tête.

— Alors bien sûr, ce minerai-là est mélangé à du quartz et d'autres cochonneries, il faut le travailler, le traiter & l'amalgamer pour en faire de l'argent, mais bon, il est là.

J'ai regardé le gâteau puis ai de nouveau hoché la tête.

— Tu vois que le glaçage est plus épais à certains endroits qu'à d'autres ? Vu que je l'ai écrasé, hein ?

Oui de la tête.

— Maintenant observe : même écrasé comme il est, il reste toujours d'un seul morceau, malgré les tours, les détours et les retours. (Il m'a tendu l'assiette pour que je voie mieux.) Toujours en un seul morceau, OK ?

Je ne comprenais pas tout ce qu'il disait, mais je voyais bien ce qu'il voulait dire.

— OK.

Titus Jepson a reposé l'assiette & repris le couteau. Avec, il a fait trois petites entailles sur le dessus du gâteau.

— Ça, a-t-il poursuivi, ce sont les ravins du mont Davidson. Celui-ci, c'est le Ravin Ophir. (Et il a versé un peu de café à l'endroit indiqué.) Cet autre, c'est un petit ruisseau qui s'écoule du Ravin Ophir. On l'appelle le « Ruisseau mexicain » en souvenir de deux frères – des Mexicains miséreux – qui vivaient ici à l'époque de la fondation de la ville. Ce ruisseau passait sur leur propriété. Ils avaient échangé leur eau contre une petite partie d'une mine, et avaient baptisé leur filon « la Mine mexicaine ». En fait, c'était la partie la plus épaisse du glaçage. Les deux frères l'ont revendu quelques années après, et maintenant ils vivent dans de belles maisons, tu te doutes.

Titus Jepson a délicatement découpé un tout petit bout de gâteau. Le tenant sur la pointe du couteau, il a ajouté :

— Moi, je possède un mètre de cette Mine mexicaine, et j'en tire un joli petit revenu.

Là-dessus, il a gobé ce minuscule bout et m'a fait :

— Désolé d'avoir massacré ton gâteau. Je t'en rapporte une part ?

— Non, monsieur, ai-je répondu en prenant une bouchée de la Veine principale. Il est tout aussi bon comme ça. En plus, maintenant, je sais ce que c'est qu'un filon.

Titus Jepson me souriait en hochant la tête.

— Je t'ai appris quelque chose, à toi de m'apprendre autre chose. Dans quoi elle s'est encore fourrée, Belle ?

J'aurais dû m'en douter.

En échange du morceau de Comstock fourré — et de la leçon de géologie locale —, le propriétaire du Colombo Restaurant voulait des renseignements sur Belle Donne.

— C'est votre fille ? lui ai-je demandé.

Expression n° 4 : la Surprise.

— Ah ça, j'espère bien que non.

— Votre femme ?

— Ça me plairait. J'ai envie de faire d'elle une honnête femme, et de l'épouser. (Sur ce, il a repéré une croûte sur la table — de l'œuf séché — et il s'est mis à la gratter avec son ongle.) Mais elle a une sale habitude.

— Moi, des fois, je fais craquer mes doigts. Ma Evangeline dit que c'est une sale habitude.

Jepson a fait non de la tête & m'a regardé dans les yeux. Les siens étaient humides.

— Belle, c'est autre chose. J'ai bien peur qu'elle devienne Toxicomane.

— C'est quoi, ça ? ai-je voulu savoir.

— Quelqu'un qui fume de l'opium. Dès qu'elle a 3 $ en poche, elle court les fumer à Chinatown. J'ai essayé de la faire décrocher, mais ça ne sert à rien. M'étonnerait qu'elle change.

J'ai acquiescé. Ma Evangeline disait toujours à Pa Emmet que fumer la pipe était une sale habitude.

À ce moment-là, on a entendu du bruit dans la salle d'à côté.

— Elle est où ? ! a crié quelqu'un. (Sa voix nous parvenait étouffée, à cause de la porte.) 'ttendez que je la chope, je vais la saigner comme une truie.

J'ai failli m'étouffer.

Walt-Les-Copeaux m'avait encore retrouvé.

FEUILLE DE COMPTES 24

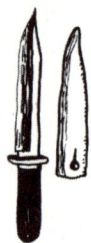

Je n'ai pas eu le temps de filer : la porte de la Salle privée pour Dames & Enfants s'est ouverte sur Walt et ses hommes.

Coup de chance, je m'étais arrêté au studio d'Isaiah Coffin – Ambrotypes & Photographies – avant de venir au restaurant, et j'avais changé de déguisement. Là, j'étais en Chinetoque : pantalon bleu trop grand, chemise à gros boutons et chapeau de paille conique avec une fausse natte accrochée derrière. Je m'étais regardé dans un miroir : ma « peau couleur gadoue » et mes « yeux noirs » bridés correspondaient carrément mieux à ce déguisement.

Walt m'a à peine remarqué. Il cherchait une petite fille en robe rose et bonnet.

Du moins…

— Elle est où ? ! a-t-il encore crié. (Il agitait son Couteau de Chasse – une arme aussi longue que mon avant-bras.) Où est Belle Donne ? On m'a dit que je la trouverais ici !

— Oh ! s'est exclamé Titus Jepson en se levant d'un bond. Holà !

— Viens là, toi ! a fait Walt en attrapant le restaurateur par le tablier. Où est Belle Donne ? On raconte qu'elle mange ici souvent.

— Je l'ignore !

— Tu sais un peu qui je suis ?

— N-n-non.

— Mon nom c'est Walt-Les-Copeaux. Dis-moi où je peux trouver cette femme ou sinon je te coupe les doigts et les orteils un par un.

— Non ! s'est écrié Titus Jepson. Je vous en supplie, pas ça. Je suis très attaché à mes doigts. Je vous jure que j'ignore où Belle se trouve !

Le serveur mexicain observait la scène, un peu à l'écart. Il serrait & desserrait les poings. La famille de blonds et la femme en noir suivaient tout ça d'un air incrédule.

Titus Jepson a hurlé quand le bout de son auriculaire gauche a sauté. Le bout de doigt est retombé dans mon assiette, en plein dans ce qui restait de gâteau.

La femme en noir s'est mise à crier & les enfants blonds à pleurer.

Une mare de sang se répandait sur la table.

— Tu vas parler, maintenant ! disait Walt en brandissant son Couteau ensanglanté. Ou sinon je continue à te découper, et pour finir, je te montrerai que *rien n'est plus beau que la mort*.

Ça l'a fait rigoler comme s'il avait sorti une bonne blague.

— C'est bon ! a hurlé Titus Jepson. Je vais parler !

— Où est Belle ?

— Sûrement dans une Fumerie d'Opium à Chinatown.

— Laquelle ? a demandé Walt en approchant son couteau de l'annulaire gauche de Jepson.

— Celle de Ah Sing ! D'habitude elle va chez Ah Sing.

— Je connais, est intervenu Extra Dub. C'est dans F. Street, un petit trou à coyotes dans la montagne.

Walt a fait signe que ça allait, et a craché du jus de chique par terre.

— Eh ben tu vois, a-t-il conclu, c'était pas si dur...

Puis, après avoir essuyé sa lame à son pantalon :

— Venez, les gars. On va faire un tour à Chinatown.

— Non ! pleurnichait Titus Jepson. Faites pas de mal à Belle. Pitié, faites pas de mal à ma Belle.

Mais les trois hommes quittaient déjà la salle. En partant, Extra Dub a braqué son revolver Colt Navy sur le plafond et tiré un coup. La détonation a fait bourdonner mes oreilles & déclenché une petite pluie de plâtre – en plus de faire crier tout le monde.

Titus Jepson avait du mal à respirer, il pleurait en agitant la tête et en serrant son poignet gauche.

— Oh non... se lamentait-il. Ils vont la découper. Ma pauvre Belle.

Je me suis levé.

Jusqu'ici, Walt et ses sbires avaient eu la main.

Il était grand temps que je fasse autre chose que m'enfuir.

— Vous en faites pas, ai-je rassuré Jepson. Je vais la trouver avant eux, et je la préviendrai.

Il m'a regardé, la figure baignée de larmes.

— Si tu aides Belle à s'en tirer, m'a-t-il dit, tu paieras demi-tarif chez moi jusqu'à la fin des temps.

FEUILLE DE COMPTES 25

Pas besoin d'être un vrai pisteur indien pour suivre Walt et ses sbires. Une fine pellicule de neige me montrait leurs empreintes. Malgré ma cheville endolorie, je les ai rattrapés à l'angle de Taylor et de D. Street. Je ne les perdais pas de vue tout en restant caché dans l'ombre des torches.

Ils avaient récupéré une bouteille de whisky et ils se la passaient les uns aux autres. À un moment, Boz a dérapé – j'ai alors remarqué qu'il avait la main droite bandée. Walt lui a tendu la main comme pour l'aider à se relever, mais il a juste empoigné la bouteille. Extra Dub a aidé Boz à se relever et ils se sont tous marrés.

J'avais intérêt à faire attention. La neige rendait la rue en pente très glissante et je n'étais pas habitué aux sandales à semelles de bois.

Et puis les trois hommes ont pris à gauche, dans F. Street – la même rue que j'avais empruntée quelques heures plus tôt. Chinatown n'avait pas la même allure, de nuit. Les fumées d'encens planaient au-dessus des cabanes, et les lanternes de papier luisaient comme des étoiles. De la main droite, j'ai sorti mon sept-coups de mon sac-médecine. Puis j'ai fourré ma main droite dans ma manche gauche et vice versa – comme j'avais vu faire des Chinetoques. Ça me permettait de cacher mon arme tout en me réchauffant un peu les mains. À un moment donné, Boz s'est retourné, alors j'ai baissé la tête et il n'y a vu que du feu.

Extra Dub semblait connaître le chemin, c'est lui qui menait les deux autres à travers le labyrinthe de cabanes et de tentes. Puis ils sont arrivés devant une petite porte en bois qui donnait directement dans la paroi rocheuse de la montagne, comme si elle ouvrait sur une grotte.

— Dub, tu montes la garde, a fait Walt. Boz et moi on va jeter un œil dedans.

Les deux desperados ont dû baisser la tête pour entrer. Dub a tiré un cigare d'une poche de sa veste & frotté une allumette contre la roche. J'ai profité de ce qu'il se penchait pour allumer son cigare : j'ai renfoncé mon chapeau sur mon front, resserré mes manches & suis passé devant lui.

Il ne m'a même pas remarqué.

La porte en bois s'est ouverte sans bruit, comme si ses charnières baignaient dans l'huile. À l'intérieur, entre l'obscurité et la fumée, je ne voyais que des ronds de lumière jaune, rouge et bleue. Il n'y avait pas un bruit, mis à part le cliquetis des éperons des deux desperados, et un *bloup-bloup-bloup* bizarre. Des gens fumaient, ici et là, et l'odeur aigre-douce rappelait celle des fleurs brûlées et me tournait la tête. J'avais reconnu le parfum de l'Opium, alors je m'efforçais de respirer par la bouche, histoire de ne pas devenir Toxicomane.

Une fois mes yeux habitués, j'ai remarqué contre les parois de la grotte des couchettes étroites, empilées sur quatre rangées. Toutes ou presque étaient occupées par un client qui dormait ou fumait. Les pipes, elles, étaient très longues et sûrement d'origine chinoise. Certaines étaient si longues que des employés, habillés comme moi, étaient chargés de les tenir.

J'ai entendu Walt qui parlait, alors je me suis tourné dans sa direction. Il s'adressait à un vieux Chinois tout petit, assis à une table. Sur cette table : une balance en bronze, des boîtes, des pièces.

Walt lui parlait petit nègre :

— Moi chercher fille blanche bastringue. Toi avoir vu elle ?

Le vieil homme a répondu quelque chose comme « Humpf ! » puis toute une volée de paroles en chinois.

J'inspectais du regard les couchettes des Toxicomanes. Belle était installée dans le coin le plus obscur, sur la couchette du bas. J'ai laissé mes sandales avec les autres, à la porte, & me suis dirigé en silence vers Belle.

Elle avait les yeux mi-clos. Quand j'ai murmuré son prénom à son oreille, elle n'a pas répondu. Elle portait sa robe rouge et rose, mais sans les cerceaux. Elle avait dû les retirer à sa crèche. *Idem* pour son chapeau et son ombrelle. Par contre, elle avait toujours son petit sac avec les perles.

J'entendais le vieux Chinois qui demandait quelque chose à Walt – sans doute de l'argent. Du coup, vu que je leur tournais le dos, j'ai glissé mon sept-coups dans une poche de mon pantalon, puis, me penchant en avant, j'ai ouvert sans faire de bruit le petit sac & passé une main dedans.

Victoire !

Ma Lettre s'y trouvait toujours. Avec en plus quelques billets, au jugé, ainsi que le sachet de poudre et les balles en plomb. Par contre, ma pièce en or avait disparu. Le cœur au galop et la gorge sèche, j'ai glissé la Lettre et deux, trois billets dans ma poche, où se trouvait déjà le Smith & Wesson. J'ai laissé un peu d'argent, le sachet de poudre et les balles, pour ne pas éveiller les soupçons de Belle.

Comme j'allais pour partir, elle a tourné lentement la tête : ses yeux mi-clos avaient du mal à se fixer sur moi. Elle ouvrait la bouche pour parler, mais je lui ai mis un doigt sur les lèvres. Puis je me suis approché de la couchette voisine et j'ai fait semblant de m'occuper des babioles qu'il y avait sur la tablette : une petite lampe à alcool qui produisait une flamme bleue, une boîte remplie d'une espèce de mastic marron & enfin une longue pipe en bambou avec son bol en argile.

J'entendais le *clic-clic-clic* des éperons de Walt & Boz qui se dirigeaient vers la couchette de Belle. Par-dessous le rebord de mon chapeau de paille, j'ai vu Walt qui la fouillait. Elle somnolait tellement qu'elle n'a presque pas protesté.

— Tiens, a fait Walt en tendant le Double Deringer à Boz. Ça te fera un souvenir.

Boz a pris l'arme de la main gauche et l'a glissée dans une poche de sa veste.

Ensuite, Walt s'est redressé et a dit :

— Cette purin de gamine a menti. La Lettre est pas là. On se casse.

— Mais c'est la Salope qui m'a tiré dessus, gémissait Boz. Je veux me venger.

De sa main gauche, il a dégainé son revolver Colt Navy et en a pressé le canon contre le front de Belle.

Elle avait beau m'avoir trahi, ligoté & dévalisé, je n'avais pas envie qu'on la tue pour autant.

J'ai donc armé mon Smith & Wesson. Il n'était peut-être pas précis, mais à moins d'un mètre je ne pouvais pas rater ma cible.

Malgré ce que j'avais promis à ma mère mourante, j'étais prêt à tuer pour sauver Belle.

FEUILLE DE COMPTES 26

Je me suis dit : « Si Boz arme son revolver, je tire. » Par chance, ça n'a pas été nécessaire.

Avant même qu'il ait pu armer, Walt lui touchait le bras en disant :

— Pas maintenant, Boz. Et surtout pas ici. Mais je te promets que tu pourras te venger.

— T'as raison, a fait l'autre. Une balle dans le crâne ça serait trop gentil. Moi, je veux la faire souffrir. C'est bon, on file. On a la gamine à retrouver.

Tandis qu'ils quittaient la Fumerie, j'ai failli m'évanouir de soulagement & aussi à cause de l'odeur de la fumée qui me tournait la tête.

J'ai essayé de réfléchir à ce que je devais faire.

J'avais récupéré ma Lettre et je devais me mettre à l'abri jusqu'au le lendemain matin, moment où je pourrais aller la présenter au Juge.

Je me disais aussi que je devais prévenir Belle, par rapport à Boz. C'est vrai qu'elle m'avait trahi, mais je ne voulais pas la voir souffrir.

Le meilleur endroit où passer la nuit, ça me semblait être justement cette Fumerie. Walt et ses sbires n'allaient pas y revenir de sitôt. Il restait des couchettes de libres en hauteur, je pouvais en prendre une.

Je suis allé voir le vieux Chinois et quand il a vu ma figure il a ouvert les yeux en grand. Expression n° 4 : la Surprise. Avant, il n'avait pas dû remarquer que je n'étais pas un petit Chinois.

J'ai sorti un billet de 1 $ en demandant :

— Combien pour la nuit ?

Plissant les yeux, il a répondu :

— 5 $ pipe et couchette.

— Je ne veux pas de pipe. Juste un endroit où passer la nuit.

— Tu crois dans pension ? Tu paies 5 $. Tu as pipe et couchette pour deux, trois heures. Après tu pars.

— Je vous en prie, l'ai-je supplié en tirant deux autres billets. Je peux vous donner 3 $. Juste la couchette, là-haut. Le temps que la dame du bas s'en aille. Pas de pipe.

Le vieux Chinetoque a fait une grimace.

— S'il vous plaît... C'est tout ce que j'ai. (Là, j'ai eu l'idée d'ajouter :) Je suis un ami de Ping.

— Ping ? a demandé l'autre. Quel Ping ?

— Le neveu de Hong Wo.

Le bonhomme a de nouveau ouvert de grands yeux. Un coup d'œil alentour puis il a grondé :

— Ça va. 1 $ pour la couchette sans pipe. Grimpe là-haut.

— Si je m'endors, vous voudrez bien me réveiller quand la dame s'en ira ?

Il a fait un petit signe de la tête et dit :

— Je réveillerai.

Je lui ai donné son dollar et suis allé m'installer sur la fameuse couchette du haut. J'ai retiré mon chapeau de paille pour m'en servir d'oreiller. En guise de matelas, il y avait une simple natte de jonc graisseuse posée à même le bois, mais j'ai très vite ressenti une bonne chaleur dans mes pieds nus. La sensation s'est répandue dans le reste de mon corps jusqu'à me réchauffer tout entier, comme si j'étais dans une baignoire bouillante. Ma cheville ne me lançait plus et je n'avais plus mal nulle part. Je ne me sentais même plus triste, juste calme. Étrangement calme.

J'ai dû m'endormir, car j'ai fait un très beau rêve. J'ai vu Ma Evangeline et Pa Emmet. Ils marchaient main dans la main, au Ciel. Le Paradis ressemblait à Virginia City mais en tout plat, sans rue en pente, avec des bâtiments en pierres précieuses, pas en bois, et des rues pavées d'or pur. Il y avait des arbres, aussi. Des arbres à lourdes feuilles vertes et aux grosses fleurs qui luisaient de rouge, de jaune et de bleu. Elles diffusaient le parfum le plus doux que j'aie jamais respiré.

Une fois, à Salt Lake City, j'ai vu une montgolfière s'élever dans le ciel. Là, j'avais l'impression que mon cœur était comme ce ballon, que je pouvais flotter en l'air et me laisser porter par la brise.

C'est là qu'on m'a secoué et que j'ai senti qu'on me giflait.

Ouvrant les yeux, j'ai fini par distinguer le visage cireux et tout ridé d'un vieillard.

On aurait dit le plus grand sage de tous les temps, il faisait plaisir à voir.

— Vite-vite ! a-t-il dit d'un air mauvais. Ta dame part, tu pars aussi !

En voulant me rasseoir, je me suis cogné la tête à la voûte rocheuse. Ça m'a rappelé de remettre mon chapeau de paille. Et le sol froid m'a rappelé de ne pas oublier les sandales qui m'attendaient à la porte. Je suis sorti dans la nuit glaciale. Il ne neigeait plus, le ciel était dégagé & on voyait un million d'étoiles qui brillaient.

Ma tête me lançait, je me sentais hébété & groggy. Mais bon, quelques bouffées d'air froid m'ont permis de reprendre mes esprits à temps pour voir Belle disparaître dans une des ruelles sombres de Chinatown. Je me suis élancé après elle. Le temps que je la rattrape, je me sentais un peu plus réveillé, mais j'avais quand même encore mal au crâne.

— Belle, l'ai-je appelée en la tirant par la manche. Belle, attendez !

Elle s'est retournée et m'a regardé, les sourcils froncés. Elle avait les cheveux défaits et des mèches qui lui tombaient sur ses épaules nues. Le brouillard qui nous entourait s'était dissipé et les lueurs des quelques lanternes encore accrochées m'ont permis de voir que sa robe rouge et rose était déchirée au niveau du corsage.

— T'es qui et tu veux quoi ? m'a-t-elle demandé.

— C'est moi, c'est P.K.

Elle me dévisagea.

— P.K. ?

— Je suis déguisé, comme un Détective. Vous ne pouvez pas retourner à votre crèche, Belle. Walt et ses hommes me cherchent et ils risquent d'aller voir là-bas. Ils sont vraiment furieux après vous, ils vous découperont vivante s'ils vous trouvent.

Elle m'a regardé, sa lèvre inférieure s'est mise à trembloter, ses yeux à pleurer.

— Oh, P.K. ! J'ai tellement peur. J'ai rêvé qu'ils étaient passés chez Ah Sing pendant que j'y étais.

— Ils sont venus. Boz a même failli vous brûler la cervelle.

— Ils ont ruiné ma plus belle robe. Ils m'ont pris ce que j'avais. Et tu dis que je ne peux même pas rentrer chez moi ! Qu'est-ce que je vais pouvoir faire ?

— Je connais un endroit sûr, ai-je annoncé. Venez avec moi. Et demain vous quitterez la ville par la première diligence.

— Oui… Oh, P.K., je m'en veux de t'avoir ligoté et dévalisé. C'est juste que j'aime trop fumer la pipe. C'est ma seule joie dans ce trou paumé.

On a pris Taylor Street, guettant Walt et ses hommes derrière les moindres ombres. Ma tête me lançait encore & entre l'air raréfié et la fumée d'opium je n'étais pas loin de me sentir mal. À un moment, j'ai dérapé mais Belle m'a rattrapé. On tremblait de froid tous les deux en arrivant dans B. Street. Il y avait toujours autant de monde et d'activité dans cette rue alors qu'il devait être dans les 2 ou 3 heures du matin. Ça me donnait une impression de sécurité, mais je n'ai vraiment poussé un ouf de soulagement que lorsqu'on s'est retrouvés devant la boutique d'Isaiah Coffin. J'ai alors glissé mes doigts frigorifiés dans mon sac-médecine, en ai ressorti la clé & ai ouvert la porte. La clochette a tinté pour nous accueillir.

Il faisait sombre, mais moins froid que dehors et la lumière des torches de la rue suffisait. J'ai montré à Belle la peau de bison et le canapé dont j'avais tellement rêvé. Elle s'est couchée sur le canapé, s'est enroulée dans la peau de bison & a fermé les yeux.

Moi aussi, j'étais fatigué mais je savais que je devais aller porter ma Lettre au Bureau du Juge à la première heure le lendemain matin. On n'allait sûrement pas me laisser entrer chez le Juge si j'étais habillé en Chinetoque. En plus, si Walt se rappelait avoir vu un jeune Chinois dans le restaurant & à la Fumerie, il risquait de découvrir le pot aux roses. Sans compter que mon pantalon était mouillé & glacé, vu que j'étais tombé dans la neige en venant.

Du coup, j'ai oublié ma fatigue, j'ai allumé une lampe et ai ouvert la penderie pour me trouver d'autres affaires.

Là, j'ai ôté ma tenue de Chinetoque & les sandales en bois, et j'ai enfilé le costume le plus chic qu'il y avait. Pantalon en serge rayé, chemise blanche en lin, gilet en velours rouge & veste bleue à boutons de cuivre. Il m'a fallu retrousser les jambes du pantalon et les manches de la chemise, mais la veste m'allait bien. J'ai déniché un vieux chapeau en tuyau de poêle et de beaux souliers vernis. J'ai bourré le chapeau de papier journal pour l'adapter à ma tête ; quant aux souliers, j'ai enfilé trois paires de chaussettes en laine pour être mieux dedans.

Tout en les laçant, je repensais à mes souliers d'école & ça m'a rappelé mes parents étendus dans une mare de sang sur le plancher de notre petite cabane de Temperance. Ça m'a donné le vertige, j'avais le cœur qui cognait dur, alors je me suis assis pour respirer à fond le temps que ça passe.

Après, je me suis relevé & me suis regardé dans le miroir.

J'essayais de me voir avec les yeux d'un inconnu.

J'avais en face de moi un petit brun aux cheveux courts, la peau couleur gadoue & les yeux noirs légèrement plissés. Mon visage n'exprimait rien. J'ai essayé de sourire mais ça ne donnait rien & ça me faisait bizarre.

J'ai dégoté un peigne, de l'huile pour les cheveux & me suis coiffé en arrière. Je ressemblais à un fils de riche banquier ou courtier. Peut-être espagnol. Ou italien. Voire des Cornouailles. Les mineurs de Dayton qui viennent des Cornouailles ont les cheveux et les yeux très noirs.

J'ai pris mon accent le plus guindé pour prononcer « tout à fait ». Il n'est pas mal, mon accent guindé : ma mère adoptive me l'a fait travailler pendant les deux ans que je l'ai connue pour que je n'aie pas l'air d'un petit sauvage.

J'ai vérifié que la Lettre se trouvait toujours dans mon sac-médecine. J'avais oublié que j'avais encore l'affiche **WANTED** et deux billets de banque. J'ai glissé mon Smith & Wesson à sept coups dans la poche droite de mon pantalon. On aurait dit qu'elle était faite pour. J'avais promis à Ma Evangeline que je ne tuerais jamais personne, mais ça me rassurait quand même de l'avoir sur moi.

Il n'y avait pas de couverture dans la penderie, alors je me suis rabattu sur un lourd pardessus en laine d'un officier nordiste.

J'ai éteint la lampe et suis retourné dans le studio pour m'assurer que Belle n'avait pas filé.

Elle dormait à poings fermés en ronflant un peu. Allongée comme ça, roulée dans la peau de bison, devant le tableau des Grandes Plaines, elle me rappelait un peu ma mère indienne.

Je me suis couché derrière le canapé, sur un tapis, ai sorti mon Smith & Wesson, en ai vérifié le barillet puis l'ai posé par terre près de moi.

Sous le tapis, le sol était dur & froid, et je ne pensais pas arriver à trouver le sommeil, mais sitôt que j'ai eu fermé les yeux, je me suis endormi comme une souche.

FEUILLE DE COMPTES 27

Le lendemain matin, c'est le tintement de la clochette & l'odeur du café frais qui m'ont réveillé.

J'ai ouvert les yeux.

Je me trouvais dans une pièce dont une partie du plafond était en verre et me laissait voir un ciel bleu.

L'espace d'un instant, je ne voyais plus trop où j'étais.

Puis tout m'est revenu d'un coup.

J'avais passé la moitié de la nuit dans une Fumerie d'Opium de Chinatown et à présent je protégeais une Colombe de Suie, Belle, des trois desperados qui voulaient nous torturer et nous tuer.

La porte s'est refermée et, en regardant sous le canapé, j'ai vu une paire de chaussures noires bien cirées et deux bas de pantalon gris.

Puis une voix s'est exclamée :

— Bonté divine ! Mais qui êtes-vous donc ?

— Oh, bonjour, monsieur, a fait Belle d'une voix pas vraiment réveillée. (J'entendais le canapé grincer.) Je m'appelle Belle Donne. Vous êtes ?

— Isaiah Coffin, propriétaire de cet établissement. Et je vous somme de me dire ce que vous faites sur mon canapé.

Il avait un accent guindé, comme Ma Evangeline m'avait appris. J'en ai déduit qu'il avait eu une bonne éducation.

Belle lui a répondu :

— Je me cache ici parce qu'il y a trois desperados qui veulent me tuer. P.K. ? Tu es là ?

— Oui, m'dame, ai-je répondu en me levant.

— Fichtre ! a fait Isaiah Coffin en me voyant apparaître derrière le canapé. Mais que se trame-t-il dans mon studio ?

Le soleil entrait par la fenêtre orientée à l'est et illuminait l'homme qui se tenait devant la porte fermée. Isaiah Coffin portait un chapeau en tuyau de poêle, une redingote bleue & une cravate rouge. Les traits de son visage étaient symétriques. Il avait les cheveux châtain clair, les yeux gris, une moustache & un bouc blonds. Dans une main il tenait une clé, dans l'autre une cafetière. Il avait aussi un journal sous le bras.

— Je suis un ami de Ping, ai-je annoncé. Il m'a donné une clé de votre boutique.

— Ce Ping ! s'est exclamé Isaiah Coffin tout en posant sa cafetière, son journal et en rangeant sa clé dans sa poche. Il ne perd rien pour attendre !

— Oh pardon ! s'est alors écrié Ping qui entrait sur les talons du propriétaire. Je suis désolé ! J'avais dit il ne touche rien.

Il a ouvert de grands yeux en découvrant Belle. Puis il les a plissés, m'a regardé & a marmonné des mots que je n'ai pas compris.

Sans faire attention à Ping, Isaiah Coffin a accroché son chapeau au portemanteau puis, une grimace aux lèvres, m'a demandé :

— Est-ce là un de mes costumes ? (Et à Belle :) Est-ce ma peau de bison ?

— Oui, monsieur, a dit Belle. Toutes mes excuses.

Et elle a légèrement écarté la peau pour montrer sa robe déchirée.

Isaiah Coffin a fait des yeux tout ronds en voyant dans quel état elle était. Ping aussi.

— Bonté divine ! s'est écrié le photographe en se cachant les yeux comme si le soleil l'éblouissait. Un peu de décence, madame, je vous en conjure.

— Mais c'est que je n'ai rien d'autre à me mettre.

Indiquant d'un geste la penderie, Coffin déclara :

— Allez trouver de quoi vous vêtir. Mais laissez-moi votre robe en échange. Quant à toi ! (Il s'adressait à présent à moi.) Tu prétends être un ami de Ping ?

— Pas mon ami, est intervenu le Chinois. Il sera bientôt riche. Il me paiera 500 $ et vous remboursera habits. (Se tournant vers moi :) Pas vrai ?

— Oui, monsieur, ai-je répondu. C'est exact. D'ici environ une heure je serai millionnaire.

— Et tu as dit que tu t'appelais comment ? a repris Isaiah Coffin.

Il avait une façon bien à lui de se tenir, à la fois très droit mais les épaules un peu en arrière.

— P.K. Pinkerton, ai-je dit de ma voix la plus guindée.

— P.K. Pinkerton... Pas banal.

— Isaiah Coffin. Pas banal.

— Touché...

Il avait une lueur étrange dans le regard.
J'ai dit :
— De quoi ?
— *Touché*, a-t-il répété. C'est une façon de dire que tu m'as bien eu.

Sur ce, il a pris une tasse et s'est servi du café noir.
— J'ai un faible pour le café, moi aussi, ai-je annoncé. Noir, sans sucre.
— Tiens donc...

Il a pris une tasse à thé d'un service de décoration & l'a remplie.
— Ping ? a-t-il ensuite appelé. Veux-tu aussi du café ?
— Non, patron. Je préfère le thé.

Il m'en voulait encore.
— Moi, j'aime bien le café, a dit une voix de femme de l'autre côté du paravent. Avec de la crème et trois sucres.
— Ping, a repris le photographe. Va donc chercher de la crème au Colombo Restaurant.

Et il lui a tendu un petit pot décoré de boutons de roses.

Ping m'a lancé un dernier regard assassin en sortant de la boutique.

Je me suis assis sur le canapé. Il restait un peu de la chaleur de Belle. J'ai soufflé sur mon café et en ai bu une gorgée. Je n'ai pas oublié de relever mon petit doigt comme m'avait appris Ma Evangeline. Je commençais à trouver que mes nouveaux habits faisaient de moi un nouveau P.K., plus supérieur, plus sûr de lui.

— Mets-toi à l'aise, m'a dit Isaiah Coffin en relevant un sourcil.
— Merci bien, ai-je répondu.

Il a roulé des yeux et est venu s'asseoir à côté de moi.

— Dis-moi, qui sont les « desperados » qui pourchassent cette jeune femme ?

— En fait, c'est moi qu'ils pourchassent. Walt-Les-Copeaux, Extra Dub et Boz Burton. Ils ont tué mes parents adoptifs à Temperance et les ont scalpés pour faire accuser les Indiens.

Isaiah Coffin ne souriait plus, il était blanc comme un linge.

— Walt-Les-Copeaux ? a-t-il répété.

— Tout à fait. On l'appelle comme ça parce qu'il aime découper ses victimes tout en récitant le poème « Le Corbeau », de Poe.

Là-dessus, j'ai sorti l'affiche **WANTED** de mon sac-médecine & l'ai tendue au photographe.

Il l'a dépliée et a ouvert des yeux tout ronds.

— Eh ben pu-in ! s'est-il exclamé. Excuse mon langage.

Je savais que ce n'était pas son langage qu'il fallait excuser, mais lui-même pour avoir utilisé un mot qui risquait de l'envoyer rôtir en enfer. Je commençais à me dire que les habitants de cette ville juraient tous comme des charretiers.

Je rangeais l'affiche dans mon sac-médecine lorsque la porte s'est ouverte dans un tintement et que Ping a passé sa tête à l'intérieur :

— Colombo Restaurant est fermé.

La voix toujours guindée, j'ai tenté d'expliquer :

— Sans doute est-ce dû au fait que Titus Jepson a perdu un bout de son auriculaire hier soir et qu'il cherche à préserver ses autres doigts.

— Mais pu-in ! a juré Isaiah Coffin. (Cette fois, il a oublié de me demander d'excuser son langage.) Va en chercher ailleurs, de la crème. (Puis, à moi :) Pourquoi te recherche-t-il, ce desperado ?

— J'ai en ma possession un document qu'il veut me prendre. M. Dan De Quille, du *Territorial Enterprise*, affirme que c'est le Saint-Graal de la région de Comstock et que son porteur pourrait bien devenir millionnaire.

Isaiah Coffin a bu une gorgée de café, puis a plongé son regard dans sa tasse.

— P.K., vieux frère, tu ne devrais pas accorder ta confiance au premier venu. Ni raconter à tout le monde que tu possèdes une lettre de grande valeur qui pourrait faire de son porteur un millionnaire.

— C'est un bon conseil, ai-je dit en buvant un peu de café. Je ne sais jamais à qui je peux faire confiance ou pas.

— Si tu me permets un autre conseil, dans cette ville, méfie-toi de tout le monde. La seule raison qui pousse les gens à venir ici, c'est le dieu Argent. Ils n'ont tous en tête que l'or, l'argent ou la fortune en général.

— Vous aussi ?

— Moi aussi. (Là-dessus, il a terminé son café & posé sa tasse par terre.) Si je peux te suggérer un nom, je te recommande de faire confiance à M. S.B. Rooney – notre pasteur. Encore que je ne puisse jurer de rien puisque je n'ai jamais mis les pieds dans son église.

À ce moment-là, je l'ai vu qui ouvrait des yeux tout ronds en regardant par-dessus mon épaule. Expression n° 4 : la Surprise.

Je me suis retourné, Belle nous rejoignait. Elle portait un bonnet blanc et une robe noire boutonnée jusqu'au menton. Elle se réchauffait les mains dans un manchon en fourrure.

Isaiah Coffin s'est levé et a dit :

— Vous voilà métamorphosée, Miss Donne.

— Je sais, a rétorqué Belle. Une horreur, trouvez pas ?

— Du tout. C'est très charmant.

— P.K., m'a-t-elle dit ensuite. J'ai bien entendu, tu as récupéré ta Lettre ?

— Oui. Et je vais de ce pas la porter au Bureau du Juge dans A. Street.

— Je crains que ça ne soit pas possible.

Sur ce, elle a laissé tomber son manchon : elle tenait à la main un revolver Colt Baby Dragoon qu'elle braquait sur nous.

— Les mains en l'air, tous les deux, a-t-elle ordonné. File-moi la Lettre, P.K. Et pas de blague.

Je me suis dit : « Cette Belle… Elle m'a encore eu. »

Et aussi : « Je n'arrive même pas à sentir quand on va me faire un sale coup. »

Et enfin : « Je ne serai jamais un bon Détective. »

FEUILLE DE COMPTES 28

Mon Épine m'avait trahi, mais mon Don – mes excellentes facultés d'observation – pouvait encore me tirer d'affaire.

Belle Donne avait armé son Baby Dragoon et le pointait sur moi. La crosse du revolver était en ivoire. C'était celui de la penderie.

— Donne-moi cette Lettre, a ordonné Belle, et tout ira bien.

— Ça n'est pas juste, ai-je dit. J'ai risqué ma vie pour vous sauver.

— Exact. C'était très gentil de ta part. D'ailleurs je n'ai pas envie de te tirer dessus. Mais si tu ne me laisses pas le choix… Donne-moi cette Lettre.

— Très bien.

Je me suis levé.

— Tu fais quoi, là ? s'est-elle écriée.

J'ai menti :

— La Lettre est dans ma poche.

Je me suis levé pour pouvoir glisser une main dans ma poche et en ai ressorti mon Smith & Wesson.

Aussitôt, Belle m'a visé aux jambes et a pressé la détente. Rien.

— C'est quoi, ce bordel ? a-t-elle fait.

J'ai armé mon sept-coups.

— Votre revolver, c'est celui de la penderie, je l'ai reconnu. Il est déchargé et cassé. Maintenant à vous de lever les mains.

— Tu n'oseras jamais.

Elle affichait l'Expression n° 3 : le Dégoût.

J'ai tiré un coup dans le plafond, à deux petits doigts de la grande lucarne en verre. Ça a fait pleuvoir de la poussière et du plâtre. J'ai réarmé.

Belle a débité un chapelet de jurons que je ne peux pas répéter ici, tout en levant les mains.

Isaiah Coffin pouffait en baissant les siennes.

— Mains en l'air *tous les deux*. (M'adressant à Belle :) Vous, asseyez-vous sur le canapé.

— Pu-in de toi, a-t-elle craché.

Elle a obéi quand même.

— Monsieur Coffin, vous voudrez bien ôter votre cravate et lui lier les mains dans le dos ?

— Il faudrait choisir : ou je garde les bras en l'air, ou je ligote Miss Donne.

— Ligotez-la. Ensuite je vous attache à elle.

Isaiah Coffin a dénoué sa cravate et s'est mis à lier les poignets de Belle.

— Je ne comprends pas pourquoi tu me traites de la sorte, a-t-il fait.

— Vous m'avez recommandé de ne faire confiance à personne. C'est un excellent conseil.

— Touché... a-t-il encore dit. (Puis, ayant terminé de ligoter Belle :) Voilà. Et maintenant ?

— Ôtez vos souliers et retirez les lacets.

Isaiah Coffin s'est accroupi et a obéi.

— Détache-moi, P.K., me disait Belle pendant ce temps. On partagera les gains, fifty-fifty.

— J'ai déjà un associé, lui ai-je rétorqué. Et il ne devrait pas tarder à nous rapporter la crème. Monsieur Coffin, vous voulez bien m'envoyer vos chaussures ? Ensuite vous vous ligoterez les chevilles avec les lacets.

Le photographe a poussé un gros soupir mais s'est exécuté.

La suite était plus risquée. Il me fallait lui attacher les poignets de la main droite tout en braquant mon revolver sur lui de la gauche. Mais ça s'est bien passé. Après, j'ai fait un nœud entre les liens des poignets de Coffin et ceux de Belle.

Ils étaient assis dos à dos sur le bord du canapé, les poignets bien serrés avec tous les nœuds que j'avais pu faire.

— Maintenant vous fermez les yeux, leur ai-je ordonné, et vous comptez jusqu'à cent à voix haute.

Dès qu'ils ont commencé à compter, je suis allé mettre la petite pancarte FERMÉ à la porte. Ensuite je suis sorti et j'ai refermé à clé derrière moi. Avant de partir, j'ai voulu m'assurer que mes deux prisonniers avaient toujours les yeux fermés. J'ai regardé par la fenêtre.

Belle avait ouvert un œil qu'elle a refermé sitôt qu'elle m'a repéré.

J'ai désarmé mon sept-coups & l'ai rangé dans ma poche. Puis j'ai tapoté mon sac-médecine, que je tenais sous ma chemise. J'ai senti la Lettre – ouf.

Comme j'allais pour me diriger vers le Bureau du Juge, j'ai vu Ping qui venait vers moi. Il rapportait le pot rempli de crème et faisait bien attention à ne pas en renverser. Je n'avais pas envie de lui expliquer en détail pourquoi j'avais ligoté son patron, alors, avant qu'il ne m'ait remarqué, je me suis réfugié dans la boutique d'à côté, celle du marchand de tabac.

La boutique était très étroite, on aurait dit un long couloir dont les parois étaient couvertes d'étagères bourrées à craquer de boîtes et de blagues à tabac. Il y avait aussi des pipes & des cigares. Et même une statue d'Indien en bois coloré devant la porte.

À l'intérieur, l'odeur me rappelait Pa Emmet & l'espace d'un instant ma vue s'est brouillée. J'ai cligné des yeux & c'est passé.

— Bonjour, a fait une voix de fille. Je peux t'aider ?

Je me suis retourné, c'était la fille de la veille.

— Je regarde juste, ai-je répondu.

— Tu me rappelles mon cousin Moshe. (Puis, me tendant sa main :) Je m'appelle Becky Bloomfield. Et toi ?

Je lui ai serré la main, qu'elle avait chaude et moite.

— P.K.

Elle avait le teint pâle & les cils les plus longs que j'aie jamais vus. Sans me lâcher la main, elle a continué :

— La boutique appartient à mon père. Son prénom c'est Salomon mais tout le monde l'appelle Smiley. Moi, mes amis m'appellent Bee, parce que dans notre langue ça veut dire « Abeille » et que je suis douce comme du miel. Là, on va bientôt s'installer dans un nouveau local dans C. Street. Le temps qu'on vende ici, mon père me laisse tenir la boutique après l'école et le week-end. Tu vas à l'école, toi ? Moi je suis inscrite à la First Ward School, dans la classe de Miss Feather.

J'ai réussi à récupérer ma main & ai répondu :

— Je vais à l'école à Dayton.

— Tu habites à Dayton ? a-t-elle fait en battant des cils.

Elle se tenait un peu trop près à mon goût, alors j'ai reculé d'un pas.

Elle s'est rapprochée d'un pas.

— Et tu as quel âge ? Moi, j'ai 11 ans mais tout le monde dit que je fais plus.

— 12.

Nouveau pas en arrière. Là, quelque chose me rentrait dans les omoplates & j'ai compris que c'était la statue d'Indien.

Bee Bloomfield s'est rapprochée de moi. Son haleine sentait la pâte dentifrice mentholée Sozodont. La même que Ma Evangeline utilisait les jours de fête pour avoir les dents blanches. Bee m'a demandé :

— Tu voudrais bien m'embrasser, P.K. ?

— De quoi ?

— Adelicia dit qu'elle l'a déjà fait & elle est plus petite que moi. Pareil pour Hannah & Susan. Je suis la seule de ma classe à ne pas encore avoir embrassé un garçon.

Elle avait fermé les yeux & tendait ses lèvres vers moi.

— Je n'aime pas qu'on me touche, lui ai-je dit. Au revoir !

J'ai réussi à m'éclipser juste à temps. À tous les coups elle a dû embrasser la statue en bois.

Je me suis précipité dans la rue, ai renfoncé mon chapeau en tuyau de poêle, traversé Taylor Street & pris la direction du Bureau du Juge.

Je me demandais : « C'est quoi cette ville où ceux qui ne veulent pas vous tuer cherchent à vous embrasser ? »

FEUILLE DE COMPTES 29

Malgré la neige de la nuit dernière, il faisait presque chaud. Le soleil du petit matin peignait la silhouette de la ville en longues ombres bleues sur la pente du mont Davidson. Le temps était vraiment surprenant. Hier il faisait chaud. Dans la nuit il avait neigé. Là, le ciel était bleu & le soleil faisait fondre la neige. Il n'en restait que quelques traînées à l'ombre des bâtiments. Le milieu de la rue était déjà transformé en fleuve de boue par le passage des Bogheis & des Chariots de Quartz.

En tout cas, ce temps radieux me redonnait le moral. D'autant que, pour une fois, je n'avais pas de desperados armés à mes trousses. J'avais récupéré mon précieux Document & d'ici une heure – plaise à Dieu – j'aurais embarqué dans une diligence à destination de Chicago.

J'ai donc traversé la rue boueuse pour passer du côté ouest de B. Street, direction le nord. Mes souliers faisaient un sacré boucan sur le trottoir en bois. En passant devant la Halle aux Viandes Fulton, j'ai fait un grand détour pour éviter le chien marron, puis j'ai traversé Union Street sans encombre. De l'autre côté de B. Street, je voyais l'entrée de service de l'International Hotel, et le mât de 12 mètres de haut qui trônait sur son toit. Arrivé à l'angle de Sutton et B. Street, j'ai pris à gauche dans la rue transversale.

Il n'y avait pas de trottoir & la neige fondue formait un petit torrent. J'avais parcouru à peu près la moitié de la rue quand un cheval venant en sens inverse s'est mis à déraper : il a pris peur, son cavalier a failli le laisser s'emballer & me piétiner.

Je me suis calé contre le mur en brique avant de terminer mon ascension pour me retrouver dans A. Street. J'ai murmuré une petite prière de remerciement tellement j'étais soulagé de retrouver une rue plate. Là-dessus, je me suis posé deux minutes, le temps de reprendre mon souffle, de m'assurer que personne ne me suivait & de me repérer.

De l'autre côté de A. Street, en diagonale, il y avait les locaux du *Territorial Enterprise*. Juste en face : le Bureau du Juge – de là où j'étais, je voyais l'enseigne qui pendait.

J'attendais de pouvoir traverser Sutton Street, lorsque j'ai remarqué un grand bonhomme qui traînait à l'angle opposé. Il portait un chapeau noir mou, un cache-poussière couleur biscuit & avait la plus grosse pomme d'Adam qu'il m'ait été donné de voir. C'était Extra Dub.

Ça m'a glacé sur place & mon cœur s'est emballé.

Au lieu de traverser Sutton, j'ai traversé A. Street, direction le trottoir ouest. De là, j'ai noté la présence d'un autre individu suspect, à une quinzaine de mètres de moi. Il était adossé à un pilier en bois juste en face du Bureau du Juge. Lui aussi portait un chapeau noir et un cache-poussière beige. Quand il s'est tourné vers moi pour cracher par terre, j'ai vu qu'il avait le nez cassé, et deux petits yeux dont l'un louchait légèrement vers l'autre. C'était Boz. J'ai baissé la tête vite fait pour qu'il ne croise pas mon regard.

Sur ce, j'ai pris une grande inspiration et traversé la rue boueuse quand la circulation l'a permis. Je suis allé frapper à la porte du *Territorial Enterprise*, toujours marquée **PONY EXPRESS**. Sans attendre de réponse, j'ai tourné la poignée en priant pour que la porte s'ouvre.

Grâce à Dieu, elle s'est ouverte & j'ai pu me mettre à l'abri.

Première surprise : les locaux étaient vides et la Presse typographique silencieuse.

Je me suis dirigé vers la fenêtre pour regarder dans la rue.

À gauche, je voyais Boz adossé à sa colonne ; à droite, Extra Dub faisant les cent pas. Du coup, je suis allé voir ce qui se passait au niveau du Bureau du Juge. Dans la rue passaient tout un tas de gens & de chariots. Des chevaux étaient attachés à un poteau devant le Bureau du Juge, ça m'empêchait de bien voir. Puis un homme est venu récupérer sa monture, l'a enfourchée puis est parti – c'est là que j'ai repéré Walt. Il était assis sur un banc, juste à droite en sortant de chez le Juge. Les jambes étendues & un chapeau mou enfoncé sur les yeux, il donnait l'impression de dormir. Sauf que moi, sous son chapeau, j'ai remarqué qu'il chiquait.

Il ne dormait donc pas. Il guettait mon arrivée. Et il n'était pas près de bouger.

FEUILLE DE COMPTES 30

Je suis resté un moment à épier les trois desperados depuis la fenêtre du *Territorial Enterprise*. Aucun doute possible : Walt et ses sbires avaient pris leurs marques et m'attendaient.

Je me demandais ce que je pourrais faire.

Ils ne me reconnaîtraient pas forcément dans mes habits de fils de banquier.

Sauf si Walt avait repéré ma manie de me déguiser. Ou s'il avait donné ordre à ses hommes d'arrêter tous les individus mesurant moins d'un mètre cinquante — même avec mes souliers et mon chapeau en tuyau de poêle, je ne dépassais pas le mètre cinquante.

— Je peux vous aider ? a demandé une voix dans mon dos.

Me retournant, j'avais face à moi un homme assez bizarrement vêtu. Comme il se rebraguettait, j'en ai déduit qu'il sortait du petit coin.

Il était rasé de frais, avait les cheveux brun-roux coupés court, des sourcils fournis & des favoris. Son pantalon était trop grand pour lui, sa chemise trop petite. Il sentait le savon & l'amidon.

— Nous sommes fermés aujourd'hui, a-t-il continué.

— Je voudrais voir M. Dan De Quille, ai-je expliqué.

— Il n'est pas là.

Sur ce, il a sorti une pipe & l'a glissée entre ses dents. Elle n'était pas allumée, pourtant elle empestait. J'ai reconnu aussitôt l'odeur : mélange de tabac et d'insecte mort.

— Monsieur Sam Clemens, c'est vous ?

Il s'est approché de moi & m'a regardé bien en face.

— P.K. Pinkerton ? C'est toi ?

J'ai fait oui de la tête.

Il a pouffé.

— Je ne t'avais pas reconnu. Tu t'es encore déguisé ? Pour quoi faire ?

— Walt-Les-Copeaux m'a retrouvé hier et il me prend pour une fillette qui s'habille en rose. Il fallait que je trouve autre chose.

— Quel dommage, tu étais si mignonne... Pour ma part, tu le vois, j'ai fait travailler le barbier et le marchand de savon. Je porte un costume neuf de chez M. Bach – des Bains Selfridge & Bach. Que dis-tu de mes favoris ? a-t-il demandé en me montrant son profil. « Bach trouve qu'ils ressemblent à ceux du général Burnside, d'après lui c'est la Dernière Mode.

— Où est Dan ? Et tous les autres employés ? Vous n'avez pas un journal à faire paraître ?

— L'édition de ce matin est déjà sortie. Et nous ne paraissons pas le dimanche – on fait relâche. Tous nos collaborateurs sont soit chez eux soit encore au

Old Corner Saloon. À propos, tu es une célébrité, maintenant, P.K.

De la tête de sa pipe, il tapotait un journal posé sur la grande table.

Je me suis approché pour voir ce qu'il me montrait : une petite colonne en page 3.

Le titre disait :

DOUBLE MEURTRE TRAGIQUE À TEMPERANCE

Et l'article :

> Nous avons appris hier au soir la nouvelle de la mort du Révérend Emmet Jones et de son épouse Evangeline, à Temperance, près de Como. Certains témoins affirment que le couple a été attaqué par des Indiens Païutes de la région, mais la chose n'a pas encore été confirmée. Tout acte de représailles serait donc malavisé. Ne cédez pas à la panique ! Le fils adoptif du couple, un garçon de 12 ans, a disparu à peu près à l'heure du crime. Il répond au nom de P.K., ou « Pinky », Pinkerton. Les autorités le considèrent comme le suspect numéro 1. On croit savoir qu'il aurait dérobé un document de grande valeur au Révérend et à son épouse qui avaient pourtant eu la bonté de le recueillir et de s'occuper de lui. L'enfant mesure un peu moins de un mètre cinquante, a les cheveux noirs coupés court, les yeux marron foncé et le teint cireux du fait qu'il est à moitié indien. Si vous l'apercevez, vous êtes prié de le conduire au

bureau du Marshal, qui souhaite l'interroger. La prudence est de mise, car l'enfant pourrait être armé et dangereux.

— Qui a écrit ça ? ai-je voulu savoir.
— Dan De Quille.
— Il présente les choses comme si c'est moi qui avais dépouillé et tué mes parents adoptifs. Il ne parle même pas de Walt-Les-Copeaux et de ses gars.
— Cet article est destiné à calmer Walt et ses hommes, et non à les énerver. Dan est passé au saloon hier soir pour nous expliquer ce qui lui était arrivé. (Sam Clemens s'est interrompu, il tentait d'allumer sa pipe répugnante.) Il était dans tous ses états. Il pense que Walt cherche à le découper parce qu'il t'a fait passer pour sa fille. Il prévoyait de filer à Carson City par la première diligence.
— Je suis désolé qu'il ait à fuir à cause de moi, mais ça ne lui donnait pas le droit de raconter des mensonges ni de demander aux gens de me livrer au Marshal.
— Si Dan a écrit cela, c'est uniquement parce qu'il estime que tu seras plus en sécurité en prison. Il a expliqué au Marshal ce qui s'est réellement passé. Ne sois pas trop dur avec lui, P.K.

Quand enfin Sam est parvenu à allumer sa pipe, il a ajouté entre deux bouffées :

— Il m'a aussi demandé de te dire qu'il avait eu tort de te conseiller d'aller faire voir ta Lettre au Juge. D'après lui, tu devrais d'abord la porter au Notaire.
— C'est quoi, ça, un Notaire ?

— Un notaire, m'a alors expliqué Sam Clemens, c'est un homme qui met des timbres sur les documents pour les certifier et les rendre légaux.

Je suis retourné près de la fenêtre, Walt, Dub et Boz n'avaient pas bougé de place. Ils semblaient prêts à passer la journée là.

J'ai dit au reporter :

— Donc je ne suis pas obligé de me rendre au Bureau du Juge, en face ? Je peux faire déclarer ma Lettre chez un Notaire ?

Sam Clemens a haussé les épaules.

— Je n'y comprends pas grand-chose, à ces machins-là. Mais malgré tout, oui : je crois bien que c'est ce que Dan avait en tête.

FEUILLE DE COMPTES 31

Alors même que tout était au plus sombre, une lueur d'espoir s'est allumée dans mon cœur.

Montrant du doigt la porte de derrière, j'ai demandé à Sam Clemens :

— On peut sortir par là, ou est-ce que ça donne juste sur le petit coin ?

— Si ça ne te dérange pas de zigzaguer entre les ordures et les poulets du Vieux Joe, oui, tu peux sortir par là.

— Et vous sauriez où je peux trouver le Notaire ?

— Non, a-t-il répondu en hochant la tête. Par contre, nous avons un *Répertoire d'adresses* de la ville. Ça devrait t'aider.

Le reporter est allé feuilleter un gros livre puis m'a annoncé :

— Voilà : W. Hutchins, Notaire du comté de Storey, Territoire du Nevada, B. Street en face du Virginia City Hotel.

Ensuite il a encore tourné quelques pages & ajouté :

— Quant au Virginia City Hotel, il se situe à l'angle sud-ouest de B. Street et Sutton. Pas très loin de l'International Hotel, on dirait. À deux pas d'ici, quoi. Viens voir par là.

Il me montrait la Vue panoramique de Virginia City accrochée au mur du bureau.

La veille au soir, il faisait trop sombre, cette fois je voyais mieux. Le tableau représentait Virginia City vue du ciel, depuis le sud. Le sommet de la montagne se situait sur la gauche, et la pente descendait vers le coin inférieur droit, avec cinq ou six rues qui faisaient comme des marches d'escalier. Tout autour de cette vue, le peintre avait dessiné une trentaine de bâtiments. On les voyait de face et non du ciel.

— C'est quoi, tous ces immeubles autour du tableau ? ai-je voulu savoir.

— À ce que m'a dit Dan, ce seraient des points de repère. Tiens, regarde ici.

Ça m'a bluffé. L'un des bâtiments était celui dans lequel je me trouvais : le local du *Territorial Enterprise*. On voyait l'enseigne, les deux drapeaux et la porte avec **PONY EXPRESS EXTRA** marqué dessus. À côté, il y avait même un garçon de mon âge qui vendait un journal à un élégant monsieur.

— On voit le chien marron devant la Halle aux Viandes Fulton, ai-je indiqué. Et là une quincaillerie avec un poêle et des cafetières sur le toit.

— Il y a même mon point de repère préféré, a ajouté Sam Clemens. Le Old Corner Saloon de ce cher Piper. Un bien beau tableau, vraiment.

— Mmm, ai-je fait en admirant l'œuvre.

Il y avait une étiquette collée sur le bord inférieur : Virginia City, Territoire du Nevada, 1861. Par Grafton T. Brown.

La ville avait pas mal grandi depuis un an, mais la plupart des bâtiments n'avaient pas changé. J'ai ainsi reconnu la flèche de l'église dans D. Street, les corrals des écuries de louage & les cheminées des bâtiments des mines. On voyait aussi la disposition des rues sur le flanc du mont Davidson. Surtout entre A. Street et D. Street. Avec aussi quelques bâtiments des mines.

— L'Étude de ton Notaire doit se trouver dans ce coin-ci, a dit Clemens en tapotant le verre qui protégeait le tableau, au niveau de B. Street.

— Je peux peut-être y arriver par là ? ai-je fait en indiquant un itinéraire possible.

— Et pourquoi tu ne passerais pas directement par Sutton ?

Je me suis approché de la fenêtre et ai regardé dans la rue.

— Déjà à cause du torrent de boue. Et puis parce que Walt et ses sbires m'attendent de l'autre côté de la rue.

Le reporter est venu regarder par-dessus mon épaule.

— Purin de desperados. C'est donc eux… J'aurais peut-être intérêt à sortir par-derrière, moi aussi. J'avais prévu d'aller m'offrir un joli petit costume dans C. Street. C'est le costume qui fait l'homme, tu sais, P.K. Sans habits, tu n'auras pour ainsi dire jamais la moindre influence dans notre société.

J'ai acquiescé, la tête un peu ailleurs. Je réfléchissais au meilleur itinéraire à suivre.

Sam Clemens s'est dirigé vers le portemanteau. Deux chapeaux mous y étaient accrochés. Un instant, il a hésité à prendre le plus vieux des deux, tout couvert de poussière jaune pâle. Puis il a choisi l'autre : l'air plus neuf et couleur café. Il s'en est coiffé puis s'est approché de la porte de derrière. Avant de l'ouvrir, il s'est retourné :

— Tu veux que je t'accompagne jusqu'à l'Étude du Notaire ?

J'allais accepter, mais je me suis rappelé la grande leçon de Virginia City : ne faire confiance à personne.

— Non merci, ai-je dit. J'irai tout seul.

— Comme tu préfères. Je te souhaite bonne chance et j'espère que je te reconnaîtrai à notre prochaine rencontre. Si ça n'est pas le cas, ne le prends pas mal, c'est juste que je ne suis pas doué.

— Moi pareil.

Sam m'a souri, a touché le rebord de son chapeau puis est sorti.

J'ai attendu deux minutes avant de m'approcher à mon tour de la porte.

Je l'ai entrouverte pour regarder dehors.

J'ai repéré la remise, le poulailler, le coin où on brûle les ordures & bien sûr la pente de la montagne.

Je suis sorti du local du journal en regardant bien alentour. Personne à part les poulets.

Du côté du mont Davidson, une caille faisait : « Chicago ! Chicago ! »

Je me suis dit : « Le départ est pour bientôt. »

Je montais la pente en me faufilant entre les ordures et les buissons d'armoise.

Je me suis vite retrouvé près de A. Street, dans une ruelle qui n'était qu'un marécage boueux. De là, j'ai repéré un grand bâtiment blanc surmonté d'une grosse cheminée avec une enseigne qui disait **MINE MEXI-CAINE**. De l'autre côté, je dominais la ville : le mieux que j'avais à faire était de continuer vers le nord puis de rejoindre B. Street par Carson Street, et ensuite de faire demi-tour.

J'ai inspiré à fond puis regardé vers l'horizon. Le soleil était chaud, l'air embaumait l'armoise & je sentais les battements dans la montagne, ça me rassurait.

J'ai pensé : « Je suis toujours plus heureux quand je suis tout seul. »

Et tout de suite après : « Est-ce que ça fait de moi un Sans-Cœur ? »

Une dernière bonne bouffée d'air & je me suis dirigé vers Carson Street.

Un bruit sourd m'a fait me retourner.

Un wagonnet venait de déverser son chargement de terre, de roche & autres cochonneries. Dans les boyaux de la montagne, des hommes creusaient comme des fourmis. Le wagonnet avait l'air d'être suspendu en l'air mais, quand la poussière s'est dissipée, j'ai vu qu'il roulait sur des rails soutenus par une structure en treillage – comme une moitié de pont. À présent, un mineur le ramenait dans l'autre sens, vers une ouverture pratiquée dans la paroi rocheuse.

— L'homme défigure la montagne dans sa quête de richesse, a dit une voix derrière moi.

Je me suis retourné, c'était un nègre qui dessinait, assis sur une chaise pliante. Jusque-là je ne l'avais pas remarqué parce qu'il était caché par un gros rocher.

— Des trous, des puits, des gravats, continuait-il. D'aucuns pensent que ça n'est pas grave. Ils disent que la région est déjà moche à la base. (D'un geste, il désignait les environs.) Moi, je lui trouve une beauté singulière, à cette montagne nue.

— J'aime le désert, ai-je dit. Beaucoup.

— Moi aussi.

Je n'avais jamais vu de nègre d'aussi près. Ses joues étaient lisses, il ne devait pas avoir beaucoup plus de 20 ans.

— Vous êtes un esclave en cavale ?

Ça l'a fait rigoler.

— Non, je suis libre. Depuis que je suis né, d'ailleurs – à Philadelphie.

Me rapprochant de lui, j'ai vu ce qu'il dessinait : Virginia City. Son style me rappelait quelque chose. Je me suis tourné vers lui et ai demandé :

— Vous ne seriez pas Grafton T. Brown, par hasard ?

Il a ouvert des yeux tout ronds. Expression n° 4 : la Surprise.

— Euh… mais si. On se connaît ?

— Non, par contre je viens d'admirer votre Vue panoramique de Virginia City dans le bureau du *Territorial Enterprise*. Je crois bien que c'est le plus beau dessin que j'aie vu de ma vie.

Il a découvert deux rangées de dents blanches dans un Vrai Sourire n° 1.

— Et tu t'es rappelé mon nom ?

— Je suis fort pour ça. Pas comme avec les visages.

Il a acquiescé & a posé son crayon.

— Crois-le ou non, j'ai le même problème. Mais j'ai trouvé la parade. Une astuce qui me permet de distinguer les gens.

— Vous ne voudriez pas me l'apprendre, s'il vous plaît ?

— Le truc, c'est les oreilles.

— Les oreilles ?

— Tout à fait. Si deux personnes se ressemblent, et si tu n'arrives pas à les différencier, observe leurs oreilles.

— C'est facile à dire pour vous, vous êtes un artiste.

— Tout le monde peut le faire. Ce n'est qu'une question d'entraînement. Toi, par exemple, tu as de jolies oreilles : avec des lobes plats et un peu carrés & un pavillon qui décrit une boucle douce. Le lobe, c'est la partie que les dames se percent pour y accrocher des pendants. Le pavillon, c'est toute la partie autour du trou de l'oreille. Regarde les miennes, tu remarques quelque chose de spécial ?

J'ai examiné son oreille gauche.

— Vous avez les oreilles rondes et petites par rapport à votre tête. Les lobes aussi sont ronds.

— Bien, a-t-il dit avant de se pincer un lobe entre le pouce et l'index. Et mes lobes, tu les trouves épais, minces ou entre les deux ?

— Gros. Mais bon, je n'aurais aucun mal à vous reconnaître, vous êtes pour ainsi dire le seul nègre que j'aie vu dans cette ville.

— Tu serais surpris de savoir combien nous sommes à Virginia. (Nouveau sourire.) Les Blancs prétendent que nous nous ressemblons tous, mais je peux en dire autant de tous ces mineurs barbus. Et j'ai aussi du mal à distinguer les Chinetoques. Sans parler des Indiens. C'est pour ça que je fais attention aux oreilles des gens, autant qu'à leur visage.

— Vous vivez à Virginia ?

— Non, à San Francisco. Je ne viens ici qu'une ou deux fois l'an pour me changer les idées et modifier mes vues de la ville en fonction des changements. Tu n'imagines pas ce qu'elle a pu se développer en à peine un an.

— Vous êtes déjà allé à Chicago ? lui ai-je demandé.

— Une fois, oui. Il faisait très froid et il y avait un vent de tous les diables. C'est de là que tu viens ?

— Non, mais je compte y aller un jour.

— Tu devrais venir à San Francisco. Ça oui, c'est une jolie ville. Elle ressemble beaucoup à Virginia, d'ailleurs, mais avec l'océan à la place du désert. Et un climat plus doux.

Pendant que nous parlions, le vent s'était levé & il nous envoyait du sable et de la poussière d'armoise dans la figure.

— Et voici le Zéphyr de Washoe, a annoncé Grafton T. Brown. Je peux remballer mes affaires pour aujourd'hui.

Là-dessus, il a rangé ses crayons dans une poche de sa veste & refermé son carnet à dessins.

Le vent gémissait & menaçait d'emporter nos chapeaux.

On s'est mis à descendre la pente de la montagne et j'ai demandé à l'artiste :

— Ce vent est vraiment violent. Comment vous l'avez appelé, là ?

— Les gens d'ici disent que c'est le Zéphyr de Washoe. Il lui est déjà arrivé d'emporter des toitures et même des bâtiments entiers.

— À la maison, notre dictionnaire définit le zéphyr comme « une brise chaude ». Là, on est plus proches de la tempête.

— Humour local, a déclaré Grafton T. Brown avec un sourire, tout en renfonçant sa tête entre ses épaules & en relevant le col de sa veste. Les gens d'ici sont un peu pervers : une mule qui brait à tue-tête, ils l'appellent un Canari de Washoe ; et ce vent, là, un Zéphyr. Les mineurs ne s'arrêtent même pas de travailler le dimanche pour aller à l'église, par contre ils iront tous assister à l'enterrement de cette pauvre Fille qui s'est fait tuer au Bastringue.

— Une Fille au Bastringue ? ai-je demandé.

Disant ça, je m'étais brusquement arrêté de marcher, et Grafton T. Brown aussi.

— C'est ça – une de celles qui habitent dans D. Street. Une Colombe de Suie.

L'espace d'un instant, j'ai eu peur qu'il parle de Belle. Mais je l'avais laissée ligotée à Isaiah Coffin dans le studio de celui-ci moins d'une heure auparavant.

— Elle s'appelait comment, cette Fille de Bastringue ?

— Sally Sampson, dite « Sally la Bêcheuse », ou « la Petite Sally ». Quelqu'un l'a égorgée.

— Qui ça ?

J'avais la bouche sèche.

— Personne ne le sait.

J'étais près de vomir. Et si Walt et ses hommes avaient confondu la Petite Sally et Belle ? Avec des Tueurs impitoyables comme eux, il fallait s'attendre à tout.

Le vent soufflait dans mon dos, comme s'il voulait me pousser vers la ville.

Que faisais-je là à rêvasser sur les pentes du mont Davidson ?

Je devais aller montrer ma Lettre au Notaire, et le plus tôt serait le mieux.

FEUILLE DE COMPTES 32

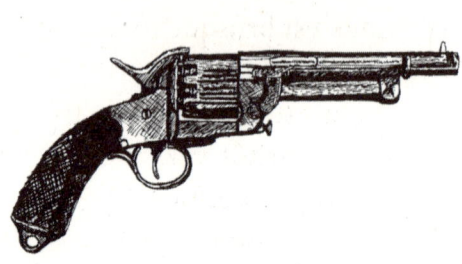

Sans même dire au revoir à l'artiste, je me suis mis à courir.

Je n'ai pas tardé à me retrouver près de l'endroit où ils mettent leurs gravats. Je me suis arrêté net en haut d'une espèce de montagne de déchets. La terre était encore détrempée à cause de la neige fondue, j'ai failli me casser la figure. En contrebas, c'était rempli de terre, de blocs de roche & de bouts de bois pourris. Mais ça ne ressemblait pas aux tas qui se formaient près des mines : ceux-là étaient lisses et pointus, comme des fourmilières, parce qu'ils étaient formés par la poussière fine des Concasseurs de Quartz.

Devant moi, c'était bien une Décharge : l'endroit où le wagonnet de tout à l'heure avait déversé les cochonneries récupérées dans les puits et les tunnels.

J'aurais sûrement dû en faire le tour mais j'avais hâte d'aller trouver le Notaire de B. Street, côté est, derrière l'International Hotel. Les mugissements du vent me poussaient à ne pas perdre une seconde. On aurait dit qu'ils annonçaient un malheur.

Je me suis donc lancé sur les rochers, les bouts de planches et les gravats. Une ou deux fois, j'ai failli tomber quand un caillou a roulé sous mon pied ou qu'une planche a basculé. Mais j'ai pu garder l'équilibre.

Arrivé au pied de cette colline de déchets, un garçon aux yeux pâles s'est brusquement relevé & a voulu m'arrêter. Mais j'arrivais trop vite & du coup on s'est rentrés dedans & on est tombés par terre. Je me suis relevé pour repartir aussitôt vers la ville. Sauf qu'à ce moment-là j'ai repéré deux autres garçons qui s'étaient eux aussi levés pour me barrer la route, avec un quatrième qui s'approchait derrière eux.

Le premier s'était remis debout, il plissait les yeux – Expression n° 5 : le Soupçon.

— Qu'est-ce tu fais sur notre tas ? a-t-il demandé. T'es du Gang des Sauvages ?

— Nan, l'est pas des Sauvages, a fait un rouquin. (Il tenait à la main un bâton aussi gros que mon bras, et le brandissait comme une lance.) Y doit être des chicos. Visez ses habits.

— Laissez-moi passer, leur ai-je dit.

Ils devaient avoir 10 ou 11 ans à peine, mais on aurait dit une bande de fouines acculées par un prédateur. Je me suis rappelé qu'on était samedi, et que donc ils n'avaient pas école.

Ils portaient de vieux pantalons & chemises.

Moi, une chemise blanche, un pantalon en serge, un gilet, une veste & un chapeau en tuyau de poêle. Sans oublier mes gros souliers.

Deux d'entre eux allaient pieds nus.

Un cinquième garçon est arrivé derrière moi & m'a attrapé par le bras, juste au-dessus du coude.

— On peut pas te laisser passer, a annoncé le premier garçon. Nous on est le Gang des Mexicains et toi t'es sur notre Territoire. T'es notre prisonnier.

Voilà que ça recommençait, comme avec Olaf & ses copains.

Sauf que là, je n'avais franchement pas le temps.

J'ai dégagé mon bras & sorti mon sept-coups de ma poche. Aussitôt je l'ai armé & ai tiré en l'air. Dehors, comme ça, la détonation n'a pas fait un gros vacarme, surtout avec le vent qui soufflait. Mais ça a suffi à faire reculer les Mexicains. Une seconde ou deux, ça a senti la poudre, le temps que le vent chasse la fumée. J'ai réarmé mon revolver & l'ai braqué successivement sur les cinq garçons.

— Laissez-moi passer, leur ai-je ensuite ordonné.

Ils m'ont laissé passer.

Quand je les ai eu dépassés, j'ai désarmé mon sept-coups & l'ai rangé dans ma poche puis me suis mis à courir. Je culpabilisais un peu d'avoir tenu en joue des petits de mon âge. Qu'auraient dit Pa Emmet & Ma Evangeline ? En même temps, j'étais en mission. Je devais me rendre chez le Notaire.

Un coup d'œil par-dessus mon épaule. Comme je le craignais, les Mexicains me suivaient. L'un d'eux avait déniché un arc & une flèche. J'ai ressorti mon revolver et ils ont tous bondi pour se cacher derrière une baraque qui servait de cabinets. Alors j'ai de nouveau rangé mon arme & pris mes jambes à mon cou, me faufilant entre les cabanons, les remises et les tas d'ordures jusqu'à A. Street.

Retour au point de départ.

Je ne suis même pas allé voir si Walt et ses hommes m'attendaient toujours devant le Bureau du Juge. J'ai préféré m'engager dans une ruelle entre deux bâtiments. À vue de nez, elle devait déboucher dans B. Street.

À un moment, la ruelle faisait un T, il fallait prendre soit à gauche soit à droite.

J'étais occupé à me demander par où j'avais intérêt à passer quand une flèche est venue se ficher dans la palissade du bâtiment devant moi. Ça m'a décidé d'un coup. Je me suis élancé par la gauche, puis j'ai pris à droite & suis ressorti dans B. Street, près de chez le maréchal-ferrant. De l'autre côté de la rue, il y avait une écurie de louage et à côté le Fashion Saloon. À ma droite, j'ai repéré le drapeau qui flottait sur le toit de l'International Hotel. L'Étude du Notaire se trouvait entre lui & moi. J'y étais presque.

J'ai ressenti une démangeaison familière dans ma nuque. Je me suis retourné : ils étaient là – les derniers membres du Gang des Mexicains qui me suivaient. Il a suffi que je glisse une main dans ma poche pour qu'ils foncent se cacher derrière chez le maréchal-ferrant.

J'avais intérêt à arriver chez le Notaire au plus vite.

Le vent se déchaînait, il faisait claquer les volets.

Comme j'allais pour traverser B. Street, un morceau de toiture en étain a valdingué à côté de moi. Au niveau de mon cou. Un poil plus à droite et je n'avais plus de tête.

À croire que Virginia City elle-même en voulait à ma peau.

Cet objet volant a fait se cabrer un attelage de chevaux, ce qui a interrompu la circulation. J'en ai profité pour traverser la rue. De ce côté-là, il n'y avait pas de trottoir et j'étais obligé de slalomer entre les tas de purin devant l'écurie de louage.

« Plus que quelques mètres, je me disais, et ça ira mieux. »

Ensuite je me suis mis à courir et le vent m'envoyait de la poussière dans les yeux. C'est pour ça que je n'ai pas vu arriver cet homme en noir.

Il sortait du Fashion Saloon & recomptait sa monnaie devant les portes battantes quand je l'ai percuté. Quelques pièces d'or sont tombées dans la gadoue. Le bonhomme a poussé un juron & voulu m'attraper par le col, mais je m'étais déjà relevé et je filais en courant.

Sauf que je n'ai pas couru longtemps. Je me suis heurté à deux jambes de colosse vêtues d'un pantalon gris et jaune à carreaux. Au-dessus, il y avait un torse en chemise noire aussi solide qu'un bloc de quartz. Mais le pire, c'était la figure. L'une des plus moches que j'aie jamais vues. Cet homme portait une grosse moustache noire & avait des yeux qui regardaient dans deux directions différentes.

— Laissez-moi passer, lui ai-je dit.

— Tu ne vas nulle part, gamin, a-t-il répliqué en pointant sur moi un énorme revolver. Tu bouges, t'es mort.

L'arme du grand moche était un de ces gros Le Mat qu'utilisent les officiers sudistes. Moitié revolver, moitié fusil. Le canon du dessus tirait neuf balles de calibre .40 ; celui du bas ne tirait qu'un seul coup, mais ça aurait suffi à m'arracher la tête.

— Tu lui rends, a fait le grand moche.

Je l'entendais à peine, tellement ça soufflait fort.

— Que je lui rende quoi ?

— Les pièces d'or que t'as chourées à Jace.
— Je ne lui ai rien pris.
— Alors pourquoi est-ce que tu cours comme un lapin ?
— Je dois aller chez le Notaire. Son Étude est juste derrière vous, de l'autre côté de la rue. Laissez-moi passer, s'il vous plaît.

L'homme braquait son arme entre mes deux yeux.
— T'es bête ou quoi, gamin ?
— Je suis pas bête. Je suis même intelligent.
— Ben pourquoi t'as pas peur, alors ?
— Mais si, j'ai peur. Et aussi je suis en colère.
— T'en as pas l'air.
— Ça, c'est parce que je suis un Accident de la Nature.

Le bonhomme a ouvert de grands yeux & dit :
— Dis donc, Jace. Viens un peu voir ça. Je crois que ce gosse est encore plus doué que toi pour cacher ses émotions.

L'homme que j'avais bousculé nous a rejoints. Je n'avais pas envie de tourner la tête, et de toute façon je le voyais du coin de l'œil. Il était grand, mince et portait des habits noirs. Il recomptait ses pièces d'or.
— Je te présente Poker Face Jace, a fait le bigleux. Moi, on m'appelle Stonewall. T'as peut-être entendu parler de nous.
— Non, monsieur. Jamais.

J'avais répondu sans bouger d'un poil.

Le bigleux a pressé le canon de son arme sur mon front.
— Jace a qu'un mot à dire et je te fais sauter la cervelle. Tu me crois ?

— Oui, monsieur. Je vous crois.

Poker Face Jace a pris la parole :

— T'es pas mort de trouille ?

Il avait l'accent sudiste.

— Si, monsieur.

— On dirait pas.

Poker Face Jace est venu se mettre face à moi. J'ai pu voir ses yeux : marron foncé, sans expression. J'ai compris que je l'avais déjà vu quelque part. C'est lui le joueur de poker qui m'avait rattrapé dans ses bras quand j'avais sauté du premier étage du saloon. Cette fois-là, je portais une robe rose et un bonnet. Je me demandais combien de temps il allait mettre pour me reconnaître.

— T'as pas l'air bien inquiet, a-t-il jugé.

Jace avait la peau pâle & ses cheveux grisonnaient sur ses oreilles. Ailleurs – mais son chapeau en dissimulait la plus grande partie –, ils étaient noirs. Comme sa moustache, ses sourcils et ses yeux. Ses vêtements aussi étaient noirs – du chapeau jusqu'aux bottes. Le vent fouettait son cache-poussière noir et en a écarté les pans : la crosse en noyer d'un petit pistolet dépassait de la poche droite de son pantalon.

Il a pris un cigare & l'a examiné.

— Pourquoi tu cours comme ça ?

— J'ai le Gang des Mexicains à mes trousses.

Ce n'était pas tout à fait vrai, mais un rapide coup d'œil sur la droite m'a permis de repérer deux garçons mexicains qui m'épiaient de l'autre côté de la rue. L'un était prêt à me décocher une flèche, l'autre tenait un caillou pointu dans chaque main. Quand Jace et Stonewall se sont tournés vers eux, les gamins ont pris la poudre d'escampette.

— Les petits merdeux, a craché Jace. Malgré ça, ta figure ne montrait aucune peur ; ni maintenant alors que t'as un flingue collé à ton front. (Il a frotté une allumette contre le mur & allumé son cigare en protégeant la flamme de sa main.) T'as raison, Stonewall. Il est encore plus fort que moi. Baisse donc ton arme.

Stonewall a désarmé son Le Mat & l'a pointé en l'air.

— Il te manque des pièces, Jace ?

L'autre a tiré quelques bouffées de son cigare avant de répondre :

— Nan. Tout est en ordre.

Stonewall a grogné, puis il a rengainé son revolver – acier bleuté & crosse en noyer.

Des badauds s'étaient arrêtés et nous regardaient, un peu éberlués, alors même que le vent soulevait leurs robes ou leurs manteaux.

Jace a retiré son cigare de sa bouche & en a étudié le bout allumé.

— Maintenant que ces gosses t'ont lâché, tu ne voudrais pas rentrer deux minutes avec moi, qu'on discute ?

J'ai regardé son visage. Impossible d'y lire quoi que ce soit.

— J'ai le choix ? ai-je demandé.

Jace a penché la tête en arrière pour recracher de la fumée. Puis il a dit que non.

— Alors je viens.

FEUILLE DE COMPTES 33

Les portes battantes du Fashion Saloon se composaient de lattes de bois. Jace tenait la droite ouverte, Stonewall la gauche. J'ai inspiré un grand coup & suis entré à l'intérieur. Il faisait sombre, j'ai mis un moment à m'adapter à l'obscurité. Le sol était couvert de sciure que le vent avait repoussée contre le bar, côté droit.

En face du comptoir, il y avait des tables en pin toutes simples. D'autres encore au fond de la salle. Certaines étaient rondes, d'autres carrées. Ça sentait la bière éventée, la fumée de cigare & la sueur. Une grosse dame tenait un orgue de Barbarie sur ses genoux et jouait « Camptown Races ». Trois mineurs dansaient avec des Filles de Bastringue quasi nues.

— Par ici, m'a fait Jace.

Il avait déjà traversé la moitié de la salle. La sciure de bois y était plus épaisse. Elle étouffait le son de mes gros souliers.

Il m'a fait signe de m'installer à une des tables du fond, près d'une fenêtre dont la vue filait jusqu'à l'horizon. Dehors, on voyait la poussière que le vent chassait, & aussi un chapeau qui est passé en volant.

— Purin de Zéphyr, a pesté Jace en suivant le chapeau des yeux.

Il a tiré une chaise pour moi.

J'ai hésité.

Ma mère indienne m'avait appris à toujours m'asseoir dos à un mur, de sorte que personne ne puisse m'attaquer par-derrière. Cette fois, je n'avais pas le choix, j'ai obéi sans rien dire. Jace s'est installé face à moi. Lui, j'ai remarqué qu'il s'était mis dos au mur. Il gardait son chapeau.

Un bruit derrière moi m'a fait me retourner. C'était le patron qui refermait deux grandes portes. Aussitôt, l'atmosphère s'en est trouvée plus silencieuse, plus calme mais aussi plus sombre.

Je me sentais comme pris au piège.

À tous les coups, Poker Face Jace avait lu l'article de Dan De Quille & compris qui j'étais. Et comme tout le monde, il voulait mettre la main sur mon « document de grande valeur ».

— Tu bois quoi ? m'a-t-il demandé.

Il avait retiré son cigare de sa bouche & en faisait tomber la cendre dans le cendrier en cuivre.

— De l'eau.

— À Virginia, personne ne boit l'eau. Elle contient de l'arsenic, de la plombagine et du cuivre. Elle n'est bonne que pour la lessive.

— Du café, alors. Noir.

— Stonewall ? Apporte-nous du café et deux tasses. Puis tu monteras la garde au bar.

— Ça roule, patron.

Jace me regardait, je le regardais. Tous ses traits étaient droits. Son nez, sa bouche. Et même ses sourcils noirs.

Je me demandais bien ce qu'il comptait me faire.

Il a tiré quelques bouffées de son cigare qu'il a projetées vers le plafond.

— Ton visage me dit quelque chose. On se connaît ?

Ne sachant quoi répondre, je n'ai rien répondu.

— Tu es vraiment impénétrable. Je n'arrive pas à dire à quoi tu penses.

— C'est mon Épine.

J'avais les mains froides & maintenant que j'étais assis mes genoux tremblaient.

— Tu dis ?

— Une Épine dans mes côtes : je ne comprends pas ce que les gens ressentent ou se disent.

Jace a fait signe qu'il comprenait.

— Et donc j'imagine que tu as aussi du mal à montrer tes émotions.

— Oui, monsieur. Des fois, même, je ne reconnais pas des gens que j'ai déjà rencontrés. S'ils se sont laissé pousser la barbe ou s'ils ont changé de coiffure, ça me trouble. Un jour, à Dayton, je n'ai pas reconnu ma mère adoptive – elle portait un bonnet neuf. Heureusement, elle a compris la situation et ne m'en a pas trop voulu. Mais c'est une Épine. Une Épine et une Malédiction.

Jace a encore tapoté son cigare au-dessus du cendrier.

— Tu t'appelles comment ?

— P.K. Pinkerton.

Il aurait sûrement fini par l'apprendre, alors…

— T'es parent de Doc Pinkerton ? a-t-il demandé, l'air surpris.

— Non. Je suis de la famille des célèbres Détectives de Chicago. Je suis le neveu d'Allan Pinkerton. Mon père était son frère Robert. Je compte aller travailler pour l'Agence Pinkerton de Chicago.

— Nous ne fermons jamais l'œil, a dit Jace.

— Vous dites ?

— C'est leur devise. Sur leur logo et leurs courriers il y a un œil avec marqué dessous « Nous ne fermons jamais l'œil ».

— Je ne connaissais pas leur devise.

— Merci, Stonewall, a fait Jace quand son compère est venu nous apporter le café & deux tasses.

Stonewall nous a servis puis est retourné se planter au bar.

J'avais toujours les mains froides. J'ai serré la tasse pour me les réchauffer.

Jace a posé son cigare dans le cendrier & bu une gorgée de café.

— P.K., ton Épine & ta Malédiction, pour moi c'est une Aubaine. Et je crois même pouvoir t'aider.

— Comment ça, m'aider ?

Mes mains se réchauffaient un peu mais j'avais toujours la tremblote au niveau des genoux.

Il a repris son cigare & en a aspiré une bouffée.

— As-tu déjà entendu parler du poker ?

— Oui, monsieur. J'y ai même joué dans le convoi qui nous emmenait vers l'Ouest.

Jace recrachait la fumée en acquiesçant.

— Et le pharaon ?

— De nom seulement, pas les règles.

— Pas grave. Si tu comprends le poker, tu sauras jouer à d'autres jeux. L'expression « poker face », ça te dit quelque chose ?

— Oui. C'est quand le visage n'indique pas si on a un bon jeu ou non.

Jace s'est penché en avant pour faire tomber la cendre de son cigare.

— Tout juste, P.K. « Poker face », ça désigne un visage qui n'exprime aucune émotion. Ni le plaisir de tirer une quinte royale. Ni la déception de ne sortir que des petites cartes. Des types avec un visage aussi impénétrable que le tien, je n'en ai croisé qu'un. Un Indien.

— Je suis moitié sioux.

— Je m'en doutais. (Il s'est appuyé contre le dossier de sa chaise.) Tu vois, P.K., il m'a fallu des années pour parvenir à faire ce que tu fais naturellement.

— Sauf que ça ne sert que si on sait lire les expressions des autres joueurs. Moi, par exemple, chaque fois que j'ai joué, j'ai toujours perdu.

— Bien vu ! T'es vraiment un petit futé, toi.

— Oui, monsieur. Je suis futé. Vous me montrez un truc, je ne l'oublie jamais. Et aussi je suis fortiche pour les gros calculs de tête.

Jace relevait un sourcil.

— 9 fois 9 ? m'a-t-il demandé.

— 81.

— 30 fois 22, moins 10, divisé par 5 ?

— 130.

— Et 138 fois 3 567 ?

J'ai réfléchi une minute, visualisant les chiffres dans ma tête. Puis j'ai répondu :

— 492 246.

— Pu-in... a fait Jace.

Il a adressé un regard à Stonewall avant de se mettre à m'étudier. Puis il a glissé une main dans sa poche de poitrine et en a ressorti un jeu de cartes. Il les a mélangées, en a tiré sept & les a disposées en éventail dans sa main droite. Il me les a montrées, le temps de compter jusqu'à trois, puis les a retournées sur la table.

— J'avais quoi ? m'a-t-il demandé.

— Reine de pique, 3 de cœur, 5 de carreau, reine de carreau, valet de trèfle, 10 de pique et as de pique.

Jace retournait les cartes à mesure que je les nommais. J'avais tout juste.

— Pu-in, a-t-il refait. Tu es une vraie mine d'or, P.K. Si j'arrivais à t'apprendre à lire dans les pensées des gens, tu serais le meilleur joueur de poker à l'ouest du Mississippi.

J'ai fait non de la tête.

— J'ai promis à ma mère mourante que je ne tuerais jamais, ni ne boirais, ni ne jouerais aux jeux d'argent.

Jace m'a observé un instant. Je ne déchiffrais pas son expression.

— Et tes promesses, tu les tiens toujours ?

— J'essaie.

Un coup d'œil à Stonewall puis un hochement de tête.

— Un génie honnête, Stonewall. Un mélange bien déprimant.

Stonewall a répondu par un grognement avant d'avaler une gorgée de bière.

Jace a repris son cigare en bouche & plissé les yeux.

— Ton café, tu le bois ou tu comptes le caresser jusqu'à ce soir ?

— Je le préfère froid.

Il a retiré son cigare de sa bouche.

— Dis-moi, P.K., quelle est à ton avis la partie la plus honnête du corps d'un homme ?

— Vous dites ?

— Quand tu cherches à comprendre ce qu'une personne ressent, quelle partie de son corps tu regardes ?

— Sa figure.

— La figure est la partie la plus *malhonnête* du corps. La plus honnête, c'est celle qui est la plus éloignée du visage.

— Les pieds ?

— Les pieds, a-t-il acquiescé.

FEUILLE DE COMPTES 34

Du bout de son cigare, Jace me montrait une table.
— Tu vois ces joueurs de poker ?
J'ai regardé dans la direction qu'il indiquait. Il y avait là quatre hommes élégants – des épiciers ou des employés de banque. L'un d'eux avait la figure grêlée, il distribuait les cartes.
— Observe leurs pieds, a soufflé Jace.
J'ai obéi. Les hommes récupéraient leurs cartes & les examinaient.
— Tu ne remarques rien ?
— Quand ils ont pris leurs cartes, leurs pieds ont un peu bougé. Surtout ceux du chauve avec la grosse moustache. Les siens s'agitent.
Jace faisait oui de la tête.
— Moi, je dirais carrément qu'ils dansent. Ce type croit détenir la main gagnante.
— Et vous voyez ça à ses pieds ?
— Pardi ! Il n'y a que les gens heureux qui dansent.
— Mais pourquoi il fait ça ? Les autres ne vont pas le remarquer ?

— Il n'a même pas conscience de bouger les pieds. Et ses adversaires non plus. Ils se concentrent uniquement sur les parties de leur corps que les autres peuvent voir.

Ça m'a scié. J'avais encore du mal à le croire, mais la théorie de Jace s'est vérifiée quelques minutes plus tard, quand le chauve a raflé la mise. Les autres joueurs n'avaient aucune idée de ce que ses pieds fabriquaient sous la table.

Jace a retiré son cigare de sa bouche, j'ai senti le bout de sa botte me frôler le pied tandis qu'il changeait de position. Puis il a repris son cigare et s'est penché vers moi.

— Les pieds ne mentent pas, P.K. Quand Stonewall t'a fait entrer ici, j'ai lu ta peur non pas sur ta figure mais sur tes pieds. Ils n'étaient pas pointés vers moi. Après, quand tu t'es assis, tu as calé tes chevilles contre les pieds de la chaise & t'es installé sur le bord du siège. Tu te réchauffais les mains contre ta tasse de café. Quand on a peur, on a les mains froides. Par contre, maintenant tes pieds sont pointés vers moi, je me trompe ?

J'ai vérifié. Il avait raison. Comment pouvait-il le savoir ?

— Comment pouvez-vous le savoir ? Vous ne voyez quand même pas à travers le plateau de la table ?

— Il y a trois secondes, je t'ai effleuré les pieds du bout de ma botte. T'as pas senti ?

— Si. Mais j'ai cru que vous changiez juste de position. Et ça veut dire quoi, que mes pieds soient pointés vers vous ?

Léger sourire de Jace.

— Ça prouve que ce que je te raconte t'intéresse.

Nouveau coup d'œil à mes pieds – toujours dans la même position.

Il avait raison. Ce qu'il racontait m'intéressait.

Et même plus que ça encore.

S'il m'aidait à comprendre les gens, j'arriverais peut-être à surmonter mon Épine pour devenir un bon Détective & marcher dans les pas de mon père.

Je regardais Jace dans les yeux.

Tout à coup, il s'est penché vers moi, si près que je sentais le café et la fumée de cigare dans son haleine.

— L'autre signe que tu me donnes, a-t-il dit, c'est que le noir de tes yeux s'est agrandi. (Il s'est calé contre le dossier de sa chaise & me regardait par-dessous son chapeau.) Ça ne se contrôle pas. Quand on est intéressé ou excité, on a les pupilles qui se dilatent légèrement. Et quand on voit une chose qui nous déplaît, elles se rétractent. La plupart des gens ne prêtent pas attention à de si petits détails. Moi, si.

J'ai eu une idée.

— C'est pour ça que vous m'avez fait asseoir en face de la fenêtre ? Pour que mon visage soit bien éclairé ?

— Bravo, P.K. Avec un peu d'entraînement, je pourrai t'apprendre mes petits tours.

— Sauf que j'ai promis à ma mère de ne jamais jouer à des jeux d'argent. C'était son vœu de mourante.

Jace a repris son cigare & en a tiré une bouffée.

— Tu me l'as déjà dit. Et je n'ai rien contre. Comme ça tu ne me feras pas concurrence. (Il recrachait la fumée en l'air.) Mais tu pourrais m'aider… Tu penses que feu ta mère y verrait un inconvénient ?

J'ai réfléchi un instant.

— Non, ai-je fini par dire en me frottant la nuque. Je ne crois pas, non.

Sourire de Jace.

— Quand quelqu'un se frotte la nuque comme tu viens de faire, ça signifie en général qu'il ne dit pas toute la vérité.

Là encore, j'étais scié. Il avait raison. Ma Evangeline aurait sûrement vu un inconvénient à ce que j'aide quelqu'un à jouer pour de l'argent. Je ne me l'étais pas encore avoué, mais Jace, lui, le savait. J'étais admiratif.

— Au poker, a-t-il continué, on peut arriver à mentir avec son visage, mais sûrement pas avec tout son corps. Autre exemple. Tu vois cette dame, là-bas ? Elle dit oui tout en faisant non de la tête. À ton avis, quel message est sincère ?

— Le non ?

— Tout à fait. Elle ment avec sa bouche et dit la vérité avec son corps.

Là-dessus, Jace a mis les pieds sur la table, chevilles croisées, & a basculé sa chaise en arrière. Il avait les épaules contre le mur. Il a mis les mains derrière la tête et ramené les coudes en avant.

— Ceci, m'a-t-il expliqué, est la position d'un patron sûr de lui. Et ça… (Il a baissé son chapeau sur ses yeux.)… c'est la posture d'un homme détendu qui pique un roupillon. Mais en fait j'observe tout.

J'ai fait oui de la tête. Il donnait bien l'impression de dormir, mais en me penchant vers lui j'ai pu voir son regard qui balayait la salle.

— Viens t'asseoir à côté de moi, P.K. Je vais te donner ta première leçon.

Je regardais Poker Face Jace tout en réfléchissant.

Il fallait que je me rende chez le Notaire pour récupérer l'argent de ma Lettre. Mais Jace offrait de m'apprendre à comprendre les gens. Je trouvais ça plus important. J'aurais donné n'importe quoi en échange. Y compris ma Lettre.

FEUILLE DE COMPTES 35

J'ai approché ma chaise de celle de Jace & me suis rassis. Puis je l'ai basculée en arrière & ai posé les pieds sur la table. J'essayais de cacher mon regard comme lui, mais le bord de mon chapeau en tuyau de poêle n'était pas assez large.

— On va commencer par les bases, a annoncé Jace, puis on progressera étape par étape. Je vais t'apprendre quelle est la partie la plus honnête du corps et on finira par celle qui ment le plus. Toi, en échange, tu m'aideras ce soir. Marché conclu ?

Il me tendait la main.

— Marché conclu, ai-je répondu en la lui serrant.

Il avait les doigts frais, fermes & lisses.

— Avant tout, a-t-il repris, je vais te montrer une petite chose toute bête qui va t'ouvrir les yeux pour toujours. Regarde les quatre joueurs de poker. Ils fument tous le cigare. Quand un type crache la fumée en l'air, c'est le signe qu'il est heureux et sûr de lui. S'il la crache vers le bas, ça veut dire quoi d'après toi ?

— Qu'il n'est ni heureux ni sûr de lui ?

— Correct. Autre point, plus le type souffle vite, plus ses sentiments sont forts. S'il souffle sa fumée rapidement et vers le bas, c'est sans doute qu'il est en colère. Et s'il la recrache tout doucement du coin des lèvres, c'est qu'il déprime.

J'ai observé les quatre hommes & constaté aussitôt que Jace disait juste. Je n'en revenais pas, de ne jamais avoir remarqué quelque chose d'aussi simple et d'aussi vrai.

Les quelques heures qui ont suivi, je n'ai plus pensé au meurtre de mes parents adoptifs, ni à la mort de ma mère indienne et de mon père, Robert Pinkerton. Pas plus qu'à Belle Donne, Isaiah Coffin, Dan De Quille ou Titus Jepson. Je ne me suis même pas demandé si Walt & ses sbires m'attendaient toujours devant le Bureau du Juge ou si l'Étude du Notaire était encore ouverte. J'étais trop occupé à observer les gens.

Je regardais les hommes qui jouaient aux cartes & recrachaient leur fumée de cigare tantôt en l'air tantôt en bas.

Je regardais les cochers assoiffés s'installer au bar et commander une bière bien fraîche, les pieds pointés vers le barman.

Je regardais les mineurs épuisés & je devinais qui était ami avec qui.

Je regardais les Filles de Bastringue qui descendaient des chambres pour soulager les mineurs de leur paie le temps d'une ou deux danses. Jace me montrait comment reconnaître lesquelles appréciaient leur partenaire & lesquelles faisaient semblant. Il y en avait qui disaient non avec la tête et oui avec la bouche.

L'après-midi a fait place au soir sans que je m'en aperçoive.

La musique était agréable mais je ne me laissais pas entraîner.

Ce qui me captivait, c'étaient les leçons de Poker Face Jace.

Il ouvrait pour moi les Portes de la Connaissance. Comme si on ôtait un Voile de devant mes yeux. Les signes étaient là depuis le début, sauf que je ne les avais jamais vus. L'astuce, m'expliquait Jace, consistait à regarder non pas les visages, mais les habits, les accessoires, les corps et les façons de se tenir. Cet après-midi, on s'est surtout concentrés sur les pieds.

Jace m'a appris douze choses à retenir. Je ne les ai pas notées sur le moment parce que je retiens tout très facilement, mais je les répète ici, dans l'intérêt de celui qui trouvera mon histoire.

1. Les pieds sont la partie la plus honnête du corps parce qu'on n'a pas toujours conscience de ce qu'ils font.
2. Si une personne les écarte, c'est qu'elle se sent forte & des fois aussi en colère.
3. Si elle bascule un pied sur le talon, les orteils relevés, c'est qu'elle est heureuse.
4. Si les pieds s'agitent ou se mettent à danser, la personne est excitée & heureuse.
5. Si un pied se met à gigoter ou à taper, la personne n'est pas contente.
6. Si un pied bat la mesure alors qu'il n'y a pas de musique, la personne est nerveuse ou a envie de partir.
7. Si la personne se tient face à vous mais que l'un de ses pieds ou les deux ne sont pas dirigés vers vous, c'est qu'elle n'a pas réellement envie d'être avec vous.

8. Souvent, un pied ou les deux pointent dans la direction que la personne veut prendre.

9. Une personne assise les jambes allongées & les chevilles croisées se sent détendue & sûre d'elle.

10. Les chevilles calées contre les pieds d'une chaise indiquent que la personne est nerveuse ou cherche à se contrôler.

11. En général, si les gens croisent les jambes, c'est qu'ils sont en face d'une personne qu'ils apprécient.

12. Le fait de toucher délibérément le pied de quelqu'un sous une table indique presque toujours quelque chose. Entre un homme & une femme, c'est le désir.

Quand Jace a eu terminé sa liste, je lui ai demandé ce qu'il voulait dire par « désir ».

Il a alors demandé à Stonewall de lui servir un whisky et d'en profiter pour s'en offrir un & de nous rapporter aussi du café frais & du gâteau.

Stonewall a donc commandé le café, apporté le whisky & trois verres sur la table puis est retourné au bar chercher le gâteau. Jace a rempli un verre & me l'a tendu. J'ai fait non de la tête, alors il en a bu une gorgée.

— P.K., m'a-t-il ensuite demandé, qu'est-ce que tu sais sur les hommes et les femmes, et ce qu'ils font ensemble ?

— J'ai déjà vu des chevaux s'accoupler, des chiens aussi. Et une fois un homme et une femme derrière la Mercerie de Temperance.

— Bon, eh bien parfois ça ne se limite pas à l'accouplement. Il y a aussi du désir.

D'un mouvement de la tête, il indiquait une jolie Mexicaine qui descendait d'une des chambres. Elle portait une robe très décolletée & plusieurs hommes sont allés la trouver, comme des clous attirés par un aimant.

— Ah, ai-je fait. Ce désir-là. Elle les attise.

— Tu n'éprouves jamais de désir ? a voulu savoir Jace.

— Non. Ce que les hommes et les femmes font ensemble, je trouve ça débile et bizarre.

— Tu as quel âge ?

— 12 ans.

Jace a pris une nouvelle gorgée de whisky avant d'ajouter :

— Tu verras les choses différemment d'ici quelques années.

— Ça m'étonnerait.

Il a haussé les sourcils puis s'est penché en avant, le regard braqué sur moi.

— Excuse-moi de te poser la question, mais dis-moi, P.K. : tu es un garçon ou une fille ?

Je l'ai dévisagé, incrédule.

Pourquoi me demandait-il cela ?

Personne ne m'avait jamais posé cette question.

Est-ce parce que je portais une robe rose la fois où il m'avait rattrapé dans le saloon et que là il venait de me reconnaître ?

Ou à cause d'autre chose ?

Je restais à le regarder sans répondre.

Jace examinait le bout de son cigare.

— L'Ouest est parfois dangereux pour une fillette. Ici, dans la région de Comstock, il doit bien y avoir dix hommes pour une femme. Si ce n'est plus.

Indiquant d'un geste la Mexicaine de tout à l'heure, il a ajouté :

— C'est pour ça que des filles comme Mercedes s'enrichissent rapidement. Elles se font payer autant qu'elles veulent pour une danse. Sauf que d'ici un an elle sera peut-être morte, la faute à trop de drogue, trop de désespoir, ou un coup de couteau en travers de la gorge comme cette pauvre Petite Sally – il paraît que ce serait un amant jaloux qui l'aurait tuée.

Jace tirait sur son cigare.

Moi, j'avais tellement de questions à lui poser que je ne savais pas par où commencer. Du coup je bouillais intérieurement.

Jace a recraché la fumée vers le bas puis a déclaré :

— Une dizaine d'hommes pour une femme, c'est pas naturel. Les journaux racontent qu'on est des gros bourgeois, ici à Virginia City, avec notre école, nos maisons avec leurs jolis petits jardins, notre église & nos bals de charité & l'eau courante qu'on a installée. Mais ça reste un endroit dur pour une femme. Ou une fille, a-t-il précisé en me regardant. Si j'avais une fille, peut-être bien que je l'habillerais en garçon, ça serait plus sûr.

À cet instant précis, Stonewall revenait avec du café frais & remplissait nos tasses. Un serveur chinois le suivait, il a posé sur notre table trois assiettes de gâteau fourré à la vanille. Puis il nous a donné à chacun un couteau, une fourchette et une serviette en lin.

Jace a remercié Stonewall d'un signe de tête. Son compère a pris une chaise pour se joindre à nous.

De mon côté, je savais enfin ce que j'allais dire :

— Il y a un verset de la Lettre de Paul aux Galates qui dit… ai-je commencé.

Aussitôt Jace a levé la main pour m'interrompre :

— T'avise pas de me citer les Écritures. Stonewall tolérerait peut-être, moi pas.

Stonewall affichait un petit sourire en prenant une première bouchée de gâteau.

Jace a fait de même.

Il est resté quelques instants à mâcher en silence.

Puis il m'a adressé un clin d'œil.

— Tu es peut-être un Accident de la Nature, P.K., mais alors tu es un accident qui va nous rapporter pas mal de sous.

Dans ma tête, je me disais : « Les sous c'est bien. Mais ce que vous m'avez appris vaut tout l'or & l'argent de la région. »

FEUILLE DE COMPTES 36

Plus tard ce même soir, Poker Face Jace m'emmenait à l'International Hotel, où il avait sa Chambre Ensuite. On est entrés côté B. Street, en passant devant l'Étude du Notaire – qui était fermée.

Dans le couloir de l'hôtel, il y avait des tapis turcs, des plantes vertes, des crachoirs en cuivre & des lampes à pétrole accrochées aux murs. J'étais bien content de porter mes habits « chicos ».

À la réception, Jace a demandé au portier de faire monter trois repas dans sa Chambre Ensuite. Le temps qu'il commande, mes yeux sont tombés sur la grande horloge de l'hôtel & je n'en revenais pas. Il était près de onze heures du soir. Je n'avais pas vu passer le temps.

Une fois qu'on a été dans sa chambre, toutes lumières allumées, Jace a ôté son chapeau & sa veste, & les a accrochés à des patères derrière la porte. C'était la première fois que je le voyais tête nue. Ses cheveux commençaient à lui manquer sur le dessus. J'ai compris qu'il devait avoir 40 ans – l'âge qu'avait eu Pa Emmet l'an dernier –, ou plus.

La chambre de Jace était une des plus belles que j'aie jamais vues : rideaux en velours rouge, papier peint à rayures, tapis à motifs. Il y avait aussi des tables en bois poli, des chaises capitonnées, une cheminée en marbre & un crachoir en cuivre. Le balcon donnait sur C. Street. J'y suis sorti quelques secondes mais le vent a bien failli m'emporter jusqu'au canyon. S'il avait fait jour, j'aurais sûrement pu profiter d'une vue imprenable sur Virginia City & ses environs. Et ça n'était pas tout – je me dis que c'est de là que vient le nom de Chambre Ensuite, parce qu'il y a toujours quelque chose à découvrir –, il y avait aussi deux chambres et une armoire à glace. Glace dans laquelle j'ai vu se refléter un grand lit en bois.

— Vise un peu ce que l'argent permet d'acheter… disait Jace.

Il avait versé de l'eau dans une vasque & s'en aspergeait la figure.

— Il me semble que la ferronnerie du bâtiment à elle seule a coûté beaucoup d'argent. Plus de 4 000 $, ai-je indiqué.

Jace se séchait à l'aide d'une serviette en lin tout en acquiesçant.

— C'est ce que tout le monde court après.

Quelqu'un a frappé doucement à la porte & Stonewall est allé ouvrir. Un Chinois en tablier blanc nous apportait notre repas sur une petite table à roulettes. Il a déplié une pièce de tissu blanche qu'il a étendue sur une table de poker près de la cheminée. Puis il a disposé les couverts en argent & enfin tous les plats : côtelettes de porc, purée de patates, haricots verts, biscuits & beurre – sans poils dedans, le beurre.

On a mangé tous les trois au coin du feu. Après ça, on a eu tarte aux pommes & fromage avec du café noir. J'avais faim, ça faisait du bien. Comme on mangeait en silence, j'en ai profité pour inspecter la chambre, voir toutes les jolies choses que l'argent permet d'acheter. L'Ensuite de Jace était plus grande que notre cabane à Temperance.

La tarte terminée, Jace a envoyé Stonewall au studio d'Isaiah Coffin avec ma clé.

Quand on a été seuls, il s'est calé sur sa chaise & s'est allumé un cigare.

— Qu'est-ce qui t'amène à Virginia, P.K. ?

J'ai pris le temps de réfléchir, j'hésitais à lui dire la Vérité. Mais comme j'avais besoin d'apprendre tout ce qu'il pourrait m'enseigner, j'ai fini par lui dire :

— Mes parents adoptifs se sont fait tuer hier. Et leurs meurtriers sont à mes trousses.

Jace a relevé les sourcils.

— Qui ça, leurs meurtriers ?

— Walt-Les-Copeaux et deux de ses hommes.

— Voilà qui n'arrange pas mes affaires, a commenté Walt tout en se penchant sur sa droite pour faire tomber la cendre de son cigare dans les flammes. J'ai entendu parler de ce Walt. (Il s'est rassis.) Mais pourquoi venir à Virginia City ?

— Pour m'éloigner le plus possible de lui.

— Ça a marché ?

— Non. Walt et ses sbires sont en ville. Et ils me recherchent toujours.

— Et pourquoi te recherchent-ils ?

J'ai hésité un instant, puis ai répondu :

— Parce que je sais que c'est eux qui ont tué mes parents adoptifs.

— Là tu mens, P.K.

— Comment vous avez deviné ?

— La première fois que tu as hésité, tu te demandais si tu pouvais me faire confiance. Et tu as regardé de côté. La seconde fois, juste là, tu préparais un mensonge et tes yeux ont regardé de l'autre côté. Pourquoi Walt te court-il après ?

Je me demandais ce que Jace ferait quand il serait au courant pour ma Lettre. Et puis j'ai décidé que ça n'avait aucune importance, du moment qu'il continuait ses leçons.

— J'ai une Lettre.

— Fais voir.

J'ai défait le premier bouton de ma belle chemise & en ai sorti mon sac-médecine. Je l'ai ouvert, les mains tremblantes (ça ne m'a pas échappé), puis ai tendu ma Lettre à Poker Face Jace.

— Je te remercie, P.K.

Il m'a regardé un bon moment avant de déplier la Lettre. Pendant qu'il la lisait, j'ai remarqué qu'il avait les doigts longs, pâles et effilés. Avec des ongles impeccables.

Quand enfin il a replié la Lettre, il m'a dit :

— On a sûrement dû te dire que ce document peut te rendre immensément riche. Faire de toi un millionnaire.

— Oui. À condition que ça ne soit pas un faux. Il faut que je le fasse voir au Notaire de B. Street pour qu'il l'authentifie, puis au Juge pour qu'il déclare qu'il m'appartient.

— Ça me semble correct.

Sur ce, il m'a rendu la Lettre. Elle ne paraissait pas l'intéresser. Ça m'a surpris.

— P.K. ? a-t-il fait.

— Oui, monsieur ?

— Ne tombe pas amoureux de l'or. L'or est un leurre & un piège. L'or rend les hommes fous et conduit des familles entières à la ruine.

— Je croyais que c'était de l'argent qu'on cherchait, dans la région.

— L'argent. L'or. Pareil, tout ça.

— Mais vous, vous aimez les deux.

— Non. Moi, j'aime la monnaie. Nuance. (Il tirait sur son cigare, mais celui-ci s'était éteint. Ça l'a fait grimacer.) P.K., tu viens de me montrer que tu me faisais confiance. En récompense, je vais t'offrir le meilleur conseil qui soit.

— J'écoute.

Je me suis rendu compte que j'étais assis sur le bord de ma chaise – à tous les coups j'avais les pupilles dilatées.

Poker Face Jace a frotté une allumette & l'a approchée du bout de son cigare tout en aspirant par l'autre extrémité. Il faisait tourner le cigare jusqu'à ce qu'il brûle bien partout.

— Il existe trois types de personnes dans cette ville, a-t-il dit ensuite. Tout d'abord, les gros richards – les propriétaires des mines qui ont sous leur responsabilité des milliers d'hommes. Ensuite, ces mineurs eux-mêmes, justement. Tous les jours ils risquent leur vie ; et leur seul espoir de s'enrichir, c'est la spéculation. Ce sont eux les plus bêtes. Enfin, tu as les vendeurs de biens et de services. Les plus malins, ceux-là. Ils finissent par s'enrichir, oui, mais ils doivent travailler dur. Si tu veux réussir dans cette ville – comme dans n'importe quelle ville minière –, ne te fais surtout pas mineur. Au contraire, vis sur le dos de ceux qui exploitent les mines.

J'ai acquiescé. Ça se tenait. Ça correspondait aussi à ce que Pa Emmet m'avait toujours dit sur la Cupidité & le Dieu Argent.

Jace a craché une bouffée de cigare en l'air.

— Et puis tu as aussi les gens comme moi. Dont le travail consiste à délester de leur argent les individus des trois catégories précédentes.

La porte s'est ouverte, Stonewall est entré. Il avait récupéré mes habits d'Indien & mes mocassins chez Isaiah Coffin.

— Tout s'est bien passé ? lui a demandé Jace en allant récupérer une couverture dans l'armoire. Tu ne t'es pas fait agresser par un photographe susceptible ou une Fille de Bastringue ?

Stonewall a secoué la tête et m'a tendu mes affaires. Et aussi la clé du studio. Je l'ai rangée dans mon sac-médecine.

— Tu vas remettre ta chemise en daim, m'a dit Jace. Ensuite tu passeras cette couverture sur tes épaules. Stonewall va te conduire dans un saloon à 25 dans C. Street.

— C'est quoi, un « Saloon à 25 » ?

— Un endroit où on te fait payer 25 ¢ le verre ou le cigare, alors qu'ailleurs c'est moitié moins cher. Stonewall t'y amènera. Mais tu ne devras pas montrer que tu le connais. Juste tu le suivras à l'intérieur, puis tu t'assiéras par terre. La tête baissée. Tu vas te faire passer pour un petit mendiant païute. Sauf qu'en fait tu observeras les pieds des types avec lesquels je jouerai au poker.

Jace a terminé son café & examiné sa tasse. Elle était en porcelaine, décorée de fleurs bleues et roses.

— Stonewall, apporte-moi la...

Il n'avait pas achevé sa phrase que son complice lui tendait déjà une coupe en fer-blanc. Un signe de tête de Jace, et Stonewall me la donnait.

— Tu te serviras de cette coupe, continuait Poker Face Jace. Si l'un de mes adversaires a les pieds qui dansent, je veux que tu l'agites légèrement. Juste un peu, compris ? Pas comme des maracas. Ensuite tu la reposes, l'anse tournée vers le type qui a la meilleure main.

— C'est tricher.

— Pas vraiment, a fait Jace en s'essuyant les lèvres & la moustache à sa serviette. Si tu regardais ses cartes, là oui, je dis pas.

J'ai réfléchi un instant.

— D'accord, ai-je fini par conclure.

— Si tu vois un gars donner un coup de pied ou les ramener sous sa chaise, qu'est-ce que ça veut dire ?

— Qu'il a de mauvaises cartes ?

— Sûrement. Dans ce cas, tu gardes la coupe, mais tu orientes l'anse vers le type nerveux. Vu ?

— Vu. La main est bonne : j'agite la coupe puis la repose. L'homme est nerveux : je garde la coupe.

— Et n'oublie pas d'orienter l'anse. Tout en restant discret. Bon, en général, les saloons à 25 n'acceptent pas les mendiants, mais j'aurai filé 50 ¢ au barman pour qu'il tolère un Indien avec Couverture.

J'ai fait signe que je comprenais.

— Si j'estime qu'on risque d'être découverts, je veux que tu décampes. Comme signal, je dénouerai ma cravate et la glisserai dans ma poche de devant. Tu pourras revenir dans cet hôtel mais à condition que personne ne te voie. Stonewall te montrera l'entrée des fournisseurs. Tu te sens à la hauteur ? Tu sauras te débrouiller seul si nécessaire ?

— Oui. Je suis fortiche pour passer sans me faire voir.

— Bien. Maintenant va te changer dans la chambre d'à côté.

FEUILLE DE COMPTES 37

Je suis donc allé me changer dans la chambre de Jace.

Une très belle chambre, d'ailleurs. Avec un grand lit en bois, une immense armoire et du papier peint à rayures. J'ai retiré mon pantalon et ma chemise « chicos » et c'est avec plaisir que j'ai renfilé mes habits en daim. La couverture était jaune pâle & je n'avais jamais vu de mendiant indien en porter d'aussi belle. J'ai quand même fait comme Jace avait dit, puis suis retourné dans la pièce d'à côté.

— Pas mal, a estimé Jace en m'observant de haut en bas. Mais tu as la figure trop propre. Viens là.

Je me suis approché. Du bout des doigts de sa main droite, il a touché des cendres froides dans la cheminée puis m'a frotté le visage. Après quelques secondes de réflexion, il en a aussi mis quelques traînées sur la couverture.

— Voilà qui est mieux, a-t-il dit. Mais il manque encore quelque chose.

Il est allé récupérer sur le portemanteau un chapeau mou avec une plume de faucon coincée sous le bandeau.

— Je l'ai gagné au jeu avec un Indien la semaine dernière. J'ai bien fait de le garder.

En mettant le chapeau sur ma tête, j'ai senti une bouffée de graisse d'ours qui m'a rappelé ma mère indienne. Le chapeau était un peu trop grand, il me tombait sur les yeux. J'ai donc ressorti l'affiche **WANTED** de mon sac-médecine, l'ai froissée puis l'ai fourrée à l'intérieur avant de le ressayer. Cette fois, il ne m'empêchait plus de voir.

Jace a fait signe qu'il approuvait et a craché de la fumée en l'air.

— Retourne dans la chambre et regarde-toi dans le miroir.

Je suis allé me poster devant un miroir en pied accroché au mur. Un Indien avec Couverture, tout sale et le visage inexpressif, me regardait. J'ai remarqué que, sous le bord du chapeau trop grand, mes yeux étaient très sombres, comme ceux de Jace, si bien qu'on avait du mal à distinguer si les points noirs grossissaient ou non. Comment avait dit Jace, déjà ? Impénétrable.

J'aimais bien ce que je voyais, mais ça ne se lisait pas sur mon visage.

— Arrête de t'admirer, m'a lancé Jace depuis l'embrasure de la porte.

D'où est-ce qu'il savait ? C'est là que j'ai noté que les orteils de mon pied droit étaient relevés. J'ai reposé le pied à plat et ai regardé Jace dans le miroir. Il m'a peut-être adressé un clin d'œil, pas sûr.

— Stonewall, a-t-il ensuite appelé. Conduit P.K. chez Almack. Je vous y retrouve d'ici une vingtaine de minutes.

Stonewall suçait une tranche de citron. Il l'a jetée au feu & s'est levé. Puis il est allé récupérer son manteau, son chapeau et son ceinturon.

Je suis sorti de la chambre derrière lui. Dans le couloir, je lui ai demandé :

— Vous m'auriez vraiment fait sauter la cervelle, tout à l'heure ?

Il m'observait de l'œil gauche. Le droit regardait ailleurs.

— 'videmment que non. Je voulais juste te flanquer la frousse, que tu rendes les pièces d'or que tu aurais pu chourer à Jace.

J'ai acquiescé. Ça me soulageait un peu.

— Pourquoi on vous appelle « Stonewall » ? lui ai-je ensuite demandé.

— Tu connais pas Stonewall Jackson ?

— Si, justement, le célèbre général sudiste.

— Un vrai génie militaire. J'ai pris son nom parce que je n'aime pas trop le mien.

— Moi non plus je n'aime pas trop mon nom.

Stonewall a grogné puis a ouvert une porte blanche sans numéro dessus. Un escalier étroit nous a conduits jusqu'au trottoir de C. Street.

Il était minuit passé, mais la rue semblait encore plus animée que pendant la journée. Il y avait pas mal de mineurs barbus qui donnaient l'impression de tout juste sortir du travail.

Le vent soufflait toujours et il faisait froid à présent. J'étais bien content de porter une couverture et un chapeau. J'ai noué deux coins de la couverture autour de mon cou puis ai rabattu un des deux autres par-dessus mon épaule pour bien m'envelopper. Ensuite je me suis élancé après Stonewall.

Les gens s'écartaient devant lui. Je marchais dans ses pas sans trop me laisser distancer, et personne ne m'a bousculé. De partout on entendait des cris & des rires. Une fois, j'ai même cru distinguer des coups de feu suivis de hurlements puis d'un rire. À travers les semelles fines de mes mocassins, je sentais les vibrations du trottoir. Les concasseurs de quartz fonctionnaient même en pleine nuit.

On s'est arrêtés à l'angle nord-ouest de C. Street & Taylor, près de la quincaillerie avec le poêle et les cafetières sur le toit. En diagonale, il y avait un élégant bâtiment en pierre. Des deux côtés de la porte d'entrée, des torches éclairaient une grande enseigne : **ALMACK, SALOON À HUÎTRES & ALCOOLS**. On allait pour traverser Taylor & là Stonewall a tourné sa mine patibulaire dans ma direction. Est-ce qu'il me regardait ? Je n'en étais pas sûr puisque ses yeux n'étaient déjà pas d'accord entre eux. Là-dessus il m'a dit à voix basse :

— Quand j'entre dans le saloon tu me suis, mais tu vas t'asseoir là où Jace t'a dit.

J'ai fait oui de la tête. Ensuite j'ai attendu qu'il ait traversé Taylor et soit entré dans le saloon.

Chez Almack, il n'y avait pas de portes battantes comme au Fashion Saloon où Jace m'avait emmené cet après-midi. Là, c'étaient des doubles portes normales, avec poignées en cuivre et panneaux en verre dépoli marqués **ALMACK**. Stonewall n'a pas refermé complètement derrière lui, si bien que j'ai pu me glisser à l'intérieur sans faire de bruit.

Le saloon était sombre & enfumé, comme au Fashion. Mais un rapide coup d'œil m'a permis de constater la différence entre un Saloon à 25 et ceux où on paie moitié prix : papier peint à rayures, abat-jour colorés, chandeliers. Les parquets étaient polis & cirés – l'odeur de miel se mêlait à celles de la bière, des lampes à huile & des cigares. Je me suis assis en tailleur à côté d'une fougère en pot, dos au mur, ma coupe posée devant moi.

Sur ma gauche, dans le coin opposé, il y avait une petite estrade sur laquelle un chauve barbu jouait du banjo. Il interprétait une chanson populaire à propos d'une certaine « Lorena ». C'était à la fois triste et plein d'espoir. J'ai dû me pincer pour ne pas me laisser hypnotiser.

À ma droite, il y avait le bar. Stonewall y était accoudé, un pied posé sur la petite barre en cuivre. En me voyant entrer, il s'est tourné vers le barman et lui a dit un truc. L'autre m'a regardé et a fait oui de la tête.

Un grand miroir était fixé au mur, derrière le comptoir, avec un tableau noir de chaque côté. Ils me rappelaient mon école, à Dayton, avec les lettres & nos notes dessus. Je sais pourtant lire, mais là je n'arrivais pas à déchiffrer ce qu'il y avait de marqué.

Il y avait foule chez Almack. Au bar, la plupart des hommes se contentaient de boire tandis qu'aux tables presque tous jouaient aux cartes. Une porte intérieure entrouverte me donnait un aperçu du Restaurant dans lequel on devait servir les huîtres. On entendait les gens rire & parler, et de temps en temps quelqu'un crachait dans un crachoir en cuivre. Il y avait aussi quelques femmes. Elles portaient des robes voyantes avec des dentelles, des rubans et des décolletés profonds.

Mon père adoptif devait se Retourner dans sa Tombe, à condition qu'il soit déjà enterré.

FEUILLE DE COMPTES 38

Le temps que Jace arrive, je regardais des joueurs de poker à une table carrée. C'est comme si on m'avait retiré un Voile de devant les yeux. Je voyais qui était nerveux, qui était content, qui bluffait. Au-dessus de la table, ils ne laissaient quasiment rien paraître. Mais leurs jambes & leurs pieds les trahissaient à chaque mouvement.

J'avais du mal à croire qu'ils ne s'en rendaient pas compte. Mais je me suis souvenu que moi-même je ne faisais pas attention à mes pieds avant que Jace ne m'en parle.

À ma droite, les portes se sont ouvertes & j'ai détecté une odeur à la fois nauséabonde et familière quand deux hommes sont entrés. Le parfum des lampes, de la cire & des cigares de luxe ne suffisait pas à masquer l'odeur d'insecte mort qui se dégageait de cette pipe. Sam Clemens, du *Territorial Enterprise*, et un homme très élégant avec chapeau en tuyau de poêle & canne se joignaient à nous. Sam a promené son regard dans la salle, sans prêter plus attention que cela à ma présence. Mon déguisement devait être sensass.

Les deux hommes se sont dirigés vers le bar.

— Bonsoir, monsieur Goodman, a dit le barman.

Ce M. Goodman était jeune, grand, avait la figure ronde & portait une moustache sombre.

— Bonsoir, Lorry, a-t-il répondu. Je vous présente Sam Clemens, notre nouveau Local.

— Ravi de vous rencontrer, l'a salué le barman. Vous prendrez quoi ?

— Deux bières, a annoncé M. Goodman. Marque *twain*.

Le barman a acquiescé puis tracé deux traits à la craie sur son tableau, sous les initiales J.G.

— C'est quoi, ce manège, Joe ? lui a demandé Sam Clemens en indiquant le tableau du doigt.

— Si le barman accepte de te faire crédit, tu ne paies tes consommations qu'une fois par semaine. Le reste du temps, tu viens, tu bois et tu dis au barman de noter combien de verres tu as pris : « Marque un », « Marque deux », etc. Là, *twain*, c'est « deux » en argot de chez nous.

— On dit pareil sur le Mississippi, a indiqué Sam Clemens.

— Hmm ?

— J'ai été Capitaine d'un Bateau sur le Mississippi. Et on disait « Marque *twain* » pour que l'assistant note que le fleuve avait deux brasses de profondeur.

— Vraiment ?

— Vraiment. Jamais je n'aurais cru prononcer ces mots sur le flanc d'une montagne, dans un paysage d'après guerre.

Joe Goodman a pouffé puis levé sa chope.

— J'espère que tu auras encore souvent l'occasion de les prononcer. Surtout en ma présence !

Sur ce, ils ont trinqué & bu une grande lampée de bière.

Le joueur de banjo avait attaqué un air qui court plus vite qu'une diligence emballée. Quand il a eu fini, tout le monde l'a applaudi.

J'ai entendu Sam Clemens qui disait :

— Ça n'est plus un musicien, c'est un pur-sang.

Ça a encore fait pouffer Joe Goodman, mais il s'est arrêté net. Il a tourné les yeux vers la porte. Et tous les gens présents dans le saloon aussi, y compris le banjoïste, qui n'avait même pas eu le temps d'entamer son morceau suivant.

Moi, je gardais la tête baissée mais j'ai quand même repéré les bottes de cuir noir de Poker Face Jace qui approchaient.

Quand il s'est accoudé au bar, j'ai regardé par-dessous le bord de mon chapeau. Je l'ai vu commander un cognac, après quoi les conversations ont repris. Le reporter et son ami dévisageaient Jace, & Joe Goodman s'est penché pour murmurer quelque chose à l'oreille de Sam Clemens. Il parlait trop bas pour que je l'entende.

Une des Filles de Bastringue s'est approchée de Jace. Elle a passé ses bras nus autour de son cou & a voulu l'embrasser sur la bouche. Jace a souri & a tourné la tête au dernier moment – elle n'a pu l'embrasser que sur la joue. Puis il s'est dégagé de son étreinte, lui a donné une tape sur les fesses, a pris son verre & s'est dirigé vers une des tables.

Jace a dit un mot aux quatre hommes qui y étaient assis. Sans perdre le sourire. L'un des types a souri lui aussi, fait oui de la tête puis a récupéré ses gains & s'est levé. Il est allé s'offrir à boire au bar. À voir la pointe de ses bottes relevée, je me suis dit qu'il était content que Jace ait pris sa place.

C'était une bonne place, d'ailleurs : parfaite pour Jace, toujours. Il était installé dos au mur, face à moi. Sa chaise sous une lampe à huile, le bord de son chapeau noir maintenait sa figure dans l'ombre.

Je trouvais ça futé. Ses adversaires ne pourraient pas voir ses yeux, mais lui verrait les leurs.

Mon cœur battait vite. Est-ce que notre plan allait marcher ?

Je regardais le type qui distribuait les cartes. L'instant critique, ce serait la première réaction des joueurs. J'observais leurs pieds avec la plus grande attention, toujours sans relever la tête. Dès qu'ils ont eu étalé leur jeu en éventail, leurs pieds se sont mis à bouger. Celui qui me tournait le dos a posé les siens bien à plat par terre. Celui de droite tapait des talons & la pointe d'une de ses bottes s'est levée une seconde.

J'ai agité ma coupe un petit poil, puis l'ai reposée – l'anse tournée vers le type à ma droite. Il avait le regard mou & la peau flasque. Il me faisait penser à un cocker.

Ça n'a pas loupé, le Cocker avait une bonne main, il a raflé la mise. Jace s'est montré beau joueur & l'a félicité. Tout en jouant, Jace leur racontait des anecdotes. Son visage ne trahissait aucune émotion, mais j'avais repéré une lueur amusée au niveau de ses yeux. Y compris lorsqu'il perdait. Durant les deux heures qui ont suivi, et alors même qu'il donnait l'impression de perdre aussi souvent que les autres, j'ai constaté que son tas de pièces grossissait régulièrement. Certains de ses adversaires orientaient même leurs pieds dans sa direction. Visiblement, ça ne les dérangeait pas qu'il les soulage de leurs sous. À un moment donné, Jace a fait venir Stonewall et lui a demandé d'apporter une bouteille de whisky à sa table. Mais lui-même, j'ai bien vu qu'il ne touchait pratiquement pas à son verre.

La nuit passait, j'agitais ma coupe, le tas de pièces de Jace grossissait. Tout allait bien pour lui. Il y avait du mouvement dans le bar et, au bout d'environ quatre heures, Jace avait face à lui trois nouveaux adversaires.

Il devait être sacrément tard, parce que j'avais tout le temps envie de bâiller. Un groupe de mineurs venait d'entrer, le saloon était aussi bondé qu'à notre arrivée. Il y avait deux barmans à présent & un accordéon remplaçait le banjo. Les saloons de Virginia devaient rester ouverts tout le temps, je me disais.

Jace n'avait pas encore bougé de sa place contre le mur. À sa gauche, donc à ma droite, il y avait un type dont la barbe était aussi fournie qu'un buisson d'armoise. Il disait être « spéculateur » ; il se tenait dos au bar. À sa gauche, donc dos à moi, se trouvait un employé de la banque Wells Fargo. Il avait une montre de gousset en or. Et à la droite de Jace était assis un Surveillant de la Mine, la moustache tout encrassée de tabac.

Au fil des parties, j'ai fini par repérer que l'employé de banque tirait sa montre chaque fois qu'il avait une mauvaise main. Le surveillant, lui, sifflait tout bas quand il avait du jeu. Le spéculateur crachait chaque fois qu'il était dégoûté – par ses cartes ou autre chose. Vous vous dites sûrement que ces indices étaient évidents… sauf qu'aucun des joueurs ne semblait les remarquer.

Je crois que Jace & moi, nous n'aurions pas pu les repérer de façon aussi claire si ces bonshommes ne s'étaient pas trahis par leurs pieds.

J'ai noté que, des fois, Jace ignorait mes signaux & perdait la main. Ça m'a rappelé les premières leçons d'échecs que Pa Emmet m'avait données. Il faisait exprès de commettre des erreurs & de perdre, & quand je lui demandais pourquoi il me répondait que c'était pour que je ne me décourage pas. Jace devait avoir le même but.

Les gens me donnaient des cacahuètes, des allumettes et parfois même une pièce en quittant le saloon. Je mangeais les cacahuètes & rangeais les allumettes dans ma poche. Les pièces, je les laissais dans la coupe pour faire du bruit. Un ou deux types m'ont craché dessus, mais la plupart se contentaient de m'ignorer. Comme je les ignorais.

Impossible d'ignorer Walt-Les-Copeaux quand il a fait son entrée dans le Saloon à Huîtres & Alcools, par contre. Ses deux acolytes l'accompagnaient toujours : Extra Dub avec son énorme Pomme d'Adam, et Boz Le Peureux avec son œil qui louche et son nez que je lui avais cassé. L'accordéoniste s'est arrêté de jouer, et le saloon est tombé dans le silence pour la seconde fois de la nuit. J'ai vu Stonewall qui sortait de l'ombre, près du bar. Il regardait les trois desperados, comme tout le monde.

Walt & ses sbires ont commandé une bouteille de whisky à l'un des barmans puis se sont retournés pour inspecter la salle.

Je me suis figé.

Walt recherchait un gamin de 12 ans habillé en Indien. J'avais réussi à lui échapper en me déguisant en fillette, en Chinetoque et en « chicos ». Mais là, j'avais remis ma tenue d'Indien. Walt m'avait déjà reconnu une fois. Allait-il remettre ça ?

Il faut croire que non. Il a descendu son whisky et s'est retourné pour s'en servir un autre.

Extra Dub et Boz ne m'ont pas reconnu non plus, grâce à ma couverture cradingue et à mon grand chapeau mou.

Walt a avalé son deuxième whisky puis a dit :

— Commandez-vous un verre, les gars, c'est ma tournée.

Puis, sa bouteille à la main, il s'est dirigé vers la table de Jace.

— Dégage, a-t-il ordonné au Surveillant de la Mine avant de cracher du jus de chique à ses pieds.

Le Surveillant a regardé Walt. Il a ouvert la bouche mais l'a refermée tout de suite. Et c'est en silence qu'il a ramassé ses gains & est allé au bar.

À le voir souffler la fumée de son cigare vers le bas, j'ai compris qu'il n'était pas content.

Walt a pris sa place. Il faisait face au bar, je le voyais de profil – de sa sale tronche à ses bottes. Il continuait à chiquer & s'est tourné vers moi pour cracher pendant que je le regardais. Mais il ne m'a pas reconnu.

Dans le saloon, tout le monde portait au minimum un revolver Colt Navy. Walt avait sur lui le calibre supérieur – le modèle Army – en plus du Couteau de Chasse entaché du sang d'une dizaine d'hommes & de femmes.

— À quoi on joue ? a-t-il demandé.

L'accordéoniste faisait une pause et, bien que les conversations aient plus ou moins repris, l'atmosphère était suffisamment calme pour que j'entende Walt chiquer.

— Poker, a répondu Jace. Cinq cartes.

Il battait le jeu – vite & bien, sans frimer comme certains types.

Walt a craché dans le crachoir au pied de sa chaise, s'est servi un whisky & l'a descendu d'un trait.

Jace battait toujours.

— Tu es Walt-Les-Copeaux, nan ? a-t-il fait. J'ai entendu parler de toi.

Sans bien distinguer ses yeux, je pensais qu'il devait me regarder.

— Moi aussi j'ai entendu parler de toi. Jason Francis Montgomery, dit « Poker Face Jace ». (Tirant son Couteau de Chasse, Walt s'est découpé une nouvelle chique.) Tu triches, je te transforme en cure-dent.

— Je ne triche jamais, a rétorqué Jace d'une voix aimable. M'est arrivé de bluffer, mais tricher, ça jamais.

Walt a grogné en rangeant son gros couteau.

L'employé de banque a pouffé. La loi l'autorisait à procéder à l'arrestation de Walt, surtout qu'il y avait accrochée au mur une affiche **WANTED** avec son portrait. Ça m'a surpris qu'il ne tente rien. Je me suis tourné vers Sam Clemens & Joe Goodman, mais les places qu'ils avaient occupées toute la nuit étaient à présent vides.

Jace a distribué quelques mains, moi, j'observais attentivement Walt. Première constatation : il était gaucher. Deuxième constatation : ses pieds le trahissaient autant que ceux de tout le monde. Troisième constatation : chaque fois qu'il bluffait ou était nerveux, il arrêtait de bouger, & même de chiquer. Une fois, je suis même sûr qu'il a avalé alors qu'il voulait cracher.

Ils ont joué quelques mains & Jace était en train de distribuer quand c'est arrivé.

— Qu'est-ce qui t'amène à Virginia, Walt ? lui a-t-il demandé.

Dans son coin, l'accordéoniste s'était remis à jouer – « Alice Where Art Thou » –, mais pas trop fort. J'entendais ce qui se disait.

Walt a tourné la tête, craché du jus de chique dans le crachoir puis répondu :

— Je cherche un gamin qui s'appelle Pinkerton. L'un de vous l'a vu ?

J'ai cru que mon cœur allait s'arrêter de battre.

Jace a posé un dollar en argent sur la table.

— J'augmente la mise, a-t-il dit en battant une dernière fois. Tout le monde mise pareil.

— Allan Pinkerton, a fait le Spéculateur à la barbe d'armoise en regardant les cartes tomber. Je le hais, ce fils de pute.

— Pourquoi donc ? a demandé Jace.

— Il s'est vendu aux généraux nordistes plus vite qu'une Fille de Bastringue.

— Moi par contre, est intervenu l'employé de banque, les Pinkerton, je n'ai pas à m'en plaindre. Leurs Détectives des Diligences ont permis de réduire les vols de moitié.

— Paraît qu'il a un frère, a glissé Jace en reposant le paquet pour examiner ses cartes. Un certain Robert.

— Mouais, a confirmé le Spéculateur. Une vraie plaie, celui-là aussi.

— Vous le connaissiez ?
— Vous parlez de lui comme s'il était mort… a dit le Spéculateur tout en organisant ses cartes.
— Et… ?
— Et à moins qu'il se soit fait zigouiller ces deux derniers mois, il est toujours vivant.

Cette annonce m'a tellement pris par surprise que j'ai bondi. Mon vrai père ne serait donc pas mort ?

FEUILLE DE COMPTES 39

Je n'en croyais pas mes oreilles.

Le Spéculateur à la barbe d'armoise prétendait avoir vu mon père il y avait de ça deux mois. Par chance, seul Jace avait repéré ma réaction. D'un geste de la main qui voulait dire « assieds-toi », il me demandait de me calmer.

Je me suis rassis.

Le Spéculateur à la barbe d'armoise a jeté deux pièces en or de 20 $ sur la table & les autres ont bloqué un moment.

Puis l'employé de banque a sifflé :

— Ça fait une somme, a-t-il dit.

— Ma dernière main, a expliqué le Spéculateur.

Les trois autres ont misé comme lui.

Le barbu a posé deux cartes retournées sur la table & les a fait glisser jusqu'au centre en annonçant :

— Deux cartes.

Jace lui a donné ce qu'il demandait.

L'employé de banque a posé trois cartes :

— Trois.

Jace lui en a donné trois.

Walt a posé deux cartes.

Jace l'a servi deux fois.

Puis Walt s'est penché en avant & a déclaré :

— Je sais pertinemment que Robert Pinkerton est vivant et qu'il habite à Chicago. Mais c'est pas lui qui m'intéresse. C'est le gosse. Il a un truc qui m'appartient.

Jace a posé une carte & s'en est servi une autre.

— Ça serait pas le gamin qui a tué & dévalisé ses parents adoptifs ? a demandé le Spéculateur en misant trois pièces d'or.

J'avais les mains qui tremblaient, ça faisait tinter ma coupe, alors je l'ai serrée plus fort.

— Je suis, a fait le banquier. Ils en parlaient dans le journal. Paraît que le gosse serait à moitié indien.

— Les Indiens, faudrait toujours s'en méfier, a grogné Walt en contemplant la mise de 60 $. C'est ce que je dis tout le temps mais les gens ne m'écoutent pas.

Jace a ajouté ses trois pièces d'or au petit tas :

— Y en a qui disent que ce serait un coup monté. Que le petit serait innocent.

Walt a craché son jus de chique par terre. Sans même viser le crachoir.

— Vous avez quoi ? a-t-il demandé au Spéculateur.

— Full aux sept, a annoncé celui-ci en étalant ses cartes.

— Full aux rois, a contré Jace.

Il se préparait à rafler la mise au moment où Walt a abattu son jeu, déclarant :

— Carré de dames.

Du coup, c'est le desperado qui a empoché le pactole.

Jusque-là, Jace avait gagné 720 $. Soit plus d'un an du salaire d'un reporter. J'ai jeté un coup d'œil à ma coupe. L'anse était tournée vers Walt. Ma tremblote de trouillard venait de faire perdre plus de 100 $ à Jace sur une seule main.

C'était ma faute. Je n'avais pas bien surveillé leurs pieds. J'étais trop captivé par ce qu'ils racontaient sur mon père mort qui habitait apparemment Chicago.

Et Jace en était de sa poche pour pas mal.

J'ai vu qu'il me fixait, mais je n'arrivais pas à déchiffrer son expression.

— Tu regardes quoi ? lui a demandé Walt.

Là-dessus, il s'est tourné & ses yeux sont passés sur moi. J'ai aussitôt baissé la tête mais nos regards se sont quand même croisés une seconde.

— Hé, Dub, a fait Walt. Vise un peu cette loque d'Indien à Couverture qui fait la manche. Depuis quand les mendiants ont le droit d'entrer chez Almack ?

— Depuis jamais, a répondu Extra Dub de sa voix râpeuse. (Puis, retirant son pied de la barre au bas du comptoir :) Je crois bien que c'est le gosse qu'on cherche.

— Moi pareil, a confirmé Boz. L'a le même regard froid.

Je gardais la tête baissée, faisais comme si je ne comprenais rien.

Mais l'accordéon avait cessé de jouer & on aurait entendu une mouche éterner dans le saloon. Je sentais bien que tout le monde m'observait.

— Hé, toi ! a lancé Walt. Toi, l'Indien, là ! Tu t'appellerais pas Pinky, des fois ?

Je n'ai pas relevé la tête, j'avais les yeux collés à mes pieds. La chaise de Walt a raclé le plancher & quand il s'est levé j'ai aperçu ses bottes pointées dans ma direction.

C'est là que Jace a déclaré :

— Bouge plus ou je te farcis de plomb.

J'ai redressé la tête : Jace était debout, un petit Smith & Wesson braqué sur la poitrine de Walt. Son pistolet était un calibre .32, donc plus gros que le mien mais pas autant que celui du desperado.

— Tu bouges plus, a-t-il répété.

À présent il le visait à la tête.

Walt s'est immobilisé un instant puis a comme souri. Il savait qu'on le couvrait. Extra Dub & Boz Burton pointaient leurs flingues sur Jace.

— Gaffe, Jace ! me suis-je écrié.

Trop tard… Dub avait tiré en même temps qu'un autre type. Jace s'est écroulé, touché à la poitrine. Sur ce, ça a été la grosse pagaille. J'ai entendu la détonation assourdissante du Le Mat de Stonewall & j'ai pensé qu'il tirait sur Extra Dub, vu que le barman avait saisi Boz par le bras, de sorte que son revolver arrosait maintenant le plafond. Il pleuvait du plâtre, une femme s'est mise à crier & les chaises ont valsé quand les hommes ont pris la tangente.

Moi, je ne faisais pas trop attention à tout ça.

C'est que Walt-Les-Copeaux s'approchait de moi d'un air décidé, son Couteau de Chasse à la main.

J'ai honte de l'avouer, mais sur le moment j'ai complètement oublié le Smith & Wesson à sept coups que j'avais dans ma poche. J'ai détalé comme un lapin.

FEUILLE DE COMPTES 40

Je suis sorti du saloon en courant, les oreilles qui bourdonnaient à cause des coups de feu. Dehors le jour se levait & les trottoirs étaient bondés : les gens suivaient une procession. Le vent fouettait leurs habits et j'ai entendu une fanfare qui essayait de couvrir les mugissements du Zéphyr. Je me suis faufilé entre les badauds & ai failli me faire piétiner par les chevaux tirant la voiture des pompiers pendant que je traversais la rue. Le véhicule était drapé de noir. Les pompiers portaient leur uniforme : casque, chemise de flanelle rouge, ceinture noire luisante. Pourquoi se réunissaient-ils là de si bonne heure ? Ils cherchaient à se moquer de moi ou quoi ? En tout cas ils m'empêchaient de m'enfuir.

Sans parler du vent qui me secouait et faisait voler ma couverture comme une cape dans mon dos. Il m'envoyait de la poussière dans les yeux et dans la bouche. Pendant ce temps, la fanfare se rapprochait.

Je me suis élancé entre une autre voiture & un groupe de pompiers. Le trottoir d'en face était bourré de mineurs donc il m'a fallu cavaler dans la rue, à contre-courant de la circulation. Les pompiers m'insultaient au passage mais, entre la fanfare et le vent, c'est à peine si je les entendais. Dès que je me suis trouvé au niveau d'une rue transversale, je m'y suis engagé. Elle aussi était pleine de mineurs, mais j'ai quand même réussi à me faufiler.

C'est dans B. Street que j'ai croisé la fanfare, et aussi une charrette funèbre tirée par des chevaux noirs sur la tête desquels on avait fixé un panache noir. Et ce n'est qu'à ce moment précis que je me suis rappelé : l'enterrement de la Petite Sally était pour aujourd'hui. Ça expliquait la présence de tous ces mineurs sur les trottoirs, ils attendaient le cortège. Je me suis dirigé vers une autre rue qui m'a ramené dans A. Street.

J'avais envie de vomir tellement j'avais couru, alors je me suis arrêté, penché en avant, les mains sur les genoux, pour me reposer. Mes parents adoptifs étaient morts, comme la Petite Sally. Jace avait sûrement subi le même sort – à cause de moi. Ça faisait beaucoup de morts. Et à côté de ça, mon père que j'avais toujours cru mort était bien vivant. Simplement, il n'avait jamais pris la peine de me retrouver.

Je n'avais pas encore repris mon souffle qu'une espèce de Guêpe a sifflé près de mon oreille. Sauf que ça n'était pas une Guêpe.

C'était une Balle tirée par Walt.

Le desperado avait fendu la foule à une cinquantaine de mètres de moi & me visait avec son revolver Colt Army. Le soleil n'était pas tout à fait levé, mais Walt y voyait suffisamment pour me tirer dessus et manquer de m'abattre.

J'ai couru me réfugier derrière une cabane tout en sortant mon sept-coups de ma poche.

Là-dessus, j'ai observé mon poursuivant. Walt approchait. Je lui ai tiré dessus. Ça n'a pour ainsi dire pas fait de bruit à cause du vent. Je ne suis même pas sûr que Walt ait entendu quoi que ce soit.

Un couple de cailles s'est envolé à tire-d'aile quand j'ai reculé sans le faire exprès contre le bosquet d'armoise où elles se cachaient. J'ai eu une boule au ventre en constatant que j'étais sur le point de sortir de la ville. Le soleil pointait tout juste au-dessus des montagnes à l'est. Si je gravissais encore la pente, j'allais me retrouver directement dans sa lumière.

C'est là que j'ai repéré le bâtiment blanc de la Mine mexicaine. Aucun bruit n'en sortait, aucune fumée ne se dégageait de sa grande cheminée.

Je m'y suis précipité.

Je me disais : « Il y aura des tas de recoins où me cacher, là-dedans. »

Mais une fois arrivé devant la porte, à bout de souffle & prêt à vomir après cette course dans une atmosphère aussi raréfiée, j'ai constaté que la porte était fermée à clé.

Le soleil était à présent levé, il illuminait les rails qui reliaient le bâtiment à une espèce de carré noir que je distinguais dans la montagne. Les rails étaient ceux du wagonnet de l'autre fois ; le carré noir l'entrée de la Mine mexicaine.

Le vent me mugissait dessus & le soleil braquait sur moi tous ses rayons.

J'ai pensé : « Si je trouve un coin sombre & tranquille, je pourrai réfléchir à la suite. »

J'ai donc foncé jusqu'à l'entrée de la mine, en courant après mon ombre allongée – le chapeau à plume et la couverture qui me servait de cape faisaient une drôle de silhouette.

L'entrée de la Mine mexicaine était ouverte mais déserte. J'ai pensé que tous les mineurs avaient eu la permission d'aller assister à l'enterrement de la Petite Sally. Sur une table en bois, j'ai trouvé une demi-douzaine de bougies. Je les ai fourrées dans ma poche droite, histoire que Walt n'ait pas de lumière pour me chercher. J'ai dû poser mon sept-coups le temps d'allumer une bougie à la lampe à pétrole suspendue près de l'entrée. J'étais tellement pressé qu'il ne m'est même pas venu à l'idée d'emporter la lampe.

En même temps j'ai commis une autre grosse erreur mais je ne m'en suis rendu compte qu'après.

J'ai donc filé dans ce tunnel vide qui s'enfonçait toujours plus profondément dans la montagne – à la seule lueur de la bougie que je tenais à la main.

Il faisait de plus en plus sombre.

Je me suis retourné, on ne voyait plus le jour.

J'ai ralenti pour essayer d'entendre mon poursuivant. Les terribles hurlements du Zéphyr ne parvenaient pas jusque-là. Par contre, le sang dans mes oreilles faisait un vacarme presque aussi assourdissant.

Sur quelques mètres, le chemin était éclairé par des lampes à pétrole installées dans des niches creusées dans la roche. Et ensuite plus rien. Je m'enfonçais toujours.

J'avais dû faire une soixantaine de mètres, si ce n'est plus, quand j'ai distingué une silhouette sombre devant moi, juste à la limite de la lumière vacillante que produisait ma bougie.

Là-dessus, j'ai entendu un grognement. Une grosse bête.

La main tremblante, j'ai relevé ma bougie.

Les deux yeux blanchâtres d'une créature démoniaque sont alors apparus.

J'ai bien cru mourir de peur sur-le-champ. J'ai même failli lâcher ma bougie mais à cet instant précis j'ai entendu un cheval qui s'ébrouait.

C'était bien un cheval.

Une jument harnachée qui devait servir pour le transport les jours de travail. Là, elle restait debout à attendre.

— Salut, ma belle, lui ai-je dit. N'aie pas peur.

L'écho du tunnel renvoyait ma voix toute petite.

La jument a roulé des yeux. Mes paroles craintives ne la rassuraient pas franchement.

Je me suis avancé, lui ai caressé le flanc. Elle avait le poil rude & poussiéreux, les yeux comme laiteux.

À rester depuis si longtemps dans l'obscurité, elle avait dû devenir quasi aveugle.

Une dernière tape amicale & j'ai poursuivi ma route calmement. Ma bougie éclairait faiblement la suite du tunnel et aussi trois grottes aux parois luisantes de quartz. Aucune ne s'enfonçait cependant à plus de sept ou neuf pas. J'en voyais le fond.

Il faisait chaud. Mais pas une chaleur agréable. Plutôt la chaleur étouffante d'une couverture qu'on vous plaquerait sur la figure & le nez. En plus, l'air était moite. J'en avais des picotements sur la peau.

Ça ne s'est pas arrangé quand des échos de voix me sont parvenus, depuis l'entrée de la mine. J'avais les poils de la nuque qui se dressaient.

Quelqu'un m'avait suivi.

Je devais aller plus profond.

J'ai levé ma bougie.

C'est là que je l'ai vue : une échelle qui sortait d'un trou dans le sol.

Je m'en suis approché prudemment.

Un trou noir au milieu de la terre toute noire.

Ma bougie n'éclairait pas assez pour me montrer le pied de l'échelle.

Juste les premiers barreaux du haut.

Je me suis retourné vers la pauvre jument qui attendait de travailler. Je l'ai rejointe & ai posé ma bougie sur une saillie de quartz. Puis je me suis débrouillé pour lui défaire ses attaches & lui ai tapé sur la croupe en montrant l'entrée de la mine.

— Fonce, ma belle, lui ai-je soufflé. Va foutre les jetons à Walt, va.

La jument s'est dirigée vers la sortie. Je savais bien qu'elle n'avait aucune chance de tuer Walt, mais j'espérais qu'elle lui fiche la frousse & peut-être le pousse à regagner la lumière du jour.

J'aurais bien aimé y être, moi, dans la lumière du jour.

Mais bon, je savais aussi que je devais continuer d'avancer jusqu'au retour des mineurs – là je serais en sécurité.

Du coup, j'ai pris la bougie entre mes dents, rabattu ma couverture en arrière pour dégager mes bras & me suis mis à descendre l'échelle aussi vite que la faible lumière me le permettait. Aussi, il me fallait tenir la tête penchée de sorte que la flamme ne brûle pas le bord de mon chapeau. Ça me déséquilibrait un peu & ne me facilitait pas la tâche.

On pourrait croire qu'il aurait fait plus frais et humide à mesure que je descendais. Pour la fraîcheur, c'était raté. J'ai même dû m'arrêter & retirer la bougie de ma bouche pour pouvoir m'éponger la figure & respirer correctement deux secondes. Ensuite j'ai dit une prière, remis la bougie dans ma bouche & repris la descente.

Quand enfin j'ai touché le dernier barreau de l'échelle, j'étais tellement soulagé que mes jambes ne me tenaient plus & que j'ai dû m'asseoir.

Puis j'ai regardé autour de moi & l'espace d'un instant l'étonnement a remplacé le soulagement.

Si vous avez déjà vu la charpente en bois d'une maison avant qu'on en monte les murs, imaginez la chose à perte de vue. Une centaine de gros cubes faits de rondins presque aussi gros & deux fois plus grands que moi s'étendaient dans l'obscurité devant moi, derrière, au-dessus et au-dessous. Je devais me trouver à une trentaine de mètres de profondeur & pourtant les mineurs avaient visiblement transporté là une forêt entière.

À la lueur de ma bougie, j'ai ensuite inspecté les lieux : on pouvait descendre encore. Un escalier étroit en tire-bouchon s'enfonçait dans l'obscurité brûlante et humide.

Pas question d'y mettre les pieds.

Autant plonger tout de suite dans le Puits de l'Enfer.

Reste que je n'étais séparé de Walt que par un bout de tunnel & une échelle – je savais bien qu'il me fallait encore descendre.

Au moins, je n'avais pas à tenir la bougie entre mes dents. N'empêche, j'avais l'impression d'être dans un de ces cauchemars où on tombe au ralenti.

Tout autour de moi j'avais cette structure en bois. Et j'avais beau connaître l'épaisseur de ces rondins, ils me faisaient quand même l'effet de cure-dents soutenant la montagne. Après peut-être quinze minutes d'une descente un peu étourdissante, j'ai enfin atteint le fond.

À ma grande surprise, c'est carrément une ville qui m'attendait là. Avec aussi des pioches, des haches, une petite scierie & des lanternes. J'ai même avisé des brouettes à moitié remplies de minerai, que les ouvriers devaient décharger dans des seaux pour remonter le tout *via* un système de cordes, de treuils & de poulies. J'ai alors compris que, n'importe quel autre jour, l'endroit aurait grouillé de mineurs.

Là, juste ça grouillait de rats.

Les rats, ça se mange, mais il faut vraiment être désespéré. En plus, ils étaient trop nombreux à mon goût.

Cela dit, ma bougie les a fait fuir. Je savais qu'ils se cachaient dans l'ombre. Je voyais leurs petits yeux rouges qui m'observaient.

En approchant de la paroi rocheuse, j'ai repéré ce qui devait être la Veine principale.

Le Filon de Comstock.

La Couche de Glaçage dans le Gâteau du mont Davidson. La flamme de ma bougie en faisait luire le quartz veiné de bleu – comme le marbre de l'International Hotel. Ces veines bleues, je savais que c'était de l'argent & qu'il faudrait les concasser, les filtrer, les amalgamer & les raffiner. Mais ça restait de l'argent, en couche épaisse. Et ça rendait fous les hommes comme les femmes.

Tout à coup j'ai eu la tête qui tournait & le souffle court ; la couverture que j'avais nouée autour de mon cou m'étouffait. Je l'ai dénouée puis renouée moins serrée & ça m'a passé. Je me demandais si des gens étaient déjà morts asphyxiés dans ce puits.

Puis j'ai levé ma bougie & ai fait le tour de la paroi rocheuse. J'entendais les rats qui grattaient & couinaient mais aucun ne se montrait. Je me cherchais une cachette depuis une dizaine de minutes quand j'ai senti un courant d'air chaud et humide sur mon visage.

J'allais murmurer une prière de remerciement au Seigneur quand, sans crier gare, ma bougie s'est éteinte & je me suis retrouvé plongé dans une obscurité encore plus noire qu'un taureau par une nuit sans lune.

FEUILLE DE COMPTES 41

J'étais coincé à 60 mètres sous terre dans une mine infestée de rats où il faisait plus sombre que dans un tonneau de goudron à minuit.

Et puis je me suis rappelé que des clients du Saloon à Huîtres & Alcools d'Almack s'étaient amusés à jeter des allumettes dans ma coupe de mendiant.

Je me suis mis à fouiller ma poche.

C'est là que je me suis aperçu que je n'avais plus mon sept-coups.

Ça m'a fait froid dans le dos. Je me suis revu le poser à l'entrée de la mine le temps d'allumer une bougie. Celle-là même qui venait de s'éteindre.

J'étais sans lumière ni arme à feu.

C'était le moment ou jamais de prier :

— Seigneur, ai-je dit, aidez-moi, je Vous en supplie.

J'ai inspiré bien fort puis ai enfoncé mes doigts dans la poche à l'intérieur de laquelle j'avais rangé les allumettes. J'y ai senti un petit trou & ai compris que la plupart des allumettes avaient dû passer à travers.

— Pitié, Seigneur.

Sur ce, mes doigts ont enfin rencontré une moitié d'allumette au fond d'un coin de la poche.

Je l'ai tâtée sur toute sa longueur & mon cœur s'est serré.

C'était la mauvaise moitié.

J'entendais les grattements des rats qui se rapprochaient de moi tandis que j'enfonçais mes doigts plus profondément dans ma poche.

Et là, au fin fond de la poche, coincée entre deux points de couture, se trouvait la moitié inflammable de l'allumette.

C'était ma seule chance d'éclairer l'obscurité. Alors je l'ai retirée précautionneusement de ma poche. Puis, la bougie dans ma main gauche, j'ai tenté de la main droite de la frotter contre la paroi rocheuse humide.

Premier essai, chou blanc.

Les rats se rapprochaient toujours.

Deuxième essai, chou blanc.

Un rat m'est passé sur le pied.

Enfin, au troisième essai, l'allumette s'est enflammée.

J'ai approché la flamme de la mèche de la bougie mais je tremblais tellement que je n'arrivais pas à les mettre en contact. La flamme était sur le point de me griller les doigts quand heureusement la mèche s'est embrasée. Elle a vacillé un peu, s'est stabilisée puis a brillé de mille feux.

Les rats ont décampé & j'ai poussé un ouf de soulagement, si fort que j'ai failli rééteindre la bougie. Du coup j'ai mis mon autre main en protection devant.

Et j'ai repris ma marche.

J'ai senti à nouveau le courant d'air chaud et humide : celui qui avait éteint ma bougie. Il provenait d'un tunnel situé dans l'une des zones les plus bleues de la paroi rocheuse. Tout en protégeant ma flamme, je me suis engagé prudemment dans ce passage obscur. Des pioches & des marteaux étaient entreposés contre les parois, elles-mêmes consolidées par des rondins qui faisaient comme une rangée de châssis de fenêtres à guillotine.

Le tunnel s'enfonçait en pente douce sur environ 400 mètres. De temps à autre, ça sentait l'eau mêlée d'alcali. Ma Evangeline m'avait expliqué une fois que certains puits des mines de Comstock descendaient à plus de 600 mètres de profondeur.

L'humidité empirait, la chaleur aussi & j'ai fini par atteindre une grotte toute moite d'un peu moins de 4 mètres sur 4. Terminus du tunnel. L'odeur d'alcali y était très forte.

Je me demandais d'où elle sortait, alors j'ai relevé ma bougie tout en la protégeant toujours. Sa flamme jaune me montrait plusieurs objets.

Une caisse en bois.

Quatre seaux en bois – trois à l'envers.

Une cafetière.

Des boîtes de conserve vides. (Des petites ; pas les modèles pour huîtres.)

Une pelle, une pioche & un marteau appuyés contre un mur.

Une bouteille de whisky vide.

J'ai fait un pas & ai failli trébucher sur une pancarte en bois posée par terre.

Dessus, il y avait marqué « DANJER ».

J'ai eu mal au ventre & la tête qui me tournait quand j'ai regardé ce qu'il y avait dessous. Un trou noir de près de 2 mètres de large. On aurait dit la bouche de Satan.

FEUILLE DE COMPTES 42

Je me suis approché tout doucement du bord du gouffre pour jeter un coup d'œil à l'intérieur. Impossible d'en apercevoir le fond. J'ai senti une bouffée d'alcali & me suis rappelé une autre chose que m'avait dite Ma Evangeline : certains puits aboutissent à des cours d'eau bouillante qui traversent la montagne. D'où la chaleur qu'il faisait. Une rivière d'eau bouillante coule dans les entrailles de Virginia City.

Soudain, un courant d'air chaud s'est engouffré dans le puits et a failli éteindre encore ma bougie. J'en ai allumé une autre à la première & les ai bien protégées de la main, tout près de moi pour éviter un nouveau désastre. Puis, en faisant attention à éviter le trou sans fond, je suis allé voir ce que contenait la caisse en bois.

Sur le côté, il y avait imprimé **N.B. JACOBS VIEUX BOURBON DE QUALITÉ, SAN FRANCISCO, CAL**.

En approchant mes bougies de la caisse, j'ai constaté qu'elle était encore à moitié remplie. Et sur le couvercle, on avait laissé trois bougies à moitié brûlées, un jeu de cartes, un restant de fromage moisi & quelques pages blanches d'un livre de comptes. L'humidité les avait déformées. Il y avait aussi des allumettes.

Alléluia ! J'en ai fourré quelques-unes dans mon sac-médecine de sorte à ne plus me retrouver dans le noir total.

À côté de la caisse se trouvaient les trois seaux renversés. Là, je suis assis sur l'un d'eux et j'écris mon histoire. Je me dis que les mineurs devaient venir ici pour boire du whisky, manger un morceau & jouer des allumettes au poker. Leur petit saloon souterrain. D'où sortaient les feuilles de compte, par contre, aucune idée. Elles leur servaient peut-être à compter les points ?

À part à l'entrée, il n'y a pas de courant d'air dans ce coin de la grotte, j'en ai donc profité pour fixer une bougie au couvercle de la caisse en faisant couler un peu de cire à la base. Avec l'autre, je suis retourné examiner les lieux. Le quatrième seau, à l'odeur, j'ai compris qu'il servait de toilettes. Les mineurs devaient sûrement le vider dans le Puits.

Ce qu'il y avait de bien, dans cette grotte chaude et humide, c'est que les rats n'avaient pas l'air de l'aimer. J'ai installé la cafetière de sorte à récupérer l'eau qui gouttait du plafond. J'en collecte deux, trois centimètres par heure. Elle contient le fameux mélange d'arsenic, de plombagine et de cuivre dont m'avait parlé Belle. Mais bon, vu que je dois mourir sous peu c'est pas trop grave.

J'ai eu faim, tout à l'heure, alors j'ai sorti de mon sac-médecine le couteau en silex de ma mère indienne. J'ai coupé le moisi du fromage & ai mangé le reste.

La faim est vite revenue, j'ai mangé la moisissure. Là, je mangerais du cuir tanné avec plaisir.

L'enterrement de la Petite Sally doit être terminé depuis longtemps parce que je sens les vibrations des Concasseurs de Quartz en surface, et aussi parfois une explosion qui fait carrément trembler la montagne. Par contre, aucun mineur n'est encore venu jusqu'à moi.

Où peuvent-ils bien être ? Dans une ville où les hommes travaillent vingt-quatre heures sur vingt-quatre, j'ai l'impression que cette mine est vide depuis des jours.

Il ne peut y avoir qu'une seule explication.

Walt et ses sbires se sont débrouillés pour barrer l'entrée aux mineurs, le temps de me retrouver & de me tuer.

J'ai trop chaud, je suis trempé. J'ai faim & je suis crevé. Il ne me reste quasiment plus de bougies. Mais au moins j'ai terminé mon histoire.

La fatigue m'empêche de bien voir maintenant. Alors je vais m'allonger & me reposer un peu.

Les derniers mots de cette histoire seront une prière : « Seigneur, pardonnez-moi pour toutes les erreurs que j'ai commises dans ma vie. Bénissez, s'il vous plaît, tous ceux qui ont été gentils envers moi sur le Terrain de Jeu du Diable & faites que Jace ne soit pas mort. Seigneur, accordez-moi de Vous voir au Paradis. Et faites que mes parents adoptifs & ma mère indienne s'y trouvent aussi. Amen. »

FEUILLE DE COMPTES 43

Vous avez dû deviner que je ne suis pas mort au fond du puits le plus profond de la Mine mexicaine, vu qu'il y a encore quelques pages d'écrites.

Vous aurez remarqué aussi que l'écriture est plus belle & moins effacée que quand j'étais dans la mine.

C'est que là je suis installé à une petite table devant la fenêtre de mon nouveau logement, dans B. Street – l'horizon s'étend à perte de vue. C'est l'ancienne remise de chez Bloomfield Tabac. Ça sent encore beaucoup le tabac et il n'y a pas plus de meubles que ça, mais j'ai au moins cette fenêtre. Je me suis installé un lit de camp, une table & une chaise – ça me suffit pour le moment.

Bref, je vous raconte la suite.

Quand j'avais découvert la fameuse grotte au fond du long tunnel en pente, il m'était venu une idée. J'avais arraché un long fil de ma couverture en laine et étais revenu sur mes pas. Ensuite, j'avais attaché ce fil entre deux poteaux, à hauteur de cheville. Je me disais que, au cas où Walt ou quelqu'un d'autre arriverait, ils allaient trébucher & je serais alerté.

J'ai dû m'endormir, vu que j'ai été réveillé par un juron. J'ai rouvert les yeux, il faisait Noir & Chaud.

Plus noir qu'un mur de charbon goudronné. La nuit la plus noire, c'était le plein jour, à côté. Et puis cette chaleur. J'en avais du mal à respirer. Et je baignais dans mon jus.

L'espace d'un instant j'ai cru que j'étais mort & que je me retrouvais en Enfer. Et puis j'ai senti les odeurs de whisky, d'urine, d'eau mêlée d'alcali, et tout m'est revenu. J'avais dû dormir davantage que je ne le voulais et ma bougie s'était éteinte. J'allais pour récupérer une allumette & une bougie dans mon sac-médecine, mais ça n'était pas la peine. J'avais repéré une faible lueur jaune qui s'immisçait dans ma grotte. Elle grossissait de seconde en seconde. J'en ai déduit que quelqu'un s'avançait dans le tunnel, une lanterne à la main.

Je me suis faufilé le long de la paroi rocheuse et ai tenté de soulever la pioche pour pouvoir me défendre. Elle était trop lourde. Du coup j'ai pris le marteau. Il n'était pas léger non plus, mais ça irait. Je me suis approché le plus près que j'ai osé de l'entrée de la grotte. Dos à la roche humide, j'ai prié pour que le visiteur soit un sauveteur. Le Marshal ou un mineur. Ou même Ping.

La lumière jaune se faisait plus forte, j'entendais des pas & des bruits de bouche. Et par-dessus les odeurs d'urine & d'eau teintée d'alcali, j'ai senti la lotion capillaire Bay Rum. Sur ce, le canon d'un gros revolver Colt Army est apparu comme une créature satanique sortie de son antre. Je ne voyais pas le propriétaire, juste le gros flingue. Dans la main gauche d'un homme. Entre ça et la crosse en os, j'étais sûr que c'était Walt.

Au moment où cette main pénétrait dans la grotte, j'ai brandi mon marteau au-dessus de ma tête & l'ai abattu aussi fort que j'ai pu sur le poignet de l'homme.

Le revolver a fait feu dans un vacarme qui a failli m'assourdir & en même temps la lampe s'est retrouvée par terre. On n'avait plus de lumière.

Quand mes oreilles ont arrêté de bourdonner, j'ai entendu une bordée de jurons que je ne peux pas reproduire ici. C'était Walt, plus de doutes. J'ai tiré une allumette de mon sac & l'ai frottée contre la roche. Sa flamme m'a permis de voir le desperado à moitié accroupi qui se tenait le poignet gauche, sa lampe éteinte par terre à côté de lui & son Colt Army presque à mes pieds.

J'ai soufflé l'allumette et – malgré l'obscurité totale – ai ramassé le revolver.

La voix de Walt était toute proche, il jurait toujours comme un charretier. Mais j'avais son flingue & je connaissais la disposition des lieux. Tenant son revolver dans la main droite, je me suis éloigné du desperado en me guidant de la main gauche contre la paroi rocheuse. Puis j'ai pris l'arme dans la main gauche pour frotter une allumette de la droite. Comme ça, j'ai pu repérer ma dernière bougie sur la caisse de whisky. Je l'ai allumée en tremblant et aussitôt après j'ai repris le revolver de ma bonne main.

— Purin de toi, j'ai mal ! criait Walt en serrant son poignet blessé. J'ai parcouru des milliers de kilomètres dans ce purin d'enfer et enfin je te retrouve. Autant essayer d'attraper une anguille beurrée. Et en plus tu m'as cassé le poignet.

— Pas un geste ou je vous explose les genoux, ai-je répliqué en le visant. Vous voulez quoi ?

— Tu le sais très bien. Ta Lettre, là.

— Eh ben vous ne l'aurez pas. Vous pouvez toujours vous gratter – excusez mon langage.

Walt a fait un pas vers moi.

Des deux pouces, j'ai armé son gros Colt.

— Ne croyez surtout pas que je ne le ferai pas.

— Oh-oh ! a-t-il dit en levant en l'air sa main valide, la paume face à moi. (Son autre main pendait, inutile.) Surtout t'emballe pas.

Il fouillait du regard les moindres recoins de la grotte comme s'il cherchait une arme ou autre.

Puis il m'a surpris en… souriant.

À la lueur de ma pauvre bougie, je n'arrivais pas à dire si c'était un Vrai Sourire ou un Faux.

— Je t'aime bien, Pinky, a-t-il dit sans cesser de sourire. Et je ne te veux aucun mal.

— Ah oui, ai-je rétorqué, alors pourquoi vous m'avez tiré dessus ?

Il a haussé les épaules & baissé légèrement sa main valide.

— Je cherchais juste à t'avertir. Si j'avais vraiment voulu, je t'aurais buté. En fait, si je suis venu jusqu'ici, c'est pour t'inviter à intégrer mon gang.

Il avait dit ça dans un grand sourire tout en se frottant la nuque de sa main valide.

— Intégrer votre gang ?

— Tout ce que tu as à faire, c'est me donner cette Lettre. On ira ensemble la montrer au Juge, on partagera les gains et tu viendras vivre avec moi dans une grande maison sur A. Street. D'ici la fin de l'année, j'aurai toute la ville dans ma poche.

— Pourquoi vous tenez à m'avoir dans votre gang ?

Walt chiquait toujours. Il a répondu :

— Ta mère était une squaw lakota, elle s'appelait Accroupie sur une Souche. Elle t'a pondu derrière un buisson dans un bled du nom de Calamity, près des monts Disappointment. J'ai juste ?

Je le regardais, incrédule. Comment savait-il tout cela ?

— Tu crois que ton père, c'était Robert Pinkerton, a-t-il continué. C'est faux.

Le gros revolver de Walt me tirait sur les bras mais je le gardais braqué sur le desperado.

— Vous mentez. Robert Pinkerton est mon père. Il m'a donné un bouton de sa veste de Détective du Chemin de Fer. Et il a envoyé cette Lettre à ma Mère pour qu'on soit riches.

— Nan. Cette Lettre est un faux, un très bon. Je le sais parce que c'est moi-même qui l'ai écrite.

J'ai baissé le Colt sans le désarmer.

— De quoi ? ai-je fait.

— Ta mère et moi, on avait mitonné ça ensemble. Sauf qu'entretemps elle s'est fait tuer par une bande de Shoshone et que depuis moi, je cherche à récupérer la Lettre. Elle est bien tournée. N'importe quel juge du Territoire la prendra pour une vraie.

— Mais elle porte la signature de mon père, Robert Pinkerton, comme témoin.

Walt a éclaté de rire.

— Robert Pinkerton n'est pas ton père. Et ce bouton ne lui appartient pas. Le bouton, je l'ai gagné au poker en 1852 contre un Détective du Chemin de Fer qui s'appelait Pinkerton.

C'était comme si on m'avait donné un coup de poing dans le ventre.

— Qu'est-ce que vous racontez ?

— Ce que je raconte, a répliqué Walt en souriant, c'est que je suis ton père.

FEUILLE DE COMPTES 44

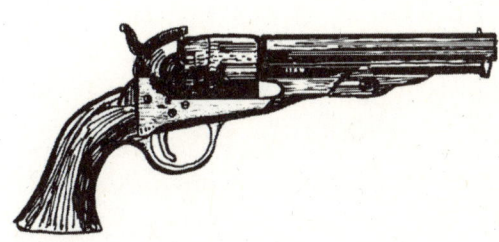

Ce n'était pas croyable.

Walt-Les-Copeaux — le desperado le plus sadique & le plus haï de la région — affirmait être mon père.

Il faisait si chaud tout d'un coup que j'étouffais.

— Vous n'êtes pas mon père, ai-je dit d'une voix que j'aurais voulue plus assurée.

— J'ai menti à ta mère. Je lui ai fait croire que j'étais Robert Pinkerton pour l'impressionner. Et ça a marché.

Mon cœur battait comme un Concasseur de Quartz. Je croyais avoir du Sang de Détective dans les veines, en fait visiblement c'était du Sang de Desperado.

— Ton fameux bouton, là, je te répète que je l'ai gagné au poker.

Il se frottait la nuque tout en souriant.

Ça m'a rappelé ce que Poker Face Jace m'avait expliqué : un menteur se reconnaît entre autres au fait qu'il se frotte la nuque.

Walt secouait la tête.

— Si tu me donnes cette Lettre, alors je saurai que je peux te faire confiance et on pourra s'associer.

Autre souvenir : Jace m'avait dit que parfois les gens hochent la tête de gauche à droite quand ils disent oui, et la hochent de haut en bas en disant non.

Jace m'avait appris à me fier au corps, pas aux paroles.

Une lueur d'espoir brillait encore dans mon cœur.

J'ai braqué le Colt sur un des genoux de Walt.

— Prouvez-moi que vous êtes mon père, lui ai-je ordonné. Dites-moi quel est mon véritable nom. Celui que ma mère indienne m'a donné.

Nouveau sourire. À la lumière de ma bougie, il avait quelque chose de maléfique.

— Ta mère t'a appelé Œil du Buisson.

Là, j'ai bien cru que j'allais m'effondrer, heureusement que j'étais assis sur un seau retourné. J'avais mal au cœur. Je voyais des petites lumières qui dansaient devant mes yeux. J'avais peut-être eu tout faux, finalement. Peut-être qu'il disait la Vérité.

Mais il s'était frotté la nuque.

Il avait fait non de la tête alors qu'il disait oui.

Et aussi il s'était arrêté de chiquer, comme lorsqu'il bluffait au poker.

Une idée m'est venue.

— Vous étiez là quand je suis né ? lui ai-je demandé.

— 'videmment. Je suis resté un an ou deux avec ta mère. Ensuite on s'est séparés. J'ai toujours regretté de ne pas être là pour t'apprendre à chasser, à pêcher, à tirer.

— Non, vous mentez. Vous n'êtes pas mon père. Je vais vous dire : quelqu'un vous a parlé de la Lettre que mon vrai père a envoyée à ma mère. Je parie même que ce quelqu'un c'était Tommy Three. C'est sûrement pour ça qu'il s'est mis avec ma Mère. Pour l'argent, pas par amour. Moi, je ne l'ai jamais aimé. Et je parie aussi que cette Lettre est authentique. Sinon vous n'auriez qu'à en fabriquer une autre.

Walt ne souriait plus ; il avait du mal à avaler sa salive.

— Tommy & ma Mère devaient venir à Virginia City. Peut-être même pour vous rencontrer. À moins que Tommy ait prévu de vous trouver seul. Sauf qu'il y a eu cette attaque et qu'ils se sont fait tuer. Vous avez retrouvé ma trace à Temperance, vous avez tué mes parents adoptifs & saccagé notre maison mais sans pouvoir mettre la main sur la Lettre. Vous m'avez suivi jusqu'à Virginia, et on vous a raconté que je n'avais pas connu mon vrai père, c'est ce qui vous a donné l'idée de vous faire passer pour lui. La personne qui vous a dit ça, c'était sûrement quelqu'un à qui j'avais révélé mon nom indien. Ça ne pouvait pas être Tommy Three, avant qu'il soit tué, vu que ma mère ne lui avait jamais dit le sien ni le mien. Le traître devait donc être un habitant de Virginia City. À tous les coups c'est ce sale menteur de Sam Clemens, pas vrai ?

Walt essayait de sourire mais même dans la pénombre je voyais que c'était un Faux Sourire.

— Je suis ton vrai père, a-t-il martelé. Donne-moi cette Lettre, fiston.

— Je ne suis pas votre fils, ai-je insisté. Si vous étiez vraiment mon père, si vous m'aviez réellement

tenu dans vos bras à ma naissance, jamais vous ne m'appelleriez « fiston ».
— Et pourquoi donc ?
— Parce que je suis une fille.

FEUILLE DE COMPTES 45

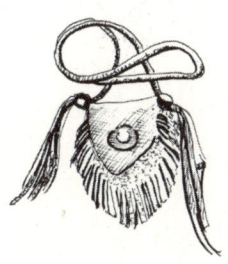

Walt, ça lui a coupé la chique. On ne m'avait jamais montré une Expression n° 4 aussi marquée. Il ressemblait à cet homme que j'avais vu une fois se prendre une ruade de mule.

— Tu es une… *fille* ?

Il avait prononcé ce mot comme si c'était une horreur.

— Parfaitement, ai-je confirmé en abaissant le lourd revolver.

— C'est impossible. Tout le monde sait que tu es un garçon. Tommy Three lui-même me l'avait dit. Et les gens de Temperance aussi. Même toi quand tu étais déguisé en fille t'avais pas l'air d'en être une.

— Ma mère indienne savait que je serais plus en sécurité si je me faisais passer pour un garçon. C'est elle qui m'obligeait à m'habiller comme ça. En même temps, ça m'allait. Et Ma Evangeline trouvait aussi que c'était bien vu. (Je me suis approché de Walt.) Et là, vous venez d'admettre que vous aviez connu Tommy Three, donc cette fois je suis sûr que vous êtes un menteur.

— T'es pas une fille. Mais t'es pas non plus comme les autres garçons. T'es ni blanc ni indien. Tu sais quoi ? (Il était passé de l'Expression n° 4 à la n° 3 & il a craché par terre.) T'es qu'un paria.

Je regardais le desperado dans les yeux ; j'avais du mal à avaler ma salive.

— Peut-être. Mais je suis aussi P.K. Pinkerton. Et maintenant je sais ce que j'ai à faire.

Alors j'ai posé le lourd revolver & sorti la Lettre de mon sac-médecine.

Ensuite, dans le plus grand calme, j'ai déchiré consciencieusement le document qui donnait au Porteur le droit de propriété sur la moitié de Virginia City & la Couche de Glaçage argenté de son sous-sol. Et j'ai laissé retomber les bouts de papier à mes pieds.

— Non ! a hurlé Walt.

Là-dessus, il m'a encore pris par surprise. Glissant sa main valide dans sa poche, il en a retiré une arme. Mon Smith & Wesson à sept coups. Il le braquait sur moi.

Je me disais : « Avec celui-là, au moins, je ne risque rien, par contre si j'arrive à le toucher avec le sien je ne suis pas obligé de le tuer. »

Donc j'ai ramassé le gros Colt à crosse en os.

Une détonation a retenti. Au même instant j'ai eu l'impression de recevoir un violent coup de poing et je me suis effondré.

Sam Clemens s'était trompé.

Apparemment, on peut toucher sa cible avec un Smith & Wesson à sept coups.

FEUILLE DE COMPTES 46

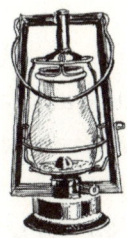

Mon épaule gauche me brûlait & ça sentait la poudre dans la grotte. Je me suis rassis et mon regard est tombé sur une tache de sang sur ma chemise en daim, au niveau de mon bras gauche. J'ai relevé la tête à la seconde où Walt réarmait le Smith & Wesson pour faire feu.

J'ai aussitôt décampé. Le desperado, lui, a fait un pas en avant.

Erreur fatale.

Vous vous rappelez le puits dont je vous ai parlé, celui qui donnait sur une rivière d'eau bouillante ? Je m'étais douté qu'un truc comme ça risquait d'arriver, alors j'avais retiré la pancarte « DANJER » et mis à la place ma couverture pour masquer le trou. Après, j'avais saupoudré le tout de terre pour parfaire l'illusion.

Quand Walt s'est avancé pour me tirer dessus, il a marché sur une couverture crasseuse recouvrant un puits d'un bon millier de mètres aboutissant à une rivière d'eau bouillante.

La première détonation résonnait encore dans la grotte lorsqu'un second coup est parti en même temps que la figure ahurie et les bras tendus de Walt disparaissaient en un éclair. Quand le second écho s'est tu, j'entendais encore les cris du desperado. De moins en moins forts à mesure qu'il approchait de l'Enfer – excusez mon langage.

Serrant mon bras blessé d'une main, je me suis relevé puis approché du bord du gouffre. J'ai regardé à l'intérieur. On n'y voyait rien, juste un trou noir et profond comme j'espère ne plus jamais en voir de ma vie.

Walt se trouvait quelque part là-dedans. Il n'avait peut-être même pas fini de tomber. Ou alors il bouillait déjà dans la rivière. En tout cas le monde était débarrassé de lui.

La lueur vacillante de ma bougie se réfléchissait sur un bout de métal dans la poussière : mon Smith & Wesson à sept coups. Il avait dû échapper à Walt au moment où il était passé à travers la couverture. Je ne suis pas sûr que Pa Emmet aurait apprécié, mais j'ai remercié le Seigneur.

J'ai contourné le gouffre pour récupérer le revolver. J'ai réussi à dégager le barillet d'une seule main puis à remplacer les cartouches usagées par des neuves.

Sur ce, je n'ai pas pu faire autrement que de vomir.

J'avais promis à Ma Evangeline de ne jamais boire d'alcool fort, mais j'avais ce goût de vomi dans la bouche et Walt avait renversé ma cafetière d'eau. Du coup, j'ai pris une bouteille de whisky dans la caisse, en ai cassé le goulot puis versé un peu du contenu dans la boîte de conserve qui me servait de verre.

Ça avait un goût atroce mais au moins ça rendait supportable la douleur dans mon bras.

Pas question de perdre la tête pour autant.

Boz et Extra Dub risquaient de me retrouver à tout moment. J'avais deux armes sur moi, je pouvais tenter de sortir de cette mine.

J'ai récupéré le Colt Army de Walt que j'avais posé sur la caisse de whisky. J'ai eu du mal à en inspecter le barillet d'une seule main, mais je me suis quand même débrouillé pour voir combien de charges il restait à l'intérieur. J'ai aussi réussi à rentrer ma chemise en daim dans mon pantalon. Ensuite, après m'être assuré que le barillet du revolver de Walt était bien entre deux compartiments, j'ai fourré le Colt sous ma chemise. Comme il était dur & que ça faisait une bosse sur ma poitrine, j'ai mis les feuilles de comptes en rembourrage. Enfin j'ai attrapé la lampe et deux, trois autres trucs qui étaient tombés par terre. Je l'ai rallumée d'une seule main.

J'avais donc une lumière qui ne s'éteindrait pas au premier courant d'air, et deux armes à feu. Que l'un des sbires de Walt se pointe, je saurais le recevoir. Évidemment, j'avais promis à ma mère agonisante de ne jamais tuer, mais rien ne m'empêchait de viser les jambes. Ça les découragerait de me suivre.

C'est franchement dur de monter un escalier en colimaçon avec un seul bras pour s'appuyer. Surtout si on est crevé, si on a la tête qui tourne & qu'on tient une lampe entre ses dents, avec une liasse de feuilles et un gros revolver sous sa chemise. Mais au bout de quelque temps, j'ai fini par arriver au niveau supérieur : la grande galerie. J'en ai profité pour poser la lampe et me reposer un peu, adossé au gros filon de quartz. Je dégoulinais de sueur, de sang et de cire.

J'ai dû perdre connaissance, vu que j'ai ensuite été réveillé par un bruit.

C'étaient des rats qui cavalaient près de moi, sans oser entrer dans le cercle de lumière de ma lampe.

Autre bruit : des pas qui descendaient l'échelle.

Je me suis relevé & ai failli perdre à nouveau connaissance, mais je me suis efforcé de respirer à fond et j'ai pu me cacher dans la pénombre.

Je me tenais derrière un gros rondin quand j'ai vu apparaître un halo lumineux au niveau de l'échelle.

J'ai passé une main sous le col de ma chemise pour en retirer le Colt Army. Une grande inspiration puis j'ai armé le revolver.

— P.K. ? demandait une voix qui me rappelait quelque chose. P.K., tu es par là ?

C'était Poker Face Jace.

— Jace ! C'est vous ? Vous n'êtes pas mort ?

Ma voix était très faible mais il m'a entendu. Je l'ai vu s'approcher de moi. Sa lampe à pétrole l'éclairait de bas en haut, j'avais l'impression qu'il souriait.

— Non, a-t-il répondu. Je suis bien vivant.

J'ai relâché le chien du Colt puis ai glissé l'arme sous ma chemise.

— Je croyais que le complice de Walt vous avait tué, ai-je dit.

— Stonewall est intervenu juste à temps. Et aussi, j'avais un jeu de cartes dans la poche de ma chemise – ça a arrêté la balle, j'ai juste été renversé en arrière. Stonewall est certain d'avoir touché un des hommes de Walt, mais ils ont réussi à s'enfuir. (Il approchait sa lampe de mon bras ensanglanté.) Et toi, ça va ?

— Ça peut aller. Walt m'a eu avec mon sept-coups mais à l'heure qu'il est il doit rôtir en enfer.

— Bonne nouvelle. Est-ce que tu pourrais prendre ma lampe ? Je vais pas pouvoir te porter tout en la tenant.

J'ai fait oui de la tête puis ai empoigné sa lampe de ma main valide.

Jace m'a pris dans ses bras & m'a ramené au pied de l'échelle. Il sentait la fumée de cigare & le café. Quel bonheur.

— Je l'ai ! a-t-il hurlé. J'ai retrouvé P.K.

— Besoin d'aide ?

La voix grave de Stonewall semblait très lointaine.

— Non ! lui a répondu Jace. Ça va aller.

Il allait pour me basculer par-dessus son épaule quand il s'est arrêté d'un coup.

— Eh, mais qu'est-ce que tu as là ? a-t-il demandé.

— C'est le revolver de Walt.

— Tu ferais mieux de me le donner.

J'ai fait ce qu'il disait. Jace a glissé le Colt sous sa ceinture & m'a pris sur son épaule. J'essayais de ne pas crier de douleur. Je tenais toujours la lampe de la main droite. Plus on montait, plus je voyais la dégringolade qu'on allait faire si jamais l'échelle cassait. Je me cramponnais à Jace & priais : surtout que je ne tourne plus de l'œil ni ne vomisse.

Quand on est arrivés en haut de l'échelle, Stonewall nous attendait avec une autre lampe.

Sa figure patibulaire avait une expression de joie, c'était bizarre à voir.

Le sang battait dans mes oreilles & mon bras me lançait. J'ai dû encore m'évanouir un instant parce que lorsque j'ai rouvert les yeux je n'avais plus la tête à l'envers. Stonewall me portait dans ses bras & Jace marchait à côté de nous, il tenait les deux lampes.

Dans le long tunnel sombre, on a croisé la jument noire. Mis à part nous trois & cette bête, la mine était déserte. Je n'y comprenais rien.

Enfin nous avons retrouvé la merveilleuse lumière jaune du jour. Le soleil éblouissant & l'air frais me faisaient l'effet d'un grand verre d'eau fraîche. Si j'en avais eu la force, j'aurais bien embrassé la terre.

Je me suis juré : « Plus jamais je ne mettrai les pieds dans un tunnel. »

Le soleil m'agressait, j'ai dû me protéger les yeux de ma main valide. Au bout d'un moment, j'ai fini par distinguer un attroupement autour de nous.

— Y a pas d'effondrement, leur a annoncé Jace. Pouvez tous retourner bosser.

— Vise un peu, m'a dit Stonewall.

D'un mouvement de la tête, il indiqua une pancarte à l'entrée de la mine :

NE PAS ENTRER. EFFONDREMENT.

— Tout cela serait donc une farce ? a demandé un homme.

On le repérait facilement, avec ses lunettes, au milieu de tous les mineurs réunis.

— Ouais, a fait Jace. Walt-Les-Copeaux vous a joué un sale tour. Mais ne vous inquiétez pas. Il est pas près de recommencer. Pas vrai, P.K. ?

— Non, monsieur.

Stonewall s'est écarté pour laisser entrer les mineurs & leur contremaître qui aboyait déjà des ordres.

Alors qu'on s'éloignait de l'entrée de la Mine mexicaine, Jace s'est penché vers moi pour me dire :

— C'est pour ça qu'on a mis tout ce temps à te retrouver. À tous les coups c'est Walt qui avait installé cette pancarte. Et tout le monde y a cru.

— Comment vous avez su que j'étais là-dedans, vous ?

On se dirigeait vers la ville, Stonewall me portant & Jace cheminant nonchalamment à côté de nous.

— Pas mal de gens ont vu Walt te courir après, a-t-il expliqué. Mais c'est une gamine qui habite pas loin, dans A. Street, qui nous a tout raconté. Elle regardait par la fenêtre dimanche matin quand elle t'a vu te précipiter dans la Mine mexicaine. Elle l'a annoncé à son père qui l'a répété au Marshal et le Marshal m'a prévenu. J'étais passé à son bureau ce matin pour voir si on avait des nouvelles de toi.

Je me suis demandé : « Qui ça peut bien être, cette fille ? »

Jace n'avait pas terminé :

— Quand on a vu Boz & Extra Dub rôder dans le coin, on s'est dit que Walt avait dû entrer dans la mine.

— Et ils sont où, maintenant, ces deux-là ? ai-je voulu savoir.

— Dès qu'ils nous ont aperçus, ils ont sauté sur leurs chevaux et ont mis les bouts. Il y a des mandats d'arrêt contre eux.

— Je suis resté là-dedans longtemps ?

— Environ trente heures.

— Un jour, pas plus ? J'aurais cru que ça avait duré une semaine.

Sourire de Jace.

— Nan. On n'est que lundi. Lundi midi. Que dirais-tu d'une tasse de café noir & d'un bon gâteau ?
— Bee.
— De quoi ?
— La fille qui vous a aidés à me retrouver, elle ne s'appelait pas Bee Bloomfield ?
— Je suis pas trop sûr. Mais la voilà qui arrive, tu n'as qu'à lui poser la question.

FEUILLE DE COMPTES 47

— Bon, a fait Sam Clemens pendant que le docteur découpait la manche de ma chemise en daim, visiblement j'avais tort. Ce petit sept-coups peut atteindre une cible, donc.

— Exactement, ai-je rétorqué. Et ça fait un mal de chien – excusez mon langage. D'toute façon, je ne vous parle pas. Vous n'êtes qu'une Vermine hypocrite & un menteur.

Nous nous trouvions dans l'annexe du *Territorial Enterprise*, dans A. Street. Sam Clemens était allé enquêter sur le soi-disant « Effondrement » de la mine et m'avait aperçu en compagnie de Jace, de Stonewall & de Bee Bloomfield. Il leur a demandé de m'amener ici puis a envoyé Horace, l'attrape-science de l'imprimeur, chercher un docteur.

J'étais étendu sur une des couchettes. Jace, Stonewall & quelques employés du journal étaient réunis autour de moi pendant que le docteur examinait mon bras. Bee Bloomfield était là aussi. Elle tenait la poêle pour le docteur.

— Pourquoi me traites-tu de Vermine hypocrite & de menteur ? a demandé Sam Clemens. Hypocrite, oui, je le confesse & il m'est aussi arrivé de mentir, mais pourquoi « Vermine » ?

— Parce que vous avez révélé mon vrai nom indien et plein d'autres trucs à Walt-Les-Copeaux.

— Il menaçait de me couper une oreille si je ne lui apprenais rien sur toi. J'ai pensé que ton nom indien serait le renseignement le plus inoffensif.

— Eh ben vous avez mal pensé. Walt-Les-Copeaux a cherché à se faire passer pour mon père. Et vu qu'il connaissait mon nom indien, il a failli me convaincre.

— C'est quoi, ton nom indien ? est intervenu Poker Face Jace. J'aimerais bien savoir.

Sam Clemens allait lui répondre mais je lui ai coupé l'herbe sous le pied :

— Je vous le défends !

— Avale ceci, m'a dit le docteur en me tendant un verre contenant un liquide jaune pâle.

Le docteur avait les cheveux blancs et portait des lunettes ovales.

— Qu'est-ce que c'est ?

— Du laudanum. Ça endormira la douleur le temps que j'extraie la balle.

Puis il m'a relevé la tête, & Bee a porté le verre à ma bouche & m'a aidé à le boire. Ça avait un goût bizarre, j'avais la bouche qui me picotait.

— Comment t'as fait pour comprendre que Walt mentait ? m'a demandé Poker Face Jace.

Je me suis rallongé.

— Il se frottait la nuque & faisait non de la tête. Mais surtout, à un moment, il a arrêté de chiquer. C'est là que j'ai su qu'il bluffait.

— Bien joué. Tu apprends vite. Moi, il m'a fallu une heure pour m'en rendre compte.

— Je suis un bon menteur, a repris Sam Clemens. J'ai rédigé un article sur seize charrettes de foin alors qu'il n'y en avait en fait qu'une seule. Par contre je ne suis pas une Vermine.

Je ressentais comme une chaleur & j'avais l'impression de flotter.

— Vos oreilles ne sont pas banales, ai-je dit à Sam Clemens. Elles sont sans lobes.

— Et les miennes ? a demandé Bee en repoussant ses cheveux pour me les montrer.

— Elles sont bien arrondies.

— Je crois que le laudanum fait effet, a estimé le docteur. Je vais pouvoir chercher la balle. (Il m'a souri.) Alors comme ça, jeune homme, vous vous appelez Pinkerton... comme moi.

— Vraiment ? ai-je fait.

— Vraiment. Je suis le docteur Thomas H. Pinkerton. Tu es parent avec les Pinkerton de Chicago ?

— C'est ce que je pensais. Là je ne suis plus trop sûr.

J'avais la nausée. Peut-être parce que Doc Pinkerton farfouillait à l'intérieur de mon bras.

— Ne te bile pas, m'a rassuré Sam Clemens. Tu n'es ni le premier ni le dernier à ne pas savoir qui est ton père.

— Ce dont je suis sûr, c'est que j'ai tout d'un Pinkerton. J'aime résoudre des énigmes et comprendre comment les choses fonctionnent. J'aime bien me déguiser aussi.

— Eurêka ! s'est exclamé le docteur en nous montrant le petit pois métallique qu'il tenait entre ses pincettes. Voici le coupable. Calibre .22.

— Pas plus gros qu'une granule homéopathique, a fait Clemens. Il en faudrait une sacrée dose pour abattre notre Pinky. En même temps, je devrais peut-être récupérer mon sept-coups.

— Si ça ne vous dérange pas, suis-je intervenu, j'aimerais bien le garder. Même si Walt m'a tiré dessus avec. Et j'espère que vous n'en parlerez pas dans le journal. Sinon, les sbires de Walt pourraient revenir se venger.

Le reporter a poussé un gros soupir avant d'acquiescer :

— C'est bon, tu peux le garder ; et, non, je n'en parlerai pas dans le journal. (Puis, à voix basse et la tête collée à la mienne :) Ton histoire vient de me donner une idée d'article – « Un massacre d'Indiens ». J'ai ta permission ?

— Et comment !

De l'autre bout de la pièce, quelqu'un a dit :

— Les mimiques et les tics, c'est peut-être bon pour Poker Face Jace, mais moi, ça ne me convainc pas. Es-tu bien certain que Walt n'était pas ton père ?

C'était l'homme avec le chapeau en tuyau de poêle & la canne que j'avais vu au saloon avec Sam Clemens.

— Lui, c'est M. Joe Goodman, a chuchoté le reporter. Propriétaire du *Territorial Enterprise*. Mon patron.

— Je suis sûr & certain, ai-je répondu à Goodman. J'ai même forcé Walt à reconnaître qu'il mentait.

— Mais comment ? ont demandé en chœur plusieurs voix.

— Facile. Je lui ai dit qu'en fait j'étais une fille. Et que s'il était réellement mon père il devrait le savoir. Ça l'a scié, et il s'est mis à bafouiller.

Ils me dévisageaient tous. Visiblement, eux aussi ça les avait sciés. Sam Clemens en avait même perdu sa pipe.

Jace promenait son regard sur toutes les personnes présentes en se frottant la nuque.

— Mais tu blaguais, P.K., pas vrai ? Tu bluffais pour l'obliger à te Montrer Sa Main, nan ?

— Oui, ai-je confirmé. (Je baignais toujours dans cette chaleur & avais encore cette impression de flotter.) C'était du Bluff pour l'obliger à me Montrer Sa Main. Ça a marché.

FEUILLE DE COMPTES 48

Le lendemain après-midi, j'ai enfin pu me rendre au Bureau du Juge situé en face des locaux du *Territorial Enterprise*. Je portais à la fois des habits d'Indien, de mineur et de fils de riche. Pour remplacer ma chemise en daim ensanglantée, Isaiah Coffin m'en avait offert une en flanelle douce, rouge délavé, et une veste bleu marine à boutons de cuivre. J'avais gardé mon pantalon en daim à franges, mes mocassins souples & aussi le chapeau mou noir avec la plume de faucon que Jace m'avait donné. Et bien sûr mon sac-médecine, bien caché sous ma chemise.

J'étais d'abord passé chez le Notaire de B. Street. Il m'avait tamponné un papier que j'apportais ensuite au Juge. La chose avait dû se savoir parce que, au moment où j'arrivais devant son Bureau, j'étais suivi par tout un groupe de badauds et d'amis, dont Dan De Quille qui rentrait tout juste de Carson City, bien ravi d'être encore en un seul morceau.

Il y avait une vingtaine de personnes dans le Bureau du Juge, tous barbus, crasseux, les cheveux en bataille, qui venaient faire valoir leurs droits. Mais en me voyant, le bras gauche en écharpe, ils se sont écartés comme la mer Rouge devant Moïse.

— R'gardez ! s'est exclamé un des mineurs. (À son accent, il venait des Cornouailles.) C'est le petit qui a buté Walt-Les-Copeaux.

— Paraît qu'il lui a collé une balle de Smith & Wesson n° 1 entre les deux yeux, a fait un autre.

— Moi, j'ai entendu dire qu'il l'avait fait valdinguer par terre avant de l'envoyer dans un puits sans fond avec de l'eau bouillante à l'intérieur.

— Si ça se trouve il a pas fini de tomber, s'est réjoui un troisième mineur en se frottant les mains.

— D'où c'est possible, ça, a demandé le premier, un puits sans fond avec de l'eau bouillante à l'intérieur ?

— Bonjour, jeune homme, m'a dit le juge.

Il avait des sourcils roux broussailleux & une moustache qui lui faisait comme deux queues de renard de part et d'autre de son nez. Un petit écriteau posé sur son bureau disait : **M. RUFUS E. ARICK, JUGE**.

— Tu viens pour faire valoir un droit ?

— Pas exactement, ai-je répondu en lui remettant une feuille de papier. Mais j'ai ceci.

M. Rufus E. Arick a regardé mon document en grimaçant.

— C'est une affiche **WANTED**. Elle concerne Walt Darmitage – alias Walt-Les-Copeaux –, recherché dans quatre États et Territoires pour meurtres, vols et tortures. La **RÉCOMPENSE** est fixée à 2 000 $. (Il a relevé la tête.) Si c'est la récompense que tu viens réclamer, tu devrais t'adresser au Marshal. Suivant !

— Une seconde, ai-je ajouté. Regardez derrière.

— Plaît-il ?

— Regardez l'autre côté de l'affiche.

M. Rufus E. Arick a fait ce que je disais. Sur l'autre côté de l'affiche, j'avais collé tous les morceaux de la Lettre que j'avais déchirée. Je les avais tous récupérés sauf un, mais c'était juste un coin de la feuille, sans importance. L'important, c'est qu'on pouvait lire ce qui était écrit, malgré les taches de sang.

Le juge a regardé la Lettre recollée. Puis il m'a regardé. Puis il a encore regardé la Lettre recollée.

— C'est là le document que tu es venu me remettre, petit ? Je ne suis pas certain qu'il soit vraiment légal.

— Regardez en bas, il a été signé au mois de novembre 1857 par Ethan Allen Grosh avec Robert Pinkerton comme témoin.

Rufus E. Arick hochait lentement la tête.

— Quand bien même, il s'est écoulé beaucoup de temps : près de cinq années. Tu vas sûrement devoir porter l'affaire au tribunal. La bataille risque de durer des mois. On ne te fera aucun cadeau.

— Qui ça, « on » ?

— La moitié des mineurs de Virginia City. Cette lettre est une menace pour eux. Les seules personnes qui vont s'enrichir, ce seront les Avocats.

Ça m'a mis le moral au fond des mocassins. J'aurais risqué ma vie pour rien du tout ?

— T'en fais pas, gamin, a dit un des mineurs. C'est comme ça que ça se passe dans le coin. Un jour tu touches le jackpot, le lendemain il te reste plus que tes bottes.

Au même instant, quelqu'un a annoncé :

— Je souhaite acheter cette Lettre.

FEUILLE DE COMPTES 49

Dans le Bureau du Juge, tout le monde s'est retourné vers la porte.

L'homme qui se tenait là portait une redingote noire & un pantalon gris. Il était blond, rasé de près et arborait de gros favoris.

— Je suis Billy Chollar, a-t-il indiqué. Le propriétaire de la Mine Chollar.

— Cette mine, m'a chuchoté Dan De Quille, occupe une trentaine de mètres du Filon de Comstock, au sud de Virginia, pas très loin de la Butte.

— M. William Morris Stewart, mon avocat, m'a conseillé d'acheter ta Lettre. Il me représente déjà dans une affaire importante et il affirme que je n'ai pas besoin de me lancer dans une nouvelle. Je te propose donc de te céder une portion de ma mine. Tu en toucheras un dividende d'au moins 200 $ par mois. Assez pour vivre confortablement, même dans cette ville.

— Mon père qui est mort disait toujours que les Avocats sont des Suppôts de Satan.

Billy Chollar s'est avancé & a ôté son chapeau. Il avait de petites poches sous les yeux qui lui donnaient un air fatigué.

— Tu vas devoir surmonter ton préjugé & engager un avocat si tu tiens réellement à faire valoir ton droit. Et je te recommande d'en choisir un bon parce qu'il devra se battre contre moi-même et tous les autres Propriétaires de Mine. Au final, d'ici une dizaine d'années tu seras peut-être l'homme le plus riche de la région. Ou bien tu seras ruiné. (Il a alors poussé un soupir & baissé les yeux.) Aujourd'hui, je regrette de ne pas m'être mis d'accord avec la Compagnie minière Potosi. Au train où vont les choses, notre procès va durer des années. (Puis il m'a regardé dans les yeux :) L'offre que je te fais est des plus généreuses.

J'ai observé ses pieds. Ils étaient dirigés vers moi. Ses épaules étaient détendues, ses mains tenaient son chapeau. Rien n'indiquait qu'il bluffait. J'ai adressé un coup d'œil à Jace. Il recrachait sa fumée en l'air & acquiesçait discrètement.

Dans ma tête j'ai eu l'impression d'entendre la voix de Pa Emmet & j'ai répété tout haut :

— L'argent est la source de tous les maux.

Ce que Sam Clemens a corrigé en :

— Le *manque* d'argent est la source de tous les maux.

C'est alors qu'un prospecteur au regard un peu fou est venu se coller à moi.

— Ton Billy Chollar doit crever d'envie de récupérer ta Lettre, gamin. Fais-le cracher, ce gros richard. Prends donc un avocat et bats-toi.

C'est ça qui m'a décidé.

— Je vous remercie, monsieur Chollar. J'accepte votre offre.

Certains ont grogné, d'autres ont applaudi. Il y en a même qui ont lancé leur chapeau en l'air.

Billy Chollar est alors venu me tendre la main.

— Sage décision, a-t-il jugé. Il n'est pas facile de résister à la Tentation dans une ville comme celle-ci. Serrons-nous la main.

Il avait la main ferme & sèche. Et il me gratifiait d'un Vrai Sourire.

— Et l'affiche **WANTED** ? est intervenu Dan De Quille. Les 2 000 $ devraient revenir à P.K.

— Je serais ravi de te conduire immédiatement chez le Marshal, a annoncé Billy Chollar en remettant son chapeau. Quand tu auras touché la récompense, tu pourras me donner l'affiche avec le contrat au verso. Ensuite tu viendras avec moi à mon Bureau et nous discuterons de la portion que je vais te céder autour d'une tasse de café. Mon boghei nous attend dehors.

Je l'ai regardé sans rien dire.

— En signe de bonne volonté, a-t-il ajouté, accepte ces 200 $ en or.

Il a sorti un portefeuille en cuir de sa redingote & s'est mis à compter des pièces d'or.

Il a voulu m'en donner dix.

J'ai hésité.

Voyant ça, Dan De Quille m'a dit :

— Je crois que tu peux lui faire confiance, P.K. En plus, t'as pas loin de cinquante témoins dans cette pièce, dont quelques reporters influents.

J'ai accepté les pièces & les ai glissées dans mon sac-médecine. 200 $, ça faisait un poids. Agréable, comme poids.

— Eh, P.K. ! s'est écriée une femme. Maintenant tu vas pouvoir partir pour Chicago, t'installer comme Détective et mener Grand Train.

Je me suis retourné : une jolie dame habillée en bleu se tenait au bras d'Isaiah Coffin. Le couple se frayait un chemin à travers les mineurs.

Je n'en revenais pas.

C'était Belle Donne.

FEUILLE DE COMPTES 50

" NOUS NE FERMONS PRESQUE JAMAIS L'ŒIL "

J'ai tiré mon Smith & Wesson de ma poche, l'ai armé et braqué sur Belle Donne.

— Oh, P.K., a-t-elle rigolé. Ne fais pas l'enfant. Isaiah et moi allons nous marier. Et nous voulions te remercier ! Si tu ne nous avais pas attachés l'un à l'autre…

Sans abaisser mon arme, j'ai jeté un coup d'œil à Isaiah Coffin.

— Ne lui faites jamais confiance, l'ai-je prévenu.

— Trop tard… Je suis fou amoureux.

— Et moi ? a dit Titus Jepson, fou de douleur.

Il serrait sa main gauche enveloppée d'un lourd bandage.

Belle l'a embrassé sur la joue.

— Navrée, cher Titus. Mais je compte devenir Actrice dès que le nouveau Melodeon ouvrira. Isaiah connaît le propriétaire, il m'a promis de me le présenter. Un jour, qui sait ? je me produirai peut-être à San Francisco, Boston ou même Chicago. (Se tournant vers moi :) On s'y verra peut-être, P.K.

J'ai désarmé mon revolver et l'ai rangé dans ma poche.

— Je n'irai pas à Chicago, ai-je annoncé.

— À Londres, alors, a proposé Isaiah Coffin. C'est dans tes moyens à présent.

— Je ne crois pas.

— San Francisco, a fait Grafton T. Brown.

Oui, lui, aussi était présent. L'artiste tenait son carnet à dessins sous le bras.

— Nan.

— Si tu restes à Virginia, m'a confié Titus Jepson, tu paieras demi-tarif chez moi jusqu'à la fin des temps. Tu mangeras du gâteau au petit déjeuner tous les jours. Du moment que tu prends un bon repas le soir.

Je me suis tourné vers Jace. Il m'a fait un clin d'œil.

— J'ai décidé de rester ici quelques années encore, ai-je déclaré.

Ce qui m'y poussait, je ne le leur ai pas expliqué, mais voilà l'idée : si je réussis à montrer à mon père Robert Pinkerton que je suis un bon Détective, peut-être qu'il sera fier de moi. Peut-être même qu'il me demandera de venir travailler avec lui dans l'agence de Chicago que dirige son frère.

En attendant, je me disais que le meilleur endroit pour apprendre le métier, c'était Virginia.

— Oui, ai-je répété, je compte rester ici.

— Pour P.K., hip-hip-hip ? s'est écrié Titus Jepson.

— Hourra ! ont hurlé en chœur toutes les personnes présentes.

Quand les cris se sont calmés, Dan De Quille m'a demandé :

— Et tu comptes te lancer dans la spéculation comme nous tous ?

— Non. Je vais plutôt monter ma propre entreprise.

— Excusez-moi, s'est alors imposée une voix de femme. Je suis Miss Prudence Feather, de la First Ward School. Et il me semble que ta place est dans ma classe.

Je l'ai reconnue : la femme en noir qui dînait au Colombo Restaurant.

— L'école, ai-je répliqué, j'ai déjà essayé. À Dayton, c'était, et les terreurs de la classe s'en prenaient à moi. Je sais lire, écrire et compter. Le reste, je devrais pouvoir l'apprendre tout seul.

— Bien dit, a approuvé Sam Clemens en crachant une bouffée répugnante. Moi-même, je n'ai jamais laissé l'école se mêler de mon éducation. J'ai commencé à travailler à l'âge de 13 ans.

— Moi à 12, a précisé Dan De Quille.

— Je t'apprendrai te battre méthode ancienne chinoise, a annoncé une voix à l'accent étranger. (Je me suis retourné : Ping jouait des coudes pour me rejoindre.) Quand tu auras payé ce que tu me dois : 500 $.

J'ai acquiescé. Je comptais bien tenir ma promesse.

— Les arts martiaux, ça peut toujours servir, a dit Isaiah Coffin. Mais si tu souhaites parfaire ta connaissance de la nature humaine et de la grande littérature, je te suggère d'emprunter quelques-unes de mes pièces de Shakespeare. Je les ai toutes.

— Je pourrais t'enseigner quelques formules latines bien utiles, a proposé Joe Goodman.

— Et l'arithmétique ? a grogné Miss Feather.

Poker Face Jace a retiré son cigare de sa bouche & l'a examiné :

— Sauf votre respect, m'dame, P.K. est sûrement meilleur en calcul que tous les gens présents ici, vous comprise.

Là-dessus, il a remis son cigare entre ses dents, a craché une bouffée de fumée en l'air puis m'a fait :

— Dis un peu à cette dame quel serait le volume d'un tunnel de 7 kilomètres de long, 4 mètres de large et 1 mètre 72 de haut.

— Attendez voir... Ça nous ferait 48 160 mètres cubes.

À son bureau, M. Rufus E. Arick a fait un rapide calcul sur une feuille de papier. Puis il m'a regardé avec l'Expression n° 4 :

— Il a raison... s'est-il étouffé.

Tout le monde ou presque a explosé de joie. Miss Feather, elle, elle a juste bougonné.

— Et aussi, ai-je ajouté, j'ai envie d'apprendre des choses qu'on n'enseigne pas à l'école. Comme de comprendre les gens, par exemple. (Je me suis tourné vers Poker Face Jace.) Les meilleurs professeurs ne se trouvent pas tous dans les écoles.

Jace m'a fait un clin d'œil. Miss Feather avait l'air moins convaincue.

Elle s'est contentée de marmonner un mot incompréhensible, puis elle a fait demi-tour & a quitté le Bureau.

— Tu dis que tu comptes monter une entreprise, a repris Dan De Quille. Tu vas l'installer à Virginia ?

— Oui, monsieur. Je vais demander à M. Sol Bloomfield s'il accepte de me louer ou de me vendre sa petite boutique de B. Street, celle qui se trouve entre le studio d'Ambrotypes & de Photographies de M. Isaiah Coffin & le Colombo Restaurant. Ça me servira à la fois de logement et de bureau.

— Mon p'tit, est intervenu un des prospecteurs. Avec un revenu de 100 $ par mois, tu n'es même plus obligé de travailler pour vivre.

— 100 $, c'est ce que je gagne au journal, a confirmé Sam Clemens. Et toi, tu n'auras même pas à lever le petit doigt. Juste à passer aux locaux de la mine pour récupérer ton or.

— Mais ouais, a ajouté un autre prospecteur. C'est notre rêve à tous, ça : prendre notre retraite & ne plus jamais travailler.

— Sauf que moi, j'ai envie de travailler, ai-je martelé. De monter mon affaire.

— Et tu as bien raison, a tranché Dan De Quille. Un homme ne devrait jamais rester oisif. Dis-nous, dans quelle branche comptes-tu te lancer ?

J'ai sorti de ma poche mon Bouton de Détective du Chemin de Fer & l'ai observé.

— Je vais me faire Détective. C'est mon Destin.

Là, ils ont presque tous éclaté de rire, comme si je blaguais.

— Le Chemin de Fer ne passe pas encore par chez nous, m'a indiqué Dan De Quille.

— Tu comptes te faire embaucher par les compagnies de diligences ? a voulu savoir Titus Jepson.

— Ou par le Marshal ? a proposé Isaiah Coffin.

— Non. Je travaillerai pour mon propre compte. J'aiderai les gens en Résolvant des Énigmes & des Crimes. Si mon travail leur convient, ils pourront me payer.

— Ce genre de choses ça fonctionne peut-être à Chicago, réfléchissait Isaiah Coffin. Mais je doute que tu aies du succès dans notre ville. Et si tu ouvrais plutôt une Mercerie ?

— Ou un bureau de tabac, renchérit Dan De Quille en désignant Sam Clemens du regard. Du bon tabac, je crois que certains dans cette ville en auraient bien besoin.

— Du moment que tu ne lances pas un journal concurrent… a fait Joe Goodman.

— Je persiste à penser que tu devrais bosser pour moi, m'a dit Jace.

— Je serai heureux de vous aider à l'occasion. Mais ma décision est prise, je serai Détective. Et mon propre patron.

— Tu sais, m'a annoncé Sam Clemens en allumant sa pipe, on raconte que le jour où Satan passait les âmes des pécheurs dans son tamis, les pires ordures ont atterri à Virginia.

— Parle pour toi ! s'est récrié un mineur barbu.

Ça a bien fait rigoler tout le monde.

Le reporter les a tous ignorés.

— Je dis simplement que, si P.K. veut réellement devenir Détective, il ne manquera jamais de travail.

— Ça me semble être une bonne idée, a jugé M. Billy Chollar. J'aimerais bien qu'on enquête sur deux ou trois personnes de ma connaissance.

— Moi pareil, a dit un prospecteur, je suis sûr que mon associé m'arnaque mais j'arrive pas à savoir comment. Je te paierais pour le suivre & trouver son truc.

— Ça s'appelle « filer » quelqu'un, il me semble, a déclaré Belle Donne. Ça m'a l'air très excitant. Tu sais, j'ai perdu un collier de rubis récemment, j'aimerais bien t'engager pour remettre la main dessus.

— Moi, c'est des bons Scoops que je voudrais que tu me déniches, a dit Sam Clemens. Des Scoops que je puisse publier. Je te donnerais 1 $ ou 2 en échange de pistes intéressantes.

Dan De Quille hochait la tête.

— Je reste sceptique. Mais je te souhaite bonne chance.

— Alors, à laquelle de nos affaires vas-tu t'attaquer en premier ? m'a demandé Titus Jepson.

— Avant toute autre chose, ai-je répondu, je vais demander à M. Grafton T. Brown ici présent s'il accepte de me peindre une enseigne pour mon bureau.

L'intéressé a accepté d'un signe de la tête en ajoutant :

— Avec plaisir. Que veux-tu que je marque sur cette enseigne ?

J'ai réfléchi un instant puis la réponse m'est venue :

— P.K. Pinkerton, Détective Privé. Nous Ne Fermons Presque Jamais L'Œil.

Aussitôt tout le monde a crié Bravo & des hommes m'ont raccompagné jusqu'au boghei de Billy Chollar en me faisant passer d'épaules en épaules.

En général, je n'aime pas qu'on me touche.

Là, ça ne m'a pas gêné.

Le ciel était bleu, le soleil était chaud. Dans un buisson d'armoise, une caille criait : « Chicago ! Chicago ! »

Je me suis dit : « Pas tout de suite. Je reste encore un peu ici. »

Du côté de la mine, on sifflait la pause déjeuner, les Canaris de Washoe brayaient à tue-tête & dans un saloon un orgue de Barbarie égrenait les notes de « Camptown Races ».

Et sous ce vacarme familier j'entendais les battements de la montagne, comme s'il s'agissait du cœur de Dieu.

GLOSSAIRE

• **ALCALI** • produit chimique que l'on rencontre dans la terre et l'eau de certaines régions du Nevada.

• **AMBROTYPE** • l'un des premiers types de photographies, inventé dans les années 1850.

• **CALIBRE** • diamètre des balles de pistolet, mesuré en centièmes de pouce.

• **CANARI DE WASHOE** • expression ironique d'argot par laquelle les gens de Virginia City désignent une mule qui brait à tue-tête.

• **CHAPEAU EN TUYAU DE POÊLE** • type de chapeau cylindrique immortalisé notamment par le président américain Abraham Lincoln.

• **CHINETOQUE** • terme d'argot désignant les Chinois, et parfois par extension les Asiatiques en général.

• **CHIQUE** • morceau de tabac à mâcher.

• **COLOMBE DE SUIE** • dans cet ouvrage, cette expression désigne les femmes qui travaillaient dans les saloons ou les maisons closes.

• **COMSTOCK** • la couche d'argent située dans le sous-sol de Virginia City avait été baptisée « Filon de Comstock » en référence à l'un de ses premiers exploitants. Le nom serait par la suite étendu à toute la région.

• **CRACHOIR** • ustensile en métal dans lequel les clients des saloons et autres établissements crachaient leur salive lorsqu'ils chiquaient.

• **CRÈCHE** • mangeoire pour les bestiaux ; en argot, ce terme désigne un logement.

• **CRÉSUS** • roi mythique à la fortune fabuleuse.

• **DAN DE QUILLE** • nom de plume de William Wright, journaliste à Virginia City.

• **DERINGER OU DERRINGER** • petit pistolet à un ou deux coups ; facile à dissimuler, il tirait de grosses balles.

• **FILLE DE BASTRINGUE** • femme qui travaillait dans les saloons.

• **FILON** • couche de minerai précieux.

• **GRAFTON T. BROWN** • artiste afro-américain libre, célèbre surtout pour ses paysages urbains.

• **GROSH** (frères) • Hosea et Ethan Grosh ont selon toute vraisemblance découvert le filon d'argent du sous-sol de Virginia City. Ils sont hélas morts avant d'avoir pu en tirer bénéfice.

• **LABORATOIRE DES ESSAIS DES MONNAIES** • endroit où l'on peut apporter un échantillon de minerai afin d'en déterminer la valeur.

• **LAKOTA (OU SIOUX)** • caractérise la langue et le nom d'un peuple amérindien du Dakota du Sud.

• **MARK TWAIN** • l'un des plus célèbres auteurs américains – de son vrai nom Sam Clemens.

• **MONT DAVIDSON** • montagne à l'intérieur de laquelle se trouvait le Filon de Comstock, et sur laquelle était bâtie Virginia City.

• **NOTAIRE** • personnage public autorisé à émettre des documents officiels et/ou à les déclarer légaux.

• **PINKERTON DETECTIVE AGENCY** • agence de détectives privés fondée en 1850 à Chicago par Allan Pinkerton.

• **POTOSI** • compagnie minière de Virginia City baptisée ainsi en référence à une montagne de Bolivie riche en argent.

• **SAC-MÉDECINE** • petite besace dans laquelle certains Amérindiens transportaient des substances magiques.

• **SAM CLEMENS** (voir Mark Twain) • reporter pour le *Daily Territorial Enterprise* de 1862 à 1864.

• ***TERRITORIAL ENTERPRISE* (OU *DAILY TERRITORIAL ENTERPRISE*)** • premier quotidien publié à Virginia City à partir de 1860.

• **VIRGINIA CITY** • ville minière du Nevada fondée en 1859, peu après que de l'argent eut été découvert sur le site.

• **WASHOE** • nom d'un lac situé à l'ouest de Virginia City ; désigne aussi la région environnante, ainsi qu'une nation amérindienne locale.

• **WELLS FARGO** • Wells Fargo & Co. : établissement fondé en 1848 pour le transport et l'entrepôt des sommes d'argent et de l'or.

Composition Nord Compo

Cet ouvrage a été imprimé en Espagne
par RODESA

« Pour l'éditeur, le principe est d'utiliser des papiers composés de fibres naturelles, renouvelables, recyclables et fabriquées à partir de bois issus de forêts qui adoptent un système d'aménagement durable. En outre, l'éditeur attend de ses fournisseurs de papier qu'ils s'inscrivent dans une démarche de certification environnementale reconnue. »

20.2869.4 – ISBN 978-2-01-202869-2
Dépôt légal 1ère publication : janvier 2013
N° d'impression :

Édition 01 – janvier 2013

Loi n° 49-956 du 16 juillet 1949
sur les publications destinées à la jeunesse.